HOLMAN
New
Testament
Commentary

Galatians, Ephesians, Philippians & Colossians

GENERAL EDITOR

Max Anders

AUTHOR

Max Anders

HOLMAN
REFERENCE

NASHVILLE, TENNESSEE

Holman New Testament Commentary
© 1999 B&H Publishing Group
Nashville, Tennessee
All rights reserved

ISBN 978-0-8054-0208-7

Dewey Decimal Classification: 226.6
Subject Heading: BIBLE. N.T. GALATIANS-COLOSSIANS
Library of Congress Card Catalog Number: 98-39365

Anders, Max.
       Galatians-Colossians / Max Anders
          p.   cm. — (Holman New Testament commentary)
       Includes bibliographical references.
       ISBN 0-80540-208-X (alk. paper)
       1. Bible. N.T. Galatians-Colossians—Commentaries. 2. Bible. N.T.
Galatians-Colossians—Commentaries.   I. Title.   II. Title: Galatians-
Colossians.   III. Series
       BS2625.3G36   1999   98–39365
       226.6'.07—dc21   CIP

15 16 17 18 19 20   19 18 17 16 15

Contents

Contents

Editorial Preface

Today's church hungers for Bible teaching, and Bible teachers hunger for resources to guide them in teaching God's Word. The Holman New Testament Commentary provides the church with the food to feed the spiritually hungry in an easily digestible format. The result: new spiritual vitality that the church can readily use.

Bible teaching should result in new interest in the Scriptures, expanded Bible knowledge, discovery of specific scriptural principles, relevant applications, and exciting living. The unique format of the Holman New Testament Commentary includes sections to achieve these results for every New Testament book.

Opening quotations from some of the church's best writers lead to an introductory illustration and discussion that draw individuals and study groups into the Word of God. "In a Nutshell" summarizes the content and teaching of the chapter. Verse-by-verse commentary answers the church's questions rather than raising issues scholars usually admit they cannot adequately solve. Bible principles and specific contemporary applications encourage students to move from Bible to contemporary times. A specific modern illustration then ties application vividly to present life. A brief prayer aids the student to commit his or her daily life to the principles and applications found in the Bible chapter being studied. For those still hungry for more, "Deeper Discoveries" take the student into a more personal, deeper study of the words, phrases, and themes of God's Word. Finally, a teaching outline provides transitional statements and conclusions along with an outline to assist the teacher in group Bible studies.

It is the editors' prayer that this new resource for local church Bible teaching will enrich the ministry of group, as well as individual, Bible study, and that it will lead God's people to truly be people of the Book, living out what God calls us to be.

Holman Old Testament Commentary Contributors

Holman New Testament Commentary Contributors

Vol. 1, Matthew
ISBN 978–0-8054-0201-8
Stuart K. Weber

Vol. 2, Mark
ISBN 978–0-8054-0202-5
Rodney L. Cooper

Vol. 3, Luke
ISBN 978–0-8054-0203-2
Trent C. Butler

Vol. 4, John
ISBN 978–0-8054-0204-9
Kenneth O. Gangel

Vol. 5, Acts
ISBN 978–0-8054-0205-6
Kenneth O. Gangel

Vol. 6, Romans
ISBN 978–0-8054-0206-3
Kenneth Boa and William Kruidenier

Vol. 7, 1 & 2 Corinthians
ISBN 978–0-8054-0207-0
Richard L. Pratt Jr.

Vol. 8, Galatians, Ephesians, Philippians, Colossians
ISBN 978–0-8054-0208-7
Max Anders

Vol. 9, 1 & 2 Thessalonians, 1 & 2 Timothy, Titus, Philemon
ISBN 978–0-8054-0209-4
Knute Larson

Vol. 10, Hebrews, James
ISBN 978–0-8054-0211-7
Thomas D. Lea

Vol. 11, 1 & 2 Peter, 1, 2, 3 John, Jude
ISBN 978–0-8054-0210-0
David Walls and Max Anders

Vol. 12, Revelation
ISBN 978–0-8054-0212-4
Kendell H. Easley

Holman New Testament Commentary

Twelve volumes designed for Bible study and teaching to enrich the local church and God's people.

Series Editor	Max Anders
Managing Editors	Trent C. Butler & Steve Bond
Project Editor	Lloyd W. Mullens
Marketing Manager	Greg Webster
Product Manager	David Shepherd

Galatians 1

You Were Born to Be Free

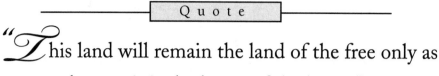

"This land will remain the land of the free only as long as it is the home of the brave."

Elmer Davis

LETTER PROFILE

- Written not to one church but to all the churches in the region of Galatia.
- Probably written to churches Paul helped establish during one of his missionary journeys to the region.
- Written to help offset the influence of false teachers, who taught that to be saved Gentiles must keep the Mosaic Law in addition to believing in Christ.
- Theme: We are saved by grace and must live by grace, not by law, for no one can keep the law.

REGION PROFILE

- Galatia was a region, not a city, in modern Turkey.
- People of the region were Celtic (originating in the British Isles, especially Ireland), who migrated to this area because of conflict with the Romans in their homeland.
- At the time of the New Testament, Galatia became a Roman province.
- Boundaries of Galatia are uncertain, but it may have contained the cities of Pisidian Antioch, Iconium, Lystra, and Derbe.

AUTHOR PROFILE—PAUL THE APOSTLE

- Jew, born in Tarsus, near the Lebanese border in modern Turkey.
- Roman citizen.
- Prominent, highly educated Jewish religious leader (Pharisee).
- Dramatically converted to Christianity, A.D. 35.
- Primary apostle to the Gentiles.
- Tireless missionary.
- Imprisoned in Rome, A.D. 67, during reign of Nero.
- Died in prison, A.D. 68.

IN A NUTSHELL

In chapter 1, Paul explains to the Galatian Christians: I am astonished that you are turning away from the gospel of grace which I taught you to a system of works and law. Anyone who teaches you this should be accursed. I learned this message from Jesus himself, as the church leaders in Jerusalem will verify.

Galatians

You Were Born to Be Free

I. INTRODUCTION

Coup in Grenada

*I*n the fall of 1983, a coup occurred on the Western Caribbean island of Grenada. Cuban-backed communists overthrew the government and installed a totalitarian dictatorship. Under martial rule, the people instantly lost their freedom and liberty. Over one hundred dissenters, including fifty children, were rounded up and marched into the fort of the capital city of St. George. They completely disappeared. A local pastor relayed the terror of living in the midst of this oppression. He believed that these innocent children were killed and dumped at sea.

This ploy did not go unnoticed. President Ronald Reagan quickly deployed a military rescue team to Grenada. They struck in the middle of the night. Within a day, the island was free again. The people of Grenada learned that liberty is most precious when it is suddenly taken away.

A similar coup occurred in the first-century church. Jewish believers—frequently called Judaizers—invaded the Galatian churches and through legalism stole the people's freedom in Christ. They denied Paul's message that salvation and maturity were through grace by simple faith in Christ. Rather, they taught that "Unless you are circumcised, according to the custom taught by Moses, you cannot be saved" (Acts 15:1; compare Gal. 6:2). Not only did these Judaizers contradict Paul's message of grace, but they also denied his apostleship.

Sadly, many Galatian believers began believing these false teachers. They submitted to circumcision and other Old Testament laws to win God's approval, gain eternal life, and mature in Christ. With all the external regulations, they felt like slaves as they tried meticulously to obey the law. Therefore, they were no longer free in Christ.

Then "to the rescue" came Paul, the liberator. His "smoking gun" was a six-chapter defense of grace known to us as "Galatians." In this letter, Paul went to the very fort of legalism and through closely reasoned biblical logic destroyed its errors. His bold defense of grace restored the Galatians and saved the early church from a cultic division. Because the message of Galatians frees Christians from the oppression of legalism, it has been called the

"Magna Carta" of Christianity. Martin Luther, the father of the Reformation, loved Galatians and considered it the best of all books. He even compared his love for this book with his love for his wife, Katherine. Luther said, "The epistle to the Galatians is my epistle. To it I am, as it were, in wedlock. It is my Katherine."

So read and appreciate this book that was the catalyst for the Reformation. Read on and develop a deep fondness for the courageous apostle Paul, our freedom-fighting hero. This defense of the gospel preserved grace for the Galatians and us.

II. COMMENTARY

You Were Born to Be Free

> **MAIN IDEA:** *Paul, the messenger of grace, is trustworthy because he received his message directly from God, and it dramatically changed his life.*

A Greeting (vv. 1–5)

> **SUPPORTING IDEA:** *The risen Christ is our only source of salvation and with the Father our only source for mission.*

1:1. Paul is the author of the Book of Galatians. God called him to be an apostle and sent him on the special mission of evangelizing the Gentiles. The opening of Galatians is unusual for Paul. In most of his letters, he begins with a thanksgiving for the recipients, but in Galatians he omits this customary praise. Why is this omission significant? Because Paul was alarmed that the Galatians had fallen into the lethal trap of legalism. He was astonished that they questioned his authority as an apostle. Therefore, as a surgeon going after the tumor, Paul avoided small talk and cut in immediately to declare his case. Since his message and apostleship were being questioned, Paul began, even in this greeting, to present his divine credentials. No human institution nor any individual sent him. Jesus Christ, the resurrected One, along with God the Father was the only reason he became an apostle to the Gentiles.

1:2. This letter was not only from Paul but also from **all the brothers with me**. Paul's companions included Barnabas and others from Antioch (see Acts 13:1). Paul mentions these recognized coworkers to legitimize further his apostleship and authority.

Throughout this chapter Paul cites his association with the apostles and key church leaders as a way to substantiate his credibility and apostleship.

Paul and his associates addressed this letter to the various churches in the Roman province of Galatia.

1:3. Grace and peace summarize Paul's gospel of salvation. Grace, God's unmerited favor, is the source of salvation (Eph. 2:8–9). When a person believes in Jesus Christ, he or she receives salvation and peace with God, others, and self. Thus, grace leads to peace. Peace represents life in its wholeness or fullness, a life filled with a sense of satisfaction that only God can give.

1:4. Grace not only saves us from the penalty of sin; it also delivers us from the power of sin. We have been rescued from the enslaving power of this present evil age—a world ruled by Satan, full of cruelty, tragedy, temptation, and deception. Later in chapter 5 Paul will explain how grace works in our lives to give us this power over sin's slavery. Christ accomplished the victory over sin through the voluntary gift of himself to us in dying on the cross. This was all according to God's eternal plan to bring us salvation.

1:5. Forever we will praise God for his grace which saves us from both the penalty and power of sin. To give glory to God:

> Is to praise, to recognize the importance of another, the weight the other carries in the community. In the Psalms people give such glory to God, that is they recognize the essential nature of his Godness that gives him importance and weight in relationship to the human worshiping community. (Comp. Pss. 22:23; 86:12; Isa. 24:15). . . . Divine glory means that humans do not seek glory for themselves (Matt. 6:2; John 5:44; 1 Thess. 2:6). They only look to receive praise and honor from Christ (Rom. 2:7; 5:2; 1 Thess. 2:19; Phil. 2:16) ("Glory," *Holman Bible Dictionary*, 557).

Ⓑ The Distortion of the Gospel of Grace Condemned (vv. 6–10)

SUPPORTING IDEA: *For Christians to submit to legalistic teachers is almost beyond comprehension and deserves strong condemnation.*

1:6. Paul was astonished the Galatians were **so quickly deserting** (like a military desertion) from the gospel of grace. This meant they were deserting God, turning their backs on him. It was almost beyond Paul's comprehension that they, having once been delivered from the bondage of law, would go back into this religious prison. Paul calls the Judaizer's blend of law and grace a **different gospel,** thus declaring that mixing law with the gospel is a distortion of truth. Even today, this Galatian error is repeated when people say, "This is what you have to do to be saved; join our church, obey our rules, submit to our baptism, practice our liturgy, worship the way we do, work hard, prove your worth, and earn God's love. In the end, if you are good enough, God will accept you." A works-based gospel is different from the message of grace.

1:7 In fact, a works-based, human-effort driven gospel is no gospel at all. How is a demand for impossible human achievement good news? Anyone who presents a way of salvation that depends in any way on works, rather than God, has contaminated the gospel message. They confuse honest, sincere believers. They have no gospel, no good news.

1:8. A hypothetical case shows the seriousness of legalism's perversion of grace. Through hyperbole (a deliberate exaggeration for emphasis), Paul declares that anyone who preaches a mixture of grace and law is worthy of eternal condemnation. A teacher who requires others to obey the law as a requirement for salvation is leading others to a Christless eternity. Paul uses strong language because he is dealing with a life-or-death situation. You must choose: the gospel of grace Paul preached or the gospel of works the perverters preached.

1:9. *Ditto!* Paul repeated his curse for effect. Any person who preaches a gospel that requires more than God's grace for salvation deserves to suffer in hell for eternity.

1:10. Paul's critics accused him of preaching "easy believism" because he did not include the law as grounds for salvation and Christian maturity. They claimed Paul watered down the gospel, by omitting the law, to increase his popularity among the Gentiles. Through two rhetorical questions, Paul adamantly denies the charge and states clearly that his motive is to please only God. He was concerned with preserving truth not increasing his **approval** ratings. To please people is to desert Christ. You must choose: serve people's fickle pleasures or serve the faithful Christ.

The True Source of the Gospel (vv. 11–12)

> **SUPPORTING IDEA:** *Paul's gospel of grace is true because it came directly from God.*

1:11. The Judaizers knew that if they could undermine Paul's apostolic authority they could defeat his message of liberty. So Paul now defends his apostleship and message. The Judaizers said Paul perverted the gospel by omitting the Law of Moses; in reality, the Judaizers perverted the gospel by adding legalism. Paul now presents the first reason the Galatians should listen to him and not the false teachers: the gospel is not man-made (compare v. 1). No human mind apart from God's revelation would dream up a plan of salvation wholly dependent on God's grace and the death of his Son.

1:12. This first reason leads to the inescapable conclusion: If Paul's gospel is not man-made, then it is God-made. While the Galatians had been taught by humans (originally by Paul and later by these false teachers), Paul had been taught directly by Christ, the highest authority. The gospel of grace that Paul preached is true because it came directly from God.

Ⅾ The Truth of the Gospel Presented (vv. 13–24)

SUPPORTING IDEA: *Paul's gospel of grace is true because it dramatically changed his life.*

1:13. Paul now presents his second proof that his gospel of grace is true: his own miraculous life change. Paul is living proof that God changes lives (see 2 Cor. 5:17). He knew that his testimony was powerful evidence not only of the reality and relevance of God but also of the credibility of his ministry. Paul began his testimony by reminding the Galatians of who he had been. (see Acts 9; 22; 26 for a deeper understanding of his past). Rabbi Saul of Tarsus set out to destroy the infant church of Jesus. The church feared him greatly.

1:14. Not only did he persecute the church, Rabbi Saul advanced up the Jewish ranks. As a Pharisee, he had been one of the strictest Jews of his day (Phil. 3:4–6), stricter than even these legalistic teachers who now opposed the gospel of grace. Paul knew well the legalism that the false teachers were teaching the Galatians. Prior to his conversion he had been such a loyal legalist that he even tried to destroy Christianity (Acts 7).

1:15. What happened to change Rabbi Saul into apostle Paul? God dramatically intervened in his life. Christ appeared to Saul on the Damascus road and brought about his conversion (Acts 9). Why did God do this? It was all part of God's eternal plan to take the good news to the whole world. God had planned Paul's part in this eternal mission even before Paul was born. Paul did not enter the missionary work and develop the missionary gospel message on his own. God was responsible for it all. He called Paul.

Thus, Paul shows that both his conversion and his commission were from God rather than man. His conversion from persecutor to preacher could only be explained as a miracle of God and a great proof of his authenticity and apostolic authority. What greater credibility could one have for ministry!

1:16. Paul played one last trump card against his opponents. His entire mission was based on revelation. God had shown Jesus Christ to Paul. This was the basis of his apostolic office, for only one who had witnessed and could personally testify to Christ's resurrection could be an apostle (Acts 1:22). On the Damascus road, Jesus appeared to Paul in person.

From that point on, Jesus lived in Paul, and Paul was in Christ. That meant Christ could work through Paul to reveal himself to others. Paul's unique mission was to take the gospel to the Gentiles. How did he train for that mission? After his conversion he could have gone directly to Jerusalem to learn more from the apostles but did not. Indeed, Paul **did not consult any man.**

1:17. Paul stayed away from Jerusalem. Instead, he went to Arabia and then back to Damascus. His purpose in going to Arabia was to pray, study, and be alone with the Lord. It was three years before he went to Jerusalem (Gal. 1:18). Interestingly, the apostles were taught by the Lord for three years; now it was Paul's turn to spend three years also being trained by Christ. It was a dramatic change to go from persecutor to apostle of Christ. Paul needed this time to be taught by the Lord so his Christian theology could be forged.

1:18–19. Paul traveled to Jerusalem to spend **fifteen days** with Peter and James. Because Paul had been taught by the Lord for three years, he could now fellowship with the key apostles as a peer and not as a pupil. Apostolic peer rather than peerless persecutor!

1:20. The heat of the argument with his opponents becomes apparent here. Paul swears an oath in the presence of God.

1:21. While Paul visited Peter and James, he learned of a plot to kill him (Acts 9:29). Therefore, he fled to Syria and Cilicia. Cilicia was Paul's home province (Acts 21:39; 22:3) the capital of which was Tarsus, Paul's home city. Thus, after escaping from Jerusalem, Paul returned home to evangelize (see Acts 15:23).

1:22. Since Paul spent only fifteen days in Jerusalem, a province of Judea, he **was personally unknown to the churches of Judea**.

1:23–24. When they heard how Saul, the persecutor, was now Paul, the preacher, they praised God. His new life astonished and encouraged them.

In summary, false teachers in Galatia were teaching that to be saved and mature in the faith Gentile believers had to follow Jewish laws and customs, especially the rite of circumcision. Faith in Christ was not enough. This message was undermining the good news that salvation is a simple gift based on faith in Christ and not a reward for certain good deeds. This false message was in direct opposition to the gospel of grace that Paul preached. Additionally, in order to discredit Paul's message, the false teachers sought to discredit Paul. Thus, to defend himself and his gospel of grace, Paul argues convincingly that the gospel of grace is true because it came directly from God and it dramatically changed his life.

MAIN IDEA REVIEW: *Paul, the messenger of grace, is trustworthy because he received his message directly from God and it dramatically changed his life.*

III. CONCLUSION

Fight or Switch?

Is conflict incongruent with Christian compassion? Not at all! When confronted with theological error, Paul would rather "fight than switch."

Without occasional fights, the battle for truth would be lost. Just as without U.S. military intervention in Grenada, that nation and possibly many more could have lost their freedom.

When the weapons of legalism fired upon Paul, he knew that pacifism would mean certain defeat. So he began in chapter 1 to defeat legalism by rolling out the double cannons of revelation and testimony. His amazing conversion "packed quite a punch" and began the dismantling of legalism's forces.

PRINCIPLES

- Perversion of the truth is more difficult to spot than blatant falsehood.
- God has given us only one way by to be saved—through Jesus Christ.
- A teacher may be sincere and still be sincerely wrong.
- Your testimony is a powerful witnessing tool.
- The gospel is true because it comes straight from God and it changes lives.

APPLICATIONS

- Beware of people who say we need more than simple faith in Christ to be saved.
- If you have never put your faith and trust in Christ to save you, then tell him now that you believe and accept him as your Savior.
- Thank God that you are free from the burden of having to earn his love and approval.
- List three changes Christ has made in your life.
- Enjoy the fact that God is working in your life.
- Pray and ask him to work even more.

IV. LIFE APPLICATION

Searching for the Keys to Heaven

Have you heard the story of the man searching for his keys under the street light? His friend saw him and stopped to help. After some minutes he asked, "Exactly where did you drop your keys?"

"In my house," the man answered.

"In your house? Then why are we looking out here?"

"Because the light is better out here."

You'll never find what you are looking for unless you look in the right place. Today people are looking for spiritual life, but like this confused man they are looking in the wrong places. Originally the Galatians knew where to find the key to salvation. They had heard Paul's message and had been saved by putting their faith in Jesus Christ. Now they were confused. They began to listen to the legalists who said that they needed both the keys of faith and good works (the law) to be saved. Confused, the Galatians were looking for the key to salvation and Christian maturity in the wrong place.

Sadly today many people are also looking in the wrong place for the key that unlocks a relationship with God. Even churchgoers aren't applying the key of grace to unlock salvation and a relationship with God. Christian author and marketing expert, George Barna writes:

> Undoubtedly, one of the rudest awakenings I have ever received in my efforts to help churches grow was the discovery, born out of research, a few years ago that half of all adults who attend Protestant churches on a typical Sunday morning are not Christian! For years, I had been lulled into the comforting but erroneous notion that every Sunday morning I was singing praises to God with the convinced.

> Little did I realize that a huge portion of those in churches across the land—yes, even those sitting in *my* pew, in my Sunday School class—were nonbelievers (George Barna, *Evangelism That Works*, Ventura, CA: Regal Books, 1995, 38).

Additionally, Barna's copious research tells us that over eighty million people in America are unchurched. He estimates that of the 2.2 million people who die each year in America "that more than 1 million of those people . . . will go to hell (*Evangelism That Works*, 11, 47).

Thus, each day as we spend time with our family and friends, as we rub shoulders with work associates, as we talk to people around our towns and cities, as we go to church, we are in a missionary field. We, who know Christ, can tell them the plan of salvation and thereby put the right key in their hand. Are you concerned about the spiritual plight of people? Do you have a passion to see people delivered from the emptiness of legalism? Are you endeavoring to put the key of salvation in others' hands so that they can unlock the door that leads to a personal relationship with Christ and a future in heaven?

V. PRAYER

O Lord, without Paul's boldness the purity of your gospel might have been lost. Remind me that no human teacher is infallible. Thank you that your Scriptures are infallible. Help me to be like the Bereans who "examined the Scriptures every day to see if what Paul said was true." As I discover your truth, help me to share it faithfully with others so that they can know your grace, forgiveness, and salvation. In the name of Christ, I pray. Amen.

VI. DEEPER DISCOVERIES

A. A different gospel (v. 6)

In verses 6–7, Paul states that the Galatians **are turning to a different gospel—which is really no gospel at all.** The word for *gospel* is *euangelion* which means "good news." From this Greek word comes our English words *evangelist* ("one who preaches the good news") and *evangelism* ("the act of telling others the good news").

These false teachers in Galatia (believed by many to be the Judaizers) were adding a type of legalism to the Christian gospel. They thought that it was absolutely necessary for Gentile converts to Christianity to become circumcised and observe the Jewish Old Testament law. In effect, they were teaching that one must become a Jew before one could become a Christian! In Philippians 3, the apostle calls them "dogs," a term of reproach and contempt that Jews commonly used in referring to non-Jews (Gentiles).

Here, Paul is contrasting the good news of Christ with what the Galatians are embracing. He uses two different Greek words in verses 6 and 7. The first is *heteros,* the second *allos. Allos* refers to something of the same kind but numerically distinct. *Heteros* refers to a difference in quality or kind. Jesus promised another (*allos*) Comforter (John 14:16).

The Holy Spirit would be a distinct personality but not a different (*heteros*) kind of *Paraclete.* Now the language of Paul is clear. He bemoans the fact that the Galatians are turning to a "different" gospel, which is really "not another" gospel. They had changed categories. They think the gospel is defined in an entirely different way than Paul has defined it. What they now followed was not the glad, good news that men can be saved through faith in Christ but the very depressing idea that one must work for his salvation. It was heterodoxy, "different opinion"; not orthodoxy, "straight opinion." There is only one true gospel, Paul would say, only one way of salvation. That is not found in the law, but in Christ (See Richard Trench, *Synonyms of the New Testament,* London: Macmillan, 1876, IV, 173).

B. Eternally condemned (vv. 8–9)

The Greek word Paul uses here is *anathema.* It means "accursed, damnation" with the idea of going to hell. Hermann Cremer elaborates: "The essential idea of the noun is *devoted to destruction,* something given up to death on account of God" (*Biblio-Theological Lexicon of New Testament Greek,* Edinburgh: T. & T. Clark, 1878, 547 as quoted by Ralph Earle, *Word Meanings in the New Testament,* Kansas City: Beacon Hill Press, 1986, 269–270). That is the regular meaning of *anathema* in the NT. Some have tried to weaken its force in one or two places to the sense of excommunication. Cremer objects to this. He holds that the word "denotes not punishment intended as discipline, but *a being given over,* or *devotion to divine condemnation"* (p. 548). In other words, in the NT it always has the idea of a curse attached to it, as it did in the secular Greek of that time.

Donald Guthrie adds: "It implies the disapproval of God, Indeed, 'anathema' is the strongest possible contrast to God's grace. . . .The essence of the gospel itself was at stake. If the false teachers were directly contradicting the gospel of the grace of Christ, they could not possibly avoid incurring the strong displeasure of Christ" (*Galatians*, Grand Rapids: Eerdman's, 1973, 64).

C. Revelation from Jesus Christ (v. 12)

Revelation in the Scriptures is more than having an insightful thought or an "aha!" experience. God has revealed himself through general revelation in the physical universe, through special revelation in the Bible, and in the sending of his Son to earth. The Greek word for "revelation" is *apocalypsis* from which we get our English word *apocalypse.* Often, the final book of the Bible, Revelation, is referred to as "The Apocalypse." David Dockery states: "The word *revelation* means an uncovering, a removal of the veil, a disclosure of what was previously unknown" ("Revelation of God," *Holman Bible Dictionary*, 1181). Merrill F. Unger comments about revelation: "A term expressive of the fact that God has made known to men truths and realities which men could not discover themselves" (*Unger's Bible Dictionary*, Chicago: Moody Press, 1966, 922). Most evangelicals believe that God's special revelation is complete in the Bible.

Specifically, in this verse, Paul has in mind the disclosure that Jesus Christ gave him in the vision during his Damascus road experience. Daniel G. Bagby notes: "Christ and no one else revealed the nature and content of the gospel Paul preached. That gave Paul his claim to be an apostle and authenticated his preaching over against his opponents. His vision of Jesus transformed his life" (*The Disciple's Study Bible*, ed. Trent C. Butler, Nashville: Homan Bible Publishers, 1988, 1491). See Ephesians 3:2–6.

VII. TEACHING OUTLINE

A. INTRODUCTION

1. Lead story: Coup in Grenada
2. Context: In the first chapter of Galatians, Paul begins to refute legalism—the belief that faith alone in Jesus Christ is not sufficient for salvation and Christian maturity. Legalists taught that a person must be

circumcised and keep the Old Testament law to have a relationship with God and have eternal life. Every time Paul established a new church, these false teachers would swoop down on the church and disseminate this legalistic heresy. As a result the church's proselytes would lose their freedom in Christ. By trying to earn God's favor through good works, they would get on an endless treadmill of religion, void of love, joy, and peace.

3. Transition: In chapter 1, we observe Paul defending himself from the attacks of the Judaizers. They have denied both his message of grace and his apostleship. Paul expresses shock that the Galatians are doubting his message of simple faith in Christ and are engaging in legalism. He pronounces judgment on the false teachers who are propagating this Christian aberration. We will learn that the best defense when our credibility is being attacked is a personal relationship with Christ (1:11–12) and the effect that relationship has had on our lives (1:13–24). In no uncertain terms, Paul states that his message is true because he received it directly from God and because it dramatically changed his life. Elmer Davis wrote in *But We Were Born Free,* "This land will remain the land of the free only as long as it is the home of the brave." Just as a country can remain free only because of the courage of its people to defend it, even so Christians can remain free only by defending the freedom of grace. The law leads to bondage, while grace leads to freedom.

B. COMMENTARY

1. Greeting (vv. 1–5)
   a. Author—Paul (vv. 1)
   b. Recipients—Christians in Galatia (vv. 1)
   c. Blessing—(vv. 3–5)
2. The Perversion of the Gospel of Grace Condemned (vv. 6–10)
   a. Astonishment when Christians pervert the gospel of grace (vv. 6–7)
   b. Condemnation for those who pervert the gospel of grace (vv. 8–10)
3. The Truth of the Gospel of Grace Presented (vv. 11–24)
   a. True because it came from God (vv. 11–12)
   b. True because it changes lives (vv. 13–24)

C. CONCLUSION: SEARCHING FOR THE KEYS TO HEAVEN

VIII. ISSUES FOR DISCUSSION

1. What does Paul mean by "the present evil age"? Do you have any alternative choice but to live in this present evil age?
2. What substitute gospels do people teach today that tempt people to depend on something besides Christ for security and salvation? How do you talk to people who believe such gospels?
3. What attitudes, actions, and habits do you have that show the world you are trying to please God and not people?
4. How did you hear the gospel for the first time? How do you know it is not something made up by human imagination?

Galatians 2

The Fight for Freedom

| Q u o t e |

"*The* price of freedom is eternal vigilance."

T h o m a s   J e f f e r s o n

Galatians

IN A NUTSHELL

In chapter 2, Paul informs the Galatian Christians: I am a true apostle, and two proofs demonstrate that my gospel of grace is true. First, it is true because the apostles and leaders in Jerusalem approved my gospel of grace and authenticated my apostleship. Second, my gospel of grace is true because I confronted and corrected the apostle Peter when he was showing preference to the Judaizers and their false system of legalism. Such a bold and uncontested act validates my apostolic authority and message.

The Fight for Freedom

I. INTRODUCTION

Heavenly Deception in Washington, D.C.

In 1974, The Church of Latter-Day Saints completed a tabernacle in Kensington, Maryland. For nighttime interstate travelers around the Maryland perimeter of Washington, D.C., the surreal appearance of this beautiful, gothic structure bathed in celestial light is a familiar sight. Adorned with lofty spires and the statue of an angel, it appears to the uninitiated to be an awe-inspiring Christian building. A first hint comes when you realize its subtle architecture includes no crosses. The doctrinal differences between Mormonism and Christianity are just as subtle but still real and immensely important. Just as their buildings bear no crosses, so their faith has no central role for the cross of Christ.

Mormons will tell you that they believe in Jesus, yet they do not believe that he is the only way of salvation, and they believe things that are contrary to what Jesus taught. They believe that ultimately humans will become divine. They do not believe the Bible is God's final and authoritative revelation of himself to us. They do not claim the Bible is infallible. They do not believe in a literal heaven and hell. Jesus taught these things. Since Jesus claimed to be the Truth, one must choose between the credibility of Jesus and the credibility of Mormon doctrine. One cannot completely trust both.

They claim to believe in Jesus, but then they teach that Jesus Christ is not enough. One must, Mormon doctrine teaches, do other things in addition to believing in Jesus. Males control the eternal fate of the family. At age twelve, boys begin to advance through the ranks of the Aaronic priesthood, attaining the offices of deacon, teacher, and priest. Then, in the Melchizedek priesthood, males can advance through the offices of elder, high priest, patriarch, seventy, and apostle. These offices afford the male, and presumably his family, higher and higher degrees of exaltation in the afterlife. This means people reach only degrees of glory, never having any type of eternal punishment. All achieved through Jesus "plus."

In Paul's day the Judaizers said the same things: "Believe in Jesus Christ, but we have something wonderful to add to what you believe." They preached "the gospel plus Moses." In our day these counterfeits of the gospel of grace preach "the gospel plus" their extra-biblical beliefs, their religious organization, their rules, regulations, and special revelations. In response to such false teachings that go beyond the gospel of grace, Paul said in Galatians

1:8, if anyone **should preach a gospel other than the one we preached to you, let him be eternally condemned!**

Paul continues defending the gospel of grace in chapter 2. He defends his apostleship and message by presenting two authenticating interactions: (1) his approval by the Jerusalem leaders, and (2) his correction of Peter's legalism—both of which substantiated the gospel and his apostleship.

II. COMMENTARY

The Fight for Freedom

MAIN IDEA: *Paul proves that he preached the true apostolic gospel because his message was endorsed by the Jerusalem leaders (2:1–10) and because he exercised apostolic authority by rebuking and correcting Peter (2:11–21).*

A Paul's Apostolic Authority and Message Endorsed (vv. 1–10)

SUPPORTING IDEA: *The leaders in Jerusalem endorsed the gospel Paul preached and affirmed his apostleship.*

2:1. In Galatians 2, Paul continues to defend himself. Apparently, his critics had not only attacked the authority of his gospel but had also said he was a renegade, opposed to and independent from the apostles in Jerusalem. After responding to their first charge, he responded to the second charge by pointing out that the **Jerusalem** apostles had, in fact, endorsed his message. They affirmed that he was part of their team. Many scholars believe this meeting with Paul and the Jerusalem apostles was the Jerusalem Council meeting recorded in Acts 15. Paul is accompanied at this meeting by **Barnabas** and **Titus.** Titus, being a Gentile, was a test case to see if the Jewish leaders in Jerusalem would require him to be circumcised.

2:2. Paul's second trip to Jerusalem following his conversion was in response to a revelation. The purpose of this meeting with the Jerusalem apostles was to clarify the apostles' position on the Christian's relationship to the Jewish law. Jerusalem did not force Paul to come to them for their official stamp of approval. God sent Paul to Jerusalem to bring unity in the mission of the church. If the leaders in Jerusalem sided with the legalistic, false teachers who required Gentile Christians to be circumcised and keep the whole law, then Paul said he would have **run my race in vain.** It would be futile for him to preach a grace message if the Jerusalem leaders preached a legalistic one. He talked to those **who seemed to be leaders.** Paul's reference to these leaders becomes more clear in verses 6 and 9.

2:3–5. The purpose for bringing Titus to Jerusalem is now revealed. Titus was a test case to see if the Jerusalem leaders would allow a Gentile to be a Christian without being circumcised. The false teachers (Judaizers) said he must be circumcised and Paul adamantly said, "No!" Paul knew that both Jews and Gentiles were accepted into the church by faith alone in Jesus Christ. Paul won this battle, for Titus was **not . . . compelled to be circumcised, even though he was a Greek.** The Judaizers wanted to make Christians **slaves** by requiring them to observe the Old Testament laws' rules and ceremonies, especially circumcision. Paul stood absolutely firm because **the truth of the gospel** was at stake. To impose circumcision on Titus would be to deny that salvation was by faith alone and to affirm the law as the means to God's acceptance.

2:6. The Jerusalem leaders **added nothing to** his **message.** They recognized that it was from God. They approved its truthfulness and completeness. They endorsed Paul and received him as a fellow apostle. We do not know Paul's tone of voice here as he spoke of **those who seemed to be important.** We do not know if he was simply acknowledging his lack of information or whether there is a subtle "put-down" in his voice. He may have been making the point to the Judaizers that his authority for what he preached came from God, and therefore, he was not intimidated by the Judaizers who, to bolster their own bluster, appealed to the Jerusalem apostles as their authority. It need not have been a slight of the apostles themselves, however. They may have been totally unaware of the controversy between the Judaizers and Paul.

2:7–9. Several times Paul refers to the leadership in the Jerusalem church. In verse 2, he refers to "those who seemed to be leaders." In verse 6, he refers to "those who seemed to be important." In verse 9, he talks of **those reputed to be pillars.** Each time, the reference seems to be, according to our modern American intuition, more indignant. We sense a rising temperature in Paul's rhetoric. We ought not to jump to this conclusion, however.

On the one hand, Paul may have been voicing his dissatisfaction and even indignation with the leadership of the church in Jerusalem over several issues. First, he may have been angered by those who wanted Titus to be circumcised, feeling that the leadership of the apostles was inadequate on this issued. Or he may have been put off by Peter's handling of the Jew/Gentile controversy (see vv. 11–14). Paul may have felt that the leadership, whom he now names as the apostles Peter, James, and John, had caved into pressure from the Judaizers and legalists in the church.

On the other hand, his indignation may have been directed solely at the Judaizers working among his beloved Gentile churches. The Judaizers may have tried to diminish Paul's authority by emphasizing the apostolic authority of Peter, James, and John. In doing so, they could support their own opposition to Paul's teaching, tearing him down by lifting up the Jerusalem apostles. Indignant at the Judaizers' presumption and opposition, Paul may have been saying, "You claim that these Jerusalem apostles are the big shots around here. Well, listen up. My authority comes from God and is just as valid. I'm just as much a leader as they are."

James, Peter, and John recognized that God had called Paul to take the gospel to the Gentiles just as he had commissioned Peter to take it to the Jews. The approval of the Jerusalem leadership silenced the false teachers' accusations that were seeking to discredit both Paul and his message. The acceptance and approval of the Jerusalem leaders was sealed when they extended to Paul **and Barnabas the right hand of fellowship**. Paul knew that his words had not convinced the Jerusalem apostles of his ministry. Rather, they saw God's grace in his ministry.

2:10. The apostles only request was that Paul **remember the poor** who were among the Jewish believers in Jerusalem. The Jerusalem leaders may have surmised that after their approval of Paul's ministry to the Gentiles he would not feel a responsibility to aid the poor in the Jerusalem church. On his third missionary journey, however, Paul raised a large offering from the Gentile Christians for the Jewish Christians in Jerusalem (1 Cor. 16:1–3). Such giving promoted love and unity among the Gentile and Jewish Christians.

B Paul's Authority and Message Illustrated (vv. 11–21)

> **SUPPORTING IDEA:** *Paul was a true apostle because he admonished and corrected Peter's accommodation of the false teachers. Only a true apostle could rebuke and correct Peter.*

The Lapse of Peter (vv. 11–13)

2:11. Having presented his acceptance by the Jerusalem leaders, Paul turns to an incidence that illustrated his apostolic clout. He exercised his apostolic authority with the strongest church leader—Peter. Paul's authority as an apostle is confirmed through this correction of Peter. In this section, Paul comes to **Antioch** and corrects Peter, the leader of the Jews, **because he was clearly in the wrong** by giving the appearance that he was siding with the false teachers. By assuming the authority to correct Peter, Paul shows his authority and the truth of his message of grace.

2:12. Peter, a Jew, was eating and fellowshipping with the Gentiles. When some of the Judaizers (**the circumcision group**) arrived, Peter **began to draw back and separate himself from the Gentiles.** He was afraid of what the Judaizers would think. Peter thought by avoiding the Gentiles he would not offend James's legalistic, judaizing friends. By identifying with them, Peter was promoting their false, legalistic beliefs. Peter by his actions was compromising grace. These men were probably not *sent* by James, an apostle and the half brother of Jesus, but were probably part of his church in Jerusalem.

2:13. The other Jews, including **Barnabas**, joined Peter in standing with the Judaizers and ostracizing the Gentiles. They were guilty of **hypocrisy** because they were professing to be one with the Gentiles, yet by their actions they denied their oneness. The pressure must have been intense because even Barnabas, who was from Cyprus—a Gentile center—succumbed. He had been with Paul on a missionary journey to reach the Gentiles.

The Correction by Paul (vv. 14–21)

2:14. Paul knew he had to confront Peter before his actions damaged the church. Therefore, Paul reprimanded Peter publicly **in front of them all** for supporting division between the Jews and Gentiles. Such segregation went against **the truth of the gospel** that Jew and Gentile were equal and one in Christ. Paul uses a rhetorical question in this verse to reprimand Peter: "**You are a Jew, yet you live like a Gentile.** Now you want the Gentiles to live like Jews. What kind of inconsistency is that?"

2:15. It is inconsistent and illogical for privileged **Jews by birth**, who rejected the keeping of their very own law as the way to salvation, to now burden the Gentiles with the keeping of that very same law. The phrase **Gentile sinners** was probably spoken in irony. Quite often, the Jews could not mention Gentiles without calling them "Gentile sinners." Yet, in Paul's eyes, the sinners were the Judaizers, not the Gentiles, Christian believers in his church.

2:16. Verse 16 is one of the most important verses in Galatians because in it Paul states the content of the gospel of grace. This is the first time Paul uses the word *justified* which means "to declare righteous." Justification is the act of God, whereby he declares the believing sinner righteous in Jesus Christ. Negatively, Paul says **a man is not justified by observing the law.** Stated positively, justification is **by faith in Christ Jesus.** Negatively, Paul has rebuffed the false teachings of the Judaizers which Peter had supported by his behavior in Antioch. Positively, he has presented the true, grace path to righteousness.

2:17. The opponents to this message of grace argued that if people aren't under law then they will freely sin. They reasoned that people could believe in Christ but then live as they wanted and by their sinful actions make Christ a promoter of sin. Paul answers this accusation with an emphatic, "No!" Grace leads to freedom from sin's slavery to obey God, not license to disobey him.

2:18. A person who rebuilds (that is, returns to) the law after believing in Christ will find himself a **lawbreaker.** No one except Jesus can keep the law perfectly. So to put one's relationship with God on a legalistic basis is to make oneself a lawbreaker.

2:19. In verses 19–20 Paul teaches about the transformation that occurs in believers. He is continuing to correct Peter for cowering to a legalistic system that is powerless to change lives. Paul uses the death and resurrection motif in each verse. First, Paul states **through the law I died to the law.** Paul may have meant by this that, when he tried to live up to the law, he saw that it was impossible. He saw that the penalty for failing to live up to the law was death. Seeing his clear condemnation according to the law drove him into the arms of grace, to rely on Jesus to save him.

Or he might have meant that, when he saw that the law was insufficient to save him, he turned his back on the law and made it no longer of any influence in his life.

Or he might have meant that the law demanded death for sin. Christ died because he took our death penalty upon himself. By believing in Christ, his death pays for the death that the law required of us. Because I am united with Christ by faith, the law killed not only him but all who are joined to him by faith. Therefore, the believer has died to the law. Since we have died, the law must acquit us of further punishment. So through fulfilling the law by dying in Christ, we are now free from the law.

Whatever Paul meant, the result is that he no longer is under the jurisdiction of the law. It is powerless over him.

2:20. Now Paul expands upon verse 19. He **died to the law** (v. 19) by being **crucified with Christ.** He lives **for God** (v. 19) because **Christ lives in** him. Believers are in union with Christ. We are united with him in his death, burial, and resurrection. Thus, we died with him to the law (see Rom. 6).

Again, we are uncertain as to what Paul meant by **I have been crucified with Christ.** It certainly did not mean that he was physically crucified. Dead people don't write letters. In what sense was he crucified? He may have used the sentence as a figure of speech, referring to the effects of Christ's death which every believer experiences. It might be reworded, "I have been as good as crucified, since the results of Christ's crucifixion count for me." Or he may have referred to a sense in which every believer is required to endure a similar experience of spiritual crucifixion to the desires of self. We put to death our own plans to follow Jesus. It might be reworded, "I have crucified my right to self-control in life, in the same way that Christ was crucified physically. He gave up his right to physical life; I gave up my right to self-life."

Or he may have referred to some sense in which the believer, because he is "in Christ" is seen by God as having actually died. He may have been referring to the union between the believer and Jesus, when the believer in Jesus experiences, spiritually, everything Jesus experienced. More will be said of these options in the "Deeper Discoveries" section of this chapter.

Whatever Paul meant about having died in Christ, the point is that his death severed him from the requirements of the law. Therefore, for Peter and the Judaizers to go back to the law is to visit the graveyard. Paul goes on to say that he can live for God because **Christ lives in** him. Finally, Paul says that **faith** is the principle that unlocks the life of Christ in the believer. The more we exercise **faith in Christ** the more he is free to live through us. The more we are obedient to the Scripture and the leading of the Holy Spirit, the more our life approximates what Jesus would do if he were in our shoes. In that sense, the life he lives, he lives by faith in the Son of God.

2:21. Now Paul presents his conclusion. The false-teaching Judaizers were voiding the grace of God by adding the works-oriented law to the work of Christ. Therefore, Paul says **I do not set aside the grace of God** (as the legalists did), **for if righteousness could be gained through the law, Christ died for nothing!** If humans could be right with God by obeying the law, why would he send his Son to suffer and die on a cross? Paul concludes his correction of Peter by showing the utter absurdity of turning back to the law. The very reason Christ died on the cross to pay for sin was because the law could not remove sin or impart righteousness. Grace provides what the law was powerless to provide—righteousness.

> **MAIN IDEA REVIEW:** *Paul proved that he preached the true apostolic gospel because his message was endorsed by the Jerusalem leaders and because he exercised apostolic authority by rebuking and correcting Peter.*

III. CONCLUSION

The Pure Gospel Stream

The gospel is like a pure stream. Those who drink from it receive eternal life; but when people add requirements to salvation that are unnecessary, the stream gets dirty. The false teachers in Galatia were polluting the gospel by requiring the Christians to obey Jewish law, especially circumcision in addition to believing in Christ. Many today would have us return to trying to earn God's favor through following rituals or obeying a set of rules. Whenever anyone tries to earn their salvation, they are falling into the bondage of legalism. Legalism pollutes the stream, changing it from a pure, life-giving stream to a bitter, deadly-toxic stream. When we try to earn God's favor or eternal life, we are drinking from a deadly stream.

PRINCIPLES

- When you affirm others, you give them wings to fly!
- One of the greatest needs of your family, friends, and coworkers is appreciation.
- Submission to authority is a sign of spiritual maturity.
- Confrontation is hard but often necessary.

APPLICATIONS

- Look for opportunities to affirm others.
- Express your gratitude to God and others for the good they do.
- Submit to spiritual authority which God places over you.
- Have the courage to confront someone over his sin if God shows you it is necessary.

IV. LIFE APPLICATION

The Wrong Bag

Two bank robbers in Sangus, Massachusetts, walked into a small delicatessen, pulled out their guns, and demanded all the money in the cash register. The owner stashed all the money into a brown bag and laid it on the counter. Nervously, they grabbed the bag and fled. Later, in a safe place they opened the bag to divide their haul only to be completely surprised. The bag contained two pastrami sandwiches and a slice of baklava. They couldn't believe it. In their nervous haste they picked up the wrong bag.

In the area of legalism and grace it is also easy to "pick up the wrong bag." Legalism's bag has written on it "do." Legalism has within it a long list of deeds one must do to be saved. It offers spiritual sandwiches that are low in nutriments.

Pastor and author Max Lucado gives a similar assessment of legalism when he writes:

> A legalist believes the supreme force behind salvation is you. If you look right, speak right, and belong to the right segment of the right group, you will be saved. The brunt of responsibility doesn't lie within God; it lies within you. The result? The outside sparkles. The talk is good, and the step is true. But look closely! Listen carefully. Something is missing. What is it? Joy. What's there? Fear. (That you won't do enough.) Arrogance. (That you have done enough.) Failure. (That you have made a mistake.) Legalism is slow torture, suffocation of the spirit, amputation of one's dreams. Legalism is just enough religion to keep you, but not enough to nourish you. So you starve. Your teachers don't know where to go for food, so you starve together. Your diet is rules and standards. No vitamins. No zest. Just bland, predictable religion (Max Lucado, *He Still Moves Stones*, Dallas: Word Publishers, 1993, 128–29).

In contrast to legalism stands grace. The bag of grace has written on it the word *faith*. Under "faith" is written John 3:36, "Whoever believes in the Son has eternal life." In contrast to legalism, grace has no rules, code, or ritual. It is an invitation directly from the heart of God simply to believe and receive. It has no price tag. Paul states in another passage, "For it is by grace you have been saved, through faith—and this not from yourselves, it is the gift of God—not by works, so that no one can boast" (Eph. 2:8–9).

Yes, legalism and grace are the two bags that rest on the counter of life. While the legalists may claim that their bag is full of wealth, in all reality, it is just an old bag with some dry, spiritual pastrami and baklava. The good news is that the wealth is found in grace. The bag of grace is full of forgiveness, joy, and eternal life. Which bag have you picked up? Which bag is in your possession? Legalism or grace? It will be a sad surprise to reach heaven's gate to find that your bag is full of worthless legalism. It will be a sad plight to enter eternity utterly destitute. All religion, apart from grace, is worthless legalism. Beware! Which bag is yours?

V. PRAYER

O Lord, the apostle Paul risked everything to maintain the purity of the gospel. Thank you that righteousness is in Christ and not the law. Help me to understand what it means that I am crucified with Christ. Thank you that my old sinful self died with Christ on the cross. Thank you that the new me arose with him from the grave. Give me strength not to go back to the graveyard and rummage around in the dead bones of sin. Give me the strength to live by faith because you have loved me sacrificially on the cross and continue to love me deeply today. For I pray in the wonderful name of the resurrected Christ, Amen.

VI. DEEPER DISCOVERIES

A. Right hand of fellowship (v. 9)

Fellowship translates the word *koinonia*. *Koinonia* means "association," "fellowship," or "close relationship" (BAGD, 439). You have fellowship or partnership with those with whom you have commonality. We speak of fellowship over coffee or a meal. No closer Christian fellowship compares to participating in spreading the good news to unbelievers about Christ. Shaking the right hand was a sign of friendship and trust (BAGD, 174). Ralph Earle adds: "Not only were James, Peter, and John displaying a good spirit of Christian fellowship towards Paul and Barnabas, but they were shaking hands as partners in a business enterprise. Wisely they decided on a distribution of labor. The first three were to minister to Jews; the latter two were to go to the Gentiles" (*Word Meanings in the New Testament*, vol. 4, 185).

B. Justified by faith (v. 16)

Paul uses the word *dikaioo* for *justified* with the meaning of "to be pronounced and treated as righteous" (BAGD, 197). It is a judicial act of God by which he recognizes a person as righteous and declares a person free from guilt and punishment. The result is that a person is brought into a right relationship with God.

Paul, likewise, uses *pistis* for *faith,* emphasizing the idea of trust. Faith in just anything will not do. The object of one's faith is paramount. Biblical saving faith places its entire hope and trust for salvation in Christ's completed work on the cross. We are righteous now in God's eyes if we are trusting in his Son, not in ourselves.

Leon Morris declares:

> It was common to the religions of the day, as it has been common to other religions throughout history, that they put their emphasis on what people did. People must offer sacrifice; they must honour their deity, and so on. But Christians had the revolutionary idea that nothing the worshiper could do could bring salvation. That came as a free gift from God or it did not come at all. All the sinner can do is trust Christ for this world and the next (Leon Morris, *Galatians*, Downers Grove, IL: InterVarsity Press, 1996, 86).

Also, Morris believes:

> It is plain from the New Testament teaching throughout that justification comes to the sinner by the atoning work of Jesus and that this is applied to the individual sinner by faith. That God pardons and accepts believing sinners is the truth that is enshrined in the doctrine of justification by faith (*Evangelical Dictionary of Biblical Theology,* ed. Walter Elwell, Grand Rapids, MI: Baker Book House, 1984, p. 443).

"Christians are justified in the same way Abraham was, by faith (Rom. 4:16; 5:1). Human works do not achieve or earn acceptance by God" ("Justification," HBD, 830).

C. Crucified with Christ (v. 20)

One may ask how could Paul have been crucified with Christ? Was Paul dead? Was he nailed, physically, to the cross on the same day Jesus was? Of course, the answers to these questions must be, "No." Paul was not a Christian the day Jesus was crucified. Nor was he hung on a cross that day. He may well have been nowhere near Golgotha—the hill of crucifixion. So in what way was he crucified with Christ?

The phrase can mean one of two things. It can be a figure of speech, in which case the words symbolize another truth other than physical crucifixion. Or it can be a literal crucifixion in a mystical sense. Let's look at both possibilities.

If it is a figure of speech, it might mean that Paul (and by implication, all believers) received the benefit of Christ's crucifixion. Because Christ was crucified and died spiritually in our place, we do not have to die spiritually. So, the phrase, "I have been crucified with Christ," really means "Christ's crucifixion counts for me, so that it is the same as if I had been crucified when Christ was crucified."

Alan Cole, in the *Tyndale Commentary*, prefers a "figure of speech" understanding of this phrase:

> This is a simple statement of Paul's relation to the law. It stands for a complete change in his way of looking at all things—a "reorientation of thought," to use modern jargon. He means that, as the death of Christ marked a total change in the relationship of Christ to all things...so it did for Paul. The cross was, for Christ, a complete break with this life. In one sense every human death is such a break, although there was a deeper sense in which it was true of Christ. He had perfectly fulfilled the law; we have utterly failed. But for both law is now no more. Henceforth, Paul is dead to all claims of the law to be able to commend him to God (*Galatians*, Grand Rapids: Eerdmans, 1983, 82).

If the meaning is mystical, it might mean that Paul (and by implication, all believers) actually participated somehow in Christ's death and resurrection because of the mystical union that believers have with the Lord. John MacArthur states: "In both Romans and Galatians, Paul is referring to the fact that when a person exercises faith in the Lord Jesus Christ, he is placed in transcendent spiritual union with Christ in the historical event of His death and resurrection, in which the penalty of sin was paid in full" (John McArthur, *Galatians*, Chicago: Moody Press, 1987, 59).

James Boice also prefers this option. "[Paul] may be referring to an actual participation of the believer in Christ's death and resurrection conceived on the basis of the mystical union of the believer with the Lord (cf. Rom. 6:4–8; Col. 2:12–14; 3:1–4). This . . . view is the hardest to understand, but it is the one involved here" (James Boice, *Galatians*, Grand Rapids: Zondervan, 1976).

What does it mean to be "in Christ"? It means to be so united to Christ that all the experiences of Christ become the Christian's experiences. Thus, his death for sin was the believer's death; his resurrection was (in one sense) the believer's resurrection; his ascension was the believer's ascension, so that the believer is (again in one sense) seated with Christ "in the heavenly realms" (Eph. 2:6). Because of the verb tense Paul used, he cannot be speaking of a present experience of Christ's crucifixion . . . but rather to Christ's death itself. He died with Christ; that is, his "old man" died with Christ. This was arranged by God so that Christ, rather than the old Paul, might live in him.

We may not know exactly which meaning Paul had, even though we may have our opinions. We do know the implications. We are dead to the law. Before we knew Christ, the law had a claim on us. The law was perfect and revealed to us that we were not perfect. Because we were not perfect, the law declared that we were dead, cut off, alienated from God. However, because we have been crucified with Christ, we died, either actually in some mystical way or as a figure of speech.

Because we died, we are no longer under the jurisdiction of the law. A person is only obligated to the demands of the law as long as he is alive; but when he dies, the demands of the law are severed. We do not have to die in the future because of our sin, as the law demands, because we have died in Christ. Spiritual death has been eliminated, and we are now alive in Christ.

D. I no longer live, but Christ lives in me (v. 20)

"I no longer live" is a figure of speech meaning that "I no longer have control of my thoughts, words, and deeds. I submit them to the will of God so that, as nearly as I can determine, the thoughts, words, and deeds are not the ones I would choose but the ones Jesus would choose if he were in my shoes."

"But Christ lives in me" is a simple statement of fact. Christ through the Holy Spirit, now lives in Paul. As a result, the indwelling God convicts, illumines, and leads Paul to do the things Jesus would if he were in Paul's shoes.

E. The life I live in the body, I live by faith in the Son of God (v. 20)

This statement affirms life on earth in the physical body but describes a new kind of life, a life available only because of Jesus' resurrection. It means that Paul trusts the conviction, the illumining, the leading of Christ who lives within. By faith, he tries to be obedient and faithful to all he should do. Only such devotion and obedience to the living Christ can truly be called living.

VII. TEACHING OUTLINE

A. INTRODUCTION

1. Lead story: Heavenly Deception in Washington, D.C.
2. Context: In Galatians 2, Paul has continued to defend his authority as an apostle. The Jewish legalists had claimed that Paul was not a genuine apostle. They used this claim to destroy both Paul's credibility and the gospel message. Paul describes in chapter 2 two interpersonal

encounters that substantiate both his apostleship and message. He visited Jerusalem and was confirmed by the apostles (2:1–10). Another time he exercised apostolic authority in reprimanding and correcting the apostle Peter (2:11–21).

3. Transition: As we look into chapter 2, we will see Paul presenting two final conclusive proofs that authenticate his apostleship and message of grace. The degree of sparring that Paul has done in these two opening chapters illustrates the truth in what Thomas Jefferson once said, "The price of freedom is eternal vigilance."

B. COMMENTARY
1. Paul's Apostolic Authority and Message Endorsed (vv. 1–10)
2. Paul's Authority and Message Illustrated (vv. 11–21)
   a. The lapse of Peter (vv. 11–13)
   b. The correction by Paul (vv. 14–21)

C. CONCLUSION: THE WRONG BAG

VIII. ISSUES FOR DISCUSSION

1. We do not fall into the hypocrisy of acting like Jews even though we are Christians, as did the Galatian and Jerusalem believers. What is our modern form of hypocrisy more likely to look like?
2. The Jewish Christians were inclined to think that the Gentile Christians were not true believers because of things they did or did not do. Do you know people who believe in Christ today but whose Christian faith you are prone to doubt because of things they do or do not do?
3. Do you feel you are crucified with Christ? Do you feel as though Christ lives in you? Do you feel as though you live by faith in the Son of God? If you do not, how do you reconcile your feelings with the truth of Galatians 2?

Galatians 3

The Law Condemns Us

Quote

"*T*he [role] of the law is to show us the disease in such a way that it shows us no hope of cure; whereas the [role] of the gospel is to bring a remedy to those who are past hope."

John Calvin

Galatians

IN A NUTSHELL

*I*n chapter 3, Paul gives six points to show the Galatians the superiority of grace over law. (1) By grace, salvation and the Holy Spirit are given. (2) Abraham, the father of our people, was saved by grace. (3) Grace gives redemption and salvation; the law brings condemnation. (4) Abraham was saved by grace hundreds of years before the law was given. (5) The law's purpose is to act as a guide that leads us to Christ. (6) By grace a love relationship with God and one another is obtained.

The Law Condemns Us

I. INTRODUCTION

Raging Rapids

C. H. Spurgeon, the "Babe Ruth" of the Christian ministry, told a story about two men in a boat caught in severe rapids. As they were being carried swiftly downstream toward the perilous rocks and falls, men on the shore tried to save them by throwing out a rope. One man caught the rope and was saved. The other man, in the panic of the moment, grabbed a log that was floating alongside. It was a fatal mistake! The man who caught the rope was drawn to shore because he had a connection to the people on land. The man who clung to the log was carried downstream by the rapids . . . never to be found. Faith is like grabbing the rope from shore; it's our saving connection to Jesus Christ. Good works, like grabbing onto the log, carry men to their doom.

That is the point that Paul makes in Galatians 3. In response to the Judaizers who emphasize salvation by works, Paul clearly argues that faith in Christ is superior to obedience to the law. Paul knew that the message of salvation through grace by faith in Christ is a saving "rope" that leads men to eternal life. He also knew that salvation by works, which the Judaizers preached, was a "log" that would carry anyone clinging to it to their spiritual death. Paul uses six strong arguments in this chapter to prove conclusively that grace is superior to the law.

II. COMMENTARY

The Law Condemns Us

> **MAIN IDEA:** *Six arguments prove that grace's justification by faith is superior to the law.*

A The Argument from Your Personal Experience (vv. 1–5).

> **SUPPORTING IDEA:** *The Galatians were originally saved by faith, not law. Therefore, grace is superior to the law.*

3:1. Paul is direct and stern as he calls the Galatians **foolish**. They had fallen under the bewitching, deceptive spell of the Judaizers. They accepted a message that implied the death of Christ was insufficient. Paul had been so clear in presenting the gospel that he could say: **Before your very eyes Jesus Christ was clearly portrayed as crucified**. They were now rejecting what they had seen, through Paul's preaching, with their own mind's eyes.

3:2. Paul in verses 2–5 asks four rhetorical questions to demonstrate that salvation is through faith alone. These questions concern the reception and work of the Holy Spirit. He asks (1) **Did you receive the Spirit by observing the law, or by believing what you heard?** The obvious implied answer is **by believing!**

3:3. (2) **Are you now trying to attain your goal by human effort?** Paul declares them **foolish** for having begun the Christian life by faith but trying to reach maturity through human effort. Since there was no way under the law for the Holy Spirit to sanctify, the Judaizers promoted the only means to maturity they knew: obedience to the law (compare 4:10; 5:2).

3:4. (3) **Have you suffered so much for nothing? Suffer** probably does not mean persecution as some believe but in this context may be translated *experienced*. Paul is asking, "Have you experienced so many blessings of the Holy Spirit in vain?" By turning to a works message, they were discounting the saving and sanctifying work that the Holy Spirit had exemplified in their lives.

3:5. (4) **Does God give you his Spirit and work miracles . . . because you observe the law, or because you believe what you heard?** The Holy Spirit enters the believer's life because of grace and not the law.

🅱 Argument from Abraham (vv. 6–9)

SUPPORTING IDEA: *Abraham, who lived before the law, was saved by faith. The blessings of Abraham (inheritance, sonship, and eternal life) were received by faith. Therefore, grace is superior to the law.*

3:6. The Judaizers pointed to the Law of Moses as the means to salvation. Paul demonstrates that Abraham, who preceded Moses by 430 years, was saved by faith and not self-effort. Quoting Genesis 15:6, Paul states Abraham **believed God, and it was credited to him as righteousness**. To further discredit the Judaizers' emphasis on circumcision, Paul noted that Abraham was justified prior to his circumcision (Gen. 17:24). Therefore, the Judaizers could not argue that the law and circumcision were necessary for salvation because Abraham was saved apart from both of them.

I know a man who married a woman who was extremely wealthy. When he accepted her as his wife, all her money was added to his bank account. In the same way, when Abraham placed his faith in God, all God's righteousness was added to Abraham's spiritual account. My friend became as wealthy as his wife, and Abraham became in God's eyes as righteous as God. How? God **credited to him** his own divine righteousness.

3:7–8. Abraham's real **children** are not his physical descendants but his spiritual descendants. His real children are those who believe God and are therefore justified by faith and not the law. This inclusion of the Gentiles in God's plan of salvation was revealed in God's covenant with Abraham (Gen. 12:3) and is quoted here.

3:9. While provision is made for all to be blessed, only **those who have faith** are justified.

C Argument from the Curse of the Law (vv. 10–14)

SUPPORTING IDEA: *The law cannot justify. It can only bring judgment. Therefore, grace is superior to the law.*

3:10. Paul quotes Deuteronomy 27:26 to prove that, contrary to what the Judaizers claimed, the law cannot justify and save. It can only condemn. The breaking of any aspect of the law brought a curse on the person who broke the law. Since no one can keep the law perfectly, we are all cursed. Paul, with this argument, destroys the Judaizers' belief that a person is saved through the law.

3:11. Paul quotes Habakkuk 2:4: **The righteous will live by faith**. This verse reveals that even during the time of the law people were justified by faith and not obedience to the law. The Judaizers would have been wrong in their fundamental message even if they had lived during the time of Moses, because they misunderstood the purpose and power of the law.

3:12. The works of the law and the faith of the gospel have radically different consequences.

3:13. The positive solution to the curse of the law is in **Christ** who **redeemed us from the curse of the law**. *Redeem* means "to buy out of slavery by paying a price." This word was used when someone purchased a slave for the purpose of freeing them. When Jesus died on the cross, he took our curse upon himself. Through his substitutionary atonement, Christ paid the penalty of the curse. When we believe in him, he frees us from the slavery of the law.

3:14. Christ redeemed us, on the cross, for two purposes. First, he redeemed us so that the **blessing given to Abraham** (salvation through faith) **might come to the Gentiles**. Second, **he redeemed us . . . by faith** so that the promise of the Holy Spirit could be given to all who believe (compare v. 2).

D Argument from the Permanence of Faith (vv. 15–18)

SUPPORTING IDEA: *Abraham was saved by faith 430 years before the law was given to Moses. Therefore, grace is superior to the law.*

3:15–16. The Judaizers argued that since the law came after Abraham, then the law had priority over grace (salvation by faith alone). To refute this point, Paul appeals to a permanently binding contract or will. Once a permanently binding contract is written and signed, it cannot be changed. Paul argues that God's promise of salvation by faith to Abraham was a binding contract and that nothing, not even the law, could change it. This promise of permanence was made to Abraham and his seed, Christ. The singular use of **seed** (NIV, "offspring") (compare Gen. 12:7; 13:15; 24:7) was an allusion, not to Abraham's many physical descendants, but to the coming Messiah who would be the conveyer of blessing (see Matt. 1:1).

3:17–18. Paul clarifies that the **law**, which was given **430 years** after the Abrahamic grace promise, does not nullify justification by faith. Faith is the permanent path to salvation. **The inheritance** (that is, justification by faith) was given as an unconditional gift to those who believed. Contrary to what the Judaizers taught, the message of justification given to Abraham is permanent and has priority over the later law.

E Argument from the Purpose of the Law (vv. 19–25)

> **SUPPORTING IDEA:** *The law's purpose was never to save. Its purpose has always been to be a standard that would show us the magnitude of our sin, our need for grace, and, thus, lead us to Christ. The law was a temporary measure only until faith in Christ was inaugurated. Therefore, grace is superior to the law.*

3:19. Now Paul reveals **the purpose of the law** answering the question, "Why was a change made at Sinai?" Paul answers this question by explaining the one purpose and the two characteristics of the law. The **law was added because of transgressions.** *Transgressions* means "a stepping aside from a right track." The law laid down a right track (perfect standard) and made people aware when they were deviating from that perfect path. Yet the law was temporary. Its end point was the coming of the Seed (Christ, the Messiah). It is also inferior to Abraham and faith because it needed a mediator (angels and Moses on Mount Sinai).

3:20. Because the law required mediation, it required each party to live up to the contract. The Abrahamic covenant, on the other hand, was dependent only on the commitment of **God**, who **is one.** Therefore, the law was inferior to the promise given to Abraham.

3:21–22. Another question is raised: Is there conflict between the law and the **promises of God**? Paul answers, **absolutely not!** The law was not given to impart life and a right standing with God. Its purpose was to reveal that **the whole world is a prisoner of sin** condemned under its judgment. Such condemnation created in mankind a need for forgiveness and release from the law's penalty—a need for forgiveness in Christ.

3:23–25. Before faith in Christ came, people **were held prisoners by the law**. In a final image, Paul conveys the purpose of the law. In the KJV the second half of this verse states that the law was given as our **tutor** (NASB more literal than NIV, "was put in charge"). A better translation is "custodian" or "strict nanny." In the Jewish culture a slave was assigned to each child to escort them to school and to assist in their supervision. This nanny was not a thirteen-year-old, sweet, little baby-sitter. This supervising nanny was more like a stern sergeant who had the bark of a German shepherd and the bite of a Doberman pincher. Every time the child took liberties without permission on the path to school (children like to play) or did something wrong, this authoritarian nanny pointed her finger at the child and in no uncertain terms told the child what it had done wrong and delivered the punishment. By correlating the law with this nanny image, we learn that the law was given to point out sin and to threaten a great punishment if God's people didn't straighten up. Man's very inability to obey this law perfectly, and thus earn God's approval, caused men and women to long for a better way to salvation and a relationship with God—by grace. God brought hope to mankind's hopelessness in the most amazing way by sending Jesus Christ into the world. The law led **us to Christ** for forgiveness and righteousness.

Argument from the Believer's Present Position (vv. 26–29)

> **SUPPORTING IDEA:** *Grace appropriated through faith makes us adult children of God and unites us as brothers and sisters. The law never brought this vertical and horizontal oneness. Therefore, grace is superior to the law.*

3:26–27. By grace we are God's adult children. Paul calls us **sons of God**. Under the law we were children. In verse 27, Paul explains how this adult sonship occurred. We were united with him through the baptism of the Holy Spirit (1 Cor. 12:13). This placement into the body of Christ unites all believers. In addition you **have clothed yourselves with Christ**. In Roman society, when a youth became old enough to be considered an adult, he took off his children's clothes and put on an adult's toga. This switch indicated that he had adult citizenship and responsibilities. In the same way, the Galatians had laid aside the old clothes of the law and had put on Christ's new robes of righteousness (2 Cor. 5:21; Eph. 4:23–24).

3:28. Having explained the vertical change that grace brought, now Paul shows its horizontal effect when he states **you are all one in Christ**. In Christ, human distinctions lose their significance. Regardless of race, profession, or gender, all who come to Christ must come the same way—through faith and repentance. As a result, with all distinctions erased, all believers are united in Christ. This does not mean that all distinctions are erased on the human level. A slave was still a slave in the eyes of Rome, but not in the eyes of God.

3:29. Furthermore, in Christ, believers are **Abraham's seed.** As the offspring of Abraham, we are **heirs** of the **promise** of righteousness through faith. Thus, grace is superior to the law because it unites us with God and one another in a way that the law could not.

> **MAIN IDEA REVIEW:** *Six arguments prove that justification by faith is superior to the law.*

III. CONCLUSION

Can Anyone Help Me?

"Help," the man cried as he dangled helplessly from the edge of the cliff. "Can anyone up there help me?"

"Yes," answered a heavenly voice. "I'll help you, but first you must let go."

"Let go!" gasped the man. "But then I'd fall!"

"I'll catch you," replied the voice.

After a long pause, the man called out, "Can anyone else up there help me?"

This story illustrates mankind's refusal to accept God's offer of salvation. Rather than accepting God's faith way to salvation, people cry out for another way. Paul had clearly taught the Galatians that faith in Christ was the only way. Simple faith in Christ can be scary because it seems so easy. It seems too simple to let go of the rope of good works and self-merit and have a faith relationship with God. So what did the Galatians do? They listened to the false teachers who taught that letting go of the rope of self-effort was foolish. These false teachers convinced the gullible Galatians that they can have heaven and a relationship with God by clinging to good works.

In response to the Galatians' departure from a grace salvation, Paul left no logical stone unturned in proving that salvation is by faith alone in Jesus Christ. Paul fired heavy biblical artillery in this battle against doctrinal error. In this, the first of two chapters on salvation by faith alone, Paul has fired fifty percent of his arsenal; and the legalists are already suffering terrible mental casualties as Paul decimates their erroneous beliefs. In chapter 4, Paul will unload the remainder of his mental weapons as he annihilates the heresy of legalism. The truth—justification by faith in Christ—will prevail. Emancipation from slavery to the law is about to occur. Paul can taste victory. Grace will win this theological battle.

PRINCIPLES

- Some people have mental barriers preventing them from believing in Christ. It is our responsibility to help distinguish between legalism and righteousness that comes by faith.
- Our inability to obey the Ten Commandments perfectly shows us that we need Jesus Christ as our Savior.
- If observing the law could have saved us, then God would never have sent Jesus to die on the cross.
- The law was a guardian personally taking us by the hand and leading us to Jesus Christ—our personal Lord and Savior.
- Christ breaks down the barriers that divide people (v. 28).

APPLICATION

- Recognize that God's entrance requirement for heaven is perfection.
- Realize that "all have sinned and fall short of the glory of God" (Rom. 3:23).
- Allow your imperfections to humble you before God.
- Put your faith in Jesus Christ for forgiveness and eternal life.
- Thank God that his "grace way" is the best way.
- Rejoice that you now live under God's blessing and not sin's curse.
- Do not consider yourself as inferior to or better than anyone else. We are all equal in Christ.

IV. LIFE APPLICATION

Good Windshields Don't Go into the Space Shuttle

Imagine for a moment you are a glass manufacturer and you make the windshields for the space shuttle. You have a flaw in your manufacturing process: your windshield has a bubble. You might say to the people at NASA, "Look, this windshield is only flawed in one place. All the rest of it is flawless. What's more, the one imperfection in it isn't very bad, and it occurred a long time ago. It hasn't developed any imperfections since that very first one. Besides, it is a good piece of glass. It's a better piece of glass than the glass you now use in the shuttle."

If you were the quality control engineer for the space shuttle, you might listen patiently. You might even be sympathetic. Would you accept the windshield for use in the space shuttle? Of course not! The fact that its last flaw occurred a long time ago would be irrelevant. The fact that all the rest of the windshield is perfect except that one flaw would be beside the point. The fact that it is better than any other piece of glass would not matter in the least. The only relevant piece of information is that the windshield is not perfect. Because it is not perfect, it will not go in the space shuttle. Good windshields don't go into the space shuttle, only perfect ones.

So it is with people going to heaven. Good people don't go to heaven. The Bible says in Titus 3:5, God saved us, "not because of righteous things we had done, but because of his mercy." In Ephesians 2:8–9, we read, "For it is by grace you have been saved, through faith—and this not from yourselves; it is the gift of God—not by works, so that no one can boast."

The reason good people don't go to heaven, therefore, is because they do not meet God's standard. God's standard is not goodness. It is *perfection*. Good people don't go to heaven. Perfect people do. That presents a problem because no one is perfect (Rom. 3:10,23).

How do you get perfect? You must have your sins forgiven and your imperfections eliminated. That happens when you believe in, and receive, Jesus as your personal Savior. In his ledger book of life, we each are indebted to God. Everyone owes God for their sins. We owe him spiritual death—eternal separation from him—because of our sins. Jesus, the perfect God-Man, didn't owe a debt because he never sinned. Therefore, when we believe that his substitutionary payment on the cross is sufficient to pay for our sins and we accept him as our Savior, then God writes "paid in full" on our debt. At that point, we are forgiven. Christ's righteousness is imputed to us, for 2 Corinthians 5:21 says, "God made him who had no sin to be sin for us, so that in him we might become the righteousness of God." We are spiritually born again.

Therefore, though we are imperfect, we get to heaven on Christ's merit, on Christ's perfection, not our own. There is no other way.

Everyone of us is like the flawed space shuttle windshield. In word, thought, or deed, we have all sinned. Our only hope for heaven is to believe in Christ. Is he your Savior? If not, accept him now. Bow your head, and tell Christ that you believe in his payment for sin. Tell him that you are receiving him at this very moment. The richest life-giving verse in the Bible says, "For God so loved the world that he gave his only begotten son, that whosoever believes in Him should not perish, but have everlasting life" (John 3:16, KJV).

If you have already committed your life to Christ, then never lose sight of the fact that one of your greatest purposes in life is to share this good news with others.

V. PRAYER

Lord God, this chapter of Galatians convinces me that Jesus, and he alone, is sufficient to save me. Thank you for forgiving me and giving me your righteousness. Thank you that you now see me as perfect, because Christ has given me his perfection. In your saving name, I pray. Amen.

VI. DEEPER DISCOVERIES

A. Bewitched (v. 1)

Baskaino, the term Paul uses here, has connotations of witchcraft, sorcery, and magic. It is found only here in the New Testament. Then, as now, people in many cultures, commonly believed that some people have the ability to cast a spell on others. This belief occurs frequently among those who practice the occult. By asking, "Who has bewitched you?" Paul did not indicate that he believed in or practiced magic or the occult. He was simply saying, "You people are acting as though someone has cast a spell on you. You seem blinded by those false teachers who are leading you astray." This often seems to be the only explanation for some people who appear to be on the right spiritual track and then suddenly jump the tracks and go to spiritual ruin. Only some satanic or demonic influence can adequately explain this. Though Paul certainly was aware of powerful demonic influences, he may very well have been using this phrase as a figure of speech, not as an indication of his belief that they were led astray supernaturally.

B. Children of Abraham (v. 7)

Abraham was the first Hebrew (Jew). His special relationship with God was based on faith in the living God (Rom. 4:16; 5:1). Can only Jews be children of Abraham? Clearly not! The term "children" is not used in a genealogical sense but in a spiritual sense. It refers to people who show the same spiritual characteristics as the one to which they are compared. The children of Abraham are those who, like Abraham, are related to God by faith. By "descendants of Abraham" Paul doesn't mean physical descendents of Abraham. Rather, he means those who are descended from him spiritually. Christians are children of Abraham in that they stand in right relationship with God by faith—just as Abraham did.

C. Promise of the Spirit (v. 14)

The Bible teaches that the Spirit of God was active in the lives of people in the Old Testament, but no Scripture teaches that all believers in the Old Testament were indwelt by him. The Old Testament never mentions the possibility. Rather, it records David's concern that the Holy Spirit might be taken from him (Ps. 51:11), something that seems impossible in the New Testament (Rom. 8:38–39). Jesus stressed that "he (the Holy Spirit) lives with you and will be in you" (John 14:17).

The gift of the Spirit through faith in Christ fulfills, rather than contradicts, the Old Testament promises. Christ died so the blessings God has promised Israel might be given to the Gentiles, too. Moses (Num. 11:29–30) looks forward to a time all people would receive the Spirit (compare Joel 2:28–32).

D. Transgressions (v. 19)

For "transgressions" Paul uses the Greek word *parabasis*, meaning "overstepping" an existing law (BAGD, 611). A transgression assumes there is a boundary. The giving of the law provided this boundary, marking the "playing field" of the game of life under God. Before God gave the law to Moses, human wrongdoing was recognized as *hamartia*, sin, a deviation from the correct course of conduct. When God gave the law, sin came to be seen not merely as wrongdoing but as the breaking of a specific law, the stepping over of a boundary line God has set up. This revealed the exceptional sinfulness of the human race, a brazen sinfulness willing to say to God, "I know how to conduct life better than you do. I will set out my own boundary lines and ignore yours." Without the boundary-setting law, the radical sinfulness of humans might not have become so clear and evident.

The law, therefore, is God's way of showing sin (*hamartia*) in its true light. Sin is more than simply going beyond what is right. Sin means entering the realm of what is wrong, crossing over from the realm of life with God into the realm of death. God revealed his wrath against this clear case of human defiance against him. Seeing God's wrath revealed should awaken the conscience of anyone who has crossed the boundary, disobeyed the revealed will of God, and entered into the realm of divine wrath and death. Hopefully, seeing God's wrath will make you more reluctant to sin in the future.

E. Baptized into Christ (v. 27)

Literally, *baptize* (*baptizo*) means to "dip, immerse." If a white cloth is dipped or immersed in purple dye, it identifies with the dye as it is changed from white to purple. Paul writes of Christians being "baptized into Christ." Those who have received Jesus Christ by faith have been baptized into Christ and are joined with him in a spiritual union in which they participate in his death, burial, and resurrection (Rom. 6:3–4; Gal. 2:16). Water baptism is a physical picture of what has happened to us spiritually when we were spiritually united with Christ.

VII. TEACHING OUTLINE

A. INTRODUCTION

1. Lead story: Raging Rapids

2. Context: Many times people try to earn their salvation through good works. Sadly and ignorantly, they fail because God's standard for heaven is not goodness, but perfection; and no one is perfect. It is imperative to repent of this legalistic approach because it leads only to eternal separation from God.

3. Transition: In the third chapter of Galatians, Paul begins a two-chapter defense of grace. He presents, in these two chapters, nine arguments why grace is superior to the law. While convincingly arguing that grace is superior to law, Paul also answers the question, What is the purpose of the law? John Calvin, Reformation leader and theologian, summarized the revelation of this chapter: "The office of the law is to show us the disease in such a way that it shows us no hope for cure; whereas, the office of the gospel is to bring a remedy to those who are past hope." Thank God that there is hope through faith in Christ.

B. COMMENTARY: SIX ARGUMENTS WHY GRACE'S JUSTIFICATION BY FAITH IS SUPERIOR TO THE LAW'S MERIT SYSTEM

1. The Argument from Personal Experience (vv. 1–5)

2. The Argument from Abraham (vv. 6–9)

3. The Argument from the Curse of the Law (vv. 10–14)

4. The Argument from the Permanence of Faith (vv. 15–18)

5. The Argument from the Purpose of the Law (vv. 19–25)

6. The Argument from the Believer's Present Position (vv. 26–29)

C. CONCLUSION: GOOD WINDSHIELDS DON'T GO INTO THE SPACE SHUTTLE

VIII. ISSUES FOR DISCUSSION

1. What are some ways people seek right standing with God other than the way of grace through faith? Why are these ways tempting?

2. How was Abraham a representative of the faith way of salvation even though he lived almost two thousand years before Christ? When did God initiate the faith way of salvation?
3. When did God decide that salvation should not be given only to Jews but also to Gentiles?
4. How does the law lead us to Christ?
5. What does it mean that we are all one in Christ? What distinctions have been extinguished? Which distinctions still remain true?

Galatians 4

Grace Saves Us

"*It* is doubtful if there is any greater joy on earth than the joy of being free. And the ecstasy is heightened if a person has once been in bondage, held captive by a power that is impossible to overcome. Being liberated from such clutches brings pleasure beyond description."

C h a r l e s   S w i n d o l l

Galatians

I N   A   N U T S H E L L

In chapter 4, Paul explains the glorious reality of what it means to be God's children and how awful it would be to forfeit such a privilege. Thus he warns his readers not to listen to the false teachers seducing them away from Christ and back into slavery to the law rather than freedom in Christ.

Grace Saves Us

I. INTRODUCTION

The Cookie Thief

Amazing things can happen when you are "not on the same page" with someone else. Chuck Swindoll in his book *Simple Faith* tells the story of a traveler who, between flights at an airport, bought a small package of cookies. She then sat down in the busy snack shop to glance over the newspaper. As she read her paper, she became aware of a rustling noise. Peeking above the newsprint, she was shocked to see a well-dressed gentlemen sitting across from her, helping himself to her cookies. Half-angry and half-embarrassed, she reached over and gently slid the package closer to her as she took one out and began to munch on it.

A minute or so passed before she heard more rustling. The man had gotten another cookie! By now there was only one left in the package. She was flabbergasted; but she didn't want to make a scene, so she said nothing. Finally, as if to add insult to injury, the man broke the remaining cookie in half, pushed one piece across the table toward her with a frown, gulped down his half, and left without even saying thank you. She sat there dumbfounded.

Some time later, when her flight was announced, the woman opened her handbag to get her ticket. To her shock, she discovered in her purse her package of unopened cookies. Somewhere in that same airport another traveler tried to figure out how that strange woman could have been so forward and insensitive.

That man and woman were "not on the same page," so there was total confusion and chaos. In the first-century church, the Judaizers had invented their own edition of the gospel by combining grace and legalism. Things were falling apart spiritually because they were "not on the same page" with God. By combining grace with Old Testament law, the Judaizers were producing a dangerous hybrid of Christianity, another gospel that, was, in fact, no gospel.

Therefore, in chapter 3, Paul reminds the Galatians of Christ's sacrificial death for them, asks how they got the Spirit, and shows how God's plan had always been by faith. In chapter 4, Paul presents three arguments to prove that grace is superior to the law.

II. COMMENTARY

Grace Saves Us

MAIN IDEA: *Arguments from sonship, personal relationship, and the allegory of Isaac and Ishmael conclusively prove that justification is by grace through faith and not by observing the law.*

A The Argument from Sonship for the Jews (vv. 1–7)

SUPPORTING IDEA: *As Jews, we have matured from restricted childhood under the law to privileged adult sonship under grace. It makes no sense to regress to childhood after becoming adults.*

4:1–2. Paul enumerates some of the characteristics of childhood to illustrate the spiritual immaturity of living under the law. Though a child may be the **heir** of a great estate, he still lives and functions as a **slave** until a time set by his father. Legally appointed trustees make all decisions and exercise all power over the estate even though the child may be the legal owner in cases where the father has died.

4:3. Now Paul makes his application to the spiritual condition of the Galatians. He uses first person to include himself and give the sense that they are in this together. Prior to the grace of Christ, the Christian is enslaved to **the basic principles of the world,** the ABCs of the law.

4:4. But . . . God marks the divine answer to man's slavery under the law. When the law had accomplished its purpose and man was ready for release from the bondage of the law, **God sent his Son.** He came right on schedule, arriving on the earth **when the time had fully come.** Some suggest world conditions were ripe for the spread of the gospel. The Romans had ushered in an era of relative peace through law and order. Their network of roads made travel more convenient. Widespread use of the Greek language simplified communication. At the same time, the proliferation of empty religions among many people created a spiritual hunger for something genuine. The Son had the qualifications to bring salvation to human beings. He was human, **born of a woman,** facing the same temptations and problems every human faces. He faced the same expectations each person did, being **born under law.** Jesus perfectly fulfilled God's law, being without sin, but he did this as a human being tempted in all ways as we are.

4:5. Christ came for two purposes: First, he came to **redeem those under law.** Christ paid the price of his death to free us from the slavery of the law. Second, Christ came **that we might receive the full rights of sons.** These rights come as a gift, or they don't come at all. Human effort can never secure them.

4:6. As son and heir, each Christian receives the Holy Spirit, the down payment of his or her inheritance (Eph. 1:14). The Holy Spirit moves believers to pray to God as **Abba, Father.** *Abba* is the equivalent of "Daddy." It shows the closeness children of grace have with their Father. No slave of the law had such an intimate relationship. That intimate relationship comes through the Spirit not through the law.

4:7. Paul concludes that the Galatians were **no longer** slaves but were sons and heirs. Thus, under grace we have progressed from being slaves to being sons and heirs. Grace is adulthood. Law is childhood. With the privileges of adulthood, why regress back to the law?

B Argument from Sonship for the Gentiles (vv. 8–11)

SUPPORTING IDEA: *As Gentiles, your new relationship as God's sons produces maturity. You are free from the bondage of paganism. It is illogical to revert to bondage by observing the law.*

4:8–9. Before Christ, the Galatians had been **slaves** to pagan gods such as Zeus and Hermes. When they believed in Christ, they had been delivered from this bondage. They could not claim any credit to say they had achieved a knowledge of God. God had taken all the initiative to form a love relationship with them so that he knew them. Now Paul asked them why they were turning back to the **weak and miserable** bondage of legalism which could not produce life or righteousness or freedom.

4:10. The Judaizers had persuaded the Galatians to observe the Mosaic calendar. These seasonal events included **special days** (weekly sabbaths), **months** (new moons), and **seasons** (Festivals of Passover, Pentecost, and Tabernacles). The Galatians kept these festivals to gain God's favor.

4:11. If they continued in legalism, Paul feared that his efforts on them would have been wasted. This could mean one of two things. It could mean that the Galatians were true Christians but that Paul's efforts to spur them on to spiritual maturity in Christ were not fruitful. Or it could mean that he feared that not turning from their legalism could indicate that they were never Christians in the first place.

C Argument from Their Troubled Relationship (vv. 12–16)

SUPPORTING IDEA: *The controversy over legalism separated Paul from his close friends, the Galatians. Therefore, the law cannot be mature and true because it has separated intimates.*

4:12. On his initial preaching visit to Galatia, the Galatians had embraced him warmly. Now Paul appeals to that reception and the resulting relationship to motivate them to return to grace. Paul had become like the Gentiles by rejecting the Jewish law as a way to right standing with God. Now he challenges the Galatian Gentiles to become like him by also rejecting legalism. The irony of this is that the Galatians were returning to legalism after their conversion to Christianity.

Most commentators believe the phrase **you have done me no wrong** refers to what follows in verses 13-14. The Galatian believers received Paul very well during his first visit to them, doing him no wrong.

4:13–14. Paul pleads with them based on their previous affection. He refers to the fellowship they had enjoyed during his prior visit with them on his first missionary journey (see Acts 13–14). While he was with them, he had gotten sick, and they had done him no wrong; rather, they treated him quite well. In fact, he says they **welcomed** him like **an angel of God** or **Christ Jesus himself.**

4:15. Paul wants to know why they no longer welcome him with joy. At one time they appreciated him so much that they **would have torn out** their **eyes and given them to** him. Paul may have had eye problems and, in hyperbole (deliberate exaggeration to make a point), Paul states that the Galatians loved him so much that they would have joyously given their eyes to him.

4:16. Apparently, everything had changed. The Judaizers had convinced the Galatians that Paul was not a legitimate apostle and that his gospel, by excluding the law, was deficient. Rather than embrace him, they had shunned and treated him like an **enemy** because he preached to them **the truth** of grace.

ⅅAppeal to their motives (vv. 17–20)

SUPPORTING IDEA: *Zealous opponents should not be able to woo you away from the truth of God's salvation in Christ, but you should trust the motives and actions of the one who first led you to Christ.*

4:17–18. The Judaizers' motives are now exposed. They are proselytizing the Galatians to separate them from Paul and thereby strengthen their own cause. Paul commends their zeal but regrets that this passion is so erroneously misplaced.

4:19–20. The apostle, on the other hand, had always had proper motives toward the Galatians. Now he reveals his tender love for them. Addressing them tenderly as **my dear children,** Paul compared himself to a mother in the midst of birth pangs. Paul agonized over them initially as he implored them to become Christians. Now he is agonizing over their spiritual growth. Paul longs for **Christ** to be **formed** in them. His passion is for them to be conformed to the character of Christ. This transformation is God's purpose for each believer as Christ lives in us and through us (Gal. 2:20). Paul is

perplexed by their spiritual waywardness. He wants to be with them and correct them firmly but gently.

E Argument from the Allegory of Isaac and Ishmael (vv. 21–31).

SUPPORTING IDEA: *Paul produces a final rebuttal of legalism by giving an allegorial interpretation of Abraham and his difficulties with his two wives and two sons.*

4:21–23. An allegory is a spiritual or symbolic interpretation of a story that also has a literal meaning. Isaac was born of the **free woman**, Sarah, and represents grace. Ishmael was born of the **slave woman**, Hagar, and represents the law. The birth of Ishmael was an ordinary birth to Abraham and his slave. The birth of Isaac was a supernatural birth because Abraham and Sarah were very old. It was a birth of **promise** in that Isaac was the child God promised to give to Abraham (Gen. 12).

4:24. As there was conflict between Isaac and Ishmael, so there is conflict between grace and legalism. The two women represent **two covenants**. Hagar represents the Mosaic Covenant which came from Mount Sinai. Her children are slaves. As Hagar brought forth a slave, so the law also produces slaves. In the same manner, Sarah represents the Abrahamic Covenant. Her children are free. As Sarah brought forth a free son, grace brings forth free children.

4:25–26. Now Paul compares the two women to two Jerusalems. **Hagar stands for Mount Sinai** and represents the first-century city of Jerusalem, the Jewish capital city whose inhabitants were still enslaved to the law. **Sarah** represents Jerusalem, the heavenly city of God, where all departed believers go (Heb. 12:22). Thus, only grace, represented by Sarah, leads to eternal life.

4:27. This quote from Isaiah 54:1 contrasts the future lineages of the two women. Sarah (grace) was initially barren, but she ended up with innumerable spiritual children because of the Abrahamic Covenant. She eventually surpassed the younger Hagar. The intended comparison was between the growth of Christianity (grace) and the stagnation of Judaism (law) in the first century. Paul is challenging the Galatians to choose Christ (grace) and be a part of what God was doing in their day.

4:28–31. Just like Isaac, the New Testament saints were **children of promise**. Just as Isaac was subject to Ishmael's persecution (see Gen. 21:9), so the early Christians were subject to persecution from the legalists. By applying this quote from Genesis 21:10, Paul commands the Galatians to get rid of the legalizers. Their work does not have the authority or blessing of God. It must come to an end. The Galatians must choose to be free and act on that choice by expelling the Judaizers.

> **MAIN IDEA REVIEW:** *Arguments from sonship, personal relationship, and the allegory of Isaac and Ishmael conclusively prove that justification is by grace through faith and not by observing the law.*

III. CONCLUSION

On God's Page

To have a deep and satisfying relationship with God, we must be "on the same page" with him. The Judaizers were definitely not on God's page. Erroneously, they believed that faith alone in Jesus Christ was not enough for salvation and Christian maturity. Unfortunately, they were getting the Galatians to read from their script, and consequently, the Galatians were no longer on God's page of grace.

The woman who naively and accidentally ate the man's cookies experienced great embarrassment when she realized that she was actually the guilty party. The result of the Judaizers' error was far greater than emotional embarrassment. The eternal destinies of people are jeopardized when grace is fogged over by legalism. In addition, Christianity is extremely unattractive when presented with a legalistic flavor. Legalism repels, while grace attracts.

Fortunately, for the Galatians and for us today, Paul tackled this legalistic distortion head on. With the three arguments presented in this chapter, Paul has proven convincingly that grace is superior to the law.

PRINCIPLES

- Grace is the spiritual parent of the Christian believer.
- External rules and restrictions are an indication of childhood immaturity.
- Reverting to the law is regressing to spiritual childhood.
- Grace gives you a deeply personal relationship with God (*Abba*, Father).
- Grace brings believers together, while law separates God's family.

APPLICATIONS

- You can rest in the security that you are the recipient of an unchangeable covenant with God.
- You can praise God that he is continuously maturing you toward spiritual adulthood.

- Decide what you think is the primary privilege and responsibility of being a spiritual adult.
- You can enjoy the fact that God is your *Abba* Father who loves you deeply.

IV. LIFE APPLICATION

The Irresponsible Foreign Consul

The New Testament clearly teaches that we do not live under the Law of Moses. This chapter teaches that salvation and maturity are products of faith in Christ apart from the law. Truly the message of grace is superior to the message of the law. Christ has set us free from the law (Gal. 5:1). Yet freedom does not imply a lack of responsibility.

The newspapers reported a Michigan state policeman who had stopped a man for driving seventy-five in a forty-five m.p.h. zone. The speeder reached into his pocket and flashed an official seal and signature of the U.S. Secretary of State. He informed the officer that he was the consul general of another country and therefore was immune from the law. Frustrated, the officer had no choice but to let the offender go.

That afternoon the officer clocked another speeder scorching the road at ninety-three in a fifty-five m.p.h. zone. With lights glaring and siren blaring the officer sped down the road after him. To his amazement, he discovered that the reckless driver was the same foreign diplomat. Rudely, the diplomat announced that he had no intention of keeping the speed and that he would do as he pleased. Impatiently, he honked his horn while the policeman radioed headquarters and was informed that there nothing they could do to detain the diplomat. As the officer frustratedly handed the diplomat's papers back to him, he said, "Even though you aren't subject to our laws, you could at least have some regard for the safety of our people."

This story reminds us that we as believers are not obligated to keep the avalanche of rules and regulations in the Mosaic legal system. Like the foreign consul, we are immune from the Mosaic Law. In addition, in Christ we also have complete immunity from the eternal sentence required by God for breaking his Old Testament law. This does not mean that we have an excuse to be lawless. We have no more right to live above God's moral principles found in the Mosaic Law than the consul had to live above the reasonable laws of this country. On the contrary, we have the responsibility to submit ourselves to the principle of love defined in the Scriptures. The New Testament tells us that the person who loves God and his neighbor with all his heart fulfills the Old Testament law. God has given us in the New Testament his guidelines for us to follow. When we obey them, we are loving as he loves.

If we fail to obey his New Testament commands and love as he loves, we will be no different than the reckless foreign diplomat who was acting against the spirit of the law even though he was not literally violating that law.

Freedom in Christ does not give us the right to do as we please but the power and ability to do as we ought. Paul's words in the next chapter verify these truths when he says in Galatians 5:13, "You, my brothers, were called to be free. But do not use your freedom to indulge the sinful nature; rather, serve one another in love."

V. PRAYER

O God, thank you for giving me a relationship with you that is based on grace. Thank you that grace is maturing me from spiritual childhood into Christian adulthood. When the very essence of your Word is threatened, give me wisdom, like Paul, to show that your gospel is superior to all spiritual imitators. In Christ's name, I pray. Amen.

VI. DEEPER DISCOVERIES

A. Abba (v. 6)

Abba is the Aramaic word for *father.* Jesus used it to speak of his intimate relationship with God, his heavenly Father. The word was well-known to his hearers. In ancient Israel when a little boy heard his father coming home from work in the fields, he might dash out of the kitchen doorway, run down the path, throw his arms around the knees of his approaching father, and shout, "Abba! Abba!" In English we might correctly translate it, "Daddy."

In the same way as God's spiritual children, we can speak to him as Abba. He loves us and treats us as his children, and we may love him and treat him as our father. Jesus addressed God as Abba when he prayed (Mark 14:36) and when he taught his disciples to pray the same way (Luke 11:1–2). Many of Jesus' opponents became offended at this, thinking Abba was too familiar a term to use in addressing the high and holy God. Jesus' usage established the pattern for the church's view of God and for each believer's relationship with him. Paul said we can cry out to God, "Abba," because he has adopted us into his family (Rom. 8:15).

B. Weak and miserable principles (v. 9)

Three basic interpretations seek to explain what Paul meant when he mentioned "weak and miserable principles" in verse 9 after referring to "basic principles of the world" in verse 3. The three interpretations are:

1. The Law of Moses: This is the most apparent possibility, since the entire context of the letter to the Galatians centers around the

Christian's responsibility to the law. Though the Galatian believers were Gentiles and had never been under slavery to the Law of Moses, they were in danger of becoming enslaved if they succumbed to the lure of the Judaizers and placed themselves under the law.

2. The four basic "elements of the universe" of Greek philosophy, namely, earth, air, fire, and water: These elements came to be known not just for their literal meaning but for gods, stars, and planets as well. Many pagan religions worshiped these heavenly bodies, believing they had some affect on the affairs of humans. So Paul may have referred to pagan influences which enslaved the Gentile believers.

3. Early stages of religious practice, Jewish or pagan: Perhaps this interpretation has the most to commend it. Paul's reference was to any fruitless religious beliefs and practices which a person may have before becoming a Christian.

Trying to reach God through any means other than Christ is a weak and miserable undertaking . . . weak because it does not bring righteousness and miserable because it does not bring any good result. That is, it provides no inheritance.

VII. TEACHING OUTLINE

A. INTRODUCTION

1. Lead story: The Cookie Thief

2. Context: In the fourth chapter of Galatians, we conclude the second major section of this letter. Having proved the authenticity of his apostleship in chapters 1 and 2, Paul, in chapters 3 and 4 defends the content of the gospel. Paul convincingly ties together nine arguments to prove that the gospel of grace is superior to the gospel of the law. In so doing, Paul obliterates the rational underpinnings of the Judaizers.

3. Transition: In chapter 4, we will study Paul's final three arguments for the superiority of grace to law. We will see conclusively that it is utterly impossible to mix legalism and grace. We will come to appreciate in a new way the wonder of grace. Charles Swindoll in *Grace Awakening* highlights the wonder of grace when he writes, "It is doubtful if there is any greater joy on earth than the joy of being free. And the ecstasy is heightened if a person has once been in bondage, held captive by a power that is impossible to overcome. Being liberated from such clutches brings pleasure beyond description."

B. COMMENTARY

1. Argument from Sonship (vv. 1–7)
2. Argument from Personal Relationship (vv. 8–20)
   a. Appeal not to return to the bondage of legalism (vv. 8–11).
   b. Appeal to their past relationship (vv. 12–16)
   c. Appeal to their motives (vv. 17–20)
3. Argument from the Allegory of Isaac and Ishmael (vv. 21–31)

C. CONCLUSION: THE IRRESPONSIBLE FOREIGN CONSUL

VIII. ISSUES FOR DISCUSSION

1. What full rights do we have as God's children? Why would someone give up such rights?
2. Describe what it means not to know God and be slaves to those who are not gods. To what are people enslaved today?
3. Does someone know that you love them as much as Paul loved the Galatians and that you want them to know and follow Christ as much as Paul wanted the Galatians to?
4. Who is trying to lead you away from Christ? Why?

Galatians 5

Walk in the Spirit

"*Legalists in our churches today warn that we dare not teach people about the liberty we have in Christ lest it result in religious anarchy. The Christian who lives by faith is not going to become a rebel. Quite the contrary, he is going to experience the inner discipline of God that is far better than the outer discipline of man-made rules.*"

Warren Wiersbe

IN A NUTSHELL

In chapter 5, Paul explains to the Galatian Christians: Through grace, Christ has set you free. Stand firm, and do not fall back into the slavery of the law. Yet do not use your freedom as an opportunity to sin. Do not give yourself over to the deeds of your carnal desires but rather to the deeds of the Holy Spirit.

Walk in the Spirit

I. INTRODUCTION

Cows in Prison

*W*hen I was a teenager growing up in the country, we had great fun letting the yearling calves out of the barn after a long winter. These calves had been born the summer before, so a pen in the barn was the only world they had known. They were kept there because of the severity of the northern Indiana winters. When spring came, we would open the gates that had separated the calves from the outside world. Then the calves were free to go into the field. However, the calves didn't know what to do with their newfound freedom.

On a typical day they bucked and jumped and ran around inside the pen in excitement but wouldn't leave it. Often they would run right up to where the gate used to be and slam on the brakes. From a full gallop they planted their front feet and dropped their noses to the floor as their rumps flew up in the air, stopping exactly where they would have had to stop if the gate had been there. Then they wheeled and sprinted, tail flying, for the other side of the barn.

Afterward, not having any more nerve for the bold approach, they changed strategies and inched cautiously up to the invisible barrier as if it were a snake. When they had exhausted their supply of nerve, they jerked back as though bitten. Then they ran around again on the inside of the pen like a merry-go-round run amok, bucking, jumping, and kicking the air. It would sometimes take hours for them to get up the nerve to leave, terrified of their sudden freedom, preferring the safety of their small enclosure to the unknown openness of the pasture outside.

I have often thought how these calves were like legalists, preferring the limitations and security of a set of dos and don'ts to the frightening world of walking by faith. Why would they want to stay in the barn when freedom, sunshine, and fresh air were theirs? That is the question Paul asks of the Galatian church. Having been freed from the slavery of the law, under Paul's initial visit, why would they now want to lose their freedom and go back to the bondage of the law?

Paul answers this question in chapter 5 in three ways. First, he implores them to stand firm in their freedom in Christ (v. 1). Then, he lists six negative consequences of returning to the law (vv. 2–11). Finally, he introduces the Spirit-filled life as the power to overcome sin and evil (vv. 12–26).

II. COMMENTARY

Walk in the Spirit

MAIN IDEA: *The Christian is freed from external control by the law to internal control by the Holy Spirit.*

A Freedom from the Law and Its Negative Consequences (vv. 1–12)

SUPPORTING IDEA: *The Christian is set free from the negative effects of the law, so don't return to it. You would have to keep the whole law perfectly, which you cannot. In Christ, only faith working through love avails anything.*

5:1. Christ died to set us free from slavery to the law. Our responsibility is to stand firm and not to fall back into law and sin.

5:2. Those who return to the law face six negative consequences. First, it invalidates Christ's work on the cross for **Christ will be no value to you.** By submitting to circumcision, a person demonstrated that they were not fully trusting in Christ. Instead they added their own works to what Christ had done, thus invalidating the sufficiency of Christ for salvation.

5:3. The second negative consequence of returning to the law is obligation. Once a person submits to one part of the law (circumcision), he is **obligated to obey the whole law.**

5:4–6. The third negative consequence of returning to the law is that it removes a person from the sphere of grace. While the legalist is insecure because he cannot know if he has done enough to merit salvation, the believer is secure because he has placed his **faith** in Christ and will **eagerly await** righteousness.

When Paul says **we eagerly await . . . the righteousness for which we hope,** he is referring to one of two possibilities. On the one hand he may be referring to the righteousness that grows in us slowly, day by day, as we live by faith in him. On the other hand, he may be referring to the day when our righteousness will suddenly be complete, the day when Jesus returns (Rom. 8:8–25; Col. 1:5; 2 Tim. 4:8). Both ideas are true and are taught elsewhere in Scripture. Our salvation is past, present, and future. We have been saved by Jesus' work on the cross in the past; we are saved day by day as the Spirit works within us to bring about daily righteousness, and we will be saved when we see Jesus and receive our glorified body, freed from sin to serve him in unsullied righteousness. What truly matters is the fruit of grace which is **faith expressing itself through love** (Eph. 2:10; Jas. 2:14–18). To fall from grace is to fall from love. (Falling from grace is discussed more fully in "Deeper Discoveries.")

5:7–10. The fourth negative consequence of returning to the law is that it hinders spiritual growth and development. Using the metaphor of a **race**, Paul states that the legalists had cut in on the Galatians' spiritual race and caused them to stumble spiritually. As a result, the Galatians were no longer **obeying the truth.** Turning to a yeast metaphor, Paul illustrates how quickly a little bit of legalism can contaminate a believer and, indeed, a whole church. Paul, however, expressed his confidence that the Galatians would not depart from the truth. He warned that those who are confusing them will experience God's judgment.

5:11. A fifth consequence when one retreats to legalism is the removal of the **offense of the cross.** Before Paul was converted, as a Pharisee, he preached circumcision. Now he is being accused of **still preaching circumcision.** Paul denies this accusation by pointing to the offense or stumbling block of his gospel. He omitted circumcision, and this omission was an offense to the legalists who attacked him.

5:12. The sixth and final consequence of turning to the law is anger. Paul is so angry he wishes the legalists **would go the whole way and** castrate **themselves** as did the pagan priests of the cult of Cybele in Asia Minor. This desire is not a pretty picture, but Paul is completely exasperated by these people who are preaching circumcision and sabotaging the Galatians' faith.

Ⓑ Freedom to Live a Life of Love (vv. 13–15)

SUPPORTING IDEA: *Christ gives the Christian the freedom to love others truly.*

5:13–14. In verse 1, Paul states that Christian freedom is the right and privilege of every believer. Then he points out six negative consequences of falling back into slavery. Now he warns them not to use this freedom as a license to sin. Rather than liberty being used for selfishness, the true objective of their newfound freedom is love. Quoting Leviticus 19:18, Paul summarizes the law as "**love your neighbor as yourself.**" Always remember that we are slaves commissioned to love one another (Matt. 22:39).

5:15. As a result of the legalists, this church was divided. They were **biting and devouring each other.** Their church and community of faith were on the verge of destruction. Legalism treats people harshly and often leads to divisions.

Ⓒ Freedom to Live and Love Empowered by the Spirit (vv. 16–18)

SUPPORTING IDEA: *Release from the law and the power to love are results of God's working in us by his Holy Spirit.*

5:16. The law was powerless to help a Christian overcome these sins. We may want to please God, but our sin nature continually pulls us into disobedience (Rom. 7). The answer to this battle between the old and new nature is found in the inward ministry of the Holy Spirit. To experience victory we must **live** or walk (KJV) **by the Spirit.** As we live our lives in dependence on, and obedience to, the Holy Spirit, **we will not gratify the desires of the sinful nature** (see "Deeper Discoveries").

5:17. Now Paul demonstrates the need for the Holy Spirit's enablement. The Christian will, this side of heaven, always experience conflict between the Holy Spirit and the flesh. Here flesh is not limited to the physical dimension of man but denotes anything less than and other than God in which man places trust that belongs to God alone. Paul gives a more complete description of this conflict in Romans 7.

5:18. In summary, Paul tells us that victory over sin is not the result of living under the law. Instead, it is the result of actively yielding to the Spirit. Therefore, both the first step of salvation and its ongoing steps (sanctification, growth in holiness) are brought about within us by God's Spirit working through faith. To be saved, we must have faith in Christ. To walk in God's way, we must have faith in the Holy Spirit, for he empowers us to walk in obedience.

Ⓓ Contrast of the Acts of the Flesh and the Fruit of the Spirit (vv. 19–23).

SUPPORTING IDEA: *The acts of the flesh symbolize spiritual death, but the fruit of the Spirit is evidence of spiritual life.*

5:19. In verses 19–23, Paul contrasts the acts of the flesh with the fruit of the Spirit. The acts of the sinful nature are divided into four categories. First, three sexual sins are listed. **Sexual immorality** is a broad term covering fornication, adultery, and homosexuality. **Impurity** is also a broad term referring to moral uncleanness in our thought life, speech, and actions (Eph. 5:3–4). **Debauchery** is brazen, unashamed boldness in these sexual sins. People who become desensitized through sexual exploits can eventually lose all modesty and instead can flaunt their erotic, sinful lifestyle.

5:20–21. The second category of these sinful acts is religious sin. Paul presents **idolatry and witchcraft** as two religious sins. **Idolatry** involves bowing down to pagan gods. **Witchcraft** refers to the magical potions administered by sorcerers. Through these magical potions, these sorcerers were able to control the evil powers.

Now Paul lists eight societal sins. They run the gamut from **hatred** to the actions of **discord** and **jealousy** that result in **factions**. Loving others is not easy. When the flesh controls us, interpersonal problems are the result. Finally, two alcohol-related sins are listed: **drunkenness** and **orgies**. Orgies refer to drunken sexual perversions associated with Bacchus, the god of wine. Alcohol controls people and distorts their thinking. Many people, under the influence of a few drinks, have committed grievous sexual sins. Rather than being controlled by alcohol, the Christian is to be controlled by the Holy Spirit (Eph. 5:18). While a Christian may intermittently get pulled into these sins, **those who live like this** (habitually, continually) are not Christians and will therefore **not inherit the kingdom of God.**

5:22–23. In contrast to the "acts of the flesh" presented above, those who are obedient to the Holy Spirit produce beautiful, nourishing spiritual fruit. Notice the fruit in this passage is called the fruit of the Spirit, not the fruit of self-effort. This fruit the Holy Spirit produces in the life of a faithful Christian. In other passages of Scripture, we are commanded to fulfill the individual characteristics. The answer to this seeming paradox, I believe, is that only the Holy Spirit can produce the fruit; but he will not do so unless we are striving to the best of our ability for them in faithful obedience. These fruits of the Spirit are in harmony with and not opposed to the law. However, they are not produced by the law but rather by the Spirit working through the believer's faith.

E The Solution to the Sinful Struggle (vv. 24–26)

SUPPORTING IDEA: *The Christian has died to sin and is alive to a Spirit-controlled life of righteousness.*

5:24. The struggle between our flesh and our new nature is real. Yet there is more truth to help us win this battle. Paul explains that those who know Jesus Christ do not have to respond to the flesh because they **have crucified the [flesh] with its passions and desires.** This crucifixion refers to our identification with Christ in his death and resurrection (Gal. 2:20). When Christ died, our flesh was judged. This does not mean our propensity to sin has been eradicated or rendered inoperative. We must accept that our old nature has died with Christ and that as new people we have an increasing power to resist sin (Rom. 6:10–12).

5:25–26. In addition to the flesh that is judged, Paul reminds the Galatians that they have the Holy Spirit to strengthen them against sin. We must **keep in step** by following the Holy Spirit's direction and guidance. He ends our bondage to evil desires. Finally, Paul challenges the Galatians to live a life of harmony. Conceited legalism sees no need of the Spirit's help and thinks it has accomplished salvation apart from the Spirit. Instead, it leads to arguments. Paul says to stop **provoking and envying each other**. These negative traits point to the divisions in the church caused by the legalists. The only answer to such disharmony is love empowered by the Holy Spirit.

MAIN IDEA REVIEW: *The Christian is freed from external control by the law to internal control by the Holy Spirit.*

III. CONCLUSION

Trading for Freedom

In this chapter Paul challenges us to live in freedom from the law. He gives us six excellent reasons not to live under the law (vv. 1–12). He tells us to walk in love (vv. 13–15) by the power of the Holy Spirit (vv. 13–26). He tells us how we can break free of the tyranny of sin—not that we will never sin again but that we need not be in bondage to sin.

In the book *The Trapp Family Singers*, the Trapp family falls into disfavor with the Nazis who are rising to power just before World War II. Therefore, they must escape from their lovely home in Austria to Switzerland. As Hitler's troops closed in on Austria, the von Trapp family escaped to a church, then to a roof, and finally to the country, where they climbed the mountains to freedom. They eventually made it to America, where they settled in Stowe, Vermont and became nationally famous for their lovely musical performances. They never lost their gratitude for the freedom they enjoyed in America. Even though they left behind a fortune in land, estates, and gold, they willingly traded it for freedom.

Like the von Trapp family, Jesus has given us escape from the bondage and tyranny of sin. Yes, we may have had to give up some things that the world considers valuable; but to enjoy spiritual freedom now and eternal reward in heaven, the exchange was well worth it.

PRINCIPLES

- Everybody is a slave to something . . . either good or bad. You cannot expect to harvest the fruit of God when you are sowing the seeds of evil.

- It only takes a few cancer cells of sin to infect and destroy vital spiritual organs.
- Freedom in Christ does not give us the right to do as we please, but the liberty to do as we ought.
- God must work in me so he can work through me.

APPLICATIONS

- Choose your bondages well. Make yourself a slave to Christ.
- Catch sin early. Like cancer, it spreads.
- Imitate Jesus in all you do.

IV. LIFE APPLICATION

In the Grip of Grace

Does grace promote sin? Legalists make the claim that complete forgiveness in Christ, without human effort to be "good," will give Christians the freedom to run wild, morally. They reject grace because they believe it gives Christians a license to sin. The opposite is true, however. If one has truly understood and experienced grace, it makes him want to be more holy, not more sinful. If one has tasted the fresh fruit of grace, a still resolve to be more like Jesus is the result. Quietness comes, not chaos.

Chuck Colson, founder of Prison Fellowship, tells a remarkable story of the power of grace being manifested in a prison near the city of Sao Jose dos Campos, Brazil. Twenty years ago the Brazilian government turned the prison over to two Christians, who renamed it Humaita, and began to run it on Christian principles. With the exception of two full-time staff, inmates do all the work. Families outside the prison adopt an inmate to work with during and after the term of imprisonment. Colson heard about the prison and one day visited it. He reported:

> When I visited Humaita I found the inmates smiling—particularly the murderer who held the keys, opened the gates, and let me in. Wherever I walked, I saw men at peace. I saw clean living areas, people working industriously. The walls were decorated with Biblical sayings from Psalms and Proverbs. My guide escorted me to the notorious prison cell once used for torture. Today, he told me, that block houses only a single inmate. As we reached the end of a long concrete corridor and he put the key in the lock, he paused and asked, "Are you sure you want to go in?"
>
> "Of course, " I replied impatiently, "I've been in isolation cells all over the world." Slowly he swung open the massive door, and I saw

the prisoner in that punishment cell: a crucifix, beautifully carved by the Humaita inmates—the prisoner, Jesus, hanging on a cross.

"He's doing time for the rest of us," my guide said softly. ("Making the World Safe for Religion," *Christianity Today*, 8 November 1993, 33).

Christ sets people free. We don't have to remain in bondage because Jesus has paid the price for our crime. Just as it would be absurd for a prisoner who has served his time to want to stay behind bars, even so it is absurd for us to remain in the penitentiary of sin. We are now free. We are released from the prison of sin. Christ has done our time for us.

Therefore, exercise your Christian liberty today. You have the freedom to say, "No," to sin and, "Yes," to God. That's your powerful privilege in Christ! You are no longer a slave to sin. When you accepted Jesus Christ as your personal Savior, he gave you the freedom to become a slave of righteousness. Disdain your old, damaging bondage to sin; celebrate your new, life-giving bondage to Christ. Everybody is somebody's slave. Whose slave are you? As a slave of Christ, your greatest joy will be the peaceful fruit of righteousness.

V. PRAYER

Dear Lord, progress is so satisfying and regression so saddening. You have changed me in many, many, wonderful ways. By the power of your Holy Spirit, help me to move forward and not fall back. Make me a large, green-leafed tree filled with the fruit of your Spirit. Work in me privately so you can be seen in me publicly. In you I pray. Amen.

VI. DEEPER DISCOVERIES

A. A yoke of slavery (v. 1)

Christ has freed believers from the law. Yet these Galatians were returning to a yoke of slavery. Depending on the law for life and salvation makes a work animal out of you. Someone else controls and steers your life by means of an instrument connected around your neck. You become a slave obedient to every direction. Any system—pagan idolatry or moral legalism—with rules or dos and don'ts can make slaves of its followers. It seems the false teachers were trying to get the Galatians to take up the yoke of the law. Paul countered, "Take the Spirit's gift of grace. Become what God wants to make you, not what you can make yourself. Be free from anyone's yoke. If you want to be a slave, let Christ be your master."

B. Fallen from grace (v. 4)

The phrase "fallen from grace" is often understood to mean that the Galatian believers had lost their salvation. Two reasons lead us to reject that interpretation. First, that is not the intent of Paul's statement to the Galatian believers. Paul is not talking about our security in Christ. He is contrasting law and grace. To say that they have fallen from grace is not to say that they have fallen from salvation. For Paul, grace is the means of salvation, the way or method of salvation. His opponents advocate a different way of salvation, the method of law or good works. Paul says if you choose that way of salvation instead of the grace way, then Christ is of no benefit to you. See Ephesians 2:8–9. Grace is the only way of salvation. If we reject this truth and try to work for our salvation, Christ can do nothing more to help us. We are on our own. We have rejected the grace way for the works way. We have to try to get to heaven as best we can, because Christ and his grace do not help us when we go the works way.

This is not only true for our salvation, but it is also true in living the Christian life. Grace is God's free blessing that he gives to us as we live our daily life by faith in him and obedience to his word. When we refuse the gift of grace for daily living, we close the door to God's blessing. When the Christian thus chooses works and "falls from grace," he does not thereby lose his salvation. He does close the door to spiritual growth and forfeits the peace and power that is his when he operates by grace. Because a Christian does not appropriate the grace God offers him for sanctification (spiritual growth) does not mean the believer loses the grace God gave him for justification (salvation). If saving grace were lost every time we turned our back on God's daily grace, everyone would be lost, because everyone, from time to time, turns his back on God's daily grace.

The second reason we reject the interpretation that the Galatian believers lost their salvation is that other passages in the Bible seem to teach rather clearly that you cannot lose your salvation. When an unclear, debatable passage like Galatians 5:6 meets a clear passage, the unclear passage must submit to the clear passage.

What are the clear passages? Jesus addresses this topic of believers' eternal security in the Gospel of John:

> "I am the bread of life. He who comes to me will never go hungry, and he who believes in me will never go thirsty. But as I told you, you have seen me and still you do not believe. All that the Father gives me will come to me, and whoever comes to me I will never drive away. For I have come down from heaven not to do my will but to do the will of him who sent me. And this is the will of him who sent me, that I shall lose none of all that he has given me, but raise them up at the

last day. For my father's will is that everyone who looks to the Son and believes in him shall have eternal life, and I will raise him up at the last day" (6:35–40).

"I tell you the truth, he who believes has everlasting life" (6:47).

"I am the gate; whoever enters through me will be saved" (10:9).

"I give them eternal life, and they shall never perish; no one can snatch them out of my hand. My Father, who has given them to me, is greater than all; no one can snatch them out of my Father's hand" (10:28–29).

Paul builds on Jesus' words when he says:

"For I am convinced that neither death nor life, neither angels nor demons, neither the present nor the future, nor any powers, neither height nor depth, nor anything else in all creation, will be able to separate us from the love of God that is in Christ Jesus our Lord" (Rom. 8:38-39).

The issue in eternal security is not our ability to hold onto what God has given us but his ability to hold on to us. The phrase "you have fallen away from grace" should be understood, not in the sense that grace has been taken away from the Galatians, but in the sense that they have turned their backs on it. When we decide to try to live by works, we adopt a mindset that keeps us from benefiting from God's goodness. He cannot show his goodness to us when we hide from him behind the wall of legalism. In that sense, we have fallen from grace.

C. Offense of the cross (v. 11)

The word for *offense* is *skandalon* which means "that which gives offense or causes revulsion, that which arouses opposition, and object of anger or disapproval, stain, etc." (BAGD, 753).

The cross of Christ is offensive to men. As an instrument of torture and punishment, its presence causes revulsion. Because it is associated with criminals, it causes the natural mind to wonder how it could possibly be an instrument of salvation (see Rom. 9:32–33 and 1 Cor. 1:18). The very thought of it insults human pride. How can human salvation occur without human action?

Kenneth S. Wuest points to another scandal of the cross:

The Cross was offensive to the Jew therefore because it set aside the entire Mosaic [law], and because it offered salvation by grace through faith alone without the added factor of works performed by the sinner in an effort to merit the salvation offered. All of which goes to show that the Jew of the first century had an erroneous conception of the law of Moses, for that system never taught that a sinner was accepted by God on the basis of good works (Wuest, *Galatians in the Greek New Testament,* Grand Rapids: Wm. B. Eerdmans, 1944, 146).

Eric W. Adams gives us the bottom line: "In other words, the offense to the Jews is that there is no favoritism of Jews over Gentiles; they are equal" (Elwell, 574). The scandal of the cross brings all people together on equal terms to depend on God for salvation and to give him glory for it. It robs us of all human pride and erases all human distinctions. God cannot be yoked into the human way of doing things. God's work of salvation, work done on the cross of Christ, is scandalous.

D. Live by the Spirit (v. 16)

The Bible does not define what it means to live (literally, to walk) by the Spirit. Scripture never explicitly explains this figure of speech. Other passages in the Bible help us gain a clearer understanding of what it means. The Holy Spirit works in us to do at least four major things:

1. He illumines our minds to understand the truth of Scripture. The natural man (one not born again) cannot understand the things that come from the Spirit of God, but the regenerate person, with the ministry of the Holy Spirit, understands what God has freely given us (see 1 Cor. 3:10–16).
2. The Spirit empowers us to be changed into the character of Jesus, to live the life Christ would live if he were in our shoes. By the ministry of the indwelling Holy Spirit, "we . . . are being transformed into his likeness with ever-increasing glory, which comes from the Lord, who is the Spirit" (2 Cor. 3:18). Philippians 2:13 reinforces this: "it is God who works in you to . . . act according to his good purpose."
3. The Spirit convicts us of sin. We all do things we ought not to do. We all fail to do things we ought to do. The Spirit convicts us of both kinds of wrong, convincing us that we ought to correct our wrongs. The Spirit can do this through the power of changed inner convictions (we realize we ought to do or not do something) and by making us feel guilty and/or remorseful about our actions.
4. The Spirit works in our hearts to cause us to want to do the things God wants us to do. "It is God who works in you to will . . . his good purpose" (Phil. 2:13).

From these scriptural truths we can extrapolate several things that are true of walking/living by the Spirit. Living by the Spirit means that we:

1. Pray to God and ask him to illumine our minds to truth, empower us to change, convict us of sin, and place godly desires in us.
2. Read the Scriptures so that the Holy Spirit has something to work with in illumining, convicting, empowering, and changing us.

3. Live by faith, meaning we believe the truth we understand, maintain faith in God's promises, acknowledge God's complete goodness, and accept the fact that everything he asks of us is asked so he can give something good to us and/or keep some harm from us.

4. Obey him. Our faith is manifested by obedience. If we believe God, we obey him. If we do not obey him, it is because we do not believe him. We trust and obey. As we do these things, we walk in and live by the Spirit.

E. The fruit of the Spirit (vv. 22–23)

We need to rethink a number of long-standing interpretations of the fruit of the Spirit. Because the word *fruit* is singular, commentators commonly view the nine characteristics listed under the fruit of the spirit as a unit. This would mean that all nine characteristics are always produced completely in every believer. This would be like picking a cluster of fruit from an unusual vine that always has on it a grape, banana, apple, peach, pear, plum, raspberry, blackberry, and blueberry.

Like English, the Greek language does not require the "singular" idea, but has a collective sense. All Christians have areas in which they grow more rapidly and securely than in other areas. If, since becoming a Christian, a person grew rapidly in love, patience, and kindness but still struggled with self-discipline in eating, must we deny that the growth in love, patience, and kindness has anything to do with the Holy Spirit? That goes too far. The text in no way requires us to interpret the fruit that narrowly, nor does such an interpretation line up with reality.

I also doubt interpretations that make the list of nine characteristics a complete list. Instead, I think it was intended to be representative. This becomes clearer when we contrast it, as Paul does, with the acts of the flesh in verses 19–21. Does anyone believe that the fifteen acts in those verses are an exhaustive list? For example, lying is not on the list. Gluttony is missing. Materialism is not found. Murder is omitted. This is not a complete list of sinful acts.

Nor is the ninefold fruit of the Spirit a comprehensive list of character traits for the Christian. Faith and hope—two of the three great theological virtues (faith, hope, and love: 1 Cor. 13) are missing. Are they not fruit of the Spirit? Thankfulness, gratitude, forgiveness, moral purity, and humility are highly held characteristics elsewhere in Scripture but missing here. The list here includes only some of the fruit of the Spirit.

The fruit of the Spirit are not emotions. They are character qualities determined by how we act, not how we feel. For example, we may get angry (an emotion), but if we do not act unkindly in our anger, we may still have manifested the fruit of the Spirit. We may be deeply agitated or fearful about a life circumstance and still manifest the fruit of the Spirit. How? By not rejecting God, lashing out at people, or acting immorally but rather trusting God and doing the right thing in our agitation and fear. We are sometimes led to believe that the fruit of the Spirit equals constant emotional tranquillity. Yet we often have no control over our emotions. If we get angry, we are angry, and if we tell ourselves that we ought not to be angry, it does not always make the anger go away. We can, however, control whether we sin in our anger. That is why the Bible says, "In your anger do not sin" (Eph. 4:26). It does not say the anger is necessarily sin. It does say that we are not to let our anger (an emotion) cause us to sin (an act). As long as we act properly, we are manifesting the fruit of the Spirit.

Contemplating his coming crucifixion when the sin of the world would be placed on him, Jesus was grieved and sorrowing to the point of death in the Garden of Gethsemane. Still he did not sin. He did not forfeit the fruit of the Spirit because his sorrow and grief (emotions) did not destroy his life characteristics of love, joy, and peace. He still loved people, which is why he was willing to go to the cross when he didn't have to. He still had joy: "for the joy set before him endured the cross" (Heb. 12:2). Jesus also had peace because he knew that God was in control, that he was moving all things to a good end, and that in the end all would be well.

The fruit of the Spirit are general marks and qualities of our life that are revealed in how we act toward others, even though, from time to time, emotions might *seem* to crowd them out. They, however, do not or need not.

VII. TEACHING OUTLINE

A. INTRODUCTION

1. Lead story: Cows in Prison
2. Context: In the fifth chapter of Galatians, Paul declares that the Christian is set free by Christ. He is no longer under the bondage of the law (Gal. 5:1–12), but he needs something, rather someone, to control him from within. That someone is the Holy Spirit (Gal. 5:13–26). To "live by the Spirit" (v. 16) is presented as the solution to man's battle with sinful temptations and impulses.
3. Transition: In verses 19–23 of this chapter we will see two long lists of attitudes and actions. Do you identify with more of the vices in verses 19, 20, and 21, or do you see, in verses 22–23, more virtues that are present in your life? The way to get freedom from the vices and freedom to experience the virtues is through the power of the Holy Spirit. This simple truth runs into direct opposition from the legalist.

B. COMMENTARY

1. Freedom from the Law and Its Negative Consequences (vv. 1–12)
   a. Call to freedom (v. 1)
   b. Consequences of the law (vv. 2–12)
2. Freedom to Live a Life of Love (vv. 13–15)
3. Freedom Empowered by the Holy Spirit (vv. 16–17)
4. Contrast of the Acts of the Old Nature with the Fruit of the Spirit (vv. 18–23)
   a. The acts of the old nature (vv. 18–21)
   b. The fruit of the Holy Spirit (vv. 22–23)
5. Final Directives to Experience Victory over Sin (vv. 24–26)
   a. Recognize that your old nature is dead (v. 24)
   b. Live in sync with the Holy Spirit (v. 25)
   c. Humbly treat others with respect (v. 26)

C. CONCLUSION: IN THE GRIP OF GRACE

VIII. ISSUES FOR DISCUSSION

1. In what ways does the church with its programs and rituals threaten to enslave us and thereby keep us from the freedom Christ wants us to enjoy in him? What can we do to ensure that we are not enslaved to the church? What can we do to make sure the church is enslaved to Christ?
2. How does faith express itself? What evidence of faith do you see in your own life? In the life of your church?
3. Why does freedom in Christ not give you freedom to enjoy the pleasures of the world?
4. How do you keep in step with the Spirit?

Galatians 6

Help One Another

Quote

"*It* is easy to talk about the fruit of the Spirit while doing very little about it. So Christians need to learn that it is in concrete situations, rather than in emotional highs, that the reality of the Holy Spirit in their lives is demonstrated."

J a m e s   B o i c e

IN A NUTSHELL

In chapter 6, Paul advises the Galatian Christians: In light of the gospel of grace and the power of the Holy Spirit (chap. 5), you are now free to help others. You can help them in three ways. First, you can help other Christians carry their burdens (6:1–5). Second, you can help your pastor(s) by financially supporting them. Third and finally, you can help others by serving them with pure motives.

Help One Another

I. INTRODUCTION

Pride Goes before a Fall

*I*n the 1988 presidential campaign, commentators and voters made much about the character of the candidates, especially those who were rumored to be womanizers. One of the leading candidates had ridiculed another man who had fallen under public attack for his conduct toward women. This leading candidate dared the press to follow him and try to find any misconduct on his part. The press took him up on the dare. Some time later news media published photos of this man himself on a yacht in the Caribbean with an attractive lady who was not his wife. The name of the yacht, prophetically, was *Monkey Business*. The scandal grew so large that this candidate was forced to withdraw from the campaign which he might have won.

A similar incident happened during the eighties with moral scandals that rocked the Christian television industry. A leading television evangelist was caught in a moral lapse which made headline news all over the United States for a long time. I recall hearing an interview with another television minister who leveled a scathing rebuke of the evangelist who had sinned. I was taken aback at the intensity of this attack but somewhat comforted by the thought that I wouldn't ever need to worry about this evangelist falling into immorality. However, it wasn't long before the story of this second evangelist's moral lapse was on newspapers and weekly newsmagazines across the nation.

Both the television evangelist and the leading presidential candidate were arrogant in their condemnation of others, and their own indiscretions were revealed a short time later.

Paul warned of that attitude in this final chapter of Galatians. He encouraged us to treat gently other Christians who have fallen into sin, all the time watching out for ourselves, lest we also be tempted. He went on to encourage the Galatians not to weary in doing good things, because we will eventually reap our reward from the Lord. Focusing on relationships and personal character provides a fitting end to a rather heavy doctrinal book.

II. COMMENTARY

Help One Another

> **MAIN IDEA:** *The message of grace frees us from selfishness to bear others' burdens, share financial blessings, and minister with pure motives.*

A The Freedom to Bear Others' Burdens (vv. 1-5)

> **SUPPORTING IDEA:** *Mature Christians help restore friends who fall into sin.*

6:1. In chapter 6, Paul applies freedom to our relationships. He's going to tell us that the Christian who walks in the Spirit is free from selfishness and so freed to love others unselfishly. He wants spiritual people to show concern for one another and respond properly to a fellow Christian who has fallen into grave sin. **You who are spiritual**, in this context, refers to those manifesting the fruit of the Spirit. These believers with Christlike character traits produced by the Holy Spirit encourage faltering Christians. The legalist is judgmental, harsh, and condemning toward those who struggle with sin (Acts 15:10). They know the law, and they know the consequences of falling short of obedience to the law. But they do not know mercy.

To illustrate grace, Paul presents this hypothetical case of a believer who is **caught in a sin. Caught** implies that the sin was not premeditated. The word was once used to describe a Roman legion which had been overrun by a Jewish military force. The way the spiritual one should deal with this sinning brother is to **restore him gently.** *Restore* means "to mend, as a net, or to restore a broken bone." The sinning Christian is like a broken bone that the body of Christ must reset. This delicate restoration must be done **gently**, the same word found in chapter 5 in the list of the fruit of the Spirit. A harsh, legalistic reaction to a sinning brother will only make things worse. A gentle, graceful response can help. We can only ask ourselves which response we would want if we were the one caught in a sin.

6:2. When we help carry the crushing burden of the one who has fallen in sin, we fulfill **the law of Christ** which is the principle of love (compare 5:14; John 13:34). When a fellow believer succumbs to temptation, it is not our place to judge and condemn him (Matt. 7:1-6). Rather, we are to make sure he knows we love him and want to help him overcome his weakness and grow spiritually.

6:3-4. When a Christian sins, we easily fall into the temptation of pride. We commit this sin when we compare ourselves to those who have fallen morally and feel better than they. This comparison can lead to a condescending attitude that says, "You fell, and I didn't." We may secretly be glad that something bad has happened to him. If we take on this "holier than thou" attitude, we fall into the sin of pride. We also destroy any opportunity to have a restorative influence on the struggling believer. Yet Paul tells us that rather than experience prideful feelings of superiority, we should **test** ourselves through self-examination to see if there is any prideful breach in our moral armor.

6:5. We exhibit a permissible, good pride, or gratitude to the Lord, when we are **carrying** our **own load** well. *Load* means "backpack" and signifies the responsibilities that each of us carries around. It is also the common term for the cargo a ship is designed to carry. It is improper for us to compare ourselves to a sinning Christian and to feel superior to him. Rather, we are to look at the normal, day-to-day responsibilities each of us carries around and feel a permissible good pride when we are fulfilling them responsibly.

Ⓑ Freedom to Share Financial Resources (vv. 6–10)

SUPPORTING IDEA: *Mature Christians share their financial resources with their pastor/teacher(s) as well as with others who instruct them in spiritual truth.*

6:6. Most of us are naturally selfish and must overcome this fault as we mature. Paul shows how grace frees us to share financially with others. He begins in verse 6 with a precept on generosity. He says that we **must share** our financial resources with our spiritual leaders. When a pastor-teacher shares **instruction**, then the student is to reciprocate by sharing **all good things**. Pastoring and teaching is time-consuming. The one who devotes his life to such ministry can hope to earn a living from his occupation (compare 1 Cor. 9:11–14).

6:7–9. To support his admonition to give, Paul shares a principle of cause and effect. A grave warning states that **God cannot be mocked**. Why? Because a man **reaps what he sows**. *Mocked* means "to turn up one's nose" or "treat with contempt." One who turns up his nose at God and sneers at him doesn't change this immutable "law of the harvest." Disregarding God's counsel, we will always suffer. Each of us by our thoughts, attitudes, and actions is constantly planting for a future reaping. Time may pass before the crop ripens, but the harvest is inevitable. Consider the harvest! In this application of the harvest principle, by giving (sowing) to our spiritual leaders, we can expect to reap a spiritual harvest of abundant ministry. In contrast, a Christian who fails to support his spiritual leaders is sneering at God and can expect discipline. Such a selfish Christian spends his resources to gratify his own personal desires. In contrast, the Christian who shares his finances adds interest to the capital of **eternal life**. In a broader application of this principle, remember there are no miracle crops. You reap spiritually, relationally, mentally, and physically in direct relation to what you plant. It is foolish to think that you can live irresponsibly and not suffer damaging consequences. Yet to the generous, Paul shares an encouraging promise: **Let us not become weary in doing good, for at the proper time we will reap a harvest if we do not give up**. It is discouraging to continue to do good and not see a reward. Paul challenges the Galatians to keep on giving because God promises to reward those who are faithful in the long run.

6:10. The believer is to **do good** to both **believers** and unbelievers with believers having priority. Christians in that era suffered great economic hardship as a result of rejection and persecution. With no government assistance programs, they had no one else to help but other believers. Though Christians should be willing to help anyone in need, caring for fellow believers is still a priority.

Ⓒ Freedom to Minister with Pure Motives (vv. 11–18)

SUPPORTING IDEA: *Mature Christians minister out of pure motives of love.*

6:11. Paul concludes his epistle to the Galatians by contrasting the improper motives of the legalists with his proper motives. Paul now discontinues using a scribe. In *Koine* (common) Greek quotation marks were not used. So emphasis was conveyed by enlarging the letters of the words written. Paul personally picks up the pen and writes with **large letters** to emphasize his concluding words and to validate that the letter was genuine.

6:12. The fear of others may have been a significant motive of the Judaizers. They may have been trying to accommodate the gospel to the Jews to avoid persecution by them. By including the law, they made the converted Jews happy. In contrast, by preaching the grace message which excluded the law, Paul had experienced harsh persecution at the hands of the Jews.

6:13. Other than being circumcised, some of the Judaizers did not try to keep the law, but they wanted new converts to Christianity also to be circumcised because it made them look good to the other legalists.

They bragged about the number of converts who were also circumcised.

6:14. In contrast to the Judaizers, Paul had pure motives. Paul's motive was to brag, not about himself or his merits, but about the **cross of our Lord Christ**. The Judaizers gloried in the flesh (circumcision), but Paul gloried in Christ.

The **world** was **crucified to** Paul and he **to the world**. He looked at the world as if it were on a cross; that is, he considered the world as good as dead and he as good as dead to the world.

6:15. It is easy to get caught up in the externals (of **circumcision** or **uncircumcision**). Paul says that in all reality, the externals are meaningless. **What counts** is a **new creation** produced by a new spiritual birth (compare

2 Cor. 5:17). **What counts** is God changing us from the inside out. The message of the Judaizers was powerless to change hearts. What changes hearts is faith in Christ for both salvation and spiritual growth.

6:16. **Peace and mercy** are available to those who believe in salvation by grace through faith in Christ.

6:17. **The marks of Jesus** are all over Paul's body. The word *marks* was used of the brand that identified slaves or animals. Paul had often been beaten for the sake of Christ, even in Galatia itself (Acts 14:19). Some of those who would be reading this letter would recall how Paul had nearly died to get the message of the gospel to them. Paul's stonings and beatings as an apostle of the message of grace are his final proof that he is a true apostle. These markings are his signs that he was a slave of Christ and not of the law. These physical scars were Paul's final credentials of authenticity. These signs of ownership indicated that his motive was to please God regardless of the consequences. Paul would rather fight for truth and grace than switch to falsehood and the law. These marks are Paul's way of saying, "Here me well. I've earned the right to be heard, respected, and obeyed."

6:18. Paul began his letter with the commendation of **grace** (Gal. 1:3). Now he concludes with that same blessing of grace. Throughout all the division and suspicion, Paul still ends with affection by calling them **brothers**. With all of his godly logic and now his open love, how can the Galatians refuse the appeal of this letter? How can they continue to accommodate the theological atrocities of the Judaizers? We hear nothing more about these churches, and we are led to believe that Paul persuaded them to abstain from legalism and to affirm grace. For a short moment they thought about going back to the dark prison of legalism, but finally they came to their senses and stayed out in the bright sunshine of grace's freedom.

MAIN IDEA REVIEW: *The message of grace frees us from selfishness to bear others' burdens, share financial blessings, and minister with pure motives.*

III. CONCLUSION

From the Inside Out

The law was powerless to change lives. It focused on the externals. The grace of Christ is powerful because it changes us from the inside out. Every person struggles with selfishness. We get preoccupied with our finances, our families, our loneliness, our time crunches, and our aches and pains. Yet all around us are people sharing the same problems. They are so overcome by difficulties that often they are emotionally and spiritually down. Grace frees us and empowers us by the Holy Spirit to reach out to them and to turn their heart light on through simple expressions of love. They simply need us to love them in word and deed. Are you bearing others' burdens? Do you give to support the work of your church and pastor? If everyone gave the same amount you give, how long would God's work go on? When you do serve others, what is your motive? Do you do it, like the Judaizers, to make a good impression? Or do you do it as appreciation for what God has done for you?

PRINCIPLES

- Love is bighearted not bigheaded.
- Legalism condemns while grace restores.
- You impress others with what you know. You impact others with how you love.
- Conceit is deceit. The one who toots his horn the loudest is usually in the deepest fog.
- Life is like a boomerang; what you throw is what returns to you.
- You harvest spiritually, mentally, relationally, and physically in direct proportion to what you plant. There are no miracle crops.
- Not only our deeds, but also our motives, are important.
- Spiritual change is an inside job begun with the new birth and sustained by a new power—the Holy Spirit.
- Scars for Christ here on earth produce stars from Christ there in heaven.

APPLICATIONS

- Put yourself in others' shoes before you judge them harshly for sin.
- Put yourself in others' shoes before you turn away from their material needs. We cannot help everyone, but we must be sensitive to the Lord's leading.
- Do what you can to be sure your church is meeting your pastor's needs.

IV. LIFE APPLICATION

The Futility of Living without Loving

The greatest practical demonstration of grace is love. Grace always shows itself in care and concern for others. When the legalistic Pharisees asked Jesus to name the greatest commandment, he told them the greatest commandment was to love God and others (Matt. 22:34–40). Paul reiterates the preeminence of love in his famous love chapter in 1 Corinthians 13. Therefore:

- You can dazzle us with your music.
- You can delight us with your humor.
- You can spellbind us with your speech.
- You can organize us with your administration.
- You can impress us with your giving.
- But you cannot change us without love!

A plaque hanging at a beachfront home echoes the shallow love of many people. It says, "If you think you don't have friends, buy a beach house." Another young man with a new ski boat said, "I have fair-weather friends. When the weather is fair, they come out." It's frustrating in an ever growing, impersonal world to want someone to love you unconditionally and faithfully and to hear them say either in word, attitude, or action:

- I'll love you as long as you make my heart flutter.
- I'll love you as long as you live up to my expectations.
- I'll love you as long as I need you.
- I'll love you as long as you look good to me.
- I'll love you as long as it's fun.
- I'll love you as long as I have a good reason.

Loving the lovely is a lot easier than loving the unlovely. It's much easier when it costs nothing. Yet Galatians teaches that God gives us the power through his Spirit to love others. When we are a new creation in Christ (Gal. 6:15), we have the power of the Holy Spirit (Gal. 5:16–26) to step outside of our own self-centeredness and to think of others. The goal is to go from self-centeredness to Christ-centeredness to ministry-centeredness. By the power of the Holy Spirit, we can love and serve others.

V. PRAYER

Now Lord, you know that I cannot truly love unselfishly without your grace. Forgive me for harshness when my fellow Christian has stumbled. Forgive me for feeling better about myself when others fail. Make me generous to all people, especially to those who teach and lead me at church. Thank you that I am a new creation in Christ and that you provide all that I need to love you and serve your people. May peace and mercy follow me just as Paul wished peace and mercy upon the Galatians. Amen.

VI. DEEPER DISCOVERIES

A. Tempted (v. 1)

Tempted (Greek *peirazo*) means, "try, make trial of, put to the test" (BAGD, 640). Temptation or to be tempted is not sin. Everyone experiences temptation.

Sin occurs when one yields to the temptation. Jesus was the only one to encounter temptation without succumbing to it and, therefore, not sinning.

Temptation comes from various sources. In the temptation of Jesus, Satan is the tempter (Matt. 4:1). As the principal source of temptation, Satan uses a myriad of instruments to entice men and women to disobey God and sin. Some examples include our own lust (Jas. 1:14), Christian friends (Matt. 16:22,23), and evil associates (Prov. 1:10). Temptation to sin does not come from God (1 John 2:16; Jas. 1:13). God in his providence uses events in our daily lives to test our faith. He may lead us to a place of testing, but he does not himself tempt us (Matt. 6:13).

B. Cross of Christ (v. 12)

The cross of Christ refers to all Jesus did to bring salvation, climaxing in his death on the Roman cross at Calvary. The cross brings different reactions from believers and unbelievers. The faithful see it as a call to discipleship and witness. Unbelievers like the legalists of Paul's day see it as an instrument of scorn and ridicule. To gain identity in Christ's cross is to face persecution from Christ's enemies as he was persecuted on the cross. As Daniel Arichea expresses it: "Anyone preaching the whole meaning of the cross would, of course, be persecuted by Jews. Paul accuses the false teachers of modifying the message in a way that would guarantee their remaining in good standing within the Jewish community" (*A Translator's Handbook on Paul's Letters to the Galatians*, Stuttgart: United Bible Societies, 1976, 155). In like manner Andrew H. Trotter Jr. affirms:

> Those who are compelling others to be circumcised are avoiding being persecuted "for the cross of Christ" (6:12), and Paul expressly declares that he will never boast in anything except "the cross of our Lord Jesus Christ, through which the world has been crucified to me, and I to the world" (v. 14). Thus the cross is as central to living the Christian life as it is to entering into it (Elwell, 137).

We gain salvation only through the cross, not through our works. We live out salvation by enduring the world's scorn, ridicule, and persecution. Only the way of the cross leads home to God's eternal salvation.

C. New creation (v. 15)

As believers in Christ, we are born again to a newness of life. Paul says we are a new creation. *New* (Greek *kainos*) means "in contrast to something old" (BAGD, 394). It has the sense that the old has become obsolete and should be replaced by what is new. In such a case the new, as a rule, is superior to the old (BAGD, 394). *Creation* (Greek *ktisis*) carries the idea of "that which is created as the result of that creative act" (BAGD, 455). Paul describes the

Christian as this kind of new creation. Creation is always God's work, never ours. Circumcision and other acts of law cannot be part of the new creation, for man performs them. We can be a new creation only as God chooses and creates. Only when he takes our old fleshly self and creates a new person of the Spirit are we counted among his people. Being part of his people is the only thing in the world that counts for anything.

VII. TEACHING OUTLINE

A. INTRODUCTION

1. Lead story: Pride Goes before a Fall

2. Context: Having contended that the believer is free from the law to love others by the power of the Holy Spirit, Paul now states that the Christian is free to help others. He tells us that mature people show concern in three ways. First, they lighten the loads of others. Second, they give to support financially those in need, especially their pastor-teacher(s). Third, they minister with pure motives.

3. Transition: As we conclude our study of Galatians we will get a concrete picture of the actions of a mature Christian. We will see specific actions we are now free to express toward others. In the words of the noted scholar James Boice, "It is easy to talk about the fruit of the Spirit while doing very little about it. So Christians need to learn that it is in concrete situations, rather than in emotional highs, that the reality of the Holy Spirit in their lives is demonstrated."

B. COMMENTARY

1. The Freedom to Bear Others' Burdens (vv. 1–5)

2. The Freedom to Share Financial Resources (vv. 6–10)

3. The Freedom to Minister with Pure Motives (vv. 11–18)

C. CONCLUSION: THE FUTILITY OF LIVING WITHOUT LOVING

VIII. ISSUES FOR DISCUSSION

1. In what way does your church function as a community to restore sinners and carry other believers' burdens?

Ephesians 1

Our Spiritual Blessings in Christ

I. INTRODUCTION
The Duck That Thought It Was a Dog

II. COMMENTARY
A verse-by-verse explanation of the chapter.

III. CONCLUSION
Too Easily Pleased

IV. LIFE APPLICATION
Gold among the Gravel

An overview of the principles and applications from the chapter.

V. PRAYER
Tying the chapter to life with God.

VI. DEEPER DISCOVERIES
Historical, geographical, and grammatical enrichment of the commentary.

VII. TEACHING OUTLINE
Suggested step-by-step group study of the chapter.

VIII. ISSUES FOR DISCUSSION
Zeroing the chapter in on daily life.

"The grace of God exalts a man without inflating him, and humbles a man without debasing him."

Charles Hodge

LETTER PROFILE

- Sent to the church in Ephesus. Not one church building but the total collection of Christians in the city.
- Probably delivered by Tychicus, a friend and colaborer of the apostle Paul.
- May not have been delivered exclusively to church in Ephesus but may have been circulated among other churches also.
- Paul stresses the Christian's spiritual blessings in Christ and the need to live a lifestyle that reflects those spiritual blessings.

AUTHOR PROFILE—PAUL THE APOSTLE

- Jewish-born in Tarsus, near the Lebanese border in modern Turkey.
- Roman citizen.
- Prominent, highly educated Jewish religious leader (Pharisee).
- Dramatically converted to Christianity, A.D. 35.
- Primary apostle to the Gentiles, tireless missionary.
- Imprisoned in Rome, A.D. 67, during Nero's reign.
- Died in prison, A.D. 68.

CITY PROFILE—EPHESUS

- Population estimated at 300,000.
- Capital city of the Roman province of Asia, in modern Turkey.
- A leading trade center in Roman Empire.
- Center of the worship of pagan goddess Diana. The temple of Diana was one of the wonders of the ancient world.
- A beautiful city, very sophisticated, wealthy, and pagan.

IN A NUTSHELL

In chapter 1, Paul tells the Ephesian Christians: Greetings, Ephesians. Praise be to God the Father who chose you and adopted you as his spiritual children before the foundation of the world. In Christ, you have redemption, the forgiveness of sin; you have been spiritually enlightened and enriched. In the Holy Spirit, you were sealed and made secure. I pray that you may be enlightened to understand the significance and magnitude of these blessings.

Ephesians

Our Spiritual Blessings in Christ

I. INTRODUCTION

The Duck That Thought It Was a Dog

Scientists know that ducks tend to imprint soon after birth. To "imprint" means that they attach themselves to the first thing they see after they hatch, thinking they are "that" thing. This is supposed to work *for* the duck, since, when they hatch, the first thing they normally see is a mama duck.

This phenomenon backfires, occasionally. Once, for example, a duckling was hatched under the watchful eye of a motherly collie dog. The baby duck took one look at the collie and decided that the dog was its mother. It followed the collie around, ran to it for protection, and slept with it at night. It spent the hot part of the day under the front porch with the collie. When a car pulled into the driveway, along with the dog, the duck would run out from under the front porch quacking viciously, trying to peck the tires.

Some things could not be changed, however. The duck still quacked, enjoyed the water, and flapped its wings. Sometimes it acted like a duck, and sometimes it acted like a dog.

Christians often experience a similar confusion in identity. We have been born into and grown up in a fallen world, so we have learned the ways of the world. We have become like it. When we become a Christian, we are in Christ. We die to the world and are born again, so that, spiritually, we are no longer who we once were (2 Cor. 5:17). Too often, however, we don't see ourselves correctly. We act like the thing we *think* we are, rather than what we really are. We believe and try to do the right things; but for the life of us, we cannot get it exactly right. When we least expect it, a car pulls into the driveway of our life; and we explode from underneath the front porch, quacking viciously and pecking at the tires.

Who are we? We aren't supposed to do that. We're supposed to be swimming around in clear blue lakes, bobbing for seaweed, preening our feathers, and laying eggs—not quacking at cars or harassing the cat.

Ephesians 1 helps us see who we truly are as Christians. Of course, more influences our inconsistent behavior than just negative imprinting. We are members of a fallen race, encumbered with the internal power of sin (Rom. 7). Still, if we could see ourselves more clearly and more consistently as who we really are in Christ, we would be able to live more consistently like him.

That is why the Bible spends so much time telling us who we really are. If we understand and believe it, we will be better able to live it.

So Paul tells the Ephesians who they have become in Christ and then prays that they might have the spiritual enlightenment to grasp who they have become. To do so is to enjoy the Christian life more completely and to live like Christ more consistently.

II. COMMENTARY

Our Spiritual Blessings in Christ

MAIN IDEA: *Through the ministries of God the Father, Son, and Holy Spirit, Christians have been given every necessary spiritual blessing.*

A Greeting (vv. 1–2)

SUPPORTING IDEA: *Spiritual blessings rest on the will of God to provide grace and peace to his people.*

1:1. Paul, the author of Ephesians, was an apostle, a specially gifted emissary from God, not because he chose to be, but because God called and gifted him. The letter is addressed to the **saints in Ephesus.** A *saint* is a "set apart" one. In this context, it means "set apart for God." Paul is writing his letter to Christians, all of whom are *saints* in this sense of the word, because they are faithful followers of Jesus.

1:2. **Grace and peace** represent a standard Christian greeting similar to our saying today, "How are you?" implying, "I hope you are fine." It might come across more literally as, "I hope that the grace and peace of God may be yours." The daily greeting is transformed into a godly greeting by the church's use of grace and peace as qualities essential to the Christian life and by reference to their source in God and in his Son Jesus.

B Spiritual Blessings in the Father (vv. 3–6)

SUPPORTING IDEA: *God the Father chose us and adopted us as his spiritual children.*

1:3. Paul wrote to Christians in Ephesus. Christians are saints today in the same sense of the word the Ephesian Christians were saints. Therefore, what he says of them also applies to us.

God is to be praised, or spoken well of, or blessed, because he has given us **every spiritual blessing** in Christ. We do not always feel spiritually blessed, however. As a result, we might wonder if we somehow missed out on these blessings. To make sure we do not misunderstand what he means by **every spiritual blessing**, Paul spells them out.

1:4. First, we have received the blessing of being chosen by God and adopted by him as his spiritual children. **Chose** raises the question of election or predestination, a deep and profound mystery which must be handled carefully. The Bible in some places seems to teach that God chooses those who will be saved and at least implies that he does not choose those who will not be saved. On the other hand, some verses seem to teach human freedom and responsibility. This question is dealt with more fully in the "Deeper Discoveries" section of this chapter.

This marvelous choice makes us **holy and blameless in his sight**. Because we have believed in and received Jesus as our Savior, all our sins are forgiven in him. This does not mean that true Christians never sin. It means our sin is paid for by the death of Christ. Jesus was holy and blameless. We are in Jesus; therefore, we are holy and blameless in God's sight.

This takes us beyond our understanding, but the final consequence is easy to grasp: In Christ, we have his righteousness imputed to us at the moment of salvation; and the day will come when, standing before God holy and blameless, we will be totally separated, freed, and redeemed from any vestige of sin.

1:5–6. He made us his full-fledged children by formally adopting us into his spiritual family. In adoption, a child is brought into a family and given the same rights as a child born into that family. God did this through Jesus, and it pleased him.

We have two spiritual blessings from God the Father: We have been chosen and **adopted** by him to be his spiritual children. He made this choice before the creation of the world with the result that we will someday stand before him holy and blameless. God the Father accomplished this through the work of his Son, Jesus, motivated by his desire to be kind to us and by his desire to receive praise for his grace.

𝐂 Spiritual Blessings in the Son (vv. 7–12)

SUPPORTING IDEA: *God the Son redeemed us, forgave us of our sins, enlightened us to know his will, and has given us an eternal inheritance.*

The second arena of spiritual blessings comes to us through God's Son, Jesus. Four blessings are listed: In Christ, we are redeemed, forgiven, enlightened, and enriched.

1:7. To be redeemed means to be "bought back." It carries with it the sense of being released from slavery. By being redeemed by Christ, we are freed from sin, both the penalty and the enslaving power. This **redemption** was accomplished by the death of Christ on the cross where he shed his blood and died to secure our redemption. His death paid the price for our release from sin and death.

Forgiveness goes hand in hand with redemption. We cannot have one without the other. To forgive means to give up the right to punish someone for a transgression. Making forgiveness possible was a major accomplishment in God's eyes, since it required the sacrifice of blood and the death of his Son, Jesus. This magnanimous decision to do this for us grew out of God's grace which he **lavished on us with all wisdom and understanding**.

1:8–10. We were also "enlightened" through Christ, when God **made known to us the mystery of his will**. The mystery known to believers but unknown and not understood by unbelievers is that when the time is right God will bring all things in heaven and earth to a fitting conclusion in Christ who will be the **head** or ruler of all things.

1:11. Finally, in Christ, we are enriched. We have been **chosen** and **predestined according to God's plan** to receive an inheritance which we will possess in full when we stand before him in heaven. This inheritance is not an accident or a whim. It is in keeping with God's plan for us from the beginning.

1:12. The result of these incomprehensible blessings is that God should be praised!

D Spiritual Blessings in the Spirit (vv. 13–14)

SUPPORTING IDEA: *God the Spirit sealed us, made us secure in Christ, and thus guarantees the completion of our redemption.*

1:13. The third arena of spiritual blessing is ours through the third person of the Trinity, the Holy Spirit, by whom we were made spiritually secure. To be **marked . . . with a seal** indicates authority, authenticity, and security. It is a validation of ownership. God seals, or marks, his children with the Holy Spirit, indicating that we are his, that we are authentic spiritual children, not fakes or impostors, and that we are under his protection.

1:14. The Holy Spirit is also given to us as a **deposit**, or a down payment, **guaranteeing our inheritance** in Christ. The believer is sealed until the day of redemption guaranteeing our final release from sin when we stand before God in heaven. This will either be after we die or, for those believers still alive at that time, at Christ's return. Again, this is to bring praise to God for his grace in our lives (see v. 12).

E Prayer for Enlightenment (vv. 15–23)

SUPPORTING IDEA: *Christians need to be spiritually enlightened so they may understand the hope of God's calling, the riches of their inheritance in Christ, and the greatness of God's power.*

1:15–17. The complexity and magnitude of these truths is beyond the ability of us to comprehend or appreciate fully. Therefore, Paul follows the presentation of these truths with a prayer for our enlightenment. He prays generally that the believers might have a **Spirit of wisdom and of revelation, so that [they] may know him better**. Wisdom involves the practical ability to act on what one knows and believes. Revelation is God letting you experience himself and his truth. Paul referred to it here as guiding one into God's truth and God's way of life. For us it also involves God's authoritative revelation in Scripture. Wisdom then becomes the practical ability to understand Scripture and apply its truth to daily living (see "Deeper Discoveries" for a fuller treatment of this subject).

1:18–23. Specifically, Paul prays that we might comprehend:

- our hope
- our riches
- God's power

Our **hope** is built on the promises which are ours in Christ. We need to know our spiritual future is based on the promises of God and find strength and courage in that hope to live in the present. To understand and embrace that hope in present living requires spiritual progress.

Paul also wants us to know our future **riches**. It is tempting to focus on our present need and poverty. Instead Paul challenges us to focus on what God has promised. These riches may refer to our present spiritual riches in Christ in being freed from sin and made ready for fellowship with God. They may also refer to our heavenly possession of the riches and glories of God. It's likely both aspects are meant. Such riches are part of our **inheritance**.

Finally, Paul prays that we might be enlightened to comprehend the magnitude of God's **power** which he exercised in bringing us our salvation. The power God demonstrated in raising Christ from the dead and placing him above all creation is the same power he is exercising toward us to bring about the blessings which he has promised us. Such power guarantees we will receive the hope and riches. That power is also available to us to make the hope and riches the focus of present life so that we live God's way and not the world's, seeking God's inheritance and not the world's.

MAIN IDEA REVIEWED: *Through the ministries of God the Father, Son, and Holy Spirit, Christians have been given every necessary spiritual blessing.*

III. CONCLUSION

Too Easily Pleased

This, then, is the lot of the Christian—a rich lot but one we scarcely comprehend. We have been chosen by God the Father to be his spiritual children. In Christ, our sins have been forgiven, and we have been given an inheritance that this world knows no way to measure. In the Holy Spirit, we have been sealed in Christ, made secure until our final redemption when we will see the Lord face-to-face. Clearly, the magnitude of these blessings escapes us, or else we would be more consistent in living for him than we are. That is why Paul ends the chapter by praying for us that we might comprehend the significance and magnitude of the blessings.

In *The Weight of Glory,* C. S. Lewis wrote:

> If there lurks in most modern minds the notion that to desire our own good and earnestly to hope for the enjoyment of it is a bad thing, I submit that this notion has crept in from Kant and the Stoics and is no part of the Christian faith. Indeed, if we consider the unblushing promises of reward and the staggering nature of the rewards promised in the Gospels, it would seem that our Lord finds our desires not too strong, but too weak. We are half-hearted creatures, fooling about with drink and sex and ambition when infinite joy is offered us, like an ignorant child who wants to go on making mud pies in a slum because he cannot imagine what is meant by the offer of a holiday at the sea. We are far too easily pleased (Grand Rapids: Eerdmans, 1949, 1965, 1–2).

PRINCIPLES

- God's sovereignty extends to us before the creation of the world.
- Every believer has complete salvation from God.
- Every believer has a great inheritance waiting for him in heaven.
- Every believer has the Holy Spirit within him.

APPLICATIONS

- Rest in God's love, which is expressed in his offer of complete salvation.
- Because of all God has done for you, see yourself as someone very significant.
- Enjoy the fact that you belong to God. You belong to the family of God, and when you get to heaven, you will belong there, too.
- Be grateful that God has forgiven your sin and given you eternal life.
- Thank God that he took the initiative in your relationship with him.

IV. LIFE APPLICATION

Gold among the Gravel

Paul presents a picture of a Christian which is much different from how we would naturally perceive ourselves. Without the Bible, none of us would dare to believe that all these things could be true of us. We are children of God. We have been spiritually adopted into his family according to his plan which existed before the creation of the world. Christ has redeemed us, forgiven us, enlightened us, and made us fabulously wealthy, on both a spiritual and a physical level in heaven. We have been sealed and made secure by the Holy Spirit. We are not who we once were.

To this, many of us might respond: "I want to believe all this, but I'm having trouble. I don't feel like I have infinite worth. How could I have inherent worth? I may have started out with infinite value, but look at all the things that have happened to me. Look at all the things I've done. How can God love me with all my faults and all my inherent deficiencies?"

Ah, I'm glad you asked.

God can love you the way you are now the same way you can love a gold mine. You buy a gold mine, and you are overjoyed. The gold asks, however: "How can you love me? I'm all dirty. I'm all mixed up with that worthless iron ore, and I have that sticky clay all over me. I'm contaminated through and through with bauxite and mineral deposits. I'm ugly and worthless."

You reply: "O, but I *do* love you. You see, I understand what you really are. I know you have all these imperfections; but I have plans for you. I am not going to leave you the way you are now. I am going to purify you. I am going to get rid of all that other stuff. I see your inherent worth. I know that the iron ore, clay, and mineral deposits are not part of the true you. You are temporarily mixed up with them for now, but I know how to change you from what you are now to what you can be.

"I must warn you: it won't be easy. You will go through a lot of heat and pressure, but look at this gold which I have purified from another mine. See the fine jewelry it makes? See how it glistens? Isn't it beautiful? That's what you are! Left to yourself, you would not be; but I know how to complete your beauty. I will make you beautiful, and you will make me rich."

That is how God can love us, even with our imperfections. God is not finished with us yet. We are not yet what we are going to be. One day we will fellowship, worship, and serve the Lord unhindered by sin. Until then, certainly, God wants us to serve righteousness and not sin (Rom. 6). As John writes in his first epistle:

If we claim to be without sin, we deceive ourselves and the truth is not in us. If we confess our sins, he is faithful and just and will forgive us our sins and purify us from all unrighteousness. If we claim we have not sinned, we make him out to be a liar and his word has no place in our lives. My dear children, I write this to you so that you will not sin. But if anybody does sin, we have one who speaks to the Father in our defense—Jesus Christ, the Righteous One (1 John 1:8–2:1).

On the basis of those promises, we understand that, once we are in Christ, our sin does not sever us from God. Christ's death is sufficient for our sin. God views us through the righteousness of Christ. In Christ, we are "gold in God's eyes." He knows we are still mixed up with sin, but he is going to free us totally from that some day. He knows better than we who we have become in Christ. So rejoice in the blessings you have in Christ. Glorify the Father, and give him praise. Tell others how wonderful he is. Don't keep the good news to yourself. Enjoy it and spread it.

V. PRAYER

God, grant to us that we might begin to comprehend the magnitude and significance of the blessings which you have given us. Open our minds to understand and our hearts to appreciate that we might glorify you fully. Then, grant the grace that we might live accordingly. Amen.

VI. DEEPER DISCOVERIES

A. Chosen (v. 4)

This verse poses, as directly as any verse in the Bible, the issue of the sovereignty of God and the free will of people. The historical phrasing of this dichotomy is that if God is sovereign, then do we have free wills? Verses throughout the Bible call on us to act as though we have free wills and are responsible for our actions. Yet a passage such as this suggests that we do not have free wills. Such an understanding would say that we are predestined to become Christian believers even before birth.

There is no easy solution. Scholars and laymen alike have been debating this issue for two thousand years. The greatest difficulty is, of course, that the Bible appears to teach both: that God is sovereign, and that a person has a free will. Rather than trying to decide between these two options, we need to find a way to live with them both.

Passages which suggest the sovereignty of God:

- "He chose us in him . . . he predestined us to be adopted" (Eph. 1:4–5).
- "For those God foreknew, he also predestined to be conformed to the likeness of his Son . . . And those he predestined, he also called; and those he called, he also justified; those he justified, he also glorified" (Rom. 8:29–30).
- "No one can come to me unless the Father who sent me draws him" (John 6:44).

Here you have the very clear statement of human election. That is not the complete message from the Scripture, however. Several passages support human free will:

- "Come to me, all you who are weary and burdened, and I will give you rest" (Matt. 11:28).
- "For God so loved the world that he gave his one and only Son, that whoever believes in him shall not perish but have eternal life" (John 3:16).
- "I urge, then, first of all, that requests, prayers, intercession and thanksgiving be made for everyone. . . . This is good, and pleases God our Savior, who wants all men to be saved and to come to a knowledge of the truth" (1 Tim. 2:1, 3–4).
- "[The Lord] is not wanting anyone to perish, but everyone to come to repentance" (2 Pet. 3:9).

We see that the Bible appears to teach both truths without reservation and without qualification. How do we begin to make sense out of these teachings? We begin by recognizing a fundamental principle in Isaiah 55:9: "As the heavens are higher than the earth, so are my ways higher than your ways and my thoughts than your thoughts."

It follows, then, that men cannot and should not expect to understand the Bible exhaustively. If they could, the Bible would not be divine but would be limited to human intelligence. The Bible contains some things so simple that even a child can understand them and some things so complex that the brightest minds will never understand them.

Ken Boa says, in his book *God, I Don't Understand*:

This can be illustrated by contrasting the mental ability of a dog with that of man. A dog has a limited number of bits of information that it is capable of handling. A man also has a limited number of bits of information, but he is capable of storing and working with a good deal more than his dog. Even so, there is some overlap between the dog and the man. For example, the dog can relate to its master's eating of food. The dog can be trained to lead the blind, herd the sheep, bring back the duck. It has that much ability to relate to its master's world. It cannot relate to its master's reading a book, however.

Nevertheless, there is enough common ground for a person to love a dog. It is almost impossible for anyone to love a worm or an insect. Why? Because there is no communication.

When a man does something beyond the comprehension of an animal, it must remain a mystery to that animal since it has no categories it can use to correlate this behavior. A dog can be taught to fetch the morning newspaper, but it is another matter to teach it how to read it (Wheaton, IL: Victor Books, 1975, 12).

The situation between us and God is similar, though even more exaggerated, because the distance between God's intelligence and ours is greater than between our intelligence and a dog's. Nevertheless, God can and has communicated with us; however, the communication is not always within our ability to grasp.

When the Bible presents seemingly irreconcilable information, such as human free will and divine sovereignty, rather than trying to force the two ideas together, it is more helpful to understand them as antinomies.

Webster defines *antinomy* as "a contradiction between two equally valid principles or between inferences correctly drawn from such principles." More simply, we might say that an antinomy contains two apparently mutually exclusive truths which must be held simultaneously. The sovereignty of God and the free will of people represents an antinomy.

The Bible teaches that God is sovereign. The Bible also teaches that people can make choices. If you try to merge the two ideas, you will distort truth. If you try to remove all tension between the two, you will destroy one or the other of the truths, and possibly both. We say "apparently" mutually exclusive truths because the truths cannot actually be mutually exclusive. If they were, God would become the author of the impossible and perhaps even of nonsense. They appear mutually exclusive to us because of a limitation either to our information or intelligence or both. The two truths are not mutually exclusive to God.

It is not intellectual suicide simply to believe them both. Here is why.

1. An infinite revelation will always take a finite mind beyond its intelligence. That is the case with antinomies in general, and this truth in specific. With an infinite revelation, we are simply not able to understand everything we know.

2. Antinomies exist outside Scripture. Take "light," for example. Matter cannot be energy, and energy cannot be matter. Yet light has properties of both energy and matter. That is impossible. Yet it is true. The character of light is an excellent example of an antinomy because

while the inherent contradiction within light cannot be resolved with our present laws of physics, every morning the sun comes up. Every evening we switch on lamps. And there is light.

3. If we are to know anything about God, he must reveal himself to us because he exists in a realm beyond our five senses. God did reveal himself. Through miracles, visions, dreams, direct conversation, and then, through Jesus. Much of this revelation was written down in the Scripture and superintended by God so that it was without error in the original manuscripts. We have found this God to be utterly trustworthy. We know of no errors in this revelation, and it has stood for thousands of years.

Therefore, (1) if infinite revelation, by definition, will take a finite mind beyond its intellectual capacity, and (2) unexplainable things exist all around us in the world of science and nature, and (3) God and Christ have demonstrated themselves to be reliable, it is not intellectual suicide to say, "The Bible teaches both human free will and divine election. Therefore, I will embrace them both."

Remember also that our ability to comprehend God's truth has been radically affected by the fall of man. First Corinthians 13:12 reads: "Now we see but a poor reflection; then we shall see face to face. Now I know in part; then I shall know fully, even as I am fully known." When we stand before God in heaven, we will smack our foreheads and say, "Oh, I understand." Until then, we suspend judgment: we hold the truths in tension, understanding who God is and who we are.

When we do that—when we accept both truths fully, without letting one diminish the other—we can rise up in glory at the fact that we have been known and chosen by God from before the creation of the world; and, at the same time, we can commit ourselves unreservedly to the spread of the gospel message, knowing that among those who hear the gospel some may choose salvation.

B. Adoption (v. 5)

One way the Father takes care of our past failures and makes us holy and blameless is that he changes families for us. William Barclay writes of this Roman concept of adoption in his commentary on Ephesians:

When the adoption was complete it was complete indeed. The person who had been adopted had all the rights of a legitimate son in his new family and completely lost all rights in his old family. In the eyes of the law he was a new person. So new was he that even all debts and obligations connected with his previous family were abolished as if they had never existed" (*The Letters to Galatians and Ephe-*

sians, The Daily Study Bible, Philadelphia: Westminster Press, 1959, 91–92).

That is what God has done for us. We were absolutely held in the power of sin and of the world. We belonged to the family of Adam. God, through Jesus, took us out of that family and adopted us into his. That adoption wipes out the past and makes us new.

C. Redemption (v. 7)

The Greek word for *redemption* (*apolutrosis*) means "to buy back for the purpose of setting free." Donald Gray Barnhouse, the great expository preacher of a past generation from Tenth Presbyterian Church in Philadelphia, told for years what is perhaps the best real example of the true meaning of *apolutrosis*. A boy was given a model sailboat by his father to sail in the lake in the park. One day as he was sailing it, the wind came up, broke the string, and blew the sailboat away. The boy was heartbroken.

One day, sometime later, the boy was walking past a toy store downtown. There in the window was his sailboat. Apparently, someone on the other side of the lake had found it. The boy went in the store and said, "The boat in the window is my boat, and I would like for you to give it to me." The store owner said, "I'm sorry, sonny, but that boat is mine. Someone brought it in here the other day, and I bought it from him. It is mine."

The heartbroken boy went home and told his father the story. His father gave his son the money. The next day, the young boy went back to the store to buy back his own boat. That is the picture of *apolutrosis*—to buy back, to set free.

D. Seal (v. 13)

A seal consisted, usually, of a signet ring with the insignia of an official engraved into the head of the ring. It was used to mark an image of the ring in hot wax. The image validated official documents, such as letters or public proclamations. We have the same kind of thing today. When companies form, they receive incorporation papers. Stamped onto the papers is a gold seal from the secretary of state, validating that this company was formed according to the laws of the state and that it has the approval of the secretary of state.

The issue of the seal is power. The seal is only as significant as the one owning the ring. The authority of the one owning the ring is only as important as his power, his ability to impose his will.

Alexander the Great is said to have sent an emissary to Egypt. This emissary was without weapons or military escort, but he carried the seal of Alexander the Great. He met with the king of Egypt, who stood with his army behind him. The emissary communicated to the king the message from Alexander the Great: discontinue hostilities against Alexander's interests. The king of Egypt, wishing to save face, said that he would consider the request and let the emissary know. The emissary drew a circle in the dirt around the king of Egypt, and said, "Do not leave the circle without informing me of your response." What an audacious move. The emissary was unarmed and without military support. The king could have had him drawn and quartered for such a bold move against him. One unarmed man against the entire army of Egypt. Except for one thing. The emissary carried the seal of Alexander. He carried the authority and power of Alexander. To touch the emissary was to touch Alexander. To disobey the emissary was to disobey Alexander. The king of Egypt stood in silence, then said, "Tell Alexander he has his request," and stepped out of the circle.

In addition to the power behind it, a seal can convey:

1. Security: When they threw Daniel into the lion's den, they put a stone over the entrance, sealed the seam with wax, and stamped the king's ring in it. No one dared break the seal without incurring the king's wrath. The seal was used in a similar manner on Jesus' tomb: "The tomb was made secure by putting a seal on the stone" (Matt. 27:66). No one dared break the seal without incurring the wrath of Pilate.

    In a similar manner, if we have the seal of the Holy Spirit on us, no one can tamper with us. We are secure in God because we have his seal on us.

2. Ownership: The valuable things the king owned were marked with his seal, indicating ownership. In a similar fashion, the believer is marked as God's possession by the seal of the Holy Spirit. "If anyone does not have the Spirit of Christ, he does not belong to Christ" (Rom. 8:9). "Do you not know that your body is a temple of the Holy Spirit, who is in you, whom you have received from God? You are not your own; you were bought at a price. Therefore honor God with your body" (1 Cor. 6:19).

3. Sign of authenticity: The seal indicates authenticity in Esther 3:10–12: "So the king took the signet ring off his finger and gave it to Haman . . . on the thirteenth day of the first month the royal secretaries were summoned. They wrote out in the script of each province and in the language of each people all Haman's orders to the king's satraps, the governors of the various provinces and the nobles of the various peoples. These were written in the name of King Xerxes himself and sealed with his own ring."

The spiritual meaning is this: The picture for us is clear. We are God's possession. Therefore, we are secure, having the protection of God. We are authentic children of his, for his seal verifies it.

E. Deposit (v. 14)

A deposit is literally a down payment on a purchase. In ancient documents, this word was used to refer to earnest money in the purchase of an animal or even of a slave. In the New Testament, the word also occurs in 2 Corinthians 5:1–2,5:

> Now we know that if the earthly tent we live in is destroyed, we have a building from God, an eternal house in heaven, not built by human hands. Meanwhile we groan, longing to be clothed with our heavenly dwelling. . . . Now it is God who has made us for this very purpose and has given us the Spirit as a deposit, guaranteeing what is to come.

Peter said:

> Praise be to the God and Father of our Lord Jesus Christ! In his great mercy he has given us new birth into a living hope through the resurrection of Jesus Christ from the dead, and into an inheritance that can never perish, spoil, or fade—kept in heaven for you, who through faith are shielded by God's power until the coming of the salvation that is ready to be revealed in the last time (1 Pet. 1:3–5).

> Your inheritance is secure!

So we are sealed with the Holy Spirit, meaning we are secure; we are authentic; we are God's possession. Our final redemption and complete inheritance is secure because the Holy Spirit is a down payment, a deposit, guaranteeing that the full price will be paid. This comes to us when we stand before God in our redeemed spiritual bodies.

F. Inheritance (v. 14)

Too little is made of the inheritance which we have received as children of God. We will not be able to enjoy much of this inheritance until we get to heaven, but understanding and concentrating on our inheritance will help us transfer our affections to the eternal realm. Our inheritance includes the following:

1. We will understand many things that are now incomprehensible. "In that day you will no longer ask me anything" (John 16:23). Our minds are now darkened by the presence of sin; but when our sin is removed, our minds will be free to function clearly.

2. Our true desires will be fulfilled. God is the One who alone can perfectly complete us. Augustine declared that "Thou hast formed us for Thyself, and our hearts are restless till they find their rest in Thee." Everything that we long for on earth is ultimately to be fulfilled in heaven. It is heaven that we long for. It is God whom we seek.

3. Our passions will be pure and sinless. Our fellowship and love for God will be reflected in intimate love and complete unity among other believers.

4. Physically, the troubles and distractions caused by the constant demands of weak and dying bodies will disappear. We will not get tired or diseased and will need no sleep. It will be unnecessary to spend time traveling from one place to another. We will not have to worry about clothing or food.

5. We can be comforted by *these* truths now. Throughout the Scriptures, the doctrine of the resurrection is used to provide a genuine hope for the future. Now we know God by faith, but then we will know him face-to-face. Many of us may suffer now, but then we will realize that "our present sufferings are not worth comparing with the glory that will be revealed in us" (Rom. 8:18). Even though we are surrounded by the reality of death, we can have peace and comfort in the knowledge that death will soon be swallowed up in victory (1 Cor. 15:54–55).

These are features of our inheritance. They are by no means all there is to the inheritance, but each feature gives us a taste of the entire package which is great, glorious, and good.

G. Spirit of wisdom (v. 17)

A spirit of wisdom is given through the Holy Spirit, but this spirit probably does not refer to the Holy Spirit himself, even though the word is capitalized in the NIV. The Ephesian believers were already possessed by the Holy Spirit. Nor does it seem that Paul was speaking of the human spirit, which everyone already has. The most likely meaning is that he is using the word *spirit* to mean "an attitude, a disposition, a mind-set," as we mean when we say, "The cheerleaders want to give the student body a spirit of enthusiasm." Jesus used "spirit" in this fashion in the Beatitudes when he said, "Blessed are the poor in spirit," meaning, "Blessed are those who have an attitude of humility."

Wisdom is insight into the true nature of things. This wisdom is not the "cause/effect" wisdom that the world can know; rather, it is the wisdom that stands for knowledge and understanding, of things as they truly are, as, for example, we see in Proverbs 9:10, "The fear of the Lord is the beginning of wisdom."

H. A spirit of revelation (v. 17)

Revelation in this context is a parallel idea to wisdom. It has nothing to do with the giving of new revelation on the same level as the Bible. Instead, it has to do with the "grasping or understanding of the truth of Scripture." Revelation (*apokalypseos*) means "to reveal, to unfold, or to unveil." The desire is that we might have a mind-set of fearing God so as to have understanding and an unfolding of the truth. We might paraphrase it: "I pray that your mind and heart may be tuned to receive the truth about God." In summary, Paul prays that we might be given a capacity for spiritual discernment.

VII. TEACHING OUTLINE

A. INTRODUCTION

1. Lead story: The Duck That Thought It Was a Dog
2. Context: In Ephesians 1, Paul described the spiritual blessings we have in Christ. He says we have "every spiritual blessing in Christ." As we go through our daily lives, we do not always feel so terribly blessed. Because of this, Paul does not leave it to our imagination as to what those blessings are. He enumerates them:
   * We are blessed in the Father: He chose us and adopted us as spiritual children before the foundation of the world.
   * We are blessed in the Son: He redeemed and forgave us, enlightened us, and gave us an inheritance.
   * We are blessed in the Spirit: We are sealed and made secure in Him.
3. Transition: As we look into this chapter, we will get a picture of who we have become in Christ—our true identity. When we do, we will see ourselves as God sees us and know that we have inherent and infinite worth, yet we have no more worth than anyone else. As Charles Hodge said in a very old commentary on Ephesians, "The grace of God exalts a man without inflating him, and humbles a man without debasing him."

B. COMMENTARY

1. Greeting (vv. 1–2)
   a. Author—Paul (v. 1)
   b. Recipients—Christians in Ephesus (v. 1)
   c. Blessing—grace and peace (v. 2)
2. Spiritual Blessings in the Father (vv. 3–6)
   a. Praise to the Father (v. 3)
   b. Chosen to be holy and blameless (v. 4)
   c. Adopted as spiritual children (vv. 5–6)
3. Spiritual Blessings in the Son (vv. 7–12)
   a. Redemption through his blood (v. 7*a*)
   b. Forgiveness of sin (v. 7*b*)

      c. Enlightenment of his intentions for us (vv. 8–10)
      e. Enrichment by obtaining his inheritance (vv. 11–12)
  4. Spiritual Blessings in the Spirit (vv. 13–14)
      a. Sealed by the Holy Spirit (v. 13)
      b. Secured because he is our deposit (v. 14)
  5. Prayer for Enlightenment (vv. 15–23)
      a. That we might comprehend our hope (vv. 15–18*a*)
      b. That we might comprehend our riches (v. 18*b*)
      c. That we might comprehend his power (vv. 19–23)

C. CONCLUSION: GOLD AMONG THE GRAVEL

VIII. ISSUES FOR DISCUSSION

1. How does it make you feel to know the spiritual blessings you have in Christ?
2. Which of the blessings seemed to take on the most meaning to you as you studied them? Why?
3. How do you think Paul's prayer for us in verses 15–23 could be used to guide our own prayers for ourselves and others?

Ephesians 2

Our Spiritual Union with God

I. **INTRODUCTION**
Back from the Dead

II. **COMMENTARY**
A verse-by-verse explanation of the chapter.

III. **CONCLUSION**
Occupied with Heaven

IV. **LIFE APPLICATION**
God Is Not Finished with You Yet!
An overview of the principles and applications from the chapter.

V. **PRAYER**
Tying the chapter to life with God.

VI. **DEEPER DISCOVERIES**
Historical, geographical, and grammatical enrichment of the commentary.

VII. **TEACHING OUTLINE**
Suggested step-by-step group study of the chapter.

VIII. **ISSUES FOR DISCUSSION**
Zeroing the chapter in on daily life.

Quote

"*I* must die or get somebody to die for me. If the Bible doesn't teach that, it doesn't teach anything. And that is where the atonement of Jesus Christ comes in."

Dwight L. Moody

Ephesians

IN A NUTSHELL

In chapter 2, Paul tells the Ephesian Christians: You were once spiritually alienated from God; but now, because of God's grace, you have been spiritually united with him. As Gentiles, you were once spiritually alienated from Israel, but now you have been spiritually united with them into a living spiritual temple of God.

Our Spiritual Union with God

I. INTRODUCTION

Back from the Dead

When James Calvert went out to the cannibal island of Fiji with the message of the gospel, the captain of the ship in which he traveled tried to talk him out of going. "You will risk your life and all those with you if you go among such savages," he said. Calvert's magnificent reply was, "We died before we came here."

In that sense it is possible to be dead even though you are alive. Corrie Ten Boom's life offers a modern example of this principle. Her remarkable story is told in the book *The Hiding Place*. She lived with her family in Holland just before World War II broke out. The Nazi military machine was beginning to press in on European Jews like the jaws of a vice. Jews who had any chance were fleeing Germany and other neighboring countries, but the German military machine was on the alert to capture any fleeing Jews. In response, an underground railroad was formed among compassionate people to assist the Jews to escape. Corrie Ten Boom's home was part of the underground system. Eventually, she and her sister were arrested and condemned to a German concentration camp for their part in assisting Jews.

Her life in the concentration camp was terrible beyond belief. In any civilized country, not even animals would be legally treated the way she and the thousands of other people in the camp were treated. Her sister, of weaker constitution than Corrie, died in the camp. Though on any given morning when she awoke, she was breathing and her heart was beating, Corrie, herself, was as good as dead. Only a short time stood between her and the gas chamber. Then one day, due to a clerical error, she was inexplicably freed. Snatched from the jaws of death, she was given her life back again.

Winston Churchill once said that there is nothing quite so exhilarating as being shot at and missed. That must have been how Corrie Ten Boom felt. Death shot at her but missed.

In that sense we've all been shot at. We have all died, spiritually; but God has given us a second chance. While we are dead, we may respond to his gift of life and receive new spiritual life. Chapter 2 of Ephesians tells the story.

II. COMMENTARY

Our Spiritual Union with God

> **MAIN IDEA:** *God's grace gives you life and unites you with him and with people from whom you are alienated.*

A Our Spiritual Death (vv. 1–3)

> **SUPPORTING IDEA:** *We were all once spiritually dead and were objects of God's wrath.*

2:1. In chapter 1, Paul enumerates God's spiritual blessings for us and then prays that we might be able to comprehend them. One of those spiritual blessings was forgiveness of sins and redemption by Christ. In chapter 2, Paul explains that great truth more specifically: we were spiritually **dead**, separated and alienated from God, because of our **transgressions and sins**. Later in the chapter, he talks about the consequences of this spiritual death, but for now he just establishes it as fact.

2:2. Paul describes the way we lived while we were in this spiritually alienated condition. We **followed the ways of this world**. That is, we lived according to the non-Christian value system. This value system is created and energized by Satan (**the ruler of the kingdom of the air**). This does not mean that non-Christians realize that their values are created and energized by Satan. In fact, most would probably deny it. Nevertheless, Satan, in his craftiness, places the things in front of us that we, in our sinful condition, find attractive, and, therefore, pursue as though they were our ideas. The **spirit who is now at work in those who are disobedient** is probably not the *ruler of the kingdom of the air* as the NIV translation suggests but rather an impersonal atmosphere created and energized by the ruler. Satan's kingdom encourages us to have ungodly values, attitudes, and actions, much the same way a spirit of enthusiasm at a ball game might encourage us to embrace the attitudes and actions of a sports fan. We cheer, yell, jump up and down, and otherwise act in ways that we would not if we were not under the influence of the spirit of enthusiasm. Under the spirit of Satan's kingdom we act in disobedient ways we would not normally follow.

2:3. Specifically, our Satanically energized value system motivated us to gratify illicit desires. As a result, we were **objects of wrath**, meaning God's wrath, just like all other non-Christians.

The wrath of God comes on us in this life in two ways. At times we receive the natural cause-effect consequences of violating God's principles. Galatians

6:7 tells us that we reap what we sow. For example, if we are sexually immoral, we may contract a sexually transmitted disease. If we are violent or angry, we may receive the hatred and resistance of those around us. At other times God may bring his wrath on us specifically, in direct divine judgment. Such instances would be difficult to prove, but examples of such temporal judgment can be found in the Bible (Rom. 1:18–27; Acts 5:5; 1 Cor. 11:30).

In addition to the wrath of God coming on non-Christians in this life, the wrath of God will certainly come on them after death. Hebrews 9:27 says, "Just as man is destined to die once, and after that to face judgment." For the non-Christian, this is a terrifying thing. Second Peter 3:7 reads, "The present heavens and earth are reserved for fire, being kept for the day of judgment and destruction of ungodly men." Ephesians 2:1–3 presents a hopeless picture for the non-Christian.

B Our Spiritual Life (vv. 4–10)

SUPPORTING IDEA: *Because of God's rich mercy, he has provided salvation for us by grace through faith, not through our good works, so that we cannot claim credit that is his.*

2:4. Against this bleak backdrop of the hopelessness of the non-Christian, Paul presents heartening news. God's mercy restrains his wrath. He refrains from punishing us even though we are sinners. Why? This mercy flows out of his **great love for us.** He desires to do good for those he loves, not evil. As a result he has done three things for us.

2:5. First, he **made us alive with Christ.** Our sins had made us spiritually dead. They separated us from God. The resurrected Christ overcame death. God lets us share in Christ's life. In so doing he caused us no longer to be spiritually alienated from himself. Why give us life when we deserved death? Because we earned it? Surely not! We deserved the death we got. We are alive because of God's grace, a concept we will explore further in verse 8.

2:6. Second, he **raised us up with Christ.** Life in Christ came because we experienced Christ's resurrection in the spiritual realm. We were raised up from our sin death and given opportunity for new life. Still facing life on earth where Satan reigns, we live with Christ as part of his kingdom.

Third, he **seated us with him in the heavenly realms.** That is, he has made possible and certain our resurrection from the dead and has mysteriously positioned us in heaven where Christ dwells (see 1:20). To be seated with Christ in the heavenlies is a figure of speech meaning God considers us worthy and destined to be seated with Christ in heaven when we get there. God has decided to do it, and it is as good as done. We just have to wait for a few years until it happens. The significance of being seated with Christ is much the same as being seated at the head table of a banquet where there are many important people. It is a privilege and honor, and it marks you as one of the important people. We will be important in heaven.

How will we be important? We will share with Christ in his rule as king. We will be seated on thrones (see Rev. 3:21). In fact, we already exercise power with Christ over the powers of this age. We can live lives reflecting Christ's kingdom, not Satan's. We are no longer dead in trespasses and sin. We are alive in Christ, sharing his power and authority, representing him in the battle with Satan where victory is assured through the resurrection.

2:7. God's intention in this, in addition to the natural response of love which he has for us (v. 4), is to show for eternity the magnitude of his grace toward us. The word *show* actually means "display." In the same sense that an artist might display his canvasses to reveal his skill, so God displays his redeemed children to the universe to demonstrate his grace. The grace shown in his children seated in heavenly realms is the same grace or **kindness** shown in the death and resurrection of Christ. Once supremely in Christ, God showed his loving attitude to the world. From now on he continues to show that attitude in the lives of his people whom he has delivered from the ways and ruler of this world and given protection and power in the heavenly realms.

2:8. In verse 5, Paul made the parenthetical statement, **it is by grace you have been saved**. Now, in verse 8, he picks up that idea and elaborates on it. *Grace* carries with it the idea of benevolence being bestowed on someone without that person having merited it by his actions. God was not required to offer us salvation. He would be justified in condemning all people to eternal separation from himself. In spite of the fact that our actions bring deserved judgment upon ourselves, God offered us an escape. He didn't have to, but because he loved us, he wanted to. That is *grace,* and that is what *saved* us, or delivered us, from eternal judgment. God's escape belongs to him and to his initiative alone. No part of it can be credited to you. The whole of salvation, the grace as well as the faith, is a gift of God.

He chose to make salvation possible in this way. He handed salvation to you. You did nothing but stick out a hand and accept the gift. Faith is exactly that. It is trustfully accepting from God what he has provided without totally understanding what you are receiving. Faith is giving up on being able to provide what you need for yourself and letting God give what he alone can provide.

2:9. Paul stressed this point almost redundantly. You have done absolutely nothing to earn salvation by being or doing "good." God's plan of salvation by grace places all humans on the same footing. No one may **boast** or point with pride to personal accomplishments in the realm of salvation. No person has done anything in this arena. God has done it all.

2:10. As we, his children, stand on display throughout eternity, we will be recognized as **God's workmanship**. "Workmanship" (*poiema*) is not just a result of effort or labor. It is a result of artistic skill and craftsmanship. If we could earn salvation by our own **good works**, we would not be a work of God but a work of our own selves. That cannot be and will not be. We were created in Christ Jesus to do good works, which God determined before we were ever born. God has prepared a path of good works for Christians which he will bring about in and through them while they walk by faith. This does not mean that we do a good work for God. It means that God does a good work through us as we are faithful and obedient to him. God is at work. In faith we join him in that work to the praise of his glory (see 1:6,12,14).

In summary, we were spiritually dead and the object of God's wrath. God, motivated by his love, extended mercy to us and allowed us to be delivered from his wrath by grace, through faith. God has accomplished this without our help; therefore, all the good that is done through us will be recognized as his work and not our own.

Ⓒ Our Spiritual Union (vv. 11–22)

SUPPORTING IDEA: *We once were separated from God and his people the Jews, but now, in Christ, both Jew and Gentile have been united with God as well as with one another.*

2:11. The Ephesian church seems to have experienced friction between Jewish and Gentile Christians. That would explain why Paul goes into a discussion of the relationship between those two groups at this point. In verse 11, Paul shows the Gentiles' hopeless condition before salvation by contrasting them with the Jews. God's plan of salvation in the Old Testament came through the Jewish nation. That still didn't mean that all Jews were truly redeemed. It only meant that the message of redemption came through the Jewish nation. The Ephesians, as Gentiles, did not have natural access to that message of salvation. Paul contrasts the conditions of the Jews and Gentiles to show the Ephesians how significant their salvation is.

Circumcision was a source of pride for the Jews. It was a visible sign of their historic relationship with God. Therefore, it was a term of derision—a religious slur, if you will—for the Jews to call the Gentiles **uncircumcised**. The Jewish nation had forfeited their special position with God, because, while they were physically circumcised, their heart attitude was not one of submission to God. So Paul says the Jews were called to **circumcision**, which is performed in the flesh by human hands. He implies that, while they were physically circumcised, their heart was not, as it were, circumcised (submissive to God).

2:12. Paul emphasizes that the Gentiles were:

- separate from Christ
- excluded from citizenship in Israel
- foreigners to the covenants of the promise
- without hope
- without God in the world

What a bleak litany!

Jesus was the Messiah, the Savior of the Jewish nation. The nation of Israel had been given promises (covenants) by God that they would have a Messiah. This gave them hope and afforded an avenue to God for them. Not being Jews, the Gentiles did not have these advantages. A Gentile might convert to Judaism; but then he would no longer be a Gentile but a converted Jew. Therefore, true Gentiles were utterly without hope even with their many religions and many gods. The one God did not acknowledge them because they did not acknowledge him.

2:13. God, because of his mercy and love, did not leave them in this hopeless condition. Christ abolished the distinction between Jew and Gentile. All people are now considered the same before God. His death on the cross made this wonderful thing possible.

2:14. God wants peace to be both horizontal and vertical. That is, he wants Jews and Gentiles to be at peace with one another; and he wants both of them, now reconciled to each other, to be at peace with him. Christ is the one who gives us peace with God, for **he himself is our peace**. Mutual animosity and hatred toward each other erected a wall of separation between Jews and Gentiles. Christ abolished the **wall** by making them **one** before him.

2:15. The Jews kept the law, with its commandments and regulations. Gentiles did not. This created a barrier between them. Jesus' death satisfied the law and therefore eliminated it as a barrier. Since neither Jew nor Gentile had to obey the law to find salvation, the means of distinguishing between the two kinds of people vanished. Again, this created peace between hostile parties.

2:16. God's purpose included more than simply uniting two parties previously at war. He wanted the new creation of one party now united horizontally to find vertical union with God. The cross destroyed both the human hostility and the hostility between people and God. This is true reconciliation—overcoming human barriers and breaking down walls that separate people from God.

2:17. Paul quoted Isaiah 57:19 to show the Word of God expected the Messiah to bring reconciliation of Jew and Gentile. Those **who were far away** are the Gentiles. Those **who were near** are the Jews.

2:18. Jesus, the Messiah, did preach the message of peace to Jews and Gentiles. In the cross he reconciled them to each other. He sent the Holy Spirit to all who believe. The Spirit opened the door to God's immediate presence. Here we see the Trinity's work in salvation. The Father developed a plan of grace for salvation through faith. The Son carried out the plan in his ministry to Jew and Gentile and in his death on the cross. The Spirit became the means of immediate access to God the Father.

2:19. Redeemed Jews and Gentiles are no longer estranged from each other but are **fellow citizens** of the kingdom of God. Race or nationality make no difference. All are redeemed people through Christ's cross. **God's people** represents the NIV interpretation of the Greek *hagion*, literally, "holy ones." Other interpreters see the holy ones as Israel, Jewish Christians, the first Christian generation, all believers, or the angels of heaven. The contrast may be between who the Gentiles were—aliens—and who they now are— kingdom citizens along with those who have always been kingdom citizens— Jews. In that case they have extended the meaning of holy ones so that it is no longer limited to Jews but also includes Gentiles, now meaning all believers. The reference could maintain the discussion of being seated in the heavenly realm and allude to the angels as other inhabitants there. Most likely, it is a general reference to people of God from all generations and uses the contrast of the Gentiles' previous state to enhance the understanding of their present state. Alienated foreigners with no citizenship papers, they have joined the people of God with heavenly citizenship. Not only are they citizens of a heavenly kingdom, but they are also members of a spiritual family, **God's household**.

2:20. Paul switches to the metaphor of a building and declares that both Jews and Gentiles are "stones," as it were, of a building. The building rests on a solid foundation—the faith, testimony, and life of Christ's closest followers, his apostles. It also rests on the foundation of prophets. These are usually taken as New Testament prophets who proclaim and explain the Word of God. It may well include also the work of the Old Testament prophets in laying the foundation on which Christ built.

The key is not the foundation, however, but the **cornerstone**, a term taken from Isaiah 28:16 and probably interpreted in light of Psalm 118:22. The question is which building stone is meant: the cornerstone to which all other stones of the foundation are connected, or the capstone or keystone which is the last stone placed in the top of the structure over the gate. Isaiah 28:16 apparently refers to the foundation or cornerstone, but Psalm 118:22 may refer to the top keystone. Ephesians can be interpreted in light of either imagery, but the setting of Christ as head over all things (1:10,20–23) may point to the keystone interpretation as the most appropriate here.

2:21. The stones are forming a living, spiritual temple to glorify the Lord. In the Old Testament, the presence and glory of God inhabited a literal stone building. Now God dwells not in a stone building but in the hearts of believers. Christ is the unifying factor that takes the separate stones and creates a temple. This **temple** is **holy**, set apart for God. In this temple God receives worship and praise. The hearts of believers is thus the basic worship place in God's kingdom on earth.

2:22. Paul concludes with a pointed reminder to the Gentile Ephesians. They had no room or reason for self-pity. God included them. In Christ they are being built into God's temple along with the Jewish Christians. All together they form one worship center where God lives through the presence of his Spirit.

> **MAIN IDEA REVIEW:** *God's grace gives you life and unites you with him and with people from whom you are alienated.*

III. CONCLUSION

Occupied with Heaven

We might be awed to meet the president of the United States or the queen of England, or a great statesman or scientist or educator. To meet God, however, is so far beyond our imagination that we may not have as great a sense of awe in meeting the Creator as we do in meeting one of his creatures. Not only have we met him, but we have also been spiritually united with him, having been made one of his children. This fact must become the one truth that rivets our attention to heavenly realities while we traffic in earthly affairs. It gives us the hope we need to persevere in a hostile world.

Of hope, C. S. Lewis once wrote:

> Hope is one of the theological virtues. This means that a continual looking forward to the eternal world is not, as some modern people think, a form of escapism or wishful thinking, but one of the things a Christian is meant to do. It does not mean that we are to leave the present world as it is. If you read history you will find that the Christians who did most for the present world were just those who thought most of the next.
>
> The apostles who brought about, on foot, the conversion of the Roman Empire. The great men who built up the Middle Ages, the English Evangelicals who abolished the Slave Trade, all left their mark on earth, precisely because their minds were occupied with heaven. It is since Christians have largely ceased to think of the other world that they have become so ineffective in this. Aim at heaven, and you will get earth thrown in. Aim at earth and you will get neither" (*Mere Christianity*, New York: Macmillan, 1952, 118).

PRINCIPLES

- Unforgiven sin brings death to life.
- A person is never free and independent but always follows someone—Satan or Christ.
- Salvation comes only through God's mercy in Christ.

- No one can earn salvation in any way.
- The saved do good works for God.
- Christ joins all believers in God's peace and love.
- God lives in you through the Holy Spirit.

APPLICATIONS

- Make a life inventory to see if you are performing the works of Satan or the works of Christ.
- Tell another person of your saving experience in which you let God's grace in Christ bring you eternal salvation.
- Any boasting or bragging words in your mouth should speak about Christ and not about you.
- Life separated from Christ is death no matter what it may seem to be at the moment.
- If you want hope for life now and for life eternal, then accept Christ's salvation, serving in love.
- You cannot be joined to Christ and separated in hate and mistrust from other people.

IV. LIFE APPLICATION

God Is Not Finished with You Yet!

What does it mean to be God's workmanship? I vividly remember attending, almost back-to-back, showings of the works of two major artists. The first, at the University of Notre Dame, was a display of the etchings of Rembrandt. The second was a display of most of the major works of Georgia O'Keefe at the Chicago Art Institute. Each well-known artist has a distinctive style that sets him apart from all other artists. After learning about a given artist, you often can readily identify many of his works.

If you see weird little color cubes that look like pieces of a puzzle put together wrong, you know you are looking at Pablo Picasso. If you see limp objects draped like wet laundry over foreboding landscapes, you know you are looking at Salvador Dali. If you see figures that are stretched up two or three times their normal height, you are looking at El Greco.

You can tell much about an artist by looking at his art. You can observe Van Gogh's gradual progression into insanity by looking at his succession of several self-portraits painted over a period of years. Look at Michaelangelo, and you see an idealist. Look at Norman Rockwell, and you see an optimist. Look closely at the art, and you will discover the artist. You and I are works of art; and we will be on display, in a sense, throughout eternity, to manifest to the universe the glory of God.

Now, catch yourself, resist the temptation to say, "If I'm a work of art, it isn't going to be much of a display!" The first reaction which most of us have is to denigrate ourselves. Let's look at it in another way that may help us to believe that it is true. Rather than seeing yourself as a painting, imagine yourself as a marble statue. You've heard at least one of the versions of the old story about when a sculptor was asked how he created his stone masterpiece of Robert E. Lee (or whoever it was), he said, "I just got a big block of marble and chipped away everything that didn't look like Robert E. Lee."

A sculptor will tell you that he sees his figure in the finest detail before he ever begins to chip at the stone. In that sense, he does just chip away everything that doesn't look like what he is creating.

We are, in a sense a big block of marble when we become a Christian. God, the Great Sculptor, knows, down to the last detail, what he wants that block to look like before he begins to work on us. We, however, do not usually have a clear sense of the Sculptor's goal. We look at ourselves after God has begun to shape us but before he has finished his work. We see that the neat, clean block of stone has been chipped and roughed up, but we do not see the finished product yet. In this incomplete state, we conclude incorrectly that that is all there is, that what we are now is all we will ever be.

You say, "This isn't beautiful. This isn't a work of art."

But God is not finished with you yet.

You reply, "This big corner over here doesn't look like it belongs."

But God is not finished with you yet.

"This part is chipped and rough!"

But God is not finished with you yet.

"This part over here hasn't even been touched!"

But God is not finished with you yet.

"This part needs to be sanded, smoothed, and polished."

But God is not finished with you yet.

To every imperfection we see, the answer is, "God is not finished with us yet." It won't *be* there when he is finished. We'll be perfect, complete, flawless. A tribute to the glory of our Creator. The universe will take *one* look at us and cry out, "Glory to God!"

That's what it means to be God's workmanship. But we must be patient. God is not finished with us yet.

V. PRAYER

O Lord, it is beyond our comprehension what you have done for us, not only in forgiving us of our sins but also in making us your spiritual children. We understand enough to know that of ourselves we are not worthy. Thank you for the honor. Thank you for the hope. Thank you for the joy.

VI. DEEPER DISCOVERIES

A. Dead (v. 1)

"You were dead in your transgressions and sins. . . ." What does it mean to be dead? Obviously, Paul was not referring to physical death because physically dead people do not read. Paul meant spiritual death, and yet this concept is not defined in Scripture. If we judge the nature of spiritual death by the nature of physical death, we might think that spiritual death is a cessation of being. Yet that could not be the case, because people were spiritually dead even while they were physically alive. We have to put the pieces of the puzzle together from a number of different Scripture passages to get a fuller understanding of what it means to be "dead."

The fundamental characteristic of spiritual death seems to be "separation from God," not "a cessation of being." Romans 5 gives us the soundest clue: "At just the right time, when we were still powerless, Christ died for the ungodly. Very rarely will anyone die for a righteous man, though for a good man someone might possibly dare to die. But God demonstrates his own love for us in this: While we were still sinners, Christ died for us.

"Since we have now been justified by his blood, how much more shall we be saved from God's wrath through him! For if, when we were God's enemies, we were reconciled to him through the death of his Son, how much more, having been reconciled, shall we be saved through his life!" (vv. 6–11).

When Jesus gave us new life, we were reconciled. Spiritual death, then, must be a state of being *unreconciled*, or separated, cut off, spiritually estranged from God. The penalty of that unreconciled state is eternal separation and destruction. Romans 3:23 states that all sinned, and Romans 6:23 states that the penalty of sin is death.

The solution is that Christ, who did not need to die, since he was sinless, died for us (Rom. 5:8). In doing so, he conquered death and ascended into heaven with power over death (Heb. 2:14–15). Jesus breaks the power of death over his children. His children are placed in Christ (Rom. 6:3–4), experience death with/in him (Col. 2:20), and pass from death into life (John 5:24) in him. We still die physically, but spiritually we are born again and made spiritually alive in Christ at the moment of our salvation (John 3:16).

B. Transgressions (v. 1)

"Transgress" (*paraptoma*) means, literally, "to stumble," "to slip," or "to fall"; and thus its primary reference is to a false step, a blunder. It could be used to describe someone losing the way and straying from the right road, or it could be used for a man failing to grasp and slipping from the truth. Transgression is failing to take the right road when we could have or missing the truth that we should have known. It is the failure to reach the goal we ought to have reached. It can refer to something unintentional or unpremeditated. Nevertheless, it brings spiritual death.

C. Sins (v. 1)

"Sins" (*hamartia*) is an archery term which literally means "a missing of the mark." Sin is the failure to hit the target of God's holiness. Sin is not merely murder or rape or criminal activity. Sin is also a failure to do all the good we should have done. This concept of sin includes all of us and validates the truth which Paul wrote in Romans 3:23, "For all have sinned and fall short of the glory of God." This understanding of sin ought to convince the best of persons that he cannot get to heaven by being good, because Romans 6:23 says that "the wages of sin is death."

In his *Daily Study Bible*, William Barclay writes:

> Is a man as good a husband as he might be? Does he try to make life easier for his wife? Does he inflict his moods on his family? Is a woman as good a wife as she might be? Does she really take an interest in her husband's work and try to understand his problems and his worries? Are we as good parents as we might be? Do we discipline and train our children as we ought, or do we too often shirk the issue? As our children grow older, do we come nearer to them, or do they drift away until conversation is often difficult and we and they are practically strangers? Are we as good sons and daughters as we might be? Do we ever even try to say thank you for what has been done for us? Do we ever see the hurt look in our parents' eyes and know that we put it there? Are we as good workmen as we could be? Is every working hour filled with our most conscientious work and is every task done as well as we could possibly do it?

> When we realize what sin is, we come to see that it is not something which theologians have invented. It is something with which life is permeated. It is the failure in any sphere of life to be what we ought to be and could be (*Galatians and Ephesians*, Philadelphia: Westminster, 1959, p. 96).

Seen in this light, all of us have to admit that we are all sinners.

D. Mercy (v. 4)

Mercy is a character quality of God which motivates him to refrain from inflicting punishment or pain on an offender or enemy who is in his power. God offers to extend mercy to anyone as long as that offer of mercy does not interfere with another of his character qualities. For example, God is also just, and he will not extend mercy if it sacrifices his justice. In a legal sense, mercy may involve acts of pardon, forgiveness, or the canceling of penalties. In each case mercy is experienced and exercised by a person who has power or authority over another person. The person under authority has no claim of deliverance.

Because of his mercy, God extends to everyone the offer of salvation in Christ (John 3:16), which allows them to escape the legal penalty of death under which they sit and will continue to sit if they choose to refuse God's mercy.

E. Grace (vv. 5,7–8)

Grace is the root characteristic of God which produced our salvation. We cannot understand chapter 2 unless we understand grace. *Grace* is defined as "undeserved favor freely bestowed on humanity by God." God's mercy led him to offer humanity the gift of salvation even though humanity sinned and fell away from God. Sin caused spiritual death and separated each sinner from God for eternity. God so loved the world (John 3:16) that he was unwilling to allow man to continue in this separated condition. Salvation from sin and death was created by God's grace. Humans accept it through faith in Jesus and what he accomplished on the cross, not by doing something by themselves. In salvation God forgives sin, causes a person to be born again, and brings that person to himself forever.

F. Faith (v. 8)

God's part in salvation is grace. Our part is faith. Even the faith to believe is a gift of grace (Eph. 2:8). Without faith, we cannot be saved. Without faith, it is impossible to please God (Heb. 11:6).

Some interpreters suggest that faith is believing in spite of the fact that there is nothing to believe. Or worse, faith is believing in spite of evidence to the contrary. These are inadequate, wrong definitions of faith. Biblical faith is not merely a matter of intellectually agreeing with truth. The Bible says that "the demons believe . . . and shudder" (Jas. 2:19). Biblical faith means "believing God and acting accordingly." It means accepting as true the biblical message that God in grace has provided salvation for you. It means acting on that belief by committing your life to Jesus, letting him be your Savior and taking your own hands off any attempt to win or earn salvation. It means continuing to act on that belief by letting Jesus be Savior of every minute you live, letting him guide in every decision you make, letting him determine what is right and what is wrong for you.

G. Citizenship in Israel (v. 12)

God did not choose Israel to the exclusion of all the other nations. God chose them *in order to reach* all the other nations. All along, God intended to use Israel as an evangelistic instrument to bring the other nations of the world to himself (Gen. 12:3). In Psalm 67, David invoked the blessing of God on Israel: "May God be gracious to us and bless us, and make his face shine upon us" (v. 1). Then David stated his reason for this request: That "your ways [may] be known on earth, your salvation among all nations" (v. 2). Then David encouraged the people and creation to praise God. In the final verse he returned to the original theme: "God will bless us, and all the ends of the earth will fear him" (v. 7).

God chose Israel and asked them to be obedient to his commandments. When Israel was obedient to his commandments, God promised to bless them abundantly (Deut. 28:1–14). When they were so incredibly blessed by God, the other nations of the earth would look at Israel, recognize that the hand of God was upon them, see the goodness of God, and desire to know the God of Israel because of his blessing on Israel.

This was a wonderful system. God would draw the entire world to himself by blessing his chosen people. *This* is why he chose Israel—not to exclude all other nations but to reach all the other nations of the world. Of course, Israel was not very faithful in obeying God for any length of time. The strongest spiritual period in Israel was during the latter part of David's reign and the first part of Solomon's reign. During this time, also, Israel was greater, wealthier, and more powerful than at any other time in its history. Its spiritual impact was also greater. In fact, the queen of Sheba came to Solomon in 1 Kings 10, just to see the glory of the kingdom and hear the wisdom of Solomon. When she saw it, she burst out in spontaneous eulogy to God (v. 9). This was the way it was supposed to work. People were to see the blessing of Israel and turn to God.

H. Holy temple (v. 21)

The Old Testament presented physical reality designed to picture a spiritual reality to be realized in the New Testament. For example, the tabernacle and temple of the Old Testament were designed to picture spiritual redemption in Christ. In the Old Testament, God gave his revelation to Israel and asked them to obey it. If they would, God promised to pour out on them staggering physical blessings: agricultural, military, economic, health, and every other way. In the New Testament, God gave his revelation to the church and asked them to obey it. If they would, God promised to pour out on them staggering spiritual blessings: love, joy, peace, patience, kindness, goodness, faithfulness, gentleness, self-control—the fruit of the Spirit.

God was revealing himself to the world through physical glory in the Old Testament and is revealing himself to the world through spiritual glory in the New Testament. In both cases, God's intention was to give a picture to the world of who he was through the blessing of his people. The resultant goal was that the world would want to know him because of what they saw of him in the lives of his people.

In both the Old and the New Testament, the focal point of God's blessing is the temple. The Old Testament temple was a stunning building. A fairly small building, the central part of the structure measured only thirty feet wide by ninety feet long, a mere 2,700 square feet. Many personal homes are larger than that. Yet some estimates say that it might cost more than four billion dollars to reproduce today. The inside was lavishly appointed with incredible amounts of gold, carvings, expensive wood, and marvelous tapestries. The walls were constructed of the finest stone. Two astonishing bronze pillars in front highlighted what may have been one of the most expensive buildings per square foot that has ever been constructed. First Kings 10 records that when the queen of Sheba saw all this splendor, she swooned ("she was overwhelmed"). The idea is that the people of the world would get some idea of the grandeur, glory, and power of God by looking at his physical temple, the physical site of his presence on earth.

The counterpart to the Old Testament temple is the New Testament temple, which is the totality of all believers in Jesus. Instead of God investing the New Testament temple with his physical glory, his intent is to invest the New Testament temple with his spiritual glory. Instead of gold and cedar and ivory and tapestry, he has lavished his New Testament temple with love, joy, and peace. The idea is that the people of the world would get some idea of the character of God by looking at Christians, his spiritual temple, the spiritual home of his presence on earth.

VII. TEACHING OUTLINE

A. INTRODUCTION

1. Lead story: Back from the Dead
2. Context: In the second chapter of Ephesians, Paul describes our lost and hopeless condition, then articulates how we may be redeemed. He says that we were dead in our trespasses and sins but that God has made us alive together with Christ. Then God brings both Jew and Gentile in Christ into the same spiritual temple, making them no longer two but one.
3. Transition: As we look at this chapter, we understand our true condition without Christ. We also learn that in Christ, there is no such thing as Jew or Gentile. Rather, everyone is equal in the eyes of God.

B. COMMENTARY

1. Our Spiritual Death (vv. 1–3)

a. Dead in transgressions and sins (v. 1)
b. Lived in cravings of our sinful nature (vv. 2–3)
2. Our Spiritual Life (vv. 4–10)
    a. We are made alive again with Christ (vv. 4–7)
    b. Our new birth is by God's grace (vv. 8–10)
3. Our Spiritual Union (vv. 11–22)
    a. We are brought near to God (vv. 11–13)
    b. We are made one with Jews (vv. 14–18)
    c. We are part of God's holy temple (vv. 19–22)

C. CONCLUSION: GOD IS NOT FINISHED WITH US YET

VIII. ISSUES FOR DISCUSSION

1. Describe the difference between your life in Christ and before Christ.
2. How would you define the grace of God to a person who has no relationship with God? What does the grace of God mean in your own life?
3. What is the relationship between salvation by grace and being created for good works?
4. What wall did Christ break down? Why? What is the result?
5. What does it mean to be God's dwelling?

Ephesians 3

Paul's Prayer for Power

Quote

"We cannot all argue, but we can all pray; we cannot all be leaders, but we can all be pleaders; we cannot all be mighty in rhetoric, but we can all be prevalent in prayer. I would sooner see you eloquent with God than with men."

Charles Hadden Spurgeon

IN A NUTSHELL

In chapter 3, Paul informs the Ephesian Christians: God has revealed to me a great mystery, namely that both Jews and Gentiles are united as one in the body of Christ, and he has called me to proclaim this message. For this reason, I pray that you might be strengthened with power through his spirit in the inner man so that you might mature spiritually, be able to comprehend the magnitude of God's love, and be filled with the fullness of God.

Paul's Prayer for Power

I. INTRODUCTION

Gaps in the Distance

In southern New Mexico, just a few miles north of the Mexican border, lie the Grand Floridas, a striking mountain range. The profile that the Floridas cut against the deep blue New Mexico sky is a ruggedly handsome one, with jagged edges and sharp rock formations jutting up out of the ground. As you look from the north, near Deming, New Mexico, they seem to be one gigantic, unbroken rock sculpture dropped onto the flat New Mexico wilderness.

As you ride close to the mountains on horseback, you can see that the mountains are not unbroken. The rock formation to the north is like the head of a prehistoric beast lying flat against the horizon. Behind it is the bulk of the mountain range, the body of the huge beast. The head is a rock formation that juts higher than a skyscraper, and in between the head and the vast body is a valley, a beautiful grassland of gentle slopes that lies completely hidden until you ride right up to the mountains. From a distance, you have no idea that it is there.

The same is true of some events in the Bible. For thousands of years, God kept a secret in his heart, hidden from the world, from the angels, from the priests, from the patriarchs, and from the prophets until the time came for him to reveal it through his Son to his holy apostles. The secret was that there was to be a new creation, a new living temple, a new spiritual body through which God was going to work to carry the message of salvation to the ends of the world, and in whom he was going to create his spiritual likeness. This new creation was to be comprised of both Jew and Gentile alike. This new creation is called the church.

The church was not foreseen by anything written in the Old Testament. It was a surprise. In Ephesians 3, Paul calls it a mystery, something previously unknown which has now been revealed. Paul introduces this mystery and explains it in very general terms in this chapter. Like the valley in the mountains, to see it, we must get close. After introducing this great mystery, Paul prays for the Ephesian believers, that they might be empowered to mature spiritually and to experience the fullness of God.

II. COMMENTARY

Paul's Prayer for Power

> **MAIN IDEA:** *Members of Christ's church should mature spiritually and experience the fullness of God.*

A Paul's Prayer for Power (v. 1)

> **SUPPORTING IDEA:** *A pastor will endure persecution to be able to minister faithfully to the needs of the people for whom God has made him responsible.*

3:1. Paul began a prayer for spiritual power for the Ephesian believers. Before he actually got into the body of his prayer, he interrupted himself and launched into a parenthetical discussion of the great mystery of both Jews and Gentiles being united as one in Christ. His explanation lasts through verse 13, after which he resumes his original prayer begun in verse 1.

His primary statement in verses 1–7 is basically this: "God has revealed to me the message that there is no longer a distinction between Jew and Gentile, and he has made me a minister of that message." However, he preceded that with the phrase, **For this reason.** The reason is found in 2:13–22: Jews and Gentiles have been brought near by the blood of Christ. Christ abolished the barrier between Jew and Gentile, and they are being built together into a dwelling of God in the Spirit.

We could summarize it this way: because Christ abolished the barrier between Jew and Gentile and made them one new thing (a dwelling place of God in the Spirit), I, Paul, was made a minister of this message. I'm assuming that you know that this truth was revealed to me, that Gentiles are fellow-heirs, fellow-members, and fellow-partakers with the Jews of the promises of God.

Now, having summarized it, let us look more closely at it. Paul was in prison in Rome when he wrote Ephesians. He did not consider himself to be a prisoner of Rome. He considered himself **a prisoner of Christ Jesus,** because it was out of obedience to Jesus that he was a prisoner there; and he trusted completely in the sovereignty of God. He considered his circumstances to be in the will of God so that the gospel could be spread to the Gentiles. Therefore, he considered himself a prisoner for the sake of the Gentiles.

Corrie Ten Boom wrote that she considered that wherever she was, that was just the part of the world that God wanted her to take the gospel to—even the German concentration camps. That was Paul's perspective, also.

B Paul's Great Mystery (vv. 2–13)

SUPPORTING IDEA: *God has revealed the mystery of the church, so believers are responsible to proclaim this mystery wherever God takes them and should not be discouraged because of suffering.*

3:2–5. Human teachers did not make known the revelation of this great **mystery** to Paul. The Lord himself made it known by direct **revelation**. Paul had mentioned this mystery briefly in chapter 2. It was not revealed in the Old Testament but was revealed to the **apostles and prophets** in the opening days of the New Testament.

3:6. A **mystery**, in this biblical sense, is not to be understood in the same sense of mystery in modern usage. It does not mean that the truth Paul is proclaiming is mysterious or puzzling. Rather, *mystery* is a technical term, meaning "something that has not previously been made known." The mystery is: Gentiles are fellow-heirs, fellow-members, and fellow-partakers with Jews of the promises of God.

3:7. Paul was a minister of this message, specially commissioned to take the message to Gentiles. This mystery is now termed **gospel**, good news. Just as salvation comes by grace, so this gospel mystery mission came to Paul because of God's grace (see Commentary on 2:8). This grace came to Paul as God worked in his power. Paul did not request or manipulate things to get to deliver this mystery gospel to the Gentiles. God in his grace worked it out so Paul would have this mission.

3:8. Paul considered himself to have no qualifications for the mission God gave him. He ranked last on the list of applicants. God chooses by different criteria than we do. He did not search out Paul's resumé to determine if he could do the job. God in love gave Paul the opportunity to tell Gentiles who had never heard the gospel the story of God's **unsearchable riches of Christ** (see Commentary on 1:7).

3:9. Paul's mission included more than defining the mystery. He had to show Jew and Gentile alike exactly how God planned and carried out this mystery. He had to explain how God took the message entrusted to Jews and expanded it to include every person. Paul's own call on the Damascus Road was an essential part in this **administration**. Until this time God had kept both the mystery and its administration to himself, a mystery reaching back to the time of creation. The mystery was not a recent addition to God's salvation plan for his world, just a recent revelation to his people.

3:10. Why wait until now? God saw the time was right. This mystery was more than it appeared. It was the **very wisdom of God**. Now that this stunning secret is revealed, this wisdom could now be made known throughout heaven. Who should know it in heaven? The **rulers and authorities**. As in

1:20–21 (see 1 Cor. 15:24–26; Col. 1:16; 2:10,15) these heavenly powers are angelic representatives of earthly rulers thought by some in Paul's audience to control access to God's throne. In 1:20–21, Paul showed that Christ alone had such control. Here he shows that the church is the means by which these evil forces could recognize God's plan and his operation of that plan—to create a church of Jews and Gentiles with the same way of salvation by grace.

3:11. The revealing and execution of this "church plan" is consistent with the **eternal purpose** of God. This purpose is no longer just a plan to be realized at a later date. In the cross of Christ, God's eternal plan of salvation has been realized. The church lets all the world see that plan accomplished and in action.

3:12. God's plan of salvation purposed before the world and executed in the cross clears the path to God. Through Christ a person can enter God's presence with **freedom and confidence**. The cross has provided salvation which cleanses us of sin, forgives us, makes us holy, and thus enables us to enter the presence of the Holy One.

3:13. The eternal plan accomplished in Christ was administered in many ways. These included Paul's becoming a prisoner and proclaiming this message while in chains. Paul's situation in prison could easily discourage young churches and turn them away from Jesus. Paul urged the Ephesians not to let this happen. His suffering was no reason for sadness. It helped accomplish God's plan. Through Paul's suffering the Ephesian believers gain **glory**, that is they are led to know Christ more intimately and experience salvation more fully.

ⓒ Paul's Prayer for Power Resumed (vv. 14–19)

SUPPORTING IDEA: *Spiritually mature believers strengthened by the Holy Spirit comprehend God's love and are filled with the fullness of God.*

3:14. Repeating the opening phrase, Paul resumes his original prayer which he started in verse 1. The kneeling posture (compare Luke 22:41; Acts 7:60; 9:40; 20:36; 21:5; Rom. 11:4; 14:11; Phil. 2:10) represents humility and reverent worship in contrast to the common practice of standing to pray (Mark 11:25; Luke 18:11,13).

3:15. Prayer is directed to the Father. This Father is the Father of all fathers, for every family in heaven and on earth derives its existence and its family name from the Father. Certainly such a powerful, creative Father can hear and answer the prayers about to be uttered.

3:16. The prayer has four requests which build on each other, or which flow out of each other. The first request is for inner spiritual strength. This is not the "when the going gets tough the tough get going" kind of power. This is not self-discipline or the power of positive thinking. This is not mental renewing, or self-talk, or getting a grip on yourself, or turning over a new leaf. This is a fundamental work of God from his Spirit to our spirit.

3:17. This leads to the second request, deep faith. This is not salvation. Paul was writing to Christians, and Christ takes up residence in our heart when we accept him (John 14:23). This is more than resident faith that comes with salvation. This is Christ's being at home in one's heart.

In the little booklet *My Heart Christ's Home*, Robert Munger (Downers Grove, IL: InterVarsity Press, 1954) pictures the Christian life as a house, through which Jesus goes from room to room. In the library, which is the mind, Jesus finds trash and all sorts of worthless things, which he proceeds to throw out and replace with his Word. In the dining room of appetite, he finds many sinful desires listed on a worldly menu. In the place of such things as prestige, materialism, and lust, he puts humility, meekness, love, and all other virtues for which believers are to hunger and thirst. He goes through the living room of fellowship, where he finds many worldly companions and activities, through the workshop where only toys are being made, into the closet, where hidden sins are kept, and so on through the entire house. Only when he had cleaned every room, closet, and corner of sin and foolishness could Christ settle down and be at home. To have Christ dwell in our hearts through faith means for him to be at home in every corner of our life, because we believe his promises and therefore become obedient to his word.

The third element is a prayer for abundant love that finds concrete expression in 19a. First Paul gives the qualities needed to be able to receive this prayer. Love must become the dominant quality of life, the roots of your existence, the foundation on which all else rests. Such love in your life comes from the divine love.

3.18. The strengthening of our inner man by the Spirit allows us to let Christ be at home in all the rooms of our heart. Letting Christ be at home in all the rooms of our heart enables us to know the vast dimensions of the love of Christ.

We need foundations for our experiences and relationships. We can't handle life unless we are assured that God loves us and has accepted us, that we are dear to him, precious to him. When we know this, then we know who we are. Then we have a sense of well-being. Love gives us that. This sense of identity and being loved gives us the ability to relate to others, so we can comprehend with all the saints the magnitude of the love of God. Knowing God's love is not an individual accomplishment. It occurs only in the loving context of the church and involves the whole church, not isolated individuals.

3:19. Paul's request then is that the church and each of its members know in a personal, emotional way, as well as an intellectual one, this love of Christ. We measure this love only with cosmic dimensions and understand it only by seeing it expressed at its deepest, most intimate level in the cross. Praying that we can know it, we ultimately confess that it is beyond our full comprehension.

The final request is a prayer for God's fullness. The inner strength of the Holy Spirit, which is a gift which God gives to those who pray for it, leads to the indwelling of Christ, which leads to abundant love, which leads to God's fullness in us. That is to be satisfied with God. We all want to be filled up to the fullness of God. The only way it will happen is if we pursue him. If we pray for him to strengthen us with power by his spirit by the inner man, Christ will be at home in each room of our heart. If Christ occupies our heart, we will have a confidence and security in his love for us. If we have such confidence and security, we are able to love others. This ability to know God's love and thus love others, leads to the fullness of God in us. His presence, his power, his love, his life inhabit us. We participate fully in his kingdom on earth. That is Paul's prayer for you.

D Paul's Great Doxology (vv. 20–21)

SUPPORTING IDEA: *God should receive eternal glory for what he has done for us.*

3:20. Paul ends his discussion of the mystery of the church and his prayer for power with a spontaneous burst of praise to God. His prayer forms a great doxology to the Lord for his power and glory. We see three things emerging from this doxology. First, we see the sovereignty of God. God in his sovereignty may choose to do whatever he wills. What he can do far exceeds anything we can dream or imagine, must less ask for. God's sovereignty means our prayers can be answered far beyond even what we ask.

Second, we see the omnipotence of God. God manifests his great power in many ways. Most obviously, he manifested it when he created the world. He used that kind of power to bring Jews and Gentiles together and form them into a dwelling of God in the Spirit. The power we see in creation and in the church is the power of God that works in us in the love relationship of prayer.

3:21. Finally, we see his **glory**. The power God has manifested and continues to display has a purpose—bringing glory to him. All that God has done is to resound to his glory forever. God has done things in the church among his people and **in Christ Jesus** where his people now abide and where God completed his plan of salvation. As we see and recognize God's work in the church and in Christ, we respond in praise and worship, giving God glory.

MAIN IDEA REVIEW: *Members of Christ's church should mature spiritually and experience the fullness of God.*

III. CONCLUSION

Begging My Own Father

Paul's mission is, in the eyes of heaven, an astounding one: to communicate to the world, and particularly to Gentiles, that there is now no distinction between Jew and Gentile. That Gentiles are now fellow-heirs, fellow-members of the body, and fellow-partakers of the promise in Christ Jesus through the gospel. Because we experience the merging of the two, it doesn't seem particularly miraculous, just as jet travel doesn't seem particularly miraculous to anyone who was born after 1950. To those born in earlier eras, jet travel still holds fascination. The Bible says that the merging of Jews and Gentiles was possible only because of the wisdom of God. Miraculously, this wisdom is now to be made known through the church to the rulers and authorities in the heavenly places.

J. Wilbur Chapman used to tell the story of a gentleman who had grown up in a wealthy family but had become estranged, something like the prodigal son. Destitute and broken in spirit, the man had taken to a life of begging. He explained:

> I got off at the Pennsylvania depot as a tramp, and for a year I begged on the streets for a living. One day I touched a man on the shoulder and said, "Hey, mister, can you give me a dime?" As soon as I saw his face, I was shocked to see that it was my own father. I said, "Father, Father, do you know me?" Throwing his arms around me and with tears in his eyes, he said, "Oh, my son, at last I've found you! I've found you! You want a dime? Everything I have is yours."
>
> Think of it. I was a tramp. I stood begging my own father for 10 cents, when for 18 years, he had been looking for me to give me all that he had.

What an interesting story, and how illustrative of our lives as human beings. We go around tapping the world on the shoulder, asking for a dime, when our Heavenly Father is seeking us out to give us everything he has. We are far too easily pleased. We are content to scrounge around for crumbs, when an invitation for a banquet is laid at our feet. We are consumed with the frustrations of the world, when the fullness of God is ours.

PRINCIPLES

- God is the giver of spiritual growth and insight.
- It is valid, even important, to ask God to increase our spiritual growth and perception.
- God is glorified through our blessings.
- The "mystery," the church, is the centerpiece of God's work in the world today.

APPLICATIONS

- Pray continuously that the Lord would strengthen you with power through his Spirit in your inner being, that Christ would dwell in your hearts through faith, that you would grasp the love of Christ, and be filled to the fullness of God.
- Do the same for others you pray for.
- Treat the church with the respect the Scripture gives it.
- Find your place in God's administration of the mystery of his plan of salvation.
- Approach God with freedom and confidence.
- Search the love of God until love becomes the foundation of your life.
- Give God glory in all you do.

IV. LIFE APPLICATION

Strengthened from Within

In his book *Fearfully and Wonderfully Made*, Dr. Paul Brand (Grand Rapids: Zondervan, 1980) tells the story of the white corpuscles, the guardians and watchdogs of the body, the armed forces of your inner workings which are always on guard against foreign invasions. He writes:

> They look exactly like amoebae: amorphous blobs of turgid liquid with darkened nuclei, they roam through the body by extending a finger-like projection and humping along to follow it. Sometimes they creep along the walls of the veins; sometimes they let go and free-float in the bloodstream. To navigate the smaller capillaries, bulky white cells must elongate their shapes, while impatient red blood cells jostle in line behind them.

> Watching the white cells, one can't help thinking them sluggish and ineffective at patrolling territory, much less repelling an attack. Until the attack occurs, that is. When damage occurs to anything in the blood stream, an alarm seems to sound. As if they have a sense of smell (we still don't know how they "sense" danger), nearby white cells abruptly halt their aimless wandering. Like beagles on the scent of a rabbit, they home in from all directions to the point of attack. Using their unique shape-changing qualities, they ooze between overlapping cells of capillary walls and hurry through tissue via the most direct route. When they arrive, the battle begins.

> The shapeless white cell, resembling science fiction's creature "The Blob," lumbers toward a cluster of luminous green bacterial spheres. Like a blanket pulled over a corpse, the white blood cell

assumes the shape of the bacteria; for awhile the bacteria still glow eerily inside the white cell. But the white cell contains granules of chemical explosives, and as soon as the bacteria are absorbed the granules detonate, destroying the invaders. In thirty seconds to a minute only the white cell remains.

When the body is attacked, its inner forces resist, the body's normal functioning is reinforced in a manner that protects it from the danger. It is strengthened from within. This gives us a very accurate analogy to the Christian life. The believer in Christ is attacked continually from the forces of the world in which we live, and from the spiritual forces of evil who would destroy us, as well as our own inner magnetism which draws us to sin. And when we are under attack, we must resist, we must be reinforced in our counter attack, we must be strengthened from within. The biblical way of dealing with life's problems is to deal with our own spiritual state. The Christian method is to build up our resistance in our inner man, by the Spirit.

That is why the apostle Paul prays that **out of his glorious riches he may strengthen you with power through His Spirit in your inner being** (3:16). Whatever the attack may be, the resistance can be so strengthened that we will be made more than conquerors. This is the essential biblical teaching as to how to live in a world such as this, how to keep coping in it, and how to be "more than conquerors" in spite of everything that happens in it. The Bible challenges us not to figure out a way to eliminate our problems but rather to be strengthened by God in such a way as to live above them, not without pain and suffering, but in spite of pain and suffering.

V. PRAYER

Our Heavenly Father, grant to us that we might be strengthened with power in the inner man, that Christ might completely be at home in our hearts, that we might know the love of God which surpasses knowledge, that we might be filled up to all your fullness. Amen.

VI. DEEPER DISCOVERIES

A. Mystery (v. 3)

A mystery (*musterion*) in the biblical sense, is not a curious or imponderable thing, difficult or impossible to explain. Rather, a mystery in the biblical sense, is something which was *previously unknown* and previously unrevealed. Once it is known, it may be perfectly easy to understand.

Paul's understanding of this *musterion* was given to him directly by the Lord through personal revelation. This mystery was not made known to the

Old Testament people. That is why it was a mystery: it was previously unknown. Now through the holy apostles and prophets, it is made known.

B. The specific mystery (vv. 4–7)

What was previously unknown but now has been made known? It is that the Jews and Gentiles are joined as one in a new spiritual entity called the church. This is unheard of to the Jews. The Old Testament offered no hint of the church. The age of the church was unknown and unexpected. We have trouble understanding why Paul is making such a major issue out of this because we do not understand the degree of separation that existed between these two groups of people.

It is like saying there will no longer be blacks and whites in South Africa. It is like saying there will no longer be Catholics and Protestants in Ireland. It is like saying there will no longer be liberals and conservatives in the United States. All these are going to be made into one. That would be difficult to imagine but not as difficult as a Jew becoming one with a (spit) Gentile dog. Historically, it was remarkable. It was close to blasphemy. That is why Paul labors the point.

He then makes the point that there are three levels of unity between the Jews and the Gentiles. First, the Gentiles are fellow-heirs. The glories of God promised to the Jews will now include the Gentiles. All the eternal riches that God possesses to bestow on his people, he will bestow on Gentiles as well as Jews.

Second, the Gentiles are fellow-members. Up to this point, if anyone wanted to be a child of God, he needed to convert to Judaism—to become a Jew. No longer. Now both Jew and Gentile are members of the church, and in the church they are equal. There is no distinction. They are fellow-members of God's family.

Finally, the Gentiles are fellow-partakers. This is not adding a new thing so much as summarizing the previous two. The historical distinction between Jew and Gentile in the church is no longer valid. They partake of the blessings of God equally.

C. Stewardship (vv. 8–9)

Paul speaks, in verse 2, of his "administration" or *stewardship* to carry the message of salvation to the Gentiles. *Stewardship* could be understood here as *responsibility*. He felt a responsibility from God to take the message of salvation to the Gentiles because God had given him the new message. Just as Paul realized a responsibility to minister to others, so each of us must sense a similar responsibility. God has given each one of us a spiritual gift to minister to others. Each one of us has received knowledge which will help others prepare for their eternal destiny as well as to live their everyday lives. We are responsible, not to keep that truth to ourselves but to do what we can to spread it to others.

First Peter 4:10 says, "Each one should use whatever gift he has received to serve others." First Corinthians 12 and Romans 12 elaborate on these gifts.

Perhaps you are not gifted as a great teacher or counselor. But you can serve others, can't you? We all can. People will often say, "I don't know what my spiritual gift is." We begin refining our understanding of our spiritual gifts by serving others and trying to help wherever we can; and by serving, we get some idea of what our gifts might be.

The Bible talks much more about responsibility to do what you can for others than it does spiritual gifts. The secret to begin determining your spiritual gift is to get involved. Then use the experience to guide you into the areas which are most rewarding for you and in which you see the greatest fruit.

Each of us, like Paul, has a responsibility to minister. To do something. Setting up chairs or stuffing the bulletins may not seem like a ministry to you until you realize that a church could not have a worship service without those tasks being completed. Then you realize it is a ministry. The secret: get involved. Then God will guide you, through experience, to the place of most fruitful service.

D. The purpose of the mystery (v. 10)

The purpose of the revelation of the mystery "was that the manifold wisdom of God should be made known to the rulers and authorities in the heavenly realms."

Apparently these are angels. Others believe that it refers to, or includes, demons. However, there is no mention of spiritual conflict or opposition, nor are there any negative words to describe these authorities. In Ephesians 6, Paul refers to world forces of this darkness, spiritual forces of wickedness in the heavenly places. No such evil descriptions exist here.

Therefore, it may be best to understand them as holy angels. For some unknown reason, that which God is doing in the world through the church is a display of his wisdom to the angelic hosts of heaven, showing them a dimension of God that they cannot see in any other way.

This plan was in accord with the eternal purpose which he carried out in Christ Jesus. When an architect or a contractor builds a building, he will do it according to a blueprint, according to a plan. If a person makes a suit, he will do it according to a pattern. If a person bakes a cake, she will do it according to a recipe. So Almighty God in framing the ages did it according to a plan, a predetermined purpose in his sovereignty. He mapped it out before the foundation of the world, and the angels stand by in wonder.

E. The heart of the mystery (vv. 11–15)

The heart of the mystery which God is manifesting to the heavenly observers is *wisdom*. God's wisdom is on display. It is impossible to condense the wisdom of God. The entire New Testament does not hold it all. It includes the outpouring of the grace of God on lost man. It includes the fact that people get saved, not because of how good they are but because of how good God is. It includes that we are kept, not by our faithfulness but by God's faithfulness. It includes that God takes the fallen, the broken, the earthbound and raises them up, heals them, and makes them heavenbound.

The wisdom of God reveals itself not only in the great salvation themes in the Bible but also in the little things we see in the process of living daily life. Many things are backwards, upside down, and inside out.

> Exalting yourself lowers you;
> lowering yourself raises you.
> To keep what you have is to lose it;
> to give it away is to keep it.
> To find your life is to lose it;
> to lose your life is to find it.
> Abundance can bring poverty;
> poverty can bring abundance.
> Freedom leads to slavery;
> slavery leads to freedom.
> Cleverness can be folly;
> foolishness of God is wisdom.
> Strength leads to weakness;
> weakness brings strength.
> The first shall be last;
> the last shall be first.

Without the Scriptures revealing to us the wisdom of God, we often would travel 180 degrees in the opposite direction of God's will. We must not overlook the wisdom of God. We can learn it even as the angels learn it. It exceeds our natural mind; but the Holy Spirit illumines the receptive mind with the Word, and we understand the mystery of the ages.

F. The inner man (vv. 16–19)

The inner man is not merely our mental self. It is not merely our intellect, emotions, and will. Rather, it is the spiritual self which was reborn when we received Christ (John 3:16; Eph. 4:24). Paul distinguishes clearly between the inner man and the flesh in Romans 7. This inner man "wants to do good," "delights with God's Law," "is a slave to God's law" (vv. 21,22,25).

Paul prays that in this inner man "he may strengthen you with power through His Spirit." In 2 Corinthians 4:16, Paul writes that "outwardly we are wasting away, yet inwardly we are being renewed day by day." A part of a Christian is getting old, decaying, deteriorating. A part is also getting fresher and more vital, increasing, and becoming richer, deeper, and stronger. That is the inner man.

This inner man is the true us; this is who we are. That true "us" is recreated in the likeness of God, in holiness and true righteousness. It wishes to do good; it joyfully concurs with the law of God; it experiences no condemnation; it is not destroyed by bad circumstances; it is renewed by feeding on eternal truth. That is who *you* are. That is where God strengthens you through his spirit with power.

G. Power (v. 20)

All of us want power—power to live the Christian life, power to do that which we know we should do, and power to not do what we know we should not do. Most Christians are acutely conscious of the gaping chasm between how they ought to live and how they actually do live. Most Christians long for the power to close the gap. Paul says it can be ours.

The power that Paul prays for is not physical power; it is not intellectual power; and it is not emotional power. It is *spiritual power!* Paul prays that we might be strengthened with spiritual power. Few people have ever felt that they had the power they prayed for. Where's the power? What does it look like? How do we get it? Why haven't we felt it?

Many of us are confused as to the nature of this power. We expect something different from what is promised in this passage. We see demonstrations of miraculous power in the Bible and want to be like the people who had this power. Our attitude is, "There's no reason Christianity of this age ought to be inferior to Christianity of the Bible. If people had the power of God because of the intensity of their zeal and commitment to the Lord, then we can be equally intense and zealous and committed, and the same power will be available to us."

We want to pray and have the rain stop and then, according to our prayer, have it start raining again. We want to pray and heal someone. We want to pray and have multitudes get saved. We want power, real power. We want power always to do right and never to do wrong. We want power always to be happy, always to believe God. As we look around at the gross godlessness, the sickening sin, the ever-present evil, we want power to prevail against it. We want power—not piddling, little power but big-time power.

Paul prays that we be strengthened with power. What is the power? How does it manifest itself. What does it enable us to do? How do we know if we have it? This is easy to answer when the Lord does the extraordinary, but what about when he does not? Does that mean there is no power at work?

We can trace power through six central passages of Scripture:

1. "Now may the God of hope fill you with all joy and peace as you trust in him, so that you may overflow with hope by the power of the Holy Spirit" (Rom. 15:13).

    If you abound in hope, you have the power of God working in you. If you hope in eternal life, that hope gives you peace from fearing death and condemnation, ability to forego gratification in this world because you understand that you will receive your reward in the next, encouragement that you are not what you are going to be, hope that in the end justice and goodness will prevail, assurance that God is sovereign and that he is guiding the world toward his conclusion which will be, in the end, good for his children.

    If you have hope, you have his power working in you.

2. "We have this treasure in jars of clay to show that this all-surpassing power is from God and not from us. We are hard pressed on every side, but not crushed; perplexed, but not in despair; persecuted, but not abandoned; struck down, but not destroyed. We always carry around in our body the death of Jesus, so that the life of Jesus may also be revealed in our body" (2 Cor. 4:7–10).

    If we are motivated to carry the message of Christ to other people and we see the light of the gospel dawning in the hearts of men, we have the power of God. If we are afflicted, but not crushed, perplexed, but not despairing, persecuted, but not forsaken, struck down, but not destroyed, we have the power of God working in us.

3. "He said to me, 'My grace is sufficient for you, for my power is made perfect in weakness.' Therefore I will boast all the more gladly about my weaknesses, so that Christ's power may rest on me" (2 Cor. 12:9).

    If God has given you comfort and contentment even though you have weaknesses, then the power of God is in you. If God has used your weaknesses to minister to others, then the power of God is in you. If God has used you beyond what you expected, if you can praise him for your "thorns in the flesh," then the power of God is in you.

4. "I can do everything through Him who gives me strength" (Phil. 4:13).

    We cannot fly to the moon through Christ's strength, so what does this mean? The context is: being content whether in abundance or in want. If you are able to live in humble means with less than you would like to have, or less than you need, and still be content in the Lord, then you have the power of God. If you are able to accept the will of God in your life when it doesn't match what you would choose, then you have the power of God.

5. "Being strengthened with all power according to his glorious might so that you may have great endurance and patience, and joyfully giving thanks to the Father" (Col. 1:11–12).

   If you have attained to greater steadfastness, then the power of God is in you. If you have attained to greater patience, then the power of God is in you. If you are able joyously to give thanks to the Father, then the power of God is in you.

6. "To this end I labor, struggling with all his energy, which so powerfully works in me" (Col. 1:29). If you are motivated to give yourself in ministry to others, then the power of God is in you. If God has used you for good in the lives of other people, helping them change into the character image of Christ, then the power of God is in you.

The point is, I think, in summary, that if you are growing, becoming more like Christ, if you are motivated to serve others and help others, if you are content in him, with his will for you, even when it is not what you would choose, then you have the power of God working in you.

Without the power of God, you would not grow and become more like Christ. Without the power of God, you would not be motivated to help others and serve others; and even if you did, it would not help them much if God were not working in them. Without the power of God, you would not be content in Him. Without the power of God, these things would not be true for you. While it is not flamboyant, it is subtly miraculous; and it is evidence that you have the power of God.

We must be quiet and still and look through eyes of faith to see much of God's power. When we see these things which are signs of God at work, we must stop missing it. We must stop taking it for granted. We must stop chalking it up to cause and effect results. We must stop assuming it would have happened anyway. We must start recognizing it as the power of God. God is at work in us and through us. We have the power of God!

H. Glory (v. 21)

To give glory means to give social weight to, to define as an important personage. It means to call accurate public attention to and to proclaim the significance of someone. When we receive the blessings of God, when we are recipients of all that he wants to give us, we give social weight to God; we call accurate public attention to him, and we proclaim the significance of who he is and what he does.

The glory of God is to be the end purpose of all that we do. It is the end of what he intends to do in us. God gives us longings which he alone can satisfy. He calls us to faith and obedience to his Word. This faith and obedience result in our lives being deeply satisfying internally and glorifying to God externally.

All that he is, all that he does, is to bring glory to himself. This is not because he is some cosmic egomaniac, but because as he calls attention to himself, accurately, it reveals the true desirability of who he is. It maximizes the likelihood that others will want to know him personally and be saved from their sins.

Writing about the issue of praise and glory, C. S. Lewis said:

> The most obvious fact about praise escaped me for the longest time. I thought of praise in terms of a compliment, approval, or the giving of honor. I had never noticed that all enjoyment spontaneously overflows into praise unless shyness or something else brings it into check. The world rings with praise . . . lovers praise their mistresses, readers their favorite poet, walkers praising the countryside, players praising their favorite game . . . praise of weather, dishes, actors, motors, horses, colleges, countries, historical personages, children, flowers, mountains, rare stamps, rare beetles, even sometimes politicians or scholars. I had not noticed how the humblest, and at the same time most balanced and capacious minds, praised most, while the cranks, misfits, and malcontents praised least.

> I had not noticed either that just as men spontaneously praise whatever they value, so they spontaneously urge us to join them in praising it: "Isn't she lovely? Wasn't it glorious? Don't you think that magnificent?" The psalmists in telling everyone to praise God are doing what all men do when they speak of what they care about (*Reflection in the Psalms*, New York: Harcourt, Brace, 1958).

VII. TEACHING OUTLINE

A. INTRODUCTION

1. Lead story: Gaps in the Distance
2. Context: After having described for us our spiritual blessings in Christ (see chap. 1) and our salvation and union of Jews and Gentiles, Paul now prays for the Ephesian believers that they might be strengthened to live a lifestyle consistent with their position in Christ.
3. Transition: Paul bursts into prayer as a result of his explanation of the union of Jews and Gentiles in the body of Christ. Before the prayer has barely started to fall from his tongue, he interrupts himself to explain his role in the communication of this profound new message. Then, having explained his role, he picks up with his prayer again.

B. COMMENTARY

1. Paul's Prayer for Power (v. 1)
2. Paul's Great Mystery (vv. 2–13)
   a. Paul's revelation from God (vv. 2–5)
   b. Paul's commission to spread the revelation (vv. 6–13)
3. Paul's Prayer for Power Resumed (vv. 14–19)
   a. Spiritual power (vv. 14–16)
   b. Deep faith (v. 17)
   c. Abundant love (vv. 18–19)
4. Paul's Great Doxology (vv. 20–21)

C. CONCLUSION: STRENGTHENED FROM WITHIN

VIII. ISSUES FOR DISCUSSION

1. What responsibilities do you think you might have to further the welfare of God's great mystery, the church?
2. How would you evaluate the statement, "We glorify God most when we enjoy him most"?
3. What are some examples of God's power in your life?

Ephesians 4

Our Call to Unity and Holiness

"*C*hristians are people who are drawn together because they owe a common debt to the goodness and grace of God."

William Barclay

Ephesians

IN A NUTSHELL

*I*n chapter 4, Paul advises the Ephesian Christians: I want to encourage you to live the way God's people should live. Two particularly important things should characterize your lives. First, since you are spiritually united in Christ with all other Christians, live in unity with one another. Minister to others, and let others minister to you. In that way, you will all grow to spiritual maturity. Second, live holy lives. Put behind you the sins of the past, and live a moral and ethical lifestyle that reflects the values of Christ.

Our Call to Unity and Holiness

I. INTRODUCTION

Acting like Who We Are

*I*dentity and actions inseparably go together. From the earliest days of our childhood, our actions are linked to our identity:

1. Three-year-old Johnny falls down on the sidewalk as he is running to greet his father who has just pulled into the driveway. Johnny is tired and hungry. Two-year-old Susie just took a toy away from him. Because of all that, he cries harder than is really warranted. Daddy picks him up and says, "There, there, you're a big boy. Act like it."

   Who he is (a big boy) should affect how he acts (he shouldn't cry needlessly).

2. Princess Margaret, as a young girl, sits beside her mother, Queen Elizabeth, at the princess's first presentation to the British public. She is called upon to walk to the microphone and say a few words to the gathered dignitaries. As she prepares to stand, her mother leans over to her and says, "You are a princess. Walk like one!"

   Who she is (a princess) should affect how she walks (with dignity).

3. Eighteen-year-old Chuck has gone through twelve of the toughest weeks of anyone's life in Marine boot camp in coastal South Carolina. During the last week they are forced to crawl under rolls of barbed wire with live machine gun ammunition blazing just inches over their heads. Chuck freezes. He begins to sweat. His hands dig into the red clay beneath him as panic sweeps his soul. Just then, a friend crawls up beside him and says, "Get a hold of yourself, Chuck. You're a Marine. Act like one!"

   Who he is (a Marine) should affect how he acts under pressure (with courage).

Throughout our life, from beginning to end, our identity is linked to our actions. Who we are affects how we should act. This is the basic principle of life to which Paul appeals in our opening sentence of chapter 4. In the first three chapters he said, "You are a child of God." Now in the fourth chapter, he is saying, "Act like one." Throughout the rest of the book, he spells out for us in specific detail how we are to act.

II. COMMENTARY

Our Call to Unity and Holiness

MAIN IDEA: *You should live like the person you have become. Live in unity and mutual ministry with others and in holiness before God.*

A The Call to Unity (vv. 1–6)

SUPPORTING IDEA: *Because Jews and Gentiles have been united by God in Christ, we should manifest the spiritual unity by being united in our actions.*

4:1. Then refers back to the entire first three chapters of the book. Because of all that God has done for us in providing salvation and making us into a spiritual dwelling place of God in the spirit, a dwelling place in which Jew and Gentile are united as one, we should live like the people we have become. The fact that Paul is **a prisoner for the Lord** lends weight to the fact that we should also become prisoners of the Lord. Paul actually was in prison when he wrote Ephesians, and we are probably not in prison. Paul's physical presence in prison bore a double meaning. He would have considered himself a prisoner of the Lord even if he had been living in freedom. The point is, he had given up his freedom to follow Christ, and he was calling on us to do the same.

4:2. After calling us to walk (live) worthy of our calling in Christ, Paul describes the character qualities of the person who lives as a prisoner of Christ.

Humility does not mean to see yourself as some pitiful excuse for humanity, some low life above whom all other human beings exist, some piece of refuse at the bottom of the human pile. Rather, humility means to see yourself as God sees you: with infinite and inherent value but with no more value than anyone else. It means being willing to accept God as the authority over your life rather than insisting on being your own supreme authority. It means you are willing to order your life in such a way as to serve God by serving others. When all Christians do that, everyone's needs are met by others in a context of harmony and love.

When we fail to subordinate ourselves to others, however, we focus on meeting our own needs. This way we may accumulate to ourselves those things which we want, but we become lonely. Christians cannot be satisfied in a context of individualism and isolationism. It is not good for man to be alone. Only humility leads away from loneliness.

Gentleness or *meekness* literally means "power under control." Being meek for a week will make you realize it takes strength to be meek. War horses in the ancient world went into battle trained to protect their master. They were under the total and instantaneous control of their rider. The war horses were described as being meek. Their strength was under total control.

Moses was described as the meekest man who ever lived. Yet he was a great, dynamic, charismatic leader who challenged the power of the throne of Egypt. His strength stood under God's control.

Patience is believing God's timetable is good, no matter what it is. "O Lord, give me patience, and hurry!" is the prayer of most of us. Patience does not always come quickly. Patience is a characteristic of mature people. When we have a proper expectation, it actually helps us be patient.

Abraham received God's promises that he would have a land, many descendants, and a blessing, but he had to wait many years to see those promises fulfilled. "After waiting patiently, Abraham received what was promised" (Heb. 6:15).

God told Noah to build an ark, far from any body of water. For one hundred years he worked on it, in faithfulness. Finally when it rained, Noah received the promise and the fruit of his obedience.

Moses waited forty years between the time he gained his burden to deliver the children of Israel and the time his burden was fulfilled. Patience.

Throughout the Scriptures patience means patience. It doesn't mean that if I am patient now, maybe the Lord will see I have learned my lesson and will give me what I want sooner. Patience is waiting for God to act when, where, and how God chooses.

Forbearance in love is the willingness to put up with something or someone in a spirit of love—*agape* love, which is the commitment of my will to benefit another.

4:3. These characteristics yield unity! Preserving the **unity of the Spirit through the bond of peace** implies that we do have spiritual unity. Unity exists in Christ! Unity is maintained by the Spirit. Unity is preserved as believers make peace with one another their major priority instead of acting selfishly for personal gain and honor. Our call is not to create spiritual unity but rather to manifest spiritual unity by relational unity. Paul calls for unity in the third verse and spends the next thirteen verses elaborating on it.

4:4. Paul appeals for corporate unity in the body of Christ on the basis of the elements of spiritual unity. Each element is an isolated whole, but each element functions as a uniting factor within the larger church.

The church is **one body.** Believers may meet in many places, speak different languages, and live in different cultures. None of this separates them. They remain Christ's one body. The church obeys **one Spirit.** Many people may claim to bring God's message or teach God's truth. Such teachers and teachings may threaten to divide the people of God into theological camps. God's Spirit speaks the one truth and guides the church to unity in theology and practice. The church lives in the light of its **one hope.** Christ's resurrection has ensured the believers' resurrection to eternal life. That common goal encourages the church to act in unity now.

4:5. The church receives salvation and marching orders from **one Lord.** Christ Jesus died and rose again. He alone has the right to the church's allegiance. All other lords are false guides and promise salvation they cannot deliver. Following Christ, the church will never be divided.

The church proclaims **one faith.** The crucified, resurrected Lord is the object of that faith. To confess Jesus as Lord is to express the faith of the church and to unify oneself with all members of that church. Membership in the church comes through **one baptism.** Each member enters the baptismal waters once to confess the one faith and become a part of the one body. This baptism identifies the person as belonging to Christ and distinguishes the person from all who do not confess Christ. Thus baptism is the unifying mark of believers.

4:6. The final element of spiritual unity is **one God.** This tied the church to its Jewish heritage. The worship of one and only one God united the church. The major elements of the church's theology and practice come in ones. This calls the church to practical unity. As Christians live together and witness together, they must show unity to the world.

B The Cultivation of Unity (vv. 7–16)

SUPPORTING IDEA: *God has spiritually gifted each of us, so we should minister to others and let them minister to us. Then we will all grow to spiritual maturity.*

4:7. Verse 7 introduces the subject of our spiritual giftedness. In so doing the emphasis turns slightly from the church's unity to individual diversity. Each of us received a spiritual gift by the grace of God. That grace has not been apportioned equally. Rather Christ has chosen how to divide grace to each member. Each is distinct and different.

4:8. In verses 8–10, Paul digresses from his direct argument to provide scriptural proof. Instead of giving a direct quote of Psalm 68:18, he apparently gave a general summary of the entire psalm. Psalm 68 is a victory hymn composed by David to celebrate the conquest of a Jebusite city. It describes a victory parade up Mount Zion, going beyond the literal, historical victory parade to attribute the victory to God. Thus it talks about a figurative victory parade with God ascending, not up to Mount Zion, but up to heaven.

Historically, it was typical, after a king won a significant military victory, to bring back the spoils of war, including enemy prisoners, to display to his people. In addition, however, if there were any of his own soldiers whom the enemy had previously captured, the victorious king would bring them back and parade them before the home crowd. These were often referred to as recaptured captives—prisoners who had been taken prisoner again by their own king and then given freedom. It was a great honor to release these captives. David pictures God ascending to heaven after having been victorious against his earthly enemies and freeing those who had been captive to the forces of evil.

When he ascended on high depicts a triumphant God returning from battle on earth back into the glory of heaven. **He led captives in his train** perhaps refers to those who have been delivered from captivity to evil.

4:9-10. Jewish rabbis interpreted Psalm 68 in light of Moses' ascent of Mount Sinai. Paul interpreted it in light of the life, death, resurrection, and ascension of Jesus. **Ascended** refers to Jesus' ascension from earth to heaven (Acts 1:9-11). He ascended from earth to heaven to reign forever with his Father. Paul then explains that if God ascended he first descended. If, as seems clear, *ascended* refers to the Lord's being taken up to heaven, then **descended** seems to refer to his coming down from heaven to earth previously. **The lower, earthly regions** complicates the interpretation. This passage has historically been understood as Jesus' having descended into hell and preached a proclamation of freedom to someone there. Recently, that interpretation has fallen into disfavor. The weight of evidence and the preponderance of modern commentaries now lean toward saying that the intent of the phrase is not to point to a specific place, such as the inner core of the earth, or to "hell," but simply to refer to the incarnation.

John MacArthur writes:

> To understand the phrase "the lower parts of the earth" we need only to examine its use elsewhere in Scripture. In Psalm 63:9, it has to do with death, being related to falling by the sword. In Matthew 12:40, a similar phrase "the heart of the earth" refers to the belly of a great fish where the prophet Jonah was kept. In Isaiah 44:23 the phrase refers to the created earth. Psalm 139:15 uses it in reference to the womb of a woman where God is forming a child. The sum of these uses indicates that the phrase relates to the created earth as a place of life and death. In the majority of the uses it appears in contrast to the highest heavens (*Ephesians*, Chicago: Moody Press, 1986, 139).

Therefore "descending into hell" is certainly a possible explanation, but not a necessary explanation. The contrast is between an ascent to heaven and a descent from heaven. The descent would then be to earth, from earth to hell. The descent from heaven to earth could refer either to Christ's incarnation or to the coming of the Spirit as Christ's representative. The problems which arise from trying to interpret it as descending into hell are so formidable that MacArthur's is the generally preferred interpretation. The emphasis of the passage is on the ascent, not the descent. Christ ascended above the heavens to take his place beside the Father ruling the universe.

In order to fill the whole universe is an uncertain phrase, but may mean that Jesus, as head of the universe (Col. 1:18), resumes his position of authority over the universe and therefore the right to bestow gifts on his subjects.

4:11. This verse ties directly back to the last word of verse 7. Verse 11 picks up again the subject started in verse 7 to tell us the relationship between the call to unity and the spiritual gifts Christ has given us. Spiritual gifts are at the heart of Christ's strategy for building his church. The gifts are ministers (or ministries) for the church. While this issue is strongly debated, particularly by Pentecostal and charismatic theologians, evangelical doctrine has traditionally held that of those four gifts two of them are still in existence and two have passed away. These gifts will be looked at more closely in the "Deeper Discoveries" section. For now, it is adequate to make the observation that the apostles and prophets seem no longer to be part of God's work in the church. The church was laid on the foundation of the ministry of the apostles and prophets (Eph. 2:20). Now that that foundation has been laid, the evangelists and the pastor-teachers are being used by God to build the superstructure.

4:12. It is not the task of these gifted people to do all the work of the ministry. Their task is to **prepare God's people for works of service.** When believers are equipped and people accept the adventure of ministering to others, then the whole body is built up, matured, strengthened, and flourishes.

4:13. Diverse gifts create and build up one body in unity. This unity is in faith and knowledge of Christ. Christ does not try to build up superstars in his kingdom with superior faith or superior knowledge. He tries to build up a church unified in its faith and knowledge, each member being built up to maturity. All are to reach the **fullness of Christ.** The church's goal is that each member and thus the entire church will show to the world all the attributes and qualities of Christ. Then the church will truly be the one body of Christ.

4:14–16. The result of these spiritually gifted people's equipping the saints is that believers are not to be like children, easily persuaded and confused, jumping from one opinion or belief to the next, like **waves** on the sea being driven by gusting winds of false **teaching.** Rather, the believers are to speaking the truth in love. Speaking the truth in love is a mark of maturity, which will enable us to grow up spiritually. Immature people often fall into one of two opposite errors. They speak the truth, but without love, or they love without speaking the truth. When we do the first, we often brutalize others, pounding them with truth but doing it in an unloving way. When we do the second, we don't tell others the truth, thinking that by shielding them from the truth we are sparing them from pain. We are not, however. All we are doing is delaying their maturation. To share the truth with our fellow believers is a mark of maturity, but to do it with love, with understanding, with compassion. From Christ the whole body is gifted, and as each one uses his gift for the benefit of others, the whole body matures. We must recognize that we belong to one another, we need one another, no matter how insignificant we think our contribution is. There are no little people in the kingdom of God, as Francis Shaeffer used to say, and there are no little jobs. Just as a physical body needs red corpuscles and livers more than it needs a handsome face or beautiful hair, so we all belong; we are all necessary. We all can contribute, and when we do, we all grow to maturity in Christ.

4:14. The Ephesian church, as most of the churches Paul wrote, faced teachers with opposing viewpoints. They divided the church body into factions, each opposing the others. Their presence required the type of spiritual maturity and church unity Paul had described. Without such unity the church would act like a group of babies, each crying out because of his own pains and needs, each inconsistently saying one thing and then another, each at the mercy of cunning, deceitful teachers. To avoid infantile behavior, the church must mature into unity of the faith and of knowledge of Christ.

4:15. Such maturity involves teaching the truth in love. False teachers showed no love or care for the members; they simply wanted to get their own way. Mature believers search for the truth as a united body, loving and caring for the needs of each member. Such loving, caring search for truth allows them to grow as members of the body whose head is Christ, for Christ is the truth.

4:16. The head allows each part of the body to mature and grow, not concentrating on special knowledge and growth for a favored few. Each of the parts of the body is needed to hold the whole body together in unity. The body is truly a maturing, loving body only as each part is encouraged to grow and do its part of the work.

𝐂 The Calling to Holiness (vv. 17–24)

SUPPORTING IDEA: *You must no longer do the evil things you did before you were a Christian.*

4:17. The Gentiles in Ephesus were particularly sinful. Ephesus was a leading city of commerce and culture in the Roman Empire, the home of the pagan temple of Diana, one of the seven wonders of the ancient world. Worship of Diana involved the worst immorality of degraded pagan religion. That influence made Ephesus a wretched hive of scum and villainy, a wicked place indeed. Temple prostitution, graft, crime, immorality, idolatry, and every conceivable form of sin abounded. Many of the Christians in Ephesus came out of that kind of background. In contrast with that evil background, Paul made his appeal, "Don't live like that any longer!"

First, he says, it is futile to live like that. It leads to nothing.

4:18. Second, he says, it reflects darkened understanding, a result of having turned their backs on God. Their hearts are hard, and as a result, their mind is dark. Lives separated from God's holiness are ignorant lives. This is hard for the sophisticated, educated people of Ephesus to accept. How dare someone call them ignorant. Paul did not contend they had no knowledge. He contended the knowledge did no good in leading them to a lifestyle that pleased God. Without such a lifestyle, their minds did not function properly.

4:19. Their hard heart, which yielded a darkened mind, led to an unholy life. Paul says they have **given themselves over to sensuality**, a life without concern for the consequences of their actions. Their desire for sensual pleasure overrode every other regard. No matter what they did, such desire was never satisfied. They always wanted more. Lust not love dominated their lives. Such Gentiles certainly did not serve as models for the church. They were not mature. They did not bring unity.

4:20–21. In contrast to this former way of life, the Ephesian Christians were to live righteous lives. Paul says, "This is not how you learned from Jesus to live!" "Your hearts are no longer darkened. You have learned the truth, which is to be found in Jesus."

4:22. Living a proper Christian life involved two concepts. They must **put off their old self**. This old self was the self that was corrupted by the deceits of lust. When we were born, we were born with a sinful bent. We were separated from God. David wrote in Psalm 51:5, "Surely I was sinful at birth, sinful from the time my mother conceived me" (see Eph. 2:1–3 and commentary there).

This old self is separated from God. While it is capable of doing good in the eyes of other people, it is incapable of doing anything but evil in the eyes of God. We are born that way, and we remain that way if we do not allow God to intervene. It is who we are by nature. We are children of Adam. We possess a fallen nature as Adam did, and we are separated from God as a result. That is the old self.

To put off the old self can mean merely to accept Christ as in Colossians 3:9, where it is treated as an accomplished fact. It can mean that, once you have become a Christian, you are to leave behind the attitudes, habits, values, and actions that you had before being born again—similar to taking off an old work coat and putting on a new coat to go out for the evening. This is more in keeping with the context, since Paul goes on in verses 25–32 to describe the specifics of a changing lifestyle.

The earthly desires, or lusts, which we have are **deceitful**. They promise one thing but deliver another. Therefore, we are to be smarter than our earthly desires, recognize their deceitfulness, and as a result, turn from them.

4:23. In contrast, we are **to be made new in the attitude of our minds**. How? You are what you think. You move in the direction of what you put into your mind and what you allow your mind to dwell on. So if you are not what you want to be, then you must begin to think differently. If you are to think differently, you must put into your mind that which you want to become. If you do, the Holy Spirit will use it to change you to become what you want to be. If you don't, you will never be what you want to be. It all depends on what you put into your mind. This is what it means to be made new in the attitude of your mind.

4:24. Finally, we are **to put on the new self**. This means, we are to allow the new self to govern our activities. We are to begin living the lifestyle that corresponds to who we have become in Christ. This new holy self shows we are maturing, growing in unity with the body, and doing our part of the body's work.

🔟 The Cultivation of Holiness (vv. 25–32)

SUPPORTING IDEA: *Living like the person you have become means incorporating a formidable list of specific actions into your daily life.*

4:25. First we are to stop lying. To be taught the truth in Jesus (v. 21) means to make truth telling a habit of life. We cannot attempt to fool or deceive one another as pagans do. We must create unity in the body with one truth because we are members of one another.

4:26–27. Sometimes a Christian may legitimately become angry. Jesus became angry at times. In those times we must be extra careful how we act, for anger gives no excuse to sin. Sinning in anger would include things such as saying unkind things or acting in harmful ways toward others. We may not always be able to keep from getting angry, but we can keep from sinning when we do. When we do get angry, we should deal with it before the day is through.

When we allow our anger to become sin or when we allow ourselves to keep our anger for more than a day, it gives the devil an opportunity to gain control over our attitudes, our actions, and our relationships. It gives him a **foothold** to lead us into greater anger and more sin.

4:28. Christians are not to steal. Stealing, in its most obvious form is, either by deception or force, taking the possession of someone else. In all civilizations, stealing is considered wrong. It is a timeless and universal value. Inherently, no one wants his possessions taken from him. We have no difficulty understanding or agreeing with this command at its most obvious level.

Rather than steal, we are to work. Work has benefits. (1) It is good. It allows a person to meet his own needs and the needs of his family. It allows him to do something meaningful with his time and to make a contribution to society. (2) Work allows a person to be able to give something to others who have needs. Rather than steal from others, work allows a person to give something to others. (3) Work allows a person to support financially the advancement of the kingdom of God. Working is thus a sign of Christian faithfulness, maturity, and unity.

4:29. This is the Bible's version of, "If you can't say something nice, don't say anything at all." We are to speak only words that build up and encourage others. This one passage, if consistently obeyed, would eliminate the overwhelming majority of life's conflicts. Words of a mature Christian seek to help the listener, not harm him. Thus the ministerial gifts of Christ's grace achieve their purposes, and the unity of the body of Christ is preserved and enhanced.

4:30. Not to limit speech to wholesome, helpful words makes the Holy Spirit feel grief because of our behavior. We are not saying that you can never say anything negative. Sometimes we are forced to talk about unpleasant things, particularly in solving problems in which people are involved. Teachers, ministers, employers, coaches, lawyers, police, and so on, all find it necessary to tell the truth about someone even if it is unpleasant. Whether you are solving a problem or not, you avoid speaking unwholesome words. Your intent is to build up, not tear down, to unify, not divide.

4:31–32. Christians are to "put away" five sins: bitterness, wrath, anger, clamor, and slander. In their place, they are to "put on" three virtues: kindness, tender-heartedness, and forgiveness. Because God acts this way toward us, we should act this way toward others. Then the church will be built up, the people will be holy, and Christ's body will be unified.

MAIN IDEA REVIEW: *You should live like the one you have become. Live in unity and mutual ministry with others and in holiness before God.*

III. CONCLUSION

Grow in Groves

The church is united spiritually. All the people who make up the church are "one" with Christ and with one another. We are to live our daily lives in a manner that manifests our spiritual oneness. Then we are to live lives that manifest to the world the character of Christ. Living in unity with one another will help us to live righteous and holy lives.

California's giant sequoias have roots just barely below the surface of the ground. That seems impossible. If the roots don't grow deep into the earth, it seems that they would blow over in a strong wind. But not sequoias. They grow only in groves, and their roots intertwine under the earth's surface. So, when the strong winds come, they hold one another up.

There's a lesson there. People are like the giant sequoias. We need to grow in groves. Our roots are just below the surface. Standing alone, the winds of life would blow us over like a cheap umbrella. We need to intertwine our roots, our lifelines, with others. Then when the strong winds of life blow, they have to take all of us, or they can't take any of us. If there are enough of us, the winds can't blow that hard. We'll stand, in groves, and grow toward the sun.

PRINCIPLES

- God has given the church what it needs to be healthy, growing, and mature.
- Jesus' authority and power extend to all the universe.
- Spiritual maturity requires that we be in mutual ministry, ministering to others and allowing them to minister to us.
- There are no Lone Rangers in the church, only Three Musketeers.
- The Christian life requires that we stop doing bad things as well as start doing good things.

APPLICATIONS

- We must all accept the challenge of living like the person we have become.
- We must get involved with other Christians (in a church if that is possible) to allow them to minister to us and allow us to minister to them.
- We must get serious about sin and do whatever is necessary to turn our backs on the things of darkness.
- We must develop a love and respect for others, for only out of love will we be able to be as kind and helpful to them as we ought.

IV. LIFE APPLICATION

Christ's Orchestra

In his book, *Fearfully and Wonderfully Made*, Dr. Paul Brand writes:

A kindly looking old gentleman with a more-than-prominent nose and a face seamed with wrinkles crosses the stage. His shoulders slump, and his eyes seem sunken and cloudy—he is over ninety years old. He sits on a stark black bench, adjusting it slightly. After a deep breath, he raises his hands. Trembling slightly, they poise for a moment above a black and white keyboard. And then the music begins. All images of age and frailty slip quietly from the minds of the four thousand people gathered to hear Arthur Rubinstein.

His program tonight is simple: Schubert's *Impromptus*, several Rachmaninoff's Preludes, and Beethoven's familiar *Moonlight Sonata*, any of which could be heard at a music school recital. But they could not be heard as played by Rubenstein. Defying mortality, he weds a flawless technique to a poetic style, rendering interpretations that evoke prolonged shouts of "Bravo!" from the wildly cheering audience. Rubinstein bows slightly, folds those marvelous nonagenarian hands, and pads offstage.

I must confess that a bravura performance such as that by Rubinstein engrosses my eyes as much as my ears. Hands are my profession. I have studied them all my life. A piano performance is a ballet of fingers, a glorious flourish of ligaments and joints, tendons, nerves, and muscles. From my own careful calculations, I know that some of the movements required, such as the powerful arpeggios in *Moonlight's* third movement, are simply too fast for the body to accomplish consciously. Nerve impulses do not travel with enough speed for the brain to sort out that the third finger has just lifted in time to order the fourth finger to strike the next key. Months of practice must pattern the brain to treat the movements as subconscious reflex actions . . . finger memory, musicians call it.

I marvel too at the slow, lilting passages. A good pianist controls his or her fingers independently, so that when striking a two-handed chord of eight notes, each of the fingers exerts a slightly different pressure for emphasis, with the melody note ringing loudest. The effect of a few grams more or less pressure in a crucial pianissimo passage is so minuscule only a sophisticated laboratory could measure it. But the human ear contains just such a laboratory, and musicians like Rubinstein gain acclaim because discriminating listeners can savor their subtlest nuances of control (Grand Rapids: Zondervan, 1980, 161–62).

That's the way we are. We are Christ's Arthur Rubinstein. We are his body. We might even say, we are Christ's orchestra. We each are musicians, and we each have a part to play. Though we do not hear the full score or see all the musicians now, the time will come when we will sit in heaven with the Great Maestro. We will hear and see for the first time how it is all to sound.

Every musician will be there. Not one of them will have been lost. Every note that was to have been played on earth will have been played. When we see it all and hear it all put together, it will be a glorious symphony of praise to the Lord. For now you are a musician. You have a part to play. You are part of something larger, greater, and grander than yourself. We are creating a symphony of praise to the glory of God. When the Great Maestro raises his baton and signals you to play, as he does now, then on the downbeat, play!

You have a part. He has gifted you so that you can play it. You are worthy. You are able. Play to the glory of God.

V. PRAYER

Our Heavenly Father, thank you for uniting us with Christ and making us "one" with all other Christians. Give us a vision for the importance of living in love and unity with one another. Give us grace to live out the vision as we are empowered by your Holy Spirit and guided by Your Word. Amen.

VI. DEEPER DISCOVERIES

A. Unity (v. 3)

Why is unity such a major issue? First, it is necessary for Christians to enjoy the richness of relationships among one another. Without unity in the bond of peace, Christians will not enjoy one another. We will not enjoy life. We will not have the mutual ministry to one another that each of us needs for life to be rich and satisfying—without unity.

Also, without unity, the world will look at Christians and doubt, based on their relationships, whether Christ is real. "[I ask that] all of them may be one, Father, just as you are in me and I am in you. May they also be in us so that the world may believe that you have sent me" (John 17:21). If the world sees unity among Christians, they have a basis for concluding that Christ is sent from God. If they do not see unity among Christians, they have a basis for assuming that Christ is not sent from God. So the unity issue is a vital, strategic one in the witness of God in the world. It is not incidental.

In verses 4–6, Paul's next step is to spell out the spiritual unity on which the relational unity is based. There is one body, Spirit, hope, faith, baptism, and God. Therefore, since there is only one of these, since we are unified in this spiritual sense, we should be one in a relational sense. Spiritual unity should be manifested in relational unity.

"One body" means the body of Christ, which is a term used to describe the totality of all believers in Christ from the time of his first coming until he comes again. There is only one body. One Spirit is, of course, the Holy Spirit. There is only one. "One hope" refers to the common hope of heaven, and eternity with God. There is only one. "One faith" speaks, most likely, not of the body of truth which we believe, but rather of the common faith which we exercise in Christ for our salvation. There is only one.

To baptize means "to place into." To baptize with water means to place into water. To baptize with the Holy Spirit means to place into the body of

Christ (meaning "to become a member of"). The term *baptism* in this verse might refer to water baptism, or it might refer to Spirit baptism. If it refers to water baptism, it alludes to the outward symbol (water baptism) of the inward reality of the believer's identification with Christ. If it refers to Spirit baptism, it alludes to the Christian's being placed into the body of Christ, mirroring the meaning in 1 Corinthians 12:13, which reads: "For we were all baptized (placed) by one Spirit into one body." In my understanding *one baptism* probably does not refer to water baptism but to our baptism into the body of Christ (Rom. 6:4–7). When we were born again, we were spiritually placed into the body of Christ. This "placing into" is referred to as being baptized into the body of Christ. There is only one.

One God is, of course, the God and Father of our Lord Jesus Christ. There is only one. He is of all, over all, through all, and in all. *Of all* means that he is the God and Father of all Christians, not all people (John 1:12, Gal. 3:26). He is over all Christians, as their sovereign God. He lives through all Christians and manifests himself in them.

B. One body (v. 4)

The body being referred to here is the body of Christ, a term used to describe the totality of all believers in Christ from the time of his first coming until he comes again. Martin Lloyd-Jones spoke eloquently of the body:

> The church or body of Christ consists of people of all types and kinds and colors, from many continents and climates. The early Christians are in this body. The martyrs of the Reformation are in this body. The Puritans, the Covenanters, the first Methodists, they are all in this body; and you and I are in this body if we are truly in Christ. The Church spans the continents and the centuries. Natural abilities play no part in this matter. It matters not what you may be, whether you are ignorant or knowledgeable, clever or lacking in faculties, great or small, wealthy or poor. All these things are utter irrelevancies; this body is one. It is the Church of all the ages . . . the fullness of God's people. It is the only body, it is the unseen, mystical church. The one thing that ultimately matters for each one of us is that we belong to this body. We can be members of a visible church and, alas, not be members of this mystical unseen Church (*Christian Unity*, Grand Rapids: Baker Book House, 1980, 47).

Just as the physical body is made up of countless different parts, all of which function as an organized whole, so the body of Christ is made up of countless individual parts, all of which contribute to a larger whole. It is extremely important that we see ourselves accurately, not as individuals in an unrelated sea of humanity, but as distinct and vital members of a great spiritual body which wants us and needs us.

C. One baptism (v. 5)

To baptize means "to place into." To baptize with water means to place into water. The metaphor "being baptized with fire" means to be placed into difficult circumstances. The term *baptism* in this verse probably does not refer to water baptism but to being placed into the body of Christ.

D. Spiritual gifts (v. 7)

1. The Bible teaches clearly that each Christian is given a spiritual gift. This is a divinely determined and granted capacity for ministry, and God wants us to use it. We can't choose our spiritual gift. He gives his gifts as he sees fit. First Corinthians 12:11 says: "[The Holy Spirit] gives them (gifts) to each one, just as he determines."

2. When we minister, using our spiritual gift, the results are up to God. Each person is called upon to be faithful to exercise his spiritual gift, but the results and the consequences are up to the Lord. Exercising the gift is our work. Producing results is his. Assuming you have been responsible to your gift, you cannot claim credit when the results are abundant, and you need feel no blame when the results are meager.

   You do not need to know your gift before you can begin serving the Lord. Some have the gift of evangelism, but everyone is to do the work of an evangelist. Some have the gift of teaching, but we must all teach from time to time, not necessarily in a classroom, but in the classroom of life. Some have the gift of giving, but all of us are supposed to give.

3. We must not become overly obsessed with discovering our spiritual gift, to the extent that we feel we can do nothing until we know. Rather, we should all get busy doing things we know we should do because the Bible commands it. Then, as we get involved, we will find that some of the things we do have better results than others and are affirmed by others; and some of the things we do, we enjoy more than others. By observing results of what we have already been doing, we get insight into what our spiritual gift is. Then we can begin to direct more and more of our energies in those areas.

E. Spiritual offices of the church (v. 11)

1. *Apostles* are "sent ones." In the technical sense, an apostle fits a very strict definition: one of twelve chosen by Christ and an eyewitness of the resurrection (Mark 3:13; Acts 1:22–24). Matthias was chosen

later to replace Judas. Paul also fits this category, though he did not meet Christ personally until after Christ's resurrection and ascension into heaven.

Apostle is used in a more general sense of other men in the early church: Barnabas (Acts 14:4), Silas and Timothy (1 Thess. 2:6), and a few other outstanding leaders (Rom. 16:7; 2 Cor. 8:23; Phil 2:25). These apostles were called "representatives" (literally, "messengers") of the churches (2 Cor. 8:23), whereas the thirteen were apostles of Jesus Christ (Gal. 1:1; 1 Pet. 1:1).

Apostles in both groups were authenticated by "signs and wonders and miracles" (2 Cor. 12:12), but neither group was self-perpetuating. *Apostle* is not used in the Book of Acts after 16:4. As the apostles died out, it appears that the gift of apostle disappeared.

2. *Prophets* were also specially gifted people. They differ from those who had the gift of prophecy in 1 Corinthians 12:10. Their ministry went far beyond the ministry described in that passage. They sometimes spoke revelation from God (Acts 11:21–29) and sometimes simply expounded revelation which had been already given. In Ephesians 2:20, we read about the church "built on the foundation of the apostles and prophets, with Christ Jesus himself as the chief cornerstone." After the foundation was laid, it appears that there was no more need for those people; and the gift was not perpetuated when each of them died.

3. *Evangelists*, technically, are those who proclaim the good news, which is the meaning of "evangelize." In the New Testament, when the message of the gospel was unknown outside of Jerusalem, these evangelists were traveling missionaries and church planters. They led people to Christ and then taught the new believers the Word, built them up, and moved on to a new territory. They would have many things in common with missionaries today.

4. *Pastor-teachers* most likely refers to one person since the Greek sentence here uses a different word for *and* between these words than the word used before the other offices. That is strong evidence to suggest that this is one and the same person. The pastor-teacher ministered as shepherd of the local congregation, teaching God's Word and leading the church's ministry. Congregations in a city such as Ephesus had several pastors.

F. Lust, sensuality, impurity (v. 19)

Verse 19 uses three Greek terms to describe the Gentile lifestyle. "Sensuality" (*aselgeia*) refers to a life of sexual excess, given over to debauchery and licentious living. "Impurity" (*akatharsia*) refers to dirt and the contents of graves that make a person ritually impure. In moral language it refers to immorality, especially sexual immorality, often involving unnatural vices. "Lust" (*pleonexia*) refers to greed, covetousness, a desire for things that can never be satisfied. The Gentiles were immorally insatiable. It is easier to deny the first desire than to fulfill all that follow. Lust is deceitful. It promises pleasure, but it delivers pain; it promises satisfaction, but it delivers sorrow; it promises a bright future, but it delivers a blighted future. Stolen bread *is* sweet, but while it is in your mouth, it turns to gravel (see Prov. 20:17).

Deitrich Bonhoeffer said, "When we are tempted, we do not say, 'I hate God, and God hates me.' Rather, we simply forget about God and act as though He didn't exist, or we had never known him."

What wrong or inappropriate thing are you tempted to do, thinking you will win? You won't. Is it financial? Is it moral? Is it interpersonal? You won't win. You may win in the short run, but you always lose in the long run. Sin is like cocaine. It feels good on the front end, but on the back end it destroys.

G. Biblical view of work (v. 28)

Working is good. God is a worker, and he instituted work before the fall. Creation, of course, is a great "work"; but God continues to work now, interacting with his creation and moving it toward a purposeful end. The Bible often pictures God as a worker: divine shepherd, divine carpenter, divine farmer, divine doctor. God is a worker. Work has intrinsic value *because* God is a worker. Work has intrinsic value to us because we are like God—created in his image. We are coworkers with God.

We serve at least four significant purposes as we work:

1. Our work makes a contribution to other people. Through your work, God has designed that you serve other people. We can rightly see ourselves as contributing to the welfare of others through our work.
2. Through your work God meets your needs and the needs of your family. First Timothy 5:8 says that if anyone does not provide for his own household, he has denied faith and is worse than an infidel (literal translation of Greek word NIV renders, "unbeliever"). Our work makes a profound contribution to our lives by meeting the practical needs of our family.
3. Through your work, you are able to contribute to the needs of others. Whether a family member, a friend, or a total stranger needs financial help, you are able to help others through the money you make at work. You are also able to support ministries as well as world evangelism.
4. Through your work, you love and serve Christ. "Obey your earthly masters in everything; and do it, not only when their eye is on you and to win their favor, but with sincerity of heart and reverence for the Lord. . . . It is the Lord Christ you are serving" (Col. 3:22,24). You

go to work to worship, love, and serve Christ. Ultimately, your boss is not your employer; the Lord is.

The Bible pictures God's expectations in our work:

1. Excellence: We must do our work with excellence. How we do our work must reflect our commitment to an excellent God. Others must see that we work hard, do as well as we can, and do so because we are Christians.

2. Morality: We must keep our moral and ethical edge sharp. We do not steal from our employer in any way. We guard our speech and do not get involved in vulgar or off-color conversations. We are true to our word. We give an honest day's work for an honest day's wage. We are upright in our relationships with others, especially those of the opposite sex.

3. Relationships: We treat others with dignity and respect. We manifest regard for the worth of others, by the way we speak to them and by the way we treat them.

4. Results: We trust all results to God. Unless we believe that God is sovereign, we can become embittered against people who stand in the way of our needs, goals, or longings. If we manifest a trust in God in all things, we can be freed from the worry, anxiety, anger, bitterness, aggression, fear, or depression that often dominate the lives of others who do not trust in the Lord. Our emotional stability in difficulties must cast a favorable light on the God we serve.

Certainly, no one will succeed totally all the time in these issues, but these are the standards toward which we must all aspire as we seek to have a biblical perspective toward work. God's work must be done God's way. For most Christians it is easier to see a missionary's or pastor's work as relating to needing to be done God's way than to see their own work in that light.

How would you want a person you work with to act in day-to-day work? How would you want the person to act toward other people as he first walks in the office on Monday morning? How would you expect the person to act in resolving conflict? What kind of integrity would you want the fellow worker to have? What kind of response would you expect in stressful situations? How would you expect the person to react when you misunderstood what the person told you?

Those same standards that apply to those in full-time Christian work also apply to you because you are in full-time Christian work. God's work must be done God's way. While God gives dignity to your work, he also gives you direction. Do you perform your work with excellence? Do you organize and plan out your day? Do you try to make the greatest contribution for your employer? Do you try to be efficient and learn to do your job a better way?

What is your attitude toward others? What is the quality of your relationships? Would they describe you as caring as a Christian should be? Do you have a stability about you in the way you respond to stress? How do you respond to the opportunity for ego gratification? Are you boastful? Do you seek to serve others? What impact do you have on others?

God's work must be done God's way. You are to have an ethical edge to your life. You are to be ethically distinctive. We are to live in such a way that our lives will be unique and distinctive so that coworkers will want to know why.

VII. TEACHING OUTLINE

A. INTRODUCTION

1. Lead story: Acting like Who We Are
2. Context: Throughout our life, from beginning to end, our identity is linked to our actions. Who we are affects how we should act. This is the basic principle of life to which Paul is appealing in our opening sentence of chapter 4. He says in the first three chapters, "You are a child of God." Now in the fourth chapter, he is saying, "Act like one." Throughout the remainder of the chapter, and even the rest of the book, he spells out for us in very specific detail how we are to act.
3. Transition: Paul begins by saying: "I want to encourage you to live the way God's people should live. There are two particularly important things that should characterize your lives. First, since you are spiritually united in Christ with all other Christians, live in unity with one another. Minister to others, and let others minister to you. In that way, you will all grow to spiritual maturity, for God has created you to be interdependent. Second, live holy lives. Put behind you the sins of the past, and live a moral and ethical lifestyle that reflects the values of Christ."

B. COMMENTARY

1. The Calling to Unity (vv. 1–7)
   a. The appeal for unity (vv. 1–3)
   b. The basis of unity (vv. 4–7)
2. The Cultivation of Unity (vv. 8–16)
   a. Parenthesis regarding Christ's gift (vv. 8–10)
   b. Spiritual gifts (vv. 11–13)
   c. Spiritual maturity (vv. 14–16)
3. The Calling to Holiness (vv. 17–24)
   a. Putting off the old man (vv. 17–22)
   b. Putting on the new man (vv. 23–24)

4. The Cultivation of Holiness (vv. 25–32)

C. CONCLUSION: CHRIST'S ORCHESTRA

VIII. ISSUES FOR DISCUSSION

1. What is your greatest area of weakness when it comes to living like the person you have become? Does this weakness come from your personality and character or from your life experiences? What do you think you can do to address that issue?
2. How involved are you in a church? Is your level of involvement sufficient to allow you to grow to spiritual maturity?
3. What do you think is your greatest potential contribution to other Christians?
4. Is your greatest tendency to sin internal (attitudes, values, etc.) or external (actions, habits). How do you think the last eighteen verses in the chapter apply to your life?

Ephesians 5

Our Life of Love

I. INTRODUCTION
The Power of Example

II. COMMENTARY
A verse-by-verse explanation of the chapter.

III. CONCLUSION
Imitation of God

IV. LIFE APPLICATION
What It Takes to Have a Team

An overview of the principles and applications from the chapter.

V. PRAYER
Tying the chapter to life with God.

VI. DEEPER DISCOVERIES
Historical, geographical, and grammatical enrichment of the commentary.

VII. TEACHING OUTLINE
Suggested step-by-step group study of the chapter.

VIII. ISSUES FOR DISCUSSION
Zeroing the chapter in on daily life.

Quote

"When I have learned to love God better than my earthly dearest, I shall love my earthly dearest better than I do now."

C. S. Lewis

Ephesians

IN A NUTSHELL

In chapter 5, Paul encourages the Ephesian Christians: Be imitators of God, and walk in love. Don't let yourself fall into a life of sin. Instead, stand against sin; and try to expose it. Use your time wisely as you follow God's will. Let the Holy Spirit influence and direct your behavior. As you do, husbands, love your wives as Christ loved the church. Wives, respect and submit to your husbands.

Our Life of Love

I. INTRODUCTION

The Power of Example

*I*n his autobiography, Benjamin Franklin tells of the time he wanted to convince the citizens of Philadelphia to light the streets at night as a protection against crime and as a convenience for evening activities. Failing to convince them by his words, he decided to show his neighbors how compelling a single light could be. He bought an attractive lantern, polished the glass, and placed it on a long bracket that extended from the front of his house. Each evening as darkness descended, he lit the wick. His neighbors soon noticed the warm glow in front of his house. Passersby found that the light helped them to avoid tripping over protruding stones in the roadway. Soon others placed lanterns in front of their homes, and eventually the city recognized the need for having well-lighted streets.

That is the power of example. Samuel Johnson once wrote, "Example is always more effective than teaching." Albert Schweitzer said, "Example is not the main thing in influencing others. It is the only thing." Children become like parents; churches become like pastors; students become like teachers—all because of the power of example. There may be no greater power on earth to change the behavior of others.

Ephesians 5 begins with an appeal to this great principle: **Be imitators of God, therefore, as beloved children; and live a life of love, just as Christ loved us and gave Himself up for us.** We are to give ourselves up for God, because he gave himself up for us. Practically, then, the outworking of that "giving up of ourselves" in this context is that we should not fall into a life of sin but rather live a life of love.

II. COMMENTARY

Our Life of Love

MAIN IDEA: *Be imitators of God, and walk in love. Be filled with the Holy Spirit, and let him determine the quality of husband-wife relationships.*

A The Imitation of God (vv. 1–2)

SUPPORTING IDEA: *Imitate God, just as Jesus did, living a life of sacrifice to God.*

5:1. Just as it is natural for an earthly child to imitate his earthly father, so should the spiritual child imitate his Heavenly Father. The word *imitate* comes from the word *mimeomai*, from which we get our word *mimic*. It means "to act like."

5:2. To imitate God in this context means to walk in love. Love denies self. It is willing to give up self-interest for God's sake. Since Jesus **gave himself up for us**, we ought to give ourselves up for him. To *give oneself up* means "to follow, to obey, to live in relationship with." When we live with this attitude toward God, we please him just as a pleasant aroma pleases the one who smells it (see Lev. 1:17; 3:16; Isa. 53:10). Jesus became the sacrifice for our sins. We must become a living sacrifice, obeying him (see Rom. 12:1).

B The Avoidance of Sin (vv. 3–14)

SUPPORTING IDEA: *You should stop committing evil sins, which bring the wrath of God on people, since those are the deeds of darkness, and you are children of light.*

5:3–4. The opposite of imitating God and giving oneself up for him is living in **sexual immorality, impurity**, and **greed** (note the same Greek words for *impurity* and *greed* in 4:19). Paul says that it is not proper for these things even to be named among the children of God. These are sins of "deed." In addition to sinful deeds, there ought not to be sinful "words." **Obscenity, foolish talk, coarse joking** ought not be part of the speech patterns of Christians. Rather, we ought to speak from a heart of thankfulness to God.

5:5–7. Paul warns the Ephesian Christians not to engage in the activities of **those who are disobedient**. It might be possible to infer that if Christians engaged in these activities (immorality, impurity, covetousness) they would lose their salvation. That is not Paul's point. Paul is saying that we are not to do these things because we are no longer **those who are disobedient**. Since we are not part of them anymore, we should **not be partners with them**. It is not a matter of salvation in this instance but a matter of identification. We are not like them anymore; therefore, we ought not to live like them. If we are partners with them, we are forewarned. Such people do not share the kingdom inheritance. Rather, they endure divine wrath. No fine theological arguments can get around that simple truth.

5:8–10. It would be a gross inconsistency for a Christian to participate in the flagrant sins of non-Christians. The Ephesian Christians were once just like those who are disobedient. But no longer! Rather than doing deeds of immorality, impurity, and greed, they should do deeds of **goodness, righteousness, and truth.** Christians are no longer **darkness,** but **children of light.** Therefore, we should do deeds of light, not darkness. Only as you walk in God's light can you please him.

5:11–14. Not only ought we not to do the same sins as those who are disobedient, but we should try to expose them. Paul may be referring to exposing the sins of church members, because the church is responsible to hold its members accountable for their lifestyles. If a Christian lives in flagrant, unrepentant sin, the church is to try to get them to turn from their sin (Matt. 18:15–20; Gal. 6:1).

The context is dealing with the disobedient. This would indicate that the church should attempt to expose the sins of the non-Christian, which would be a full-time job if done very thoroughly. Society's major sins certainly need to be exposed.

Sins are exposed by shining light into sin's darkness. An amazing thing happens. Darkness can no longer hide its nature and acts in secret. All is exposed to light. Light that **makes everything visible** brings an even more radical element. Literally, this reads, everything that is revealed is (or becomes) light. Light turns darkness into light. This is the church's mission. Whether the people in darkness are church members or society members, the goal is to transform them completely from darkness to light.

The poetic passage in verse 14 may be a quote from an ancient hymn based on Scripture. It is not a direct scriptural quotation. A person who was participating in the **deeds of darkness** is to wake up and **rise from the dead,** meaning to turn from those deeds. **Christ will shine on you** may mean that Christ is pleased with the person who turns from such deeds. He is light and the source of their light. His shining light exposes all their darkness and transforms them into light.

The Filling of the Spirit (vv. 15–21)

SUPPORTING IDEA: *Allow the Holy Spirit to direct your behavior, which will result in mutual ministry and submission.*

5:15–17. The world in which we live is filled with dangers and deceptions. It is not always easy to live an enlightened life even when we want to.

We can get tripped up or ambushed by events and people without even being aware of the danger. We must be very careful to live our life rooted in wisdom, using our time wisely. Not to do so would be foolish. The will of the Lord is that we live carefully, cautiously, always matching our lifestyle with the teachings of Scripture.

5:18. Ephesus was a center of pagan worship and ritual. The Ephesian culture worshiped Baccus, the god of wine and drunken orgies. They believed that to commune with their god and to be led by him, they had to be drunk. In this drunken state, they could determine the will of their god and determine how best to serve and obey him.

Paul was talking about how to commune with the God of heaven, how to live for him, how to serve and obey him, how to determine his will. It was natural for him to draw the contrast between how the god of Ephesus is served and how the God of heaven is served. With the God of heaven, you do not get drunk with wine. Rather, you are filled with the Spirit. Being drunk with wine leads to the sexual sins and immorality of darkness described above. By being filled with the Spirit, you can determine God's will and serve him faithfully in moral living.

What does it mean to be **filled with the Spirit**? Some interpreters equate this command with instances of being filled with the Spirit in the Book of Acts in which miraculous things happened: people spoke in tongues; prophecies and visions were given; people were healed. "Be filled" in this verse (*plarao*) is not the same word as the one used in the Book of Acts (*pimplemi*), nor are the consequences the same. Rather than understanding this command in verse 18 to have anything to do with miraculous or extraordinary happenings, it is better to understand it in context. In this ethical context, it means directed, influenced, and ultimately governed by the Holy Spirit.

In Colossians 3:16, the Colossian believers are instructed to **let the word of Christ dwell in you richly.** The consequences of this are the same as the consequences here in Ephesians 5 of being filled with the Spirit. That suggests that there is a close correlation in meaning between the two.

This filling, then, is best understood, as a command for the believer to yield himself to the illuminating, convicting, and empowering work of the Holy Spirit. As he works in our hearts through his Word, our lives are brought into conformity with the will of God (v. 17). (A fuller and more technical discussion of this matter can be found in "Deeper Discoveries.")

5:19–21. Four Greek participles—**speak, make music** (melodying), **giving thanks** (thanking), and **submit** (subjecting)—in verses 19–21 modify the verb "be filled" of verse 18, describing the person filled with the Holy Spirit. The first two participles suggest the importance of music and Scripture in being filled with the Spirit. An attitude of gratitude is a third characteristic of being filled with the Spirit. Finally, an attitude of mutual submission among believers is a characteristic of being filled with the Spirit.

Following the fourth participle, *being subject* (or submitting) to one another, Paul then moves directly into three examples of relationships in which believers are to be subject to one another: husband-wife relationships, parent-child relationships, and master-slave relationships. Paul's important point is that in each of these sets of relationships the one in authority is to be submissive to the needs of those under him and those in submission are to be subject to the authority of the one over him. For example, the wife is to be subject to the authority of her husband, but her husband is to be subject to the needs of the wife. Children are to be subject to the authority of their parents, but parents are to be subject to the needs of the children. Slaves are to be subject to the authority of their masters, but masters are to be subject to the needs of their slaves. The principle is an attitude of mutual subjection, which is a mark of being filled with the Holy Spirit. It is simply a matter of fulfilling the golden rule: doing to others as we would have others do to us.

The Role of Wives (vv. 22–24,33)

SUPPORTING IDEA: *Wives are to respect their husbands and submit to them as to the Lord.*

5:22–24. The wife is to be subject to her husband as to the Lord. This does not mean that she submits to her husband in the same way and to the same degree as she does the Lord, since the husband might ask her to disobey God. Rather she serves the Lord by having a submissive heart toward her husband and by obeying him as long as it does not require her to disobey the Lord. The reason she is called upon to be subject to her husband is that the husband is the head of the wife, as Christ is the head of the church. As the church is to be subject to Christ, so the wife is to be subject to her husband. This subjection does not mean inferiority. It is clear that male and female are both created in the image of God (Gen. 1:27) and that in Christ, where personal worth is concerned, there is "neither Jew nor Greek, slave nor free, male nor female, for you are all one in Christ Jesus" (Gal. 3:28). However, in the overall scheme of things, God has placed all of us in differing positions of authority and submission. The man may be in authority at home but submissive at work. The woman may be in submission at home and in authority at work. The point is, all social order depends on people's willingness to work together and ability to determine who is the head of certain endeavors. God's intention is that the husband be the head of the relationship with his wife.

5:33. After discussing the role of the husband, Paul comes back in a summary statement in verse 33 to add that the wife is to respect her husband. In summary, she is to be subject to her husband and to respect him. **Respect** (*phobetai*) literally means "fear." It can refer, however, to the fear a person should have before God, a reverence and respect (Luke 1:50; 18:2; Acts 10:35; 1 Pet. 2:17; Rev. 14:7; 19:5). This type of reverence and regard should characterize the relationship of a wife and her husband.

🄴 The Role of Husbands (vv. 25–32)

SUPPORTING IDEA: *Husbands are to love their wives as Christ loves the church and gave himself up for her.*

5:25–27. After instructing wives to be subject to their husbands, he instructs husbands to love their wives so completely and so righteously that the wife need never fear or suffer from her life of submission. Husbands are to **love [their] wives just as Christ loved the church.** How did Christ love the church? He **gave himself up for her.** Jesus dedicated his life to the establishment and welfare of the church. He ultimately gave his life for the church. To that degree, and in that quality, the husband is to love his wife. He is to give himself up for her. He is to dedicate his life to the physical, emotional, and spiritual welfare of his wife. Following the example of Christ, he is to give his wife not only all that he has but also all that he is. When a husband loves his wife so completely, the wife need never fear submission.

Paul goes on to extend the picture of Christ and the church. Christ loved the church that he might make her holy, or set her apart for himself. He did this by the **washing with water through the word.** Some Bible teachers do not think Paul is referring to water (baptism) in this verse. They understand the water to be a figure of speech, referring to the cleansing that the Holy Spirit brings to the soul through repentance, after hearing the Word of God. It is as Jesus said in John 15:3, "You are already clean because of the word I have spoken to you." Applying water to the outside of the physical body can have no effect whatsoever to the spiritual cleansing that makes one holy. Through repentance, the water of the word reaches the innermost recesses of the soul, cleansing and making it holy.

Other scholars, however, believe that Paul is, indeed, alluding to baptism here, understanding that the early church would only have baptized someone who had truly repented. In this understanding, baptism would be an outward sign of repentance and of the spiritual cleansing resulting from the repentance, itself a result of hearing and obeying the Word. The New Testament does not suggest that baptism cleanses a person apart from repentance or that baptism apart from personal faith can save a person.

We might amplify the meaning of this phrase by saying that the true church heard the Word of Christ preached and believed it. They were born again, regenerated, washed and cleansed spiritually by believing the Word. If Paul were alluding to baptism here, then the washing of the water in baptism would be symbolic of the inner cleansing that had already taken place through the Word.

The result of this work of Christ is that the church is **radiant . . . without stain or wrinkle . . . holy and blameless**. If a husband loves his wife as Christ loved the church, his love and care will have a sanctifying influence on the wife, who will experience personal benefit and progress as a result. The wife will never be perfect, but she becomes more than she would if the husband does not love her as Christ loved the church.

5:28–32. After having presented the work of Christ for the church, Paul now comes back to the reality of husband-wife relationships. He repeats the fact that husbands are to love their wives as their own bodies. Even though the husband lives in an imperfect body, he loves it, nourishes it, and cherishes it. So he is to do the same for his wife, even though she is imperfect.

Paul repeats Genesis 2:24, establishing that a husband and wife are to become one flesh, and closes by restating that the relationship between the wife and a husband is like the relationship between Christ and the church.

> **MAIN IDEA REVIEW:** *Be imitators of God, and walk in love. Be filled with the Holy Spirit, and let him determine the quality of husband-wife relationships.*

III. CONCLUSION

Imitation of God

Two rivers may flow smoothly before they merge; but when they flow together, they often become tumultuous. Each river has its own current which collides with the current of the other river. This creates powerful undercurrents and spectacular rapids. As the rivers flow downstream, the collision of currents subsides, and the new river emerges—broader, deeper, more powerful.

So it is with good marriages. The forming of any new union may have rough water at first, but as the currents of life merge, the two become broader, deeper, and more powerful. The two truly become one. As the husband and wife imitate God, he blesses their lives with godly unity. As the two become closer to him, they become closer to one another.

PRINCIPLES

- Our lives are to be lived in constant imitation of God.
- We must be radical in our efforts to stop committing evil sins.
- Being filled with the Spirit results in ministry to one another and in mutual submission.

- Husbands must be submissive to the needs of their wives, and wives must be submissive to the authority of their husbands.

APPLICATIONS

- Take a fearless moral inventory of your life to see if there is anything you are doing that you ought to stop.
- If you are unsuccessful in stopping something you ought to stop, contact someone whom you respect spiritually, and ask him to help you.
- Husbands, rate yourself on a scale of one to ten on how well you are submissive to the needs of your wife. Make a list of things you ought to improve. Ask your wife to forgive you for your failure in that/those area(s) and commit to her and the Lord to do better.
- Wives, rate yourself on a scale of one to ten on how well you are submissive to the authority of your husband. Make a list of things you ought to improve. Ask your husband to forgive you for your failure in that/those area(s) and commit to him and the Lord to do better.

IV. LIFE APPLICATION

What It Takes to Have a Team

Long, long ago in a kingdom far away lived a man who wanted to be a football coach. He heard of a coaching position open at a college where they had recruited many of the finest football players in the land. He applied and was hired as their football coach. The day of the first game, he said: "OK, boys. I want you all to feel a part of this team. I know that a lot of you have a lot of good ideas, so when we go out on that field, I want each of you to do what he thinks is best. As for me, I will be in my office doing what I enjoy best—reading sports magazines, watching football games, and talking to other coaches."

So the team clapped their hands in unison and stormed out onto the field. The coach zipped back into his office. The team lost that day. The quarterback called a play in the huddle, but the running back didn't like it. He wanted to run a play which they had used with great success in high school, so they argued a little bit. In the end when the ball was snapped, the running back ran the play he wanted; and the quarterback ran the play he wanted. The receivers each ran the plays they wanted, and they ended up running into each other and knocking each other down.

After three downs, the punter came out to kick but had to kick into the wind. He knew it wouldn't go very far that way, and that would be embarrassing to him, so he turned around and kicked the other direction. The ball went way up into the stands. It was a long, long kick, and the punter was very happy with himself. However, they were penalized for kicking the ball the wrong direction.

The linemen felt that the other team was hitting too hard, so they decided to leave the field. If they wanted to play that rough, they could just play with someone else. Many other things happened that day which caused the team to lose badly. It seemed such a shame, because actually the players on the losing team were better than the other team; but they were not playing together, and there was no one to draw them together to play as a team, because the coach was absent.

The athletic director went into the coach's office the next day and said: "Listen, we can't play football this way. The whole purpose for hiring you was so you would be responsible to see that the team played as a team—each player making his maximum contribution. If something goes wrong, you must be there to analyze it and decide what to do to correct it.

So the next Saturday, the coach drew up a game plan and explained it to each of the players. He stayed on the sidelines and paid close attention to each play. If something was going wrong, he explained it to the players, instructed them as to what they should do, and corrected the situation.

Several times he didn't know what was wrong. He asked several of the players if they understood what was going wrong. They did. When they explained it, the coach asked them if they had any suggestions. The team followed up on the suggestions on the next play and scored a touchdown.

The team won big that day. It was a glorious day. Everyone saw how much better it was for them to play together. Not everyone could be the quarterback. So if they were not chosen to be quarterback, they willingly played the position they were assigned. Each of them gained great recognition for doing well at his own position. The team won and won and won. All of the players were happy because they all knew that they were winning as a team. The quarterback was useless alone. He needed a good offensive line, and he needed good running backs and receivers.

After they all saw how much better it was to play as a team, they decided that they would play that way all the time; and they went undefeated from then on.

Teamwork is essential any time more than one person is needed to succeed at something. In our day we are experiencing a crisis of authority, and it is easy to understand why. Sometimes, those in authority over us have mistreated us, and we have difficulty accepting authority any more. We have had presidents who have lied to us. They have been dishonest, unethical, and immoral. Heads of companies have defrauded the company and investors out of billions of dollars. Military officials have abused power. Politicians have abused power. Nationally recognized religious leaders have abused power. Educators have abused power. Doctors have abused power. Journalists have abused power. Ministers have abused power. We are living in an age of abuse of power, and understandably, this has caused a crisis of authority.

This abuse of power has filtered down to the fundamental building block of society—the home. Just as society faces a crisis of authority, so does the home. We have men who won't lead, women who won't follow, children who won't obey, and parents who won't nurture. It is every man for himself. The ship is going down, so every person is out to save his own neck.

Against the backdrop of this ominous social upheaval, the Bible still speaks; and it still speaks truth. It still speaks words which, if followed, will bring order and truth and harmony to life. If being a Christian was ever going to make a difference, it needs to make a difference now—in the home. We must not allow the attitude and experience of society to keep us from living biblically. We must each understand our biblical role and fulfill it.

V. PRAYER

Heavenly Father, may we come to hate sin because of what it does to us and what it does to you. May we turn from it more and more completely. May we be filled with wisdom and with your Holy Spirit, and may our marriages be a reflection of your work in our lives. Amen.

VI. DEEPER DISCOVERIES

A. Sin and salvation (vv. 1–5)

The question arises in passages such as Ephesians 5:5 as to whether it is possible for a Christian, because of continual and unconfessed sin, to lose his salvation. Some say this passage teaches that. However, it teaches just the opposite. It doesn't mean that a Christian who does these things (immoral, impure, covetous, idolater) will lose inheritance in the kingdom. Rather, it means that non-Christians live this way, and since the Ephesians are Christians, they ought not to live that way. It is also possible to read into this passage the implication that if a person lives a life characterized by these things, he might not be a Christian. Second Corinthians 5:17 says, "If anyone is in Christ, he is a new creation; the old has gone, the new has come!"

If nothing becomes new in a person's life after supposedly accepting Christ, the person has no confidence from Scripture that he actually did receive Christ. The person either did not really understand what it means to become a Christian, or he was not sincere in his confession. No one has a biblical basis for confidence that he is a Christian if it has made no difference in his life.

So, if a person's life is characterized by immorality, impurity, greed, filthiness, silly talk, and course jesting, Ephesians 5:5 states that he has no inheritance in the kingdom of Christ and God. The wrath of God comes upon those who are not Christians and are disobedient as a way of life.

B. Chastening (vv. 6–17)

Because of Christ, the child of God never tastes the wrath of God as the non-Christian does. For the Christian, sin will never mean separation from God and suffering the horrors of hell. The Christian has been spared from that alternative because he is safe in Christ. For the believer, sinning can mean to suffer the chastening of God. The Christian may suffer at least two different kinds of chastening.

First, there is "cause-effect chastening." For example, the biblical principle teaches that if you want to keep your life, you must give it away. One application of that principle is that if you want to have a rich and meaningful life, you must give yourself in kindness and love to others. If we conform to that law, we see kind, generous, loving people being surrounded by friends and having a life of joy and meaning. If we violate this law and act selfishly, being unkind, stingy, and taking advantage of people, we may be rich and famous; but we will be unhappy and unfulfilled. So, a cause-effect price is paid when we violate the law of love. In Galatians 6:7–8, we read, "Do not be deceived: God cannot be mocked. . . . The one who sows to please his sinful nature, from that nature will reap destruction."

Additionally, spiritual laws govern all areas of life. If we want a rich and meaningful marriage, if we want a good relationship with our children, if we want a successful vocation, if we want friends and meaningful relationships, we must obey these laws. Conform to them and succeed; violate them and fail. So on it goes throughout the Bible.

A second form of chastening is direct divine chastening. The point comes at which God is not content to let the cause-effect principle play itself out in our lives. Instead, he actively brings divine chastening into the life of the believer. We see this spelled out clearly in passages such as Hebrews 12:5–13 and 1 Corinthians 11:20–22,28–34.

Just as loving earthly parents would not let their child engage in self-destructive behavior without trying to encourage him to correct that behavior, so the Lord tries to get us to change our self-destructive behavior. The chastening the Lord brings into our lives is never retribution for our sin. Jesus paid the price for our sin, and we do not have to bear that. The loving hand of God tries to get us to change our self-destructive behavior by chastening us for our sin.

C. Filled with the Spirit (v. 18)

In Acts, in the miraculous instances of the filling of the Spirit which resulted in speaking in tongues and other extraordinary activities, the word used for "filling" is *pimplemi*. In Ephesians 5:18, when we are commanded to be filled with the Spirit, the word for "filled" is *"plarao."* These words have different meanings. In Acts when *pimplemi* is used, the results are dramatic: the person speaks in tongues, prophesies, or preaches powerful messages spontaneously. In the only two New Testament occurrences of *plarao* in the verb form, it has no extraordinary events occurring with it.

Second, we do not see the *pimplemi* filling of the Spirit after Acts 19, the last recorded incident in Acts of the message of the gospel going to Gentiles. The purpose of the miraculous manifestations of the Spirit was to validate and reinforce the message of the gospel to people who did not know Christ (Heb. 2:4).

Third, *pimplemi* is always aorist passive with the genitive case: aorist tense means that the filling did not last long and was not intended to last long. The passive indicates that the people who were filled had no control over the fact that they were filled. It was a sovereign work of God.

Plerao in this passage is imperative passive, meaning that they were commanded to let it happen and that they could control their willingness to be filled.

Fourth, the purpose of *plerao* filling is person oriented. The purpose of *pimplemi* is task oriented. The dramatic events surrounding *pimplemi* are designed to accomplish a certain task. The purpose of *plerao* is to cause a person to be filled with joy or the Spirit as a continuous state.

Dramatic misunderstanding has occurred surrounding this teaching, because people have confused the use of the two different words. They have taken the miraculous manifestations which occurred with *pimplemi* and have generalized them to try to fit Ephesians 5:18, not realizing that they weren't even the same word, not in the same context, and not the same grammatical makeup.

Regardless of what one might believe about miraculous manifestations of the Holy Spirit, I believe that when Paul commands us in Ephesians 5:18 to be filled with the Spirit he is commanding us to allow ourselves to be governed by the fullness of Christ in our lives. In Ephesians 5:18, the results of being filled with the Spirit are speaking in psalms, singing, giving thanks, and a harmony of relationships between husbands and wives, parents and children, and masters and slaves.

In Colossians 3:16, we see the exact same results of teaching with psalms, singing, thankfulness, and harmony between husbands and wives, parents and children, and masters and slaves. However, these results are produced, not by being filled with the Spirit, but by letting the Word of Christ richly dwell within you. Being filled with the Spirit and letting the Word of Christ richly dwell within you produce exactly the same results. Therefore, they must be understood to be essentially the same thing.

We are not controlled by the Holy Spirit in the same way as a hand controls the functioning of a glove. Rather, we are governed in the sense that a speed limit sign controls how fast we drive. We are governed by it, in the sense that we have yielded to its authority and are law-abiding persons.

In Acts 13:52, we see the only other occurrence of the verb form of *plerao* in the Bible. There we read, "And the disciples were filled with joy and with the Holy Spirit." Just as the disciples were filled with and governed by joy, so we are to allow ourselves to be filled with and governed by the Spirit. We do this by allowing the Word of Christ to richly dwell within us.

As we let the Word richly dwell within us, we come to understand the will of God. The Holy Spirit applies God's truth to our hearts, and as we yield to it, allowing ourselves to be governed by it, we experience the fruit of the Spirit—peace, love, and joy. Gradually, more and more, over time we are filled with the Spirit in a nonsensational manner, but a manner just as miraculous as the dramatic manifestations of *pimplemi*.

D. Submission (vv. 22–24)

The word for *submit*, is *hupotasso*. It means "to place under," "to subordinate," or "to submit." It is a word that today's society finds unpleasant. It is not an easy word to talk about, but when fully understood, it is not an odious word. Building it into the fabric of both the home and society is essential.

Hupotasso does not mean inferiority in any way. Both the husband and wife are created in the image of God (Gen. 1:27). The wife is to be in submission to the husband. The husband is to be in submission to Christ. To do so is to reflect the relationship between Jesus and the Father in the Trinity. Christ is in submission to God the Father. So you cannot attribute inferiority to the wife for being in submission to the husband unless you are also prepared to attribute inferiority to Christ for being in submission to God the Father. It is not a matter of worth, intelligence, talent, or anything else. It is simply a structure God has established, a structure in which he has also placed himself. Jesus is in submission to the Father.

The woman is to submit to her husband "as to the Lord." The woman serves the Lord by submitting to her husband. Because of the imperfect and sin-flawed world in which we live, some circumstances may arise in which the wife would not submit to her husband. This statement derives from a biblical principle concerning another matter. In 1 Peter 2:13–17, we read that we are to obey the government. It is very clear. Yet, in Acts 5:29, the rulers command this same Peter to stop preaching the gospel; and Peter's response is, "We must obey God rather than men!" The principle we can glean from these two passages then is that we are to obey government up to the point that to do so would cause clear disobedience to God. At that point, obedience to God supersedes.

That being the case, it seems a parallel situation in which wives are commanded to be in submission to their husbands. If we are not to obey government to the point of sinning against God, then it would be consistent that wives are not to obey their husbands if it meant sinning against God. If the husband commands the wife to do something immoral, she is not obligated. If he asks her to swap partners after a party or to watch or participate in something sexually immoral, she is not obligated. If he asks her to rob a bank or hurt someone, she is not obligated. If he asks her to do anything that violates God's will, she is not obligated to obey him.

Nor does submission mean that the wife manifests unquestioned acceptance of everything the husband does. In 1 Peter 3:1–7, Peter seems to describe some of the things he means by submission:

- chaste and respectful behavior
- gentle and quiet spirit
- obedience, but not in sinful things
- proper perspective: harmonious, sympathetic, brotherly, kind-hearted, humble in spirit, not returning evil for evil or insult for insult, but giving a blessing instead

If a wife exhibits chaste and respectful behavior, a gentle and quiet spirit, a general attitude of submission, and a kind heart, she might disagree with her husband and go to appropriate lengths to try to persuade her husband of her point of view without violating the spirit of this principle. The wise husband would do well to heed carefully such attempts.

E. Attitude (vv. 31–33)

Conflict in husband and wife relationships is legendary. It has been going on ever since Adam and Eve baked their first apple pie. A certain amount of it is inevitable. Billy Graham is fond of saying, tongue in cheek, that in a husband-wife relationship, if two people agree on absolutely everything, one of them isn't necessary.

We've all smiled at the story of Winston Churchill and Nancy Astor, the American-born wife of Waldorf Viscount Astor. She visited Blenheim Palace, the ancestral home of the Churchill family. In conversation with Churchill, she expounded on the subject of women's rights, an issue that was to take her into the House of Commons as the first woman member of Parliament. Churchill opposed her on this and other causes that she held dear. In some exasperation, Lady Astor said, "Winston, if I were married to you, I'd put poison in your coffee." Churchill responded, "And if you were my wife, I would drink it."

Yet conflict is not the measure of a marriage. Love is. We may have fun looking at the foibles of married couples; still we recognize marriage's serious side. The quality of a married person's life is usually measured by the quality of his marriage. If he has a good marriage, he will say he had a good life. If he had a bad marriage, he will say he had a bad life.

A good or bad marriage usually boils down, in the end, to attitude. Certainly, specific problems must be dealt with, but the success in dealing with problems usually is traced back to how badly the couple wanted to solve them.

The story is told that in England in 1840, shortly after Queen Victoria married Prince Albert, they quarreled. Albert stalked out of the room and locked himself in his private apartment. Victoria hammered furiously upon the door. From the other side of the door came, "Who's there?" "The queen of England, and she demands to be admitted!" was the loud reply. No response. The door remained locked. Victoria hammered at the door again. "Who's there?" The reply was still, "The queen of England." No response. More fruitless and furious knocking was followed by a pause. Then a gentle tap. "Who's there?" The queen replied, "Your wife, Albert." The prince at once opened the door.

Attitude! It is the basis of everything. If two people have the right attitude toward a marriage, there is nothing they cannot work out by the grace of God.

VII. TEACHING OUTLINE

A. INTRODUCTION

1. Lead story: The Power of Example
2. Context: In chapter 4, Paul encouraged the Ephesian believers to "live a life worthy of the calling you have received." Now, in chapter 5, he applies that command in five specific ways:
   (1) Be imitators of God
   (2) Avoid sin
   (3) Be filled with the Spirit
   (4) Be responsible wives
   (5) Be responsible husbands
3. Transition: As we look into this chapter, we will see clearly that to "live a life worthy of the calling you have received" will involve two primary focuses: (1) drawing near to God, and (2) pulling away from sin.

B. COMMENTARY

1. The Imitation of God (vv. 1–2)
   a. Relationships as children (v. 1)
   b. Reciprocation of sacrifice (v. 2)

2. The Avoidance of Sin (vv. 3–14)
    a. The command to avoid sin (vv. 3–4)
    b. The penalty of a life of sin (vv. 5–10)
    c. The attempt to expose sin (vv. 11–14)
3. The Filling of the Spirit (vv. 15–21)
    a. Motivated by wisdom (vv. 15–17)
    b. Commanded by God (v. 18)
    c. Characterized by love and joy (vv. 19–21)
4. The Responsibilities of Wives (vv. 22–24,33)
    a. The attitude of submission (vv. 22,33)
    b. The pattern of the church (vv. 23–24)
5. The Responsibilities of Husbands (vv. 25–32)
    a. The attitude of love and sacrifice (vv. 25–30)
    b. The pattern of Christ (vv. 31–32)

C. CONCLUSION: WHAT IT TAKES TO HAVE A TEAM

VIII. ISSUES FOR DISCUSSION

1. If being "filled with the Spirit" is essentially the same as "letting the Word of Christ dwell in you richly," how would you say you are doing, on a scale of one to ten? What do you think you could do to improve being filled with the Holy Spirit?
2. If you are a husband, do you love your wife as Christ loved the church and gave himself up for her? What are your areas of greatest strength? Greatest weakness? What can you do to capitalize on your strengths? What can you do to overcome your weaknesses?
3. If you are a wife, do you submit to and respect your husband? What are your areas of greatest strength? Greatest weakness? What can you do to capitalize on your strengths? What can you do to overcome your weaknesses?

Ephesians 6

Our Spiritual War

"*Humanity* falls into two equal and opposite errors concerning the devil. Either they take him altogether too seriously or they do not take him seriously enough."

C. S. Lewis

Ephesians

IN A NUTSHELL

In chapter 6, Paul commands the Ephesian Christians: As you continue to respond to the Holy Spirit in your life, children, obey your parents; and fathers, do not anger your children, but bring them up in the discipline and instruction of the Lord. Slaves, obey your masters; and masters, treat your slaves as you would like to be treated if you were in their shoes. Finally, recognize that this life is a spiritual war, so take up the full armor of God; and having done so, stand firm against the schemes of the devil.

Our Spiritual War

The War behind the War

*T*he name *Benedict Arnold* is synonymous with *traitor*. He has been reviled and discussed as an unfaithful American for two hundred years, but nearly two hundred years after his death, a new theory was advanced. If accurate, the theory would change dramatically our understanding of the role of this notorious figure of our Revolutionary War.

His act of treason was attempting to smuggle to the British a diagram of the West Point fort located on the Hudson River. The cannons on the walls at West Point guarded all ship traffic up and down the Hudson River. If the British had the plans to the fort, they could figure out a way to conquer it. With the cannons silenced, they could sail shiploads of soldiers up the Hudson River and attack the American forces from the rear, as well as from the coast. Such betrayal might well have been a turning point in the war.

Arnold was meeting with a British officer, John Andre, to turn the plans over to him when they were discovered. Benedict Arnold fled to the British side and became one of their finest officers. He has never been forgiven by the American public.

The question is, Why would Arnold do such a thing? What possessed one of the finest generals in the American army to defect? According to the new theory, Benedict Arnold, at heart, was not a traitor. He was an American loyalist. However, when America asked the French for help in our battle with the British, they sent so many troops to America that there were more French soldiers fighting at one time than there were American troops. Arnold became deeply suspicious of the French motives. The only reason the French would be so willing to spill such massive amounts of French blood on behalf of America was, in his opinion, if they had ulterior motives. Perhaps, he thought, they had in mind to help the Americans defeat the British and then make America a French colony instead of a British colony.

So, in Arnold's reasoning, America was going to be a colony of some country, either Britain or France. If we remained a British colony, they would rule us more or less benevolently, he felt, and would eventually give us our freedom. If we became a French colony, they would rule us like tyrants and never give us our freedom. Therefore, Arnold argued, we should sue for peace with Great Britain.

Since America was unwilling to do so, Arnold felt that the next best thing for our nation was to do something to allow the British to win the war, rather than the French. Therefore, in an act of, as Arnold would have described it, great patriotism, he attempted to turn the diagram of West Point over to the British. When that failed, he joined the British side, not to defeat America but, as he saw it, to defeat the French and drive them off our soil.

Interestingly enough, shortly after the British were defeated, the French Revolution broke out; and all the French soldiers were recalled to France. If it weren't for that, we might be French today.

I tell this to make the point that warfare is not all a matter of putting people on two sides of a line drawn in the sand and "having at it." Warfare is not always a matter of blood and guts on the front line. War is also diplomacy, espionage, negotiations, and maneuvering behind the scenes. Things going on behind the scenes can have a greater impact on the outcome of warfare than the fighting on the battlefront.

So it is with spiritual warfare. It isn't all face-to-face combat. Much of it is a great chess match behind the scenes. One of the great responsibilities of the Christian is to learn well how to play chess, how to play this serious game.

After finishing his discussion of the role of mutual submission in the lives of Christians, Paul establishes for us the central passage in all the Bible on the reality of and strategy for spiritual warfare.

II. COMMENTARY

Our Spiritual War

MAIN IDEA: *Fathers are to nurture their children while children are to obey their parents, and slaves are to obey their masters while masters are to take care of their slaves. Also, life is a spiritual war, so be sure to keep each piece of spiritual armor in place; and stand firm against the devil.*

A The Responsibilities of Families (vv. 1–4)

SUPPORTING IDEA: *Children are to be submissive to the authority of their parents while parents are to be submissive to the needs of their children.*

6:1. Children are instructed that their role in mutual submission is to **obey your parents in the Lord, for this is right.** Without learning obedience from parents, children would run wild in society. All social order depends on this. **In the Lord** does not mean that children only need to obey Christian parents. Rather, it means that they are obeying the Lord when they obey their parents. Sadly, we are living in a day when child abuse is on the rise. This causes us to mention that the same exceptions which wives have from obeying their husbands, children have in obeying their parents.

When children are asked to do something unethical, illegal, or immoral, or when they are harmed or in danger of being harmed, the command to obey would be superseded by higher biblical principles of "obeying God rather than man."

6:2–3. The fifth of the Ten Commandments, to **honor your father and mother**, is repeated here, then followed by the statement that it is the first commandment with a promise. Actually, it is the second commandment with a promise (compare Exod. 20:6). There are many potential ways to solve this apparent contradiction. Perhaps the easiest is by noting that "first" may refer to the importance rather than order. Paul's point is probably that this commandment is of extraordinary significance. The promise, that the obedient child would live long on the earth, is a general promise, not an absolute promise. Children who learn obedience tend to live better lives and tend to live longer. Drug addicts, criminals, foolish and careless people tend not to live as well or as long as well-disciplined people.

6:4. The father's role is not to exasperate his children but to **bring them up in the training and instruction of the Lord.** Growing up in a Christian home is intended to be a very positive experience for both parent and child when each plays his proper role.

🅱 The Responsibilities of Workers (vv. 5–9)

SUPPORTING IDEA: *Slaves are to be submissive to the authority of their masters while masters are to be submissive to the needs of their slaves.*

6:5–8. Slaves carry the same principle of submission to authority as we see with wives and children. They serve the Lord by serving their master. They were not to serve their masters for the external reason of pleasing others but because they wanted to please Christ. Paul reminded slaves that their service to Christ would be rewarded by God just as will be all members of God's kingdom. Slaves on earth, they are equal members of the heavenly kingdom.

6:9. Then, fulfilling his pattern, Paul moves to the master, instructing him to please the Lord by the way he treats his slave. God is in heaven, where both master and slave are of equal importance to him.

Slaves had no options in relationships with their masters. The same general principles apply in a worker's relationship with his boss. However, as with wives and children, the employee would not be obligated to do anything unethical, illegal, immoral, or to endanger himself or others. He would be free to find other employment within the will of God.

C The Demands of Spiritual Warfare (vv. 10–20)

SUPPORTING IDEA: *We are to put on the full spiritual armor of God so that we will be able to win the spiritual war against the devil.*

6:10. Paul introduces his final subject by urging the Ephesian believers to **be strong in the Lord**. When it comes to spiritual warfare, we cannot be sufficiently strong by ourselves. If we are going to have adequate strength for the spiritual battles of life, it must be the Lord's strength. Only he has the **mighty power** sufficient to win spiritual battles against the demonic enemy.

6:11. The way we are strong in the Lord is to put on the **full armor of God**. When we have this armor on, we are able to stand against the wiles and schemes of the devil. Satan is a deceiver and a destroyer (Rev. 12:9). He deceives in order to destroy. Putting on the armor, of course, is a metaphor for following certain instructions from Scripture.

6:12. The reason this spiritual armor is needed is that **our struggle is not against flesh and blood**. The picture of warfare here implies that we do not face a physical army. We face a spiritual army. Therefore our weapons must be spiritual. **Against the rulers, against the authorities, against the powers of this dark world and against the spiritual forces of evil in the heavenly realms** seems to suggest a hierarchy of evil spirit-beings who do the bidding of Satan in opposing the will of God on earth.

6:13. When we have obeyed all the instructions implicit in the **full armor of God**, we can resist Satan's attempts to deceive and destroy us. **The day of evil** is anytime during this era in history until Jesus returns. All days are evil in their potential and become evil in reality when Satan or his demons decide to use that day to attack you.

The clear implication here is that, if the Christian has all his armor on, he has the ability to **stand firm** against Satan. At times the spiritual warfare in which we find ourselves may be frightening. However, the only thing we have to fear, if our armor is in place, is fear itself. "The one who is in you [Jesus], is greater than the one [Satan] who is in the world" (1 John 4:4). "Submit yourselves, then, to God. Resist the devil, and he will flee from you" (Jas. 4:7). "Be self-controlled and alert. Your enemy the devil prowls around like a roaring lion looking for someone to devour. Resist him, standing firm in the faith" (1 Pet. 5:8–9). Scripture is utterly consistent. If we have our armor in place, if we are firm in our faith, we may resist the devil. If we do, he will flee from us.

6:14. After instructions to put on the full armor of God and the promise of the power of God in victory over the devil, Paul specifically describes the various pieces of armor. **The belt of truth** pictures the large leather belt the Roman soldier wore. It held other weapons and kept his outer garments in place. To put on the belt of truth can be understood as accepting the truth of the Bible and choosing to follow it with integrity.

The breastplate of righteousness pictures the metal armor in the shape of a human torso common to the Roman uniform. To put on the breastplate can be understood as choosing not to harbor and nurture known sin. It is striving to be like Christ and live according to his ways of righteousness.

6:15. Feet fitted with the readiness pictures the hobnailed shoes which kept the soldiers footing sure in battle. To put on these shoes could be understood as believing the promises of God in the gospel and counting on them to be true for you. Faith in these promises yields peace in the Christian's life.

6:16. The shield of faith pictures the small, round shield the Roman soldier used to deflect blows from the sword, arrow, or spear of the enemy. To take up this shield can be understood as rejecting temptations to doubt, sin or quit, telling yourself the truth and choosing on the basis of the truth to do the right thing.

6:17. The helmet of salvation pictures the Roman soldier's metal protective headgear. It does not refer to our salvation in Christ. First Thessalonians speaks of the helmet of the *"hope* of salvation," which is probably a parallel idea. That being the case, taking the helmet of salvation could be understood as resting our hope in the future and living in this world according to the value system of the next.

The sword of the Spirit pictures the soldier's weapon sheathed to his belt and used both for offensive and defensive purposes. Taking the sword of the Spirit—defined for us as the Word of God—can be understood as using Scripture specifically in life's situations to fend off attacks of the enemy and put him to flight. We see the example of Jesus using the Scripture this way in Matthew 4:1–11.

6:18. Finally, while preparing for and doing battle, we are to be on the alert and **always keep on praying**. We petition God for our own needs in the battle, and we pray for the spiritual victory of other saints.

6:19–20. Paul finishes by asking for prayer for himself in his own ministry, acknowledging the fact that he was a prisoner at the time of this writing. He sought courage from prayer to proclaim the gospel even to those in his prison.

D Encouragement for the Saints (vv. 21–24)

SUPPORTING IDEA: *Sending another Christian with good news of one's welfare can encourage the church in your absence from it.*

6:21. Paul closes with a review of his own circumstances, his intention to send Tychicus to encourage them, and a benediction. Tychicus served as a messenger for Paul to the churches (Acts 20:4; Col. 4:7; 2 Tim. 4:12;

Titus 3:12). He may have carried the letter from Paul to Ephesus. He would let the church know of Paul's situation.

6:22. Knowing Paul's situation would be an encouragement for the church just as modern churches gain encouragement from news about missionaries they know in distant places. Churches need news of God's work around the world to encourage and strengthen them in their own work with God.

6:23. Letters typically closed with a wish for good health for the readers. As with his greetings, so in the closing Paul transformed this into a spiritual benediction. He prayed for wholeness, love, and faith for the readers, qualities that only God through his Son Jesus could grant. Victors in spiritual warfare would experience these qualities in daily life.

6.24. Paul concludes with his great theological word: *grace*. The letter that centers on divine grace (1:6–7; 2:5,7–8; 4:7) and love (2:4; 3:19; 5:2,25) and on love in the church (1:15; 3:17; 4:2,15–16; 5:2,25,28,33; 6:23) concludes with the hope that God's unearned love will be experienced by those who give love to Jesus forever. Such is the situation Paul wants to create in the churches, a climate where peace, love, and grace dominate all relationships, where God is sovereign, and where Christ is loved. Such a climate is the arena for victorious spiritual warfare and for successful family living.

> **MAIN IDEA REVIEW:** *Fathers are to nurture their children while children are to obey their parents, and slaves are to obey their masters while masters are to take care of their slaves. Also, life is a spiritual war, so be sure to keep each piece of spiritual armor in place; and stand firm against the devil.*

III. CONCLUSION

Don't Let Satan Frighten You

This spiritual warfare section, then, is one of the most important passages in the Bible. It tells us what we need to know and do to be successful in the spiritual battle of life. Said in as few of words as possible: keep a clear conscience before God, and resist the devil's attempts to frighten, deceive, or tempt you.

You cannot take that statement alone. You must read into it a fuller understanding of the information we have just covered. Basically, we are to draw near to God (keep a clear conscience; don't allow known, willful sin to take root in your heart unchallenged; accept the truth of the Bible and live accordingly) and resist the devil (stand firm against him; resist his attempts to deceive you; don't be terrorized by him). Satan has no real power if your armor is on, and he will flee from you.

PRINCIPLES

- The principle of mutual submission is the key to parent-child relationships.
- The principle of mutual submission is the key to employer-employee relationships.
- We cannot win the spiritual battle against Satan in our own strength. It must be the strength of the Lord.
- If our armor is in place, we are able to stand firm against the schemes of the devil. We need not unduly fear him.
- Spiritual warfare must be undergirded with prayer.

APPLICATIONS

- If you are a parent, how well are you doing at being submissive to the needs of your child? If you are a child still under the authority of your parents, how are you doing at being submissive to their authority?
- If you are an employer, how well are you doing at being submissive to the needs of your employees? If you are an employee, how are you doing at being submissive to the authority of your employer?
- How are you doing at fighting the spiritual battle? Do you have a clear conscience? Do you have all your pieces of armor on? If not, which ones do you need to put into place? Are you undergirding your battle with prayer? Do you have others praying for you as Paul did?

IV. LIFE APPLICATION

Resting in the Finished Work of Christ

Satan is called the "accuser of our brothers" (Rev. 12:10). He stands ready to whisper venomous accusations to us in our quiet moments and hurl demonic defamations in our busy ones.

"You cheap hypocrite!" he hisses. "You worthless loser," he rasps. "You try to talk to people about Jesus, about righteousness, about faithfulness, and all the while, you have immoral thoughts, sinful attitudes, and inconsistent behavior. Who are you to talk about forgiveness? You have no right to talk to anyone about Christianity. Why don't you come back into your old life where you belong?"

And we believe him! Doing so, we go down in flames. The secret to withstanding Satan's accusations is not what we do; it is what Christ did on the cross. The secret to withstanding Satan's accusations is to rest consciously in what Jesus did on the cross. If we truly understand it, we can stand against Satan's accusations. If we don't, we might not be able to.

As John White wrote in his book *The Fight*:

God's answer to your guilty conscience is the death of His Son. Your answer to a guilty conscience is usually something you do, like confessing harder, praying more, reading your Bible, paying more than your tithe in the offering, and so on. Do you not understand? The Father does not welcome you because you have been trying hard, because you have made a thoroughgoing confession, or because you have been making spiritual strides recently. He does not welcome you because you have something you can be proud about. He welcomes you because His Son died for you. Are you blasphemous enough to suppose that your dead works, your feeble efforts can add to the finished work of a dying Savior? "It is finished!" he cried. Completed. Done. Forever ended. He crashed through the gates of hell, set prisoners free, abolished death and burst in new life from the tomb. All to set you free from sin and open the way for you to run into the loving arms of God.

Now do you understand how 'the brethren' overcame the Accuser by the blood of the Lamb? They refused to let his accusations impede their access to God. A simple confession was enough. They face the Accuser boldly saying, "We already know the worst you could ever tell us, and so does God. What is more the blood of Jesus is enough." Therefore, when you find the grey cloud descending, whether it be as you pray, as you work, as you testify or whatever, when you find the ring of assurance going from your words because of a vague sense of guilt, look up to God and say, "Thank you, my Father, for the blood of your Son. Thank you, even now, that you accept me gladly, lovingly in spite of all I am and have done—because of His death. Father and God, I come" (Downers Grove, IL: InterVarsity Press, 1976, 87).

Resist the efforts of Satan to accuse you, to bury you with guilt, to make you feel worthless and unqualified to come to Christ again. It is part of his warfare strategy to make you ineffective as a witness and unhappy as a disciple. Be on guard against his schemes. Recognize them. Stand firm against him in the strength which God provides.

When we are faced with the temptation to sin or feel buried by guilt, we are facing spiritual warfare. At that moment, we must be strong in the Lord and in the strength of his might. We must take up the armor of God and stand firm against the schemes of the devil.

V. PRAYER

Dear Heavenly Father, help us to draw near to you. Help us to resist the temptations and deceptions of Satan. Help us to want to resist him. By your grace, may we stand firm against him, victorious in the spiritual battle. Amen.

VI. DEEPER DISCOVERIES

A. Provoking children to anger (v. 4)

Verse 4 instructs us not to "exasperate your children." The Bible does not tell us what this means. Both *wrath* and *exasperate* come from the root word *anger*. A study of human and family behavior can shed some insight on how we might exasperate our children and provoke them to anger. The following examples will give us a good starting point for understanding this instruction.

1. Overprotecting children: Parents who do everything for their children and do not let them gain any degree of independence or self-determination.

2. Overdisciplining children: Parents who overly restrict where children can go and what they can do, who never trust them to do things on their own, and who continually question their judgment. Certainly, a proper amount of this is necessary. We are talking about overdoing it.

3. Expecting more than the child can ever perform: Perfectionistic parents for whom the child's performance is never good enough.

4. Expecting less of them than they can perform: Parents who discourage the child's decisions and dreams—never approving, affirming, or encouraging.

5. Failing to sacrifice for their children: Parents who make the children feel as though they are an intrusion and burden.

6. Verbal and/or physical abuse: Parents who abuse their children, either by actions, negligence, words, or attitudes.

7. Legalism: Parents who use the Bible, religion, or God to browbeat the children into behavior that is not required by scriptural teachings.

8. Imbalance: Parents who fail to balance affirmation and discipline, who affirm without discipline, who discipline without affirmation, or who do neither.

These eight things will provoke a child to anger; they will exasperate a child, and we would be well-advised to avoid them.

B. Nurturing children (v. 4)

Proverbs 22:6, a parallel passage to Ephesians 6:4, gives us additional insight on what it means to bring children up in the discipline and instruction of the Lord: "Train up a child in the way he should go, and when he is old, he will not turn from it." This is often a misunderstood verse. Many have understood it to mean something like what Chuck Swindoll wrote in *You and Your Child*:

> Be sure your child is in Sunday school and church regularly. Cement into his mind a few memorized verses from the Bible plus some hymns and prayers. Send him to a Christian camp during the summer during his formative years, and he can be educated by people whose teaching is based in the Bible. Because after all, someday he will sow his wild oats. For sure, he will have his fling. But when he gets old enough to get over his fling, he will come back to God.

This is a breakdown in understanding because of the limitations of translations. To *train up* comes from a root word which means "the palate, the roof of the mouth, the gums." The verb form of the word is used for breaking a horse and bringing it into submission. The term was used of a midwife who would rub the mouth and gums of a newborn to stimulate the child to begin nursing. It is the word used to describe "developing a thirst."

Referring to the phrase, "in the way," again, Swindoll writes:

> "In" means "in keeping with, in cooperation with, in accordance to" the way he should go. That is altogether different from your way. God is not saying, "Bring up a child as you see him." Instead, He says, "If you want your training to be godly and wise, observe your child, be sensitive and alert, so as to discover his way, and adapt your training accordingly." In Proverbs 30:18–19, the same word for "way" is used as in Proverbs 22:6. WAY is a Hebrew word that suggests the idea of "characteristic, manner, mode."

> "There are three things which are too wonderful for me, four which I do not understand: the WAY of an eagle in the sky, the WAY of a serpent on a rock, the WAY of a ship in the middle of the sea, and the WAY of a man with a maid" (Proverbs 30:18–19).

> In each case, "way" is not a specific, well-defined, narrow road or path. It is a characteristic. The one who wrote this verse is saying, "As I observe these four things, I find myself intrigued. I can't put it all together. There is a beautiful coordination, an intriguing mystery which keeps me and captures my attention." WAY is used in that same sense back in Proverbs 22:6—train up a child in keeping with his characteristics.

In every child God places in our arms, there is a bent, a set of characteristics already established. The bent is fixed and determined before he is given over to our care. The child is not, in fact, merely a pliable piece of clay. He has been set; he has been bent. And the parents who want to train this child correctly will discover that bent.

Fathers, do not provoke your children to anger, but bring them up in the instruction and training of the Lord (Nashville: Thomas Nelson, 1977, 27).

C. Parental modeling (v. 4)

The Scriptures make clear that "modeling" is a key ingredient in the parenting process. Perhaps the clearest and most complete passage is found in Deuteronomy 6:4–9. In this passage, we see four principles essential in passing on spiritual faith to children.

1.   Belief in God: "Hear, O Israel: the Lord our God, the Lord is one."

    In his book *Modern Man in Search of a Soul,* Carl Jung, the Swiss psychiatrist, wrote: "About a third of my cases are suffering from no clinically definable neurosis, but from the senselessness and emptiness of their lives. This can be described as the general neurosis of our time." He went on to write that "for the most part, these people had given up on any concept of religion, and those who did not allow for the entrance of religious thought into their lives never recovered from their neuroses. It is no small thing to say you believe in God." (Quoted in Edith Draper, *Draper's Book of Quotations for the Christian World*, Wheaton, IL: Tyndale House, 1992, 237).

    Further, Moses wrote: "Love the Lord your God with all your heart and with all your soul and with all your strength. These commandments that I give you today are to be upon your hearts."

    These words shall be on your heart, Moses writes, not merely in your head. You cannot impart what you do not possess. Do not expect that your children will have a devotion to God unless you do. Do not expect that your children will walk with God unless you do. Do not expect that Christ will make a difference in your children's lives unless he is making a difference in yours. From the time of their childhood and early adulthood, your children are likely to have less of a walk with the Lord than the parents are. If the parent's walk is weak, the children's are likely to be weaker. If the parent's walk is strong, the children's are likely to be less strong. Then, when they move into adulthood and choose their values for themselves, parental modeling will often determine if Christ is at the center of their lives.

2.   Formal instruction: "Impress them on your children."

Jesus said, you will know the truth, and the truth will set you free (John 8:32). If you do *not* know the truth, you shall be in bondage to ignorance.

Children must know the Scriptures. They must know the words of God. When Jesus was tempted in the wilderness, each time he rebuffed Satan with Scripture. It is likely that he did not quote Scripture from his capacity as an omniscient God; rather he quoted it because as a boy receiving traditional Jewish instruction in the local synagogue and in his home he sat down and memorized it.

3. Informal Instruction: "Talk about them when you sit at home and when you walk along the road, when you lie down and when you get up (Deut. 6:7).

    Moses is saying, all the times of life should be geared to revealing how scriptural truth is lived out in everyday life. If children are to be free from bondage and ignorance, they must know truth. In order to know it, they must be taught it. That is one of the reasons children should be involved in church, but if parents are depending on the church to solve all their problems, they have misplaced hopes. The home is the dominant influence in a child's life. A church will reinforce truth if it is upheld at home. If it is not upheld at home, the truth may be drowned in a sea of contradiction.

4. Cultivation of the environment: "Tie them as symbols on your hands and bind them on your foreheads. Write them on the doorframes of your houses and on you gates" (Deut. 6:8–9).

As you consider cultivating the environment to foster spiritual growth, you must consider two aspects. First, you must eliminate the negative, and then accentuate the positive in the home environment. What, in your home, encourages spiritual development in your children, and what discourages it? You reveal your value system to the world, and ingrain it in your children, by what you have in your home and by how you treat what you have in your home.

What pictures do you have on the walls? What books do you have on the bookshelf? What magazines do you subscribe to? What television programs do you watch? What music do you listen to? What friends do you invite in? What do you talk about? What recreation do you engage in?

All these things combine to create an environment in the home, and it is not neutral. It is making a significant impact on your child's worldview, on his value system, on what is important to him and not important to him. If you have things in your home that influence your child in a direction other than toward Christ, you are contributing to a spiritual breakdown as the baton is passed from your generation to your child's generation.

Each Christian home must be carefully analyzed as to the messages it sends to the children. It is building into their value system and either encouraging or discouraging Christian behavior.

There is more to this than "material" environment. A spiritual and emotional environment is created that either encourages or discourages spiritual development. What do you talk about in the home? What do you laugh at? Do you laugh? Do you affirm and encourage one another? Do you have fun together? Do you ever have people into the home and talk about spiritual things? If you do, this creates one environment. If you don't, it creates another, and the spiritual and emotional environment has an impact on the spiritual development of the children.

D. The Christian at work (vv. 5–9)

The instructions which Paul writes for slaves and masters can form principles for the Christian in the workplace. From this passage, we learn four things. Our behavior on the job is to be obedient. Our motive on the job is to serve Christ by serving our employer. Our diligence on the job is to be for the Lord, not merely for men. Our reward for the job on earth is knowing that God will reward us in heaven for our faithfulness to him.

From these principles, and from the rest of Scripture, we can learn four lessons.

1. Work is noble before God. God works. He created work. He called Adam to work before the fall. There is nothing wrong with work. Work is good. By working, we become colaborers with God in extending his creation. God intended for man to inhabit and subdue the earth. Society is God's plan for the advancement of mankind. If we are contributing to that process, we are in step with God.
2. We serve others by our job. We provide for needs and interests of others when we produce a product or service. We earn money to provide for our families and to give away.
3. You serve God through your work. No matter what you are doing, if you believe it is the job God has provided for you at this time, that is significant. You are in God's will, you are doing what God wants you to do, and you are serving God by serving your employer.

We often have the feeling that God is more pleased with people if they are missionaries or pastors. That is not true. God is only pleased when we are doing what he has given us to do. If he has given us the job of working on an assembly line, then he is as pleased with us as he is when Billy Graham does what God has for Billy Graham.

This does not mean it is wrong to change jobs if our job is difficult. This passage was written to slaves, who did not have the option of mobility. If we have the option of mobility, I see nothing in Scripture that categorically prohibits changing jobs. But we must take care that we change jobs for right reasons, not merely to escape something we should see through.

When we work for unpleasant people, we must learn to look past them, to see Christ. Colossians 3:24 says of our labor at work, "It is the Lord Christ you are serving." It is like going to war. The battle is unpleasant, but you are pleasing your commander in chief.

E. The schemes of the devil (vv. 10–20)

Ephesians 6:11 teaches us that if we put on the full armor of God we may be able to stand against the schemes of the devil. The word *schemes* in the Greek is *methodia,* from which we get the English word *method.* It has the idea of craftiness, cunning, and deception.

The apostle John summarizes the attack points of the devil in his first epistle: "Do not love the world or anything in the world. If anyone loves the world, the love of the Father is not in him. For everything in the world—the cravings of sinful man, the lust of his eyes and the boasting of what he has and does—comes not from the Father but from the world" (1 John 2:15–16).

By ourselves, we certainly are no match for his spiritual weapons.

VII. TEACHING OUTLINE

A. INTRODUCTION

1. Lead story: The War behind the War
2. Context: After describing the relationships between parents and children, and between masters and slaves, as a continuation of being filled with the Spirit, Paul launches into a discussion of spiritual warfare. He teaches that if we will put on the full armor of God we will be able to stand against the schemes of the devil. He then describes each individual piece of armor, which is a metaphor of spiritual instruction. For example, "having girded your loins with truth" means having accepted the truth of the Scripture and committed yourself to living according to it.
3. Transition: As we look at the pieces of armor and study what the spiritual picture is between each piece, we develop a picture of how we can stand firm against the attempts of Satan to deceive and destroy us.

B. COMMENTARY

1. The Responsibilities of Families (vv. 1–4)
   a. Children (vv. 1–3)
   b. Parents (v. 4)

2   The Responsibilities of Workers (vv. 5–9)
    a.   Slaves (vv. 5–8)
    b.   Masters (v. 9)
3.   The Demands of Spiritual War (vv. 10–20)
    a.   The reality of spiritual war (vv. 10–13)
    b.   The pieces of spiritual armor (vv. 14–20)
4.   Encouragement for the Saints (vv. 21–24)

C. CONCLUSION: RESTING IN THE FINISHED WORK OF CHRIST

VIII. ISSUES FOR DISCUSSION

1. If you are a parent, what are your strengths? What are your weakness? How can you capitalize on your strengths? How can you overcome your weaknesses?
2. If you are an employer, what are your strengths? What are your weaknesses? How can you capitalize on your strengths? How can you overcome your weaknesses? How about if you are an employee?
3. What pieces of armor do you have in place? What pieces are not in place? If not all the pieces are in place, what must you do to get them in place?

Philippians 1

Our Joy in Troubled Times

Quote

"The only way to survive in prison is to abandon all expectations in this world and live for the next."

Alexander   Solzhenitsyn

LETTER PROFILE

- Written to the Christians in Philippi while Paul was in prison in Rome.
- The church at Philippi was founded by people whom Paul led to Christ during his first journey to that region.
- Lydia and her family and the Philippian jailer and his family may have been part of this first church (see Acts 16:14–34).
- Epaphroditus visited Paul while he was in prison to give him a financial gift and to encourage him. Epaphroditus may have been the pastor of the church.
- The letter is written to thank the Philippian Christians for their generous financial and spiritual gifts to Paul and to address some of their practical problems.

CITY PROFILE—PHILIPPI

- A historically Greek city, named after Philip II of Macedon, father of Alexander the Great.
- Located in the northern part of what is modern Greece, near the coast of the Aegean Sea.
- In New Testament times, a Roman colony (in the Roman province of Macedonia) whose citizens had Roman citizenship.
- It was a fairly large and important gold-mining town.
- Home to many pagan religious influences.

AUTHOR PROFILE—PAUL

- Jewish-born in Tarsus, near the Lebanese border in modern Turkey.
- Roman citizen.
- Prominent, highly educated Jewish religious leader (Pharisee).
- Dramatically converted to Christianity, A.D. 35.

- Primary apostle to the Gentiles.
- Tireless missionary.
- Imprisoned in Rome, A.D. 67, during the reign of Nero.
- Died in prison, A.D. 68.

Philippians

IN A NUTSHELL

In chapter 1, Paul tells the Philippian believers: Greetings, Philippians. Timothy and I thank you for your fellowship and pray that you may be filled with the fruits of righteousness. Don't be concerned about me. My imprisonment has actually helped further the gospel here, and I know that my afflictions will exalt the Lord. Even though you, too, suffer, I want to encourage you, in your conduct, to be worthy of the gospel of the Lord.

Our Joy in Troubled Times

I. INTRODUCTION

Life Is like a Football Game

Have you ever watched a football game on television and seen players talking on the telephone? What are they doing? Talking to mom? Ordering a pizza? The quarterback throws an interception, goes off the field, picks up a phone, and starts talking to someone. Who in the world is he talking to? Of course, he's talking to someone in the press box, usually an assistant coach.

Why is he talking to a coach in the press box? Two words: vantage point. The coach in the press box is one hundred yards from the field. From there, way above the field, he can see the whole field at once. He can see the weaknesses in the opposition's defense. He can see what each player is doing on each play. So, after an interception, the coach calls the quarterback on the sideline and says, "Let me tell you why that cornerback intercepted your pass and what to do differently the next time. Next time, run with the ball rather than pass it."

Now the quarterback may say, "That will never work in a million years." How does the coach respond? He says, "Trust me. From up here I have a much better vantage point of the whole field than you can possibly have down there in the midst of play."

In the press box of life, God looks down on our circumstances. God is trying to do for us exactly what the assistant coach is trying to do for that quarterback—give us the big picture.

The apostle Paul grasped the big picture very well. As he wrote Philippians 1, he was about to be tackled for a twenty-yard loss. Under Roman house arrest, chained to a big burly Roman guard, he was waiting trial on a capital offense before none other than the mad man himself—Nero. Yet we find Paul rejoicing. How can he be doing that? How can be full of joy in the midst of adversity? The answer? Vantage point! Like a master quarterback, he's on the phone to God in the press box. He sees his circumstances from God's perspective. Therefore, he has a clear understanding of what is going on on the field and why these things are happening to him.

Getting God's big picture, vantage point, on your problems and adversities can help give you a sense of joy and peace. Philippians 1 will challenge you to rejoice in the midst of adversity by seeing God's perspective. Then like Paul you can rejoice in troubling circumstances.

II. COMMENTARY

Our Joy in Troubled Times

MAIN IDEA: *God can use our afflictions to further the gospel and exalt the Lord, so we should live exemplary lives in the face of our own afflictions.*

A Greeting (vv. 1–2)

SUPPORTING IDEA: *God brings grace and peace to his church.*

1:1. The opening has the names **Paul and Timothy**, yet only Paul was the author of Philippians. Beginning in verse 3, he begins employing the singular **I** which he consistently uses throughout the rest of the book. Both these men were **servants of Christ Jesus**. The term *servant* emphasizes their submission to God's agenda on earth.

The letter is addressed to **all the saints in Christ Jesus at Philippi**. A saint is not someone who has died but one "set apart for the purposes of God." Every person who possesses Christ—or more accurately is possessed by Christ—is a saint. Paul is writing this letter to Christian believers, followers of Jesus Christ. Therefore, **in Christ** means these individuals have accepted him as their personal Savior.

Paul makes special mention of **the overseers and deacons**. *Overseers* is another term for elders; some translations say "pastor" or "bishop." These men were the shepherds of the flock who exercised spiritual oversight over the local church (Acts 20:28). Deacons were church leaders that ministered primarily to the physical needs of the people similar to the activities in Acts 6:1–6.

1:2. Grace and peace is a standard greeting of the time among Christians that appears in most of his correspondence. It would be like saying, "I hope this letter finds you being blessed by the Lord." Grace and peace are possible only **from our Father and the Lord Jesus Christ**.

B Joy in Prayer (vv. 3–11)

SUPPORTING IDEA: *Fellowship and love should continue to abound among Christians as they are filled with the fruits of righteousness.*

1. Praise for Their Partnership (vv. 3–8)

1:3. Paul had developed a particular fondness for the Philippians as he first preached among them about ten years earlier. The Philippian believers had supported his ministry with monetary gifts and prayer. Someone has said to be "thankful" is to be "thinkful." The apostle expressed his gratitude to God **every time I remember you**.

1:4. Friends may tell you that they have been thinking of you. Usually their thoughts are positive, and your heart is warmed. An even greater encouragement comes when someone reveals to you that they have been praying for you. The Philippians' labor in the cause of Christ with Paul had given him much joy. Bill Lawrence, a professor at Dallas Theological Seminary, once said, "Happiness is based on happenings, but joy comes from relationships." No doubt the apostle Paul would agree.

1:5. Partnership in the gospel caused Paul's joy. The Philippian Christians had supported his efforts since they had trusted Christ as their Savior during Paul's evangelistic efforts among them from his second missionary journey until the present.

1:6. The apostle is confident of what God has already done and knows that the God **who began a good work in you will carry it on to completion.** When God starts a work in our lives, beginning with our salvation, he will finish it. As believers, we are to grow in the Christian life becoming more like Christ each day. This is called sanctification. Spiritual growth should continue in committed believers **until the day of Christ Jesus**, that is until Christ returns again to the earth as the angels predicted (Acts 1:11).

1:7. Paul makes no apology for his fond affection for the Philippians in being partners in the gospel of Christ. His love for them is not lessened by painful earthly circumstances, nor is their support for him lessened because of his difficulties. They sent Epaphroditus with financial support even to his jail.

1:8. God, himself, is Paul's witness for what Paul has expressed. Paul loved them with the same unconditional love Jesus exhibited during his earthly ministry, setting the pattern for relationships among all Christians.

2. Prayer for Their Righteousness (vv. 9–11)

1:9. Having expressed his love for the Philippians, Paul shares his prayer for their pursuit of Christian growth. Having described their love (v. 7), he prays for it to **abound**. Love is a primary characteristic of Christlikeness. Yet love is more than mere emotion. Love can increase **in knowledge and depth of insight.** Knowledge is spiritual wisdom found in Scripture. Insight is application of this spiritual wisdom to practical living. Christian love must be rooted in wisdom from God's Word if we are to love both God and man in greater ways.

1:10. Next Paul prays for discernment of what is best, which is a result of growth in godly knowledge and insight. Discernment here is the ability to discriminate, to examine or test things that differ. As we mature as Christians, our abilities to make choices should improve. We are to base our decisions on Scripture so that the best way is selected. The best way is both moral and ethical before God.

When this pattern is observed, our lives are **pure** and **blameless**. These words do not mean perfection or sinlessness. They refer to our motives. Paul prays that these Christians would develop a genuine lifestyle, without hypocrisy, before God and men. As in 1:7, **the day of Christ** refers to the time when Christ will come for all true believers, his church. Since we do not know when this event might occur, an incentive for living a pure and blameless lifestyle is to be unashamed before Christ should he choose to come at a time when we least expect him. We are to be ready at all times to face him.

1:11. The fruit of righteousness is Christian character or moral qualities that glorify God. Paul described these inner characteristics in Galatians 5:22–23 as the fruit of the Spirit. Our righteousness comes through our faith in Christ. As he transforms our lives, we become more like him. A relationship with Christ is necessary to achieve fruit in the Christian life. Therefore, since God is at work in us, **the glory and praise** belong not to us but to God.

Joy in Adversity (vv. 12–30)

> **SUPPORTING IDEA:** *Afflictions can actually help further the gospel. Given the gift of suffering for Jesus, you should make sure your lifestyle is worthy of the gospel.*

1. Adversity Advances the Gospel (vv. 12–18)

1:12. Paul points to his own persecution and his present imprisonment in Rome. Instead of hampering the gospel, these have advanced it. Paul appears to be reassuring the Philippians that even though his movements are restricted, mere human constraints cannot thwart the gospel.

1:13. Paul's imprisonment was not due to committing any crime. He was **in chains for Christ. The whole palace guard** along with the common people on the street understood that he was in prison due to his commitment to the cause of Christ.

1:14. With Paul not having the freedom to minister where he pleased, other believers had taken the baton or come up to the plate to **speak the word of God** in Paul's stead. Conventional or worldly wisdom would think the threat of jail would make Christians fearful of proclaiming their faith. Yet the opposite was true. God saw fit to use what looked to be a setback to gain new converts.

1:15. Paul's difficulties spawned missionary zeal based on two types of motives: selfishness and goodwill. Seizing the opportunity of the moment, some envied the success God had given Paul, while others wanted to be a part of what God was doing through Paul. Both gave people the good news of Christ's gospel.

1:16. Motivated by Paul's example, those who preach with right motives **do so in love.** Such love flows out to Paul, to unbelievers needing the gospel, and to God. Such love realizes that Paul was suffering, not for some wrong he had done, but because he preached Christ (see vv. 12–13).

1:17. Those with wrong motives seek to exalt themselves. They do not promote the gospel in sincerity. Rather they seek to further their own selfish ambitions and to **stir up trouble** for Paul. They hoped Paul would think they had taken over his place and so would be disheartened.

1:18. Some Christians wanted to harm the messenger, Paul. Yet he was not concerned for himself. He focused strictly on the message. Even though the gospel was being proclaimed with mixed motives, the message, nevertheless, was Christ. Even wrong motives could result in actions that let people come to know Jesus. So Paul emphasized the results, not the reasons, and rejoiced.

2. Adversity Exalts Christ (vv. 19–26)

1:19. Paul was detained; but the gospel was still going forth, so Paul remained encouraged. He had faith something good would happen to him. Why? Because the Philippians prayed and **the Spirit of Jesus Christ** remained at work. So Paul looked expectantly to the day he would leave prison but at the same time comprehended that he could be executed.

1:20. Whether he regained his freedom to minister outside of prison or went to be with the Lord in heaven, he did not want to **be ashamed** of his testimony for Christ. Whatever took place, he desired for Christ to be **exalted** in his body. What was required to avoid shame and ensure exaltation of Christ? **Courage!** The internal strength to live for Christ or die for Christ, whichever was required. Only such courageous living exalts Christ.

1:21. Many people believe this verse is the most important of the entire book. It demonstrates that Christ is the source of meaning for Paul. He announced: **to live is Christ.** In death the adversities of this life would be over, and he would be with Christ in heaven. Therefore, **to die is gain.**

1:22–24. Paul conveys the dilemma of his situation. The apostle was so committed to the cause of Christ that staying on earth had its advantages but so did departing and going to heaven. To live means **fruitful labor.** He could remain ministering and spreading the gospel. To die means eternity with Christ. Given a choice in the matter, Paul did not know his decision.

Being with Christ appeals to him. It would certainly be an improvement in his present circumstances. Yet he places the needs of his readers ahead of his desire. Staying lets them benefit from his ministry.

1:25–26. Paul knew Christ's mind, a mind that put the needs of others above personal desires, so Paul knew he would **remain** on earth to minister to the churches. Paul considered the welfare of fellow Christians more important than his desire to go to heaven. By enduring on earth, he could assist their spiritual growth and joy in the Christian faith. This joy is not from circumstances but from a relationship **in Christ Jesus,** the source of true joy for believers.

3. Adversity Encourages Believers (vv. 27–30)

1:27–28. God was in control of the situation. Paul could be released from prison or killed by the Romans. Just as he wanted to maintain his testimony for Christ, he longed for the Philippians to remain faithful, too. They would show faithfulness by living a life **worthy of the gospel of Christ**. Such a life would not just be legalistic, obeying moral laws. It would show forth the spirit and love of Christ in every human relationship. Paul had faced opposition to his efforts for the cause of Christ without fear. He exhorted the Philippians to do the same even as they faced opposition. They could do so but only if they did so together. The world must see a united front defending and proclaiming the gospel. No longer would divided motives of love and selfishness do. The church must face the world in **one spirit**. A fearless, unified church will astound the world. They will see the truth of the gospel. Opposing the gospel, the world faces God's destruction. Proclaiming the gospel, the church waits for God's salvation.

1:29–30. Adversity is a part of the Christian life and should come as no surprise. Those that follow Christ should expect opposition. Believers have two privileges: **to believe on him** and **to suffer for him**. Both are an integral part of Christian living. The apostle had faced opposition on many occasions throughout his ministry. The Philippians had to face **the same** struggle and wanted to know how Paul had coped with these difficulties. He encouraged them to face their adversity in the way that he had, in Christ with joy.

MAIN IDEA REVIEW: *God can use our afflictions to further the gospel and exalt the Lord, so we should live exemplary lives in the face of our own afflictions.*

III. CONCLUSION

The Press Box of Life

The feature occupant of the press box of life is not an assistant coach but God himself. God is trying to do for you exactly what that assistant coach is trying to do for that quarterback—give you the big picture. That is the challenge of the Christian life. Our problem as believers is really not our circumstances. Our problem is our perspective on our circumstances. The vantage point from which we view our situations determines whether we have joy or despondency. To have joy, we must find a way in our minds and hearts to step off the field and get a press box view of the entire field in the game of life. Then we will understand that God is bigger than our circumstances. God's perspective will give us great joy even in the midst of problems and adversity.

This joy has one important appendage. To have joy in the midst of adversity, we must be in close contact with God in heaven. Paul summarizes this intimate relationship in verse 21: **For to me to live is Christ and to die is**

gain. What does he mean? He means that Christ is his entire life. His whole life was wrapped up in knowing Christ and promoting Christ.

Only by being on the phone to God, who is in the press box, can we have joy. This final perspective—that is not dependent on outward circumstances—brings great joy. Someone has said, "Joy is the flag over the castle of the heart announcing that the king is in residence." When "Christ is your life" and on the throne of your heart, then you can know a steadfast, abiding joy. The challenge for each of us today is to get ourselves to the place where we can say, "For me to live is Christ."

PRINCIPLES

- God is bigger than my circumstances.
- From on high God understands why!
- Proper perspective produces praise.
- In Christ, life or death is a win-win situation.
- When we are ready to die, we are best prepared to live.

APPLICATIONS

- Rest in the fact that God is with you in the midst of difficulties.
- Ask God to help you see his vantage point in your circumstances.
- Hold a steady course in the midst of perplexing problems by trusting God.
- Thank God that a Christ-centered, eternal perspective brings joy.

IV. LIFE APPLICATION

The Passage of Death

A cemetery in Indiana has a tombstone which is more than one hundred years old. The epitaph reads:

Pause, Stranger, when you pass me by,
As you are now, so once was I.
As I am now, so you will be,
So prepare for death and follow me.

To which someone added:

To follow you I'm not content,
Until I know which way you went.

Death is life's only certainty, a certainty which most people don't like! Most people feel about death like Woody Allen, who said, "It's not that I'm afraid to die. I just don't want to be there when it happens." It is so ultimate. It is so final. It is so utterly inescapable.

Someone has said:

> When we look at death, we are like a hen before a cobra. We find ourselves incapable of doing anything at all in the presence of the very thing that seems to call for the most drastic and decisive action. The disquieting thought, that stares at us like a face with a freezing grin, is that there is, in fact, nothing we can do. Say what we will, dance how we will, we will soon enough be a heap of ruined feathers and bones, indistinguishable from the rest of the ruins that lie about. It will not appear to matter in the slightest whether we met the enemy with equanimity, shrieks, or a trumped-up gaiety, there we will be (*Illustrations for Biblical Preaching*, ed. Michael Green, Grand Rapids: Baker Book House, 1984, 90).

Yes, most people view death with fear. It looms as a huge shadow over all of life. Not so for the Christian. One of the great blessings for us who have accepted Christ as our Savior is that we don't have to fear death. Like Paul, we can say, "For to me to live is Christ and to die is gain." This confidant assurance that God has a place for us in heaven brings great joy.

If you know Christ as your personal Savior, then you don't have to fear death. You can see it as a home-going, a graduation, a passage. Death is a door through which we pass from this life to the next. At the point of physical death, our physical body may die, but in God's mysterious providence we are with the Lord.

Loraine Boettner, in his book *Immortality*, wrote:

> I am standing on a sea shore. A ship at my side spreads her white sails to the morning breeze and starts for the ocean blue. She is an object of beauty and strength, and I stand and watch her until at length she hangs like a speck of white cloud just where the sea and sky come down to meet each other. Then someone at my side says, "There, she is gone." Gone where? Gone from my sight, that is all. She is just as large in mast and hull and spar as she was when she left my side, and just as able to bear her load of living weights to its place of destination. Her diminished size is in me, not in her, and just at the moment, when someone says, "There she is gone," on that distant shore there are other eyes watching for her coming and other voices ready to take up the glad shout, "Here she comes," and such is dying (*Illustrations for Biblical Preaching*, 92).

V. PRAYER

Dear Heavenly Father, thank you that you are in the press box, seeing and understanding all my predicaments. Share with me your perspective on my problems. Where you are not able to reveal to me your purposes, give me the grace to trust you fully. By your Spirit, enable me to keep Christ on the throne of my life and maintain him as my chief pursuit. In him, I pray. Amen.

VI. DEEPER DISCOVERIES

A. Servants (v. 1)

Doulos (servant) literally means "slave." Paul described our relationship to God as common slaves. Timothy and Paul considered themselves completely at God's disposal, in body and soul, ready and willing to serve him in any capacity. They subjugated their own wills to God's agenda on earth.

During the Roman Empire, Rome's aggressive armies defeated many nations. Sometimes conquered people were forced to serve their captors. Looked upon as property like land, animals, or other goods, slaves were traded—bought and sold. If a slave's master was harsh, the slave had a miserable existence. A slave fortunate enough to have a benevolent owner was often treated almost like a son.

Realizing they had been bought with a price, the death of Christ in their behalf, Paul and Timothy voluntarily became servants of God. They regarded service as slaves to God as a great honor. Giving him their complete obedience and devotion, these men were willing to go anywhere and do anything, including dying, that would further God's kingdom on earth.

Believers today have been bought from the slave market of sin with the same price as these men, the death of the Lord Jesus Christ. As a demonstration of our gratitude to Christ, we should consider ourselves to be his servants. We should give him our total allegiance and devotion by being willing to seek his kingdom and place his will before our own.

Jesus vividly demonstrated what occurs when we fully surrender ourselves to God's agenda:

"But seek first his kingdom and his righteousness, and all these things will be given to you as well" (Matt. 6:33).

"Then he [Jesus] called the crowd to him along with his disciples and said: 'If anyone would come after me, he must deny himself and take up his cross and follow me. For whoever wants to save his life will lose it, but whoever loses his life for me and for the gospel will save it'" (Mark 8:34–35).

Our first priority as disciples of Christ is to seek, find, and follow the revealed will of God found in the Bible. When this happens, we do not need to worry about how our physical needs in this life will be met. God will take care of us. When we seek his kingdom and trust him to meet our needs, true joy and fulfillment come from this obedient relationship with God.

Our lives and personal agendas must be surrendered to God's plan and program. In the Bible the cross was an instrument of execution. We are to be willing to die for Christ, if necessary, as we obey his will for us.

B. Saints (v. 1)

A saint is not a super Christian but a normal Christian. *Hagioi* literally means "holy ones." To be a saint means to be "set apart," "holy," or "sanctified." A saint is separated, consecrated, and devoted to God's service by the Holy Spirit. This act takes place the moment one trusts in Christ as personal Savior. First Corinthians 1:2 clearly relates this concept: "To the church of God in Corinth, to those *sanctified* in Christ Jesus and called to be holy, together with all those everywhere who call on the name of the Lord Jesus Christ—their Lord and ours" (emphasis added).

All true believers in the Lord Jesus Christ are saints. As instruments of God, we are "holy ones" in contrast to the sinful, anti-God culture of this world. God "has rescued us from the dominion of darkness and brought us into the kingdom of the Son he loves" (Col. 1:13). We are no longer under the power and authority of the evil one, Satan, but under God's Son, Jesus Christ. As his saints we are called out to serve him rather than pursue sin. As we love him more than we love sin, through the power of the Holy Spirit, we become more sanctified. Sanctification is an ongoing process as we sin less and produce more good works or fruit. Paul speaks of this process in 1 Thessalonians 5:23: "May God himself, the God of peace, sanctify you through and through. May your whole spirit, soul and body be kept blameless at the coming of our Lord Jesus Christ."

Paul emphasized that the whole person is involved in the sanctification process.

C. Overseers and Deacons (v. 1)

The two primary officials in the early church were overseers and deacons. *Overseer* comes from the Greek *episkopos* meaning "superintendent," "guardian," or "bishop." Overseers in the Greek culture were presiding officials in a civic or religious organization. Their counterpart from Jewish culture was an elder. The terms *overseer* and *elder* are used interchangeably in the New Testament. In Titus 1:5–9, the same individuals are referred to as elders and overseers. "Elder" possibly indicates qualification (maturity and experience), while "overseer" possibly indicates responsibility (watching over God's flock).

The apostle Paul appointed elders on his first missionary journey (Acts 14:23). He instructed them to "keep watch over yourselves and all the flock of which the Holy Spirit has made you overseers. Be shepherds of the church of God, which he bought with his own blood" (Acts 20:28). To shepherd is to "pastor" the flock, the local congregation. These men are to guide the people in the truth of God's Word and guard them from doctrinal error (Titus 1:9–16). These responsibilities were entailed in overseeing the spiritual welfare of the local church. This great charge demanded that men who served in this capacity possess high personal and moral character. Paul gave instruction on the qualifications of these leadership positions in 1 Timothy 3:1–8 and Titus 1:5–9.

Women were not found to be holding the offices of overseer, pastor, or elder in the New Testament. Elders were the teachers in the church. Prior to stating the qualifications for elders/overseers and deacons in 1 Timothy 3, the apostle revealed in 1 Timothy 2:11–13: "A woman should learn in quietness and full submission, I do not permit a woman to teach or to have authority over a man; she must be silent. For Adam was formed first, then Eve."

Some maintain that Paul's prohibition was cultural for the first century as women were less educated than men. If that was the case, why did he mention the reason for his position was the order of creation with Adam, the man, being created first? It is a strong conclusion from his words that Paul did now allow a woman to be an official teacher in the assembled church. Teaching and exercising authority over other believers were primary responsibilities of elders. Since the apostle prohibits women functioning in this capacity, they are not to exercise authority over men in the local church. Women are not inferior to men; but, based on the order of creation, certain responsibilities in the church are given to men. In many churches two-thirds of the congregation are women and children. Women have scriptural freedom to have any ministry they are gifted for as long as it does not constitute having spiritual authority over men. Obviously, then, they can instruct other women (Titus 2:3–5) and teach children. Timothy, himself, was immensely influenced by the Christian faith of his grandmother and mother (2 Tim. 1:5). It seems that, scripturally, they can provide leadership in various areas as long as that leadership does not violate the principle of spiritual authority over men.

Priscilla, the wife of Aquilla, apparently had a significant role in educating Apollos, who became mighty in the Scripture. However, she apparently was able to have this ministry in connection with her husband and did not violate the principle of spiritual authority (Acts 18:26).

Even though a woman may have the scriptural freedom to conduct a certain ministry, if it is viewed culturally as a usurpation of spiritual authority, she might need to defer to the prevailing culture in order to maintain harmony in the body (Rom. 14:13,19). For example, helping to take up a collection does not seem to violate the command for women not to exercise spiritual authority over men, but in many churches this activity would not be accepted. Therefore, in order to help maintain peace in the body, the deferential thing to do might be for the woman to forego a biblical freedom for the sake of her brothers and sisters in Christ.

The Greek *diakonos* means "one who serves." A deacon was another official office in the New Testament church. The need for this position arose as the number of converts to Christ grew. The apostles were incapable of meeting all the needs of the members of the early church. Acts 6:1–6 revealed how this significant office began. Seven men were appointed by the twelve apostles to free them up from serving tables of the church's widows so they could devote all their efforts to prayer and the ministry of the Scriptures. These men were not chosen at random. They were godly men with evidence that the Holy Spirit was at work in their lives. As the church matured, more formal qualifications were given for this office (1 Tim. 3:8–12). Elders and deacons must hold many of the same qualifications. A noteworthy exception for deacons is that they are not required to teach.

The obligations of deacons involved practical service, ministering to the physical needs of the church. Even today, deacons serve with the pastors or elders. They minister to the physical needs of the congregation and their communities. The valuable ministries of deacons free the pastors and elders to give their full attention to the congregation's spiritual needs (Acts 6:2,4).

Were there female deacons or deaconesses in the early church? Disagreement exists among scholars and Bible teachers concerning 1 Timothy 3:11: "In the same way, their wives are to be women worthy of respect, not malicious talkers but temperate and trustworthy in everything."

The Greek *gunaikas* in this verse means "women." It could refer to deacon's wives or female deacons (deaconesses). The context might lend weight to their being deacon's wives, since 1 Timothy 3:12–13 returns to the word *deacon* and states that he must have only one wife and manage his family well. He does not say that deaconesses must have only one husband.

Advocates of deaconesses employ Romans 16:1 in their argument. The apostle Paul in the last chapter of Romans says: "I commend to you our sister Phoebe, a servant of the church of Cenchrea." The Greek word translated "servant" is *diakonos*. Phoebe was active in Christian ministry at Cenchrea. She may have delivered Paul's letter to the Romans. Since every Christian was to be a servant of Christ in the church, Phoebe had been able to render particular service to Paul and many others. If *deaconess* were an official leadership position in the early church, its function is not clear. Some Bible students think they performed the same duties as male deacons. Others think they ministered only to women. Still others do not think women served officially as deacons at all.

D. Partnership (v. 5)

Partnership translates the Greek *koinonia*. *Koinonia* means "association," "fellowship," or "close relationship." You have a partnership or fellowship with those with whom you have commonality. We speak of fellowship over coffee or a meal. Close Christian fellowship includes participating in spreading the good news to unbelievers about Christ.

The Philippians supported Paul's work through prayer and finances. Their common partnership was in the advancement of the gospel of Christ. These Philippian believers were longtime participants in the apostle's ministry as they had aided him from the first day when Lydia, the purple-cloth merchant (Acts 16:14), responded to the gospel. She opened her home for Paul and his early converts to meet (Acts 16:15,40). These Christian friends continued to support his ministry even while Paul was in a Roman prison.

Today, we join the efforts of missionaries and various ministries by supporting them with prayer, finances, and sometimes donating our time to labor alongside them. Christian ministry is not meant for Lone Rangers, but as a team we labor together in the Lord's harvest.

E. Day of Christ Jesus (v. 6) and day of Christ (v. 10)

Paul believed that God would produce good works in the Philippians until "the day of Christ Jesus." This future event is believed by many to be the rapture. Others believe it will be at his Second Coming. God's angels predicted that Jesus would return in Acts 1:11: "'Men of Galilee,' they said, 'why do you stand here looking into the sky? This same Jesus, who has been taken from you into heaven, will come back in the same way you have seen him go into heaven.'"

Paul elaborated on this future event in 1 Thessalonians 4:16–17:

> For the Lord himself will come down from heaven, with a loud command, with the voice of the archangel and with the trumpet call of God, and the dead in Christ will rise first. After that, we who are still alive and are left will be caught up together with them in the clouds to meet the Lord in the air. And so we will be with the Lord forever.

Since this happening could take place at any time, we should be diligent to live a life that Christ would be proud of at his return. We are to be good stewards of the time and abilities that he has entrusted us to produce good works. No more pleasing words could be heard by faithful believers from our Master than: "'Well done, good and faithful servant! You have been faithful with a few things; I will put you in charge of many things. Come and share your master's happiness!'" (Matt. 25:21).

VII. TEACHING OUTLINE

A. INTRODUCTION

1. Lead story: Life Is like a Football Game
2. Context: In the first chapter of Philippians, Paul is about to be sacked in the back field for a twenty-yard loss. He is under arrest, chained to a burly soldier, awaiting trial on a capital offense. Yet we find Paul rejoicing. How is joy possible in the midst of problems and adversity? The answer? Two words: vantage point. When we have God's perspective on our problems, we can have joy even in the most difficult trials.
3. Transition: As we look into the chapter, we initially see Paul's prayer of joy. Then we see in verses 12–26 the reason we can have joy in the midst of difficulties. We will see that the key to joy is vantage point. God's vantage point, his perspective, on our problems gives us joy.

B. COMMENTARY

1. Greeting (vv. 1–2)
2. Joy in Prayer (vv. 3–11)
   a. Joy for their partnership (vv. 3–8)
   b. Petition for their righteousness (vv. 9–11).
3. Joy in Adversity (vv. 12–30)
   a. Perspective that the gospel was being advanced (vv. 12–18)
   b. Perspective that adversity exalts Christ (vv. 19–26)
   c. Perspective that adversity encourages believers (vv. 27–30)
      (1) To stand firm (v. 27)
      (2) Not to fear (v. 28)
      (3) To accept suffering (v. 29)

C. CONCLUSION: THE PASSAGE OF DEATH

VIII. ISSUES FOR DISCUSSION

1. What adversities are you facing today? How have you reacted to these? In what ways have you sought to find God's perspective on your adversities?
2. Have you ever experienced joy in the midst of adversity? Share your experience with a member of the class or with the class as a whole. How do you describe the feeling of joy?
3. How do you pray in the midst of adversity? What do you ask for? What do you expect to receive? Have you ever asked for God's per-

spective on your adversity? Did that change the situation in any way? Did it change your reactions to the situation?

4. In your adversity have you seen Christ exalted? How? How can your response to adversity exalt Christ?

5. How do you view death? How do you react to the reality of your own approaching death? What do you think is God's perspective on your death?

Philippians 2

The Power of Humility

Quote

"*P*ride is the mother hen under which all
other sins are hatched."

C .   S .   L e w i s

Philippians

I N   A   N U T S H E L L

*I*n chapter 2, Paul admonishes the Philippian Christians: Live
unselfishly, as Jesus did, who gave up trying to advance himself. Instead, he lived to help others. When he humbled himself, God highly
exalted him, and he will do the same with you. I will send both Timothy
and Epaphroditus to you to help and encourage you in your need, so
treat them well.

The Power of Humility

I. INTRODUCTION

The Sandwich Board of Salvation

*H*arry Ironside, well-known preacher and author from a previous generation, used to tell the story of his struggle with humility. He asked an elder friend what he could do about it. His friend counseled him to make a sandwich board with the plan of salvation in Scripture on it and to wear it as he walked throught the business and shopping district of downtown Chicago for one entire day.

Ironside did it and found it to be a humiliating experience. As he was taking the sandwich board off, however, he caught himself thinking: "There's not another person in Chicago who would be willing to do a thing like that."

Yes, humility is a difficult thing. Just the moment you think you have it, you've lost it. Humility is essential to successful relationships. It is the oil that makes the intersecting gears of human personalities turn without grinding on each other.

Love and humility go together. You cannot have one without the other. Dr. Martin Luther King once said, "Love is the only force in the universe powerful enough to change an enemy into a friend." Augustine concluded, "One loving heart sets another on fire." Benjamin Disraeli saw that "we are all born for love. It is the principle of existence and its only end."

The power of love and humility is the message of Philippians 2. Here we learn that whenever people love humbly and unselfishly, especially in the midst of strained relationships, they promote unity and spread joy. The church in Philippi needed this message. Two women were disagreeing (4:2–3). Others argued and complained (v. 14). In Philippians 2, Paul shares the attitudes and actions that will restore peace to strained relationships. We need this counsel, for "keeping the peace" in our relationships is always a challenge. As we study Philippians 2, we learn from the apostle Paul how to unify relationships by humbly looking out for **the interests of others** (v. 4).

II. COMMENTARY

The Power of Humility

MAIN IDEA: *Jesus' example of humility challenges Christians to live a life of unselfishness and unity.*

A Humility toward Others (vv. 1–4)

SUPPORTING IDEA: *If you want to make God happy, be unselfish with one another, treating others the way you would like to be treated.*

2:1. In chapter 1, Paul speaks of his joy in prayer and joy in adversity as a Christian serving his God. He could rejoice in almost any circumstance. The key to this joy is a relationship with Christ. In chapter 2, Paul explains how joy comes through another aspect of the believer's life—humility toward others. He begins his appeal for humility by referring to the Philippians' experience. Because they are **united with Christ**, believers are members of his body. We have special bonds to one another due to our relationship with Christ. Our attitudes toward one another are important. The reality of our oneness in Christ is based on being encouraged by:

1. comfort from his love
2. fellowship with the Spirit
3. tenderness and compassion

2:2. Paul instructs his readers to **make my joy complete** in practical responses with the following outlook toward one another:

1. being like-minded
2. having the same love
3. being one in spirit and purpose

These sentiments are viewed by Paul as being normal for Christians. Being united in Christ, believers work together for the same purposes rather than seeking areas of disagreement and division.

2:3. After revealing the positive way for believers to behave toward one another, Paul gives negatives to avoid. Unity in love means **selfish ambition** and **vain conceit** have no place in the Christian life. Such characteristics rise from pride, not from love. Instead, humility is to characterize the Christian. We are not to exalt ourselves above others.

You are probably thinking that this is easier said than done. Yet, Jesus, himself, said: "A new command I give you: Love one another. As I have loved you, so you must love one another. All men will know that you are my disciples, if you love one another" (John 13:34–35). Biblical love is selfless. The opposite of this kind of love is selfishness. Humility does not mean putting ourselves down but rather lifting others up.

2:4. Looking out for our own interests comes naturally. We need, and receive, no instruction for that. We are instructed to look out for **the interests of others.** We are to keep an eye out to discover ways we can help others even when they do not see they need such help. The apostle stated in Galatians 6:2: "Carry each other's burdens, and in this way you will fulfill the law of Christ."

B The Humility of Christ (vv. 5–11)

> **SUPPORTING IDEA:** *Have the same attitude that Jesus did, who humbled himself and became a servant to others. As a result of his humility, God highly exalted him.*

2:5. Paul proceeds to give examples for the Philippians to emulate. The first is Christ. He is the supreme example of humility, love, and selflessness. Christ's model brings to life Paul's words. As believers are united with Christ, we are to have the same attitude as Christ, one of humility. Paul expresses the same thought in Ephesians 4:2: "Be completely humble and gentle; be patient, bearing with one another in love." All believers should share this humble, selfless mind-set of Christ.

2:6. Jesus is the preeminent example of humility. He has always been God. John 1:1 speaks of Jesus: "In the beginning was the Word, and the Word was with God, and the Word was God." As God, he did not selfishly grasp hold of or tightly hold to his position as equal with God. Instead, he was willing to leave his high position in heaven temporarily and to give himself over to serving our needs. Although he set aside the rights and privileges of being God, he remained God.

2:7. Jesus **made himself nothing** or "emptied himself." Scholars refer to this important statement as *kenosis*, from the Greek word. By becoming a man, Jesus did not lay aside his deity. Charles C. Ryrie sheds light on this event: "Christ didn't become any less God, but he chose not to use some of his divine attributes. This involved a veiling of his preincarnate glory (John 17:5) and the voluntary nonuse of some of his divine prerogatives during the time he was on earth (Matt. 24:36). For God to become a man was humbling enough, but he was willing to go even further. Christ could have come to earth in his true position as King of the universe. Instead, he took the role of a servant. The Creator chose to serve his creatures.

Jesus did not come into existence as a baby in Bethlehem. As God, he always existed. He did take on human nature as Jesus of Nazareth **being made in human likeness** but remained sinless (Heb. 4:15). Christ did not have a halo as paintings sometimes portray him. He entered this earthly life looking like an ordinary man. Had you passed him on a street, he probably would not have caught your attention.

2:8. Jesus, looking like a man, **humbled himself and became obedient to death**. Mark 10:45, speaking of Christ, declares: "For even the Son of Man did not come to be served, but to serve, and to give his life as a ransom for many." Second Corinthians 8:9 is also helpful: "For you know the grace of our Lord Jesus Christ, that though he was rich, yet for your sakes he became poor, so that you through his poverty might become rich." Even though Jesus was equal to God the Father, he submitted to his Father's will (John 5:30).

Becoming a man was humbling. Taking the nature of a servant was more humbling. Christ went still further. He humbled himself to the extent of being willing to die like a common criminal **on a cross**. Crucifixion was the most degrading kind of execution that could be inflicted on a man (*NIV Study Bible*, 1865). It was the form of capital punishment the Romans employed for foreigners and slaves. Many died in this manner. Most paid the penalty for heinous crimes. Christ's death was unique! He died but not for what he had done. He was sinless with no penalty to pay. He died for others. He died to pay the penalty for the sins of the world. Observe Galatians 3:13: "Christ redeemed us from the curse of the law by becoming a curse for us, for it is written: 'Cursed is everyone who is hung on a tree.'" Isaiah 53:6 asserts: "We all, like sheep, have gone astray, each of us has turned to his own way; and the Lord has laid on him the iniquity of us all." Jesus Christ is the Good Shepherd. The Good Shepherd laid down his life for his sheep (John 10:14–15).

2:9. Following Jesus' humility and obedience, God the Father **exalted him** to his rightful position of honor and glory. Through the miracle of resurrection from the dead, God gave new honor to the obedient, humble Son. The Lord Jesus Christ resumed his preincarnate rank and dignity seated at the right hand of God's throne (Heb. 12:2). God bestowed upon Jesus **the name that is above every name**. The exalted Christ, seated at God's right hand, was now called "Lord." He became the object of worship for the church. He became the Master instead of the servant. The church became his slaves and looked to him as their Lord. All this is a result of God's exalting the humble, obedient Son.

2:10–11. The result of Christ's humiliation was exaltation. Following his obedience, God the Father decreed **at the name of Jesus every knee should bow**. The emphasis here is on every creature in the universe acknowledging Jesus as the Lord of the created order. God's heavenly forces and his earthly church will honor Christ. Likewise, demonic powers and people who opposed Christ and his church will bow down before him (see Isa. 45:23–24). In God's heavenly precincts, in humanity's earthly home, and in the devil's domain below the earth, every tongue will worship Jesus for who he is: The Lord, the Sovereign of the universe. These verses do not mean that all will confess him as Savior, for the Bible offers no second chances after death (Heb. 9:27). This is the combination of worship from those who believe in him and acknowledgment of his power and authority by those he has defeated. The honored place the Savior now occupies and the universal acknowledgment of his lordship in the future are all **to the glory of God the Father.**

C The Humility of Paul (vv. 12–18)

SUPPORTING IDEA: *See people like Paul serve God in humility and follow their example in living the saved life day by day.*

2:12. The Lord Jesus Christ has given Christians an incredible example of selfless humility and service to follow. His example can be followed. Paul did so and called on the Philippian believers to do the same.

Paul conveyed the closeness of his relationship with the Philippians by referring to them as **my dear friends**. He commended their past obedience and urged them to **work out your salvation with fear and trembling**. He did not say "work for your salvation." Observe Ephesians 2:8–9: "For it is by grace you have been saved, through faith—and this not from yourselves, it is the gift of God—not by works, so that no one can boast." They have been saved by grace. Now they are to bring the salvation to completion, to live out the fact that they have been saved.

2:13. This outcome is possible not through human effort but because God indwells you and is working in you. Christians must demonstrate they are saved by allowing God to work through them. Salvation is by grace through faith. Saving faith surrenders all of life to God and his purpose, producing maturity demonstrated in good works. As Christians mature and allow God to work through their lives, they find God is accomplishing his purposes in them even when they are not aware of those purposes.

2:14. When you allow God to work in you, you **do everything without complaining or arguing**. Unsaved people might be expected to complain and dispute, but Christians are to have changed lives. We do the work God has for us without being negative or rebellious.

2:15. If we are obedient, we **may become blameless and pure** or "without fault" in contrast to the culture around us. Our life resembles our divine Father rather than our pagan neighbors. People recognize us as God's children (see Deut. 32:5). Believers are to be so distinct from unbelievers that we stand out as positive models. If God is working in our lives, we are to be unlike the godless society around us. We are to make them curious as to why we are not like them. Christ, himself, said that we are to be "the light of the world" (Matt. 5:14). Paul says we are to be as conspicuous in the world as stars are in the dark nighttime heavens.

2:16. How do we shine like stars in the night? How do we live out this ongoing moral example as children who reflect the perfection of the Father? We grasp hold of the gospel. The marginal note in the NIV reads, "hold on to," the normal meaning of the Greek *epexontes*. Only God's Word can give us direction and power to let God do his work in our lives and keep us pure before him.

Paul looks forward to witnessing the progress these Christians will make in their lives. They are the reason for his ministry. He wants the concluding scene of history to show that his life had meaning. As he stands at the final judgment to hear God's evaluation of his life, he wants to hear that the Philippians have indeed been the stars of the universe. Then his ministry will not be without meaning or empty. He will have run life's race victoriously. He will have completed his life's occupation successfully. He exhibits a similar anticipation in 1 Thessalonians 2:19–20: "For what is our hope, our joy, or the crown in which we will glory in the presence of our Lord Jesus when he comes? Is it not you? Indeed, you are our glory and joy."

2:17. If anyone had the right to complain, Paul did. Yet he was an example of what he preached. Facing possible death while in prison, he viewed it simply as an act of worship, a sacrifice, **a drink offering** to God. Such a liquid offering would be poured over the main sacrifice on the altar. Paul did not describe his work and suffering as that main sacrifice. Rather, the ministry of the Philippian church constituted that sacrifice. His ministry merely supplemented and completed theirs. Seeing their faith in action, he maintained his joy. His call to obedience and purity in verses 12–16 are not in vain. They are encouragements to "keep on keeping on" in the Christian race.

2:18. Paul encourages his readers to have his same attitude and rejoice with him. Without doubt, he considers it a privilege to suffer for the cause of Christ. Christ was Paul's example. He was willing to become **obedient to death** (Phil. 2:8). We, too, may experience joy under difficult circumstance if our primary purpose is serving God and others.

ⅅ The Humility of Timothy and Epaphroditus (vv. 19–30)

SUPPORTING IDEA: *Honor Christian ministers because of what they have done for Jesus in serving you and his church courageously and unselfishly.*

2:19. Paul now returns to personal matters. Timothy was with him in Rome (Phil. 1:1). As soon as he knows the outcome of his legal situation, he plans to send this faithful man to get a firsthand report of how things are in Philippi. Such a report would bring renewed cheer and hope to the imprisoned apostle who was already rejoicing over what he knew concerning them (v. 17).

2:20. Timothy stood out uniquely among the young pastors Paul mentored. Like Paul, Timothy had **a genuine interest** in their well-being. He ministered not to fulfill ambition and needs for personal success. He ministered to meet needs of the church people. What a model for today's young ministers who are too often flooded with calls to achieve success rather than to minister.

2:21. The normal human way is the way of self-interest. Protect yourself. Get what you need. If time permits, then help others. Timothy lived a different lifestyle. Like Paul, he put aside selfish interests. He concentrated on Christ's interests. He lived out the humble, self-giving life Christ had exemplified. He stood out as a bright star in the dark heavens.

2:22. Young Timothy was a living testimony of the kind of Christian Paul was instructing the Philippians to be. Paul could testify. He watched Timothy prove himself as his associate in the ministry. Paul had sent Timothy to other churches as well. In 1 Corinthians 4:17, the apostle said: "For this reason I am sending to you Timothy, my son whom I love, who is faithful in the Lord. He will remind you of my life in Christ Jesus, which agrees with what I teach everywhere in every church." We know of no family or children of Paul. He treated Timothy like a son. Every young minister needs a senior mentor as his ministerial father.

2:23. Paul still needed Timothy for a while until he saw what his own fate would be. Facing such an uncertain future, Paul still thought of the church's need and planned to send Timothy to help them just as soon as possible. Here Paul shows the fine line between total concentration on selfish concerns (v. 21) and legitimate concern for immediate personal needs (v. 23).

2:24. Paul, even with an uncertain future, anticipated being released to come see them, too. Such hope came not from confidence in the Roman legal system but from faith in what God had promised him (see 1:6,25–26).

2:25. Having placed Christ, himself, and Timothy as examples of humility before them, Paul now refers to one of their own. With Timothy and himself unable to come immediately, Paul sent Epaphroditus at once. Epaphroditus was a member of the Philippian church. He had delivered the financial gift to Paul from them (Phil. 4:18). Epaphroditus had stayed on in Rome to assist in the ministry. Thus he was the Philippians' messenger; but more, he was a colleague of Paul in the work of the ministry. He was a member along with Paul in God's army. The Philippians had sent him to care for Paul's needs. Now Paul sent him to care for their needs.

2:26. Epaphroditus had needs, too. He had been away from home too long. Homesickness plagued him. Part of the reason for homesickness was worry over the reaction of family and friends to news of his own illness. Their worries provoked deeper worries in him because he cared so deeply for them. He needed to go home. Paul needed him to go help his home church.

2:27. Friends at home had reason for worry. Epaphroditus experienced a close encounter with death. No human cause explained his continued life. Only God's mercy was responsible for that. In his providence, God chose to let the young minister live. Paul saw this as evidence of mercy in his own life, for it spared Paul added worry and sorrow at a time when his sorrow cup was already filled.

2:28. Epaphroditus' return to Philippi was not planned. **All the more eager to send him** may also mean "sending him sooner than expected." Paul expected the return of the Philippians' young minister to bring joy to the Philippians. Seeing someone alive and well who almost died brings deep satisfying joy. Paul's life, too, would improve. He would no longer have to worry about Epaphroditus' health. Nor would he need to be concerned for the Philippian church, both because they would no longer worry about Epaphroditus and because Epaphroditus could minister in Paul's stead to the church's needs.

2:29. To prevent any criticism of Epaphroditus' leaving Paul in his difficult situation or not completing the mission on which the church sent him, the apostle commanded the Philippians to welcome and honor him for his sacrificial service for the Lord. He, too, followed Christ's model of humble service. In so doing he became the example for all Christians who want to serve in such a way as to win the church's acclaim as well as that of Christ.

2:30. The Philippians must not see Epaphroditus as a sickly weakling who failed in his mission. No! He was a Christian hero. He had risked his life in service for Christ, representing the Philippian church in doing for Paul what others in the church could not do. Thus Paul praised both the individual minister and the church for their faithfulness in carrying out God's mission to him and in fulfilling Christ's purposes.

In chapter 2, Paul sets forth the humble examples of Christ, himself, Timothy, and Epaphroditus as models for them to emulate. He desires his readers to have an attitude of humility to the extent that they will unselfishly serve one another. To be truly Christlike is to follow this instruction.

MAIN IDEA REVIEW: *Jesus' example of humility challenges Christians to live a life of unselfishness and unity.*

III. CONCLUSION

Sacrificial Love

God has created us to be gregarious creatures. We need other people because we are created as social beings. God has created us so that we cannot make it alone. We must have relationships, interaction, and contact with others. This need is because we are created in the image of God, and God is a gregarious being.

Because God has created us to want and need interaction and relationships with others, he has established humanity so that we cannot have good relationships without treating others well. When I treat you well and you treat me well, then we both get our needs met in a context of love and unity. When I treat you poorly and you treat me poorly, then we are each isolated and unhappy. When Christ asks me to regard another person as more important than myself, what he wants is to give me deep, satisfying relationships with others. The harm he wants to keep from me is the barrenness of loneliness.

Therefore, the key to satisfying and sustaining relationships is sacrificial love. Philippians 2 teaches us that the people who love humbly and unselfishly spread joy and promote unity.

PRINCIPLES

- Uniters spread joy (v. 2).
- God calls us humbly to love and serve others (vv. 3–4).
- Sacrificial love is the result of God working in us (vv. 12–13).
- I shine like a star when I look out for the needs of others (v. 15).
- When you look out for the interests of others, you look out for the interests of Christ (v. 21).

APPLICATIONS

- Spread joy by spreading God's love to someone today.
- Thank God for Christ's model of humility.
- With humble attitudes and acts of love, seek to repair the strained relationships in your life.
- Honor people who "go the second mile" (v. 29).

IV. LIFE APPLICATION

Letter to My Unborn Child

In his book *The Fine Art of Friendship,* Ted Engstrom wrote of a very special husband and wife whose relationship marvelously illustrates the selfless love of Philippians 2. The husband was paralyzed. Engstrom includes a letter the husband wrote to his unborn child:

> Your mother is very special. Few men know what it's like to receive appreciation for taking their wives out to dinner when it entails what it does for us. It means that she has to dress me, shave me, brush my

teeth, comb my hair, wheel me out of the house and down the steps, open the garage, put me in the car, take the pedals off the chair, stand me up, sit me in the seat of the car, twist me around so that I'm comfortable, fold the wheelchair, put it in the car, go around to the other side of the car, start it up, back it out, get out of the car, pull the garage door down, get back into the car, and drive off to the restaurant. Then, it starts all over again; she gets out of the car, unfolds the wheelchair, opens the door, spins me around, stands me up, seats me in the wheelchair, pushes the pedals out, closes and locks the car, wheels me into the restaurant, then takes the pedals off the wheelchair so I won't be uncomfortable. We sit down to have dinner, and she feeds me throughout the entire meal. When it's over, she pays the bill, pushes the wheelchair out to the car again, and reverses the same routine. When it's all over—finished—with real warmth she'll say, "Honey, thank you for taking me out to dinner." I never quite know what to say (Nashville: Thomas Nelson, 1985, 103–4).

Selfless, humble attitudes and acts of love! When you receive them, like this man, your heart overflows. Words cannot express your gratitude. Yes, as is taught in Philippians 2, people who love unselfishly spread joy and promote unity.

Just as selflessness is beautiful, inspiring, and rewarding, so selfishness is ugly, depressing, and demeaning. All war, all hate, all fighting, all conflict, all division result from selfishness. Selfishness creates hard, mean, little people. Selfishness inflicts pain. Selfishness destroys marriages, careers, churches, and lives.

We have all read stories of selfish people and shaken our heads in disapproval. Couldn't we tell our own stories? What about the time you snapped at your child simply because he had invaded your space? What about the time you gossiped about a coworker, causing friction at the office? What about the time you spoke disrespectfully of someone in authority over you? On and on it goes, stories we can tell of selfishness.

Jesus said that to lust was as bad as to commit immorality. He said that to hate was as bad as murder. Think of any story that you wouldn't want to be told in front of your church. Think of any story that brings a rush of embarrassment if it were widely known. Most likely, at the heart of it was an attitude, a word, an act of selfishness or empty conceit.

Selfishness is a "me first" mistake. Paul says, don't do things out of selfishness and empty conceit. Meditate on the humble example of Christ (2:5–11), and switch to a redemptive "you first" relational style. It will spread joy and unity and bring peace to any troubled relationship.

V. PRAYER

You have made us, O God, for deep, satisfying relationships because you are a relational God. Help me to bring joy into every context through humble attitudes and actions of love. Forgive me for being, at times, self-centered, looking out for only myself. Enable me to think of others first and to show your love toward them. In your loving name. Amen.

VI. DEEPER DISCOVERIES

A. Fellowship with the Spirit (v. 1)

In this verse Paul employed the same Greek word, *koinonia*, that in 1:5 was translated "partnership." Again, the meaning is "association," "fellowship," or "close relationship" (BAGD, 439). The basic idea is having something in common, sharing together in something, or sharing with someone.

The church, the body of Christ on earth, is not a building or denomination but a group of redeemed individuals who share a common life of fellowship. God the Father, God the Son, and God the Holy Spirit have fellowship with one another. As believers, we are unified by the Holy Spirit (Eph. 4:3–6). Being a part of the same body, we are to live in love, humility, and service to one another. A Christian who is not interested in God's work and the lives of other believers is not in fellowship with the Spirit. Such self-centeredness has no fellowship with Christ or his church. Fellowship with God's Spirit is manifested through love and relationship with other believers (1 John 4:12).

B. In very nature God (v. 6)

Paul referred to the time before Christ came to earth as a man. The term translated *nature* is *morphe,* meaning "form, essence, or expression." Before Jesus became a man, he was God. He possessed the divine essence of Godhood. He was equal with God the Father and God the Spirit. Being born as a baby in Bethlehem took nothing away from his deity. It only added humanity. Being fully God, his complete and absolute deity is here carefully expressed by the apostle.

C. Made himself nothing (v. 7)

The Greek *kenoo* literally means "to empty." The natural question is, What did Christ empty himself of? Some have argued that he emptied himself of his deity. Orthodox evangelicals go in a different direction. They believe that he set aside some of his divine attributes some of the time as he became or took the nature or form of a man.

Putting on humanity involved limitations. In becoming a man, he voluntarily set aside his rights and privileges as God the Son. Some say that Jesus gave up his majesty or manifestation of his glory as God when he acquired a human nature. In the commentary, it is mentioned that he veiled his preincarnate glory and voluntarily chose not to use some of his power. Yet, while on earth, he did give Peter, James, and John a glimpse of his true glory as he transfigured himself before them (Matt. 17:1–13). In his incarnation, or taking on humanity, Jesus was fully God and fully man. In his deity he was undiminished, and in his humanity he was perfect.

D. Appearance as a Man (v. 8)

In the incarnation, Jesus took the form of a man and looked like any other male living in first-century Israel. He had a functioning physical body. He covered his body with clothing. He got hungry, tired, and sad. His true essence or glory was veiled as he remained fully God. Even though he appeared like us, he was not totally like us in that he did not have a sinful, fallen nature (1 John 3:5). He had to be human to face the problems we face, and he had to be a man to die for us. As Hebrews 2:17–18 reveals:

> For this reason he had to be made like his brothers in every way, in order that he might become a merciful and faithful high priest in service to God, and that he might make atonement for the sins of the people. Because he himself suffered when he was tempted, he is able to help those who are being tempted.

The thought of the God of the universe becoming human is indeed mind-boggling! The mighty and magnificent Sovereign of creation put aside his great position in heaven to take a body like yours or mine!

E. Exalted (v. 9)

Jesus completed his obedient earthly mission to redeem humanity from their sinful condition and ascended back to heaven. There Jesus Christ was exalted to the highest place. The word for exalted (*huperupsoo*) means "to raise to the loftiest height" (BAGD, 842). Today, we might say he was superexalted or megaexalted. Christ in humility became a man, a servant of other people, even abasing himself to wash dirty feet. Finally, he became obedient to death on a cross for the sins of humanity. Then God the Father, pleased with his service, exalted God the Son to the highest possible place in the universe. This exaltation awarded him **the name that is above every name** and provided the answer to his high priestly prayer of John 17:5. God the Son glorified God the Father while on earth. God the Father glorified God the Son following his completed work on this planet. Jesus not only resumed his former glory but received added honor as he had triumphed over sin and death.

Hebrews 2:9 states: "But we see Jesus, who was made a little lower than the angels, now crowned with glory and honor because he suffered death, so that by the grace of God he might taste death for everyone."

The exaltation of the Savior of the world is unique. We Christians can look forward to being rewarded for obedient service. The apostle Peter writes: "Humble yourselves, therefore, under God's mighty hand, that he may lift you up in due time" (1 Pet. 5:6).

It is important to recognize Jesus Christ for who he is. Jesus is God and the Savior of men and women. In the afterlife, all will both recognize and acknowledge him for who he is and what he has done—providing the only way to God by dying for our sins. Unfortunately, rejecting Christ while alive on earth will result in separation from God and eternal punishment outside of God's presence. This fate can and should be avoided by trusting in Christ as one's Savior today!

F. Work out your salvation (v. 12)

This phrase at first glance appears to contradict other Scripture which explains that salvation is a work of God by grace through faith. The word translated *work* (*katergazomai*) means to "bring about, produce, or create." A more contemporary meaning is one of bringing to completion or "to carry out the goal or carry to its ultimate conclusion." Paul was telling the Philippians to put into practice in their daily living what God had worked in them by the Spirit. They were not told to work *for* their salvation but to work *out* the salvation God had already given them. These believers were to work it out to the finish as they grew and developed their spiritual lives. As stated previously, salvation is a work of God for man in the nature of a gift (Eph. 2:8–9); the outworking of the new life in Christ requires obedience and faith from the believer. The purpose God desires for us to achieve is Christlikeness, "to be conformed to the image of his Son" (Rom. 8:29).

It is plain that salvation is not by human works. Isaiah 64:6 gives us God's viewpoint of man's righteousness outside of his Son: "All of us have become like one who is unclean, and all our righteous acts are like filthy rags." Only through Christ's righteousness in our behalf on the cross can we be righteous before God.

G. Blameless and pure (v. 15)

Being absolutely blameless and pure is impossible this side of heaven. These terms are not referring to sinless perfection but to complete, focused devotion to doing God's will. In our public and private lives, we are to live in such a way that we would be free from accusation by the people that do not follow Christ. During his earthly life Christ instructed that: I am sending you out like sheep among wolves. Therefore be shrewd as snakes and innocent as doves (Matt. 10:16).

Christians are to live so that unbelievers cannot point an accusing finger at us. Unfortunately, due to scandals and moral failures of Christian leaders, many non-Christians cannot see any genuine distinctions between their lives and ours. In our spheres of influence, we can purpose to make our friends, neighbors, and coworkers see the difference in our lives that living for Christ makes.

H. I am being poured out (v. 17)

This phrase may be referring to Paul's entire ministry or more probably to his present imprisonment, which could well end in a martyr's death. During a later imprisonment Paul uses the same thought in 2 Timothy 4:6. Both Jewish and Greek religious practice included the use of wine poured ceremonially in connection with certain sacrifices. In Old Testament sacrifices and offerings the drink offering was considered as an additional "pleasing odor" offering (Num. 15:7). We, like Paul, can rejoice even when we are being poured out as an offering to our Lord. As we serve him, we should desire to be pleasing in his sight.

VII. TEACHING OUTLINE

A. INTRODUCTION

1. Lead story: The Sandwich Board of Salvation
2. Context: In the second chapter of Philippians, Paul is attempting to repair frictional, relational damage that had occurred in this fellowship. It began when two of the women had a disagreement (Phil. 4:2–3). Evidently these strained relationships had spread throughout the church as people argued and complained (Phil. 2:14).
3. Transition: As we look into this chapter we will see Paul challenging us humbly to love others (2:1–4). Then he will use the examples of Christ (2:5–11), himself (2:12–18), Timothy (2:19–24), and Epaphroditus (2:25–30) to challenge us to walk in their shoes and love selflessly and sacrificially. Strained relationships are inevitable, but restoration is guaranteed if we follow the principles of this chapter. We are about to learn that joy comes in the midst of strained relationships through selfless, sacrificial expressions of love.

B. COMMENTARY

1. Humility toward Others Commended (vv. 1–4)
   a. Bases for unifying, humility (v. 1)
   b. Appeal for unifying, humility (v. 2)

    c. The "me first" mistake (v. 3a)

    d. The "you first" solution (vv. 3b–4)

2. Example of the Humility of Christ (vv. 5–11)

    a. His humility (vv. 5–9)

    b. His exaltation (vv. 10–11)

3. Example of the Humility of Paul (vv. 12–18)

4. Example of the Humility of Timothy (vv. 19–24)

5. Example of the Humility of Epaphroditus (vv. 25–30)

C. CONCLUSION: LETTER TO MY UNBORN CHILD

VIII. ISSUES FOR DISCUSSION

1. How are you united with Christ? What is different about your life and attitude because you are united with him?
2. How would you describe the attitude of Christ Jesus? In what way is your attitude similar to his? In what way is it different?
3. What do you learn about the nature of Jesus Christ from reading Philippians 2? What does it mean to you to say that Jesus is God in the flesh?
4. What does it mean to you to work out your own salvation? Are you doing this? How?
5. In what way do you shine forth as different from the world? Does this give you joy or sorrow? Why?

Philippians 3

Joy in Knowing Christ

I. **INTRODUCTION**
Trying to Earn Salvation

II. **COMMENTARY**
A verse-by-verse explanation of the chapter.

III. **CONCLUSION**
Two Mistakes about God

IV. **LIFE APPLICATION**
Do I Know You?
An overview of the principles and applications from the chapter.

V. **PRAYER**
Tying the chapter to life with God.

VI. **DEEPER DISCOVERIES**
Historical, geographical, and grammatical enrichment of the commentary.

VII. **TEACHING OUTLINE**
Suggested step-by-step group study of the chapter.

VIII. **ISSUES FOR DISCUSSION**
Zeroing the chapter in on daily life.

Quote

"Joy is the serious business of heaven."

C .   S .   L e w i s

Philippians

IN A NUTSHELL

In chapter 3, Paul encourages the Philippian Christians: Have no confidence in gaining merit in God's eyes through things that you do. Righteousness is found only by faith in Christ. I forsake all things just to know him and press toward the goal of spiritual maturity. Follow me, not the people who have set their minds on earthly things.

Joy in Knowing Christ

I. INTRODUCTION

Trying to Earn Salvation

A number of years ago, I was in Mexico City, visiting the central square. This huge paved square is surrounded by grand buildings on three sides. On the fourth side is a great cathedral. I saw something on that visit which, I understand, is not all that unusual but which made a deep impression on me. A peasant woman was crawling across the great square, palms and knees being gouged by the ancient stones which pave the square. After she had crawled a while, she would stop, rise to her knees, pray a while, and then begin crawling a little farther. The slow painful crawl seemed to take forever as she tried to appease God through her self-inflicted suffering.

I saw a similar sight in Guatemala. People brought gifts to the church and lay them on the altar. They knocked on the wood of the altar, trying to get God to notice them. They lit candles and poured wine as an offering, seeking to merit God's favor.

These incidents are sad examples of how far people will go to win God's favor and earn his grace. Yet we often fall into similar bondages as we try to please God. We fear that if we get irregular in our Bible reading and prayer God will punish us. Or we feel that if we don't give money to the church God will not bless us. Or we get into the performance trap in our efforts to be accepted by God. We volunteer for everything and never say no because we fear that God will not fully love and approve of us.

If you have trouble believing that God accepts you, if you have difficulty resting in the fact that God loves you, if you feel you have to do something to earn acceptance in God's eyes, then you have something in common with the woman in Mexico. You are crawling across painful, rocky, pavement, trying to earn God's favor. These performances are a terrible burden because you can never know if you have done enough to appease him.

Today, if you are struggling with your acceptance with God, then Philippians 3 will be a breath of fresh air. From this chapter you will learn that you no longer have to perform to get God's approval. Rather, you will discover that Christ appeased God through his death on the cross. You will learn that in the midst of an unbelieving society joy comes by knowing Christ and doing his will.

II. COMMENTARY

Joy of Knowing Christ

MAIN IDEA: *Righteousness cannot be gained by our works; it is found only by faith in Christ. Therefore, forsake all things just to know him and press toward the goal of spiritual maturity, keeping in view the goal of your eternal home in heaven.*

Knowing Christ Exposes False Teachers (vv. 1–3)

SUPPORTING IDEA: *Do not be fooled by false teachers who think that physical acts can make one acceptable to God.*

3:1. Paul marked a transition point in his letter with a term that can mean "finally" but often indicates something like "well, then, or furthermore." He is only halfway through his letter at this point. In spite of his difficult circumstances, Paul's relationship with Christ provided him with joy. He encourages us to **rejoice in the Lord**! This spirit or attitude of joy permeates this entire letter. Joy comes, however, only as one lives in the Lord. He is joy's only source. Paul consciously repeated himself, knowing repetition leads to learning. What he wrote was so important he wanted to make sure they did not miss his points.

3:2. As a father protects his children, Paul wanted to keep his spiritual children from harm. He warned them in strong language of opponents who would tempt them to false doctrine. The apostle employed sarcasm to describe those who had lost the true significance of circumcision. These men mutilate the flesh. They are unclean dogs, not qualified to enter into spiritual worship. They do evil. Be on the lookout. Know where such people are and what they are doing. Do not follow or imitate them.

A group of Jews in Paul's day attempted to distort the gospel by adding the requirement of circumcision plus faith in Christ as necessary for salvation (Acts 15:1). Their false way of salvation was evil as it could cause great confusion to the true message of Christ. They misunderstood the teachings of the Old Testament on circumcision and the Christian gospel of salvation by grace through faith. The Jerusalem Council repudiated their teachings and confirmed that true salvation was by faith in Christ alone (Acts 15:12–21). Yet these dedicated religious teachers persisted to follow Paul and create havoc among immature Christians with their Christ plus circumcision salvation message. They wanted to preserve the Jewish heritage at any cost. Paul confronted this group in his letter to the Galatians also.

3:3. In disagreement with the teachings of his opponents, Paul took over their claims as belonging to the church and not to the Jews. The opponents claimed to be the true Israel, circumcised in the flesh, being the truly spiritual ones, and glorying in their worship and goodness as measured by obedience to the law. Paul turned the tables. Believers in Christ are the true circumcision (Rom. 9:24–26; Gal. 6:16), having their hearts circumcised (see Lev. 26:41; Deut. 10:16; 30:6; Jer. 4:4; 9:25–26; Ezek. 44:7,9; Acts 7:51; Rom. 2:28–29).

Christians are the spiritual ones who worship properly, directed by God's Spirit rather than relying on external rituals and rules. Christians glory or take pride, but not in anything they do. Christians boast and glory only in Jesus Christ, the good, obedient One who fulfilled all the law. In summary then, Christians put **no confidence in the flesh**, neither in the ritual of circumcision nor in the practice of obeying a law. This stands radically opposed to the false teachers who said Gentiles had to be circumcised to be acceptable to God. The Philippians and modern readers must make the choice—glory in Christ or in human religious achievement! Genuine believers have their complete hope or confidence in Christ's finished work in our behalf on the cross rather than anything done by them for God or in God's name. Trusting in anyone or anything besides the true Messiah is foolishness.

B Knowing Christ Exposes Human Pride (vv. 4–11)

SUPPORTING IDEA: *Human credentials, especially in matters of faith, are only rubbish. All that matters is my relationship with Christ.*

3:4–6. If anyone had bragging rights about their status and achievement, Paul did. He had been:

1. circumcised according to the Jewish Law
2. born in the Israelite tribe of Benjamin
3. a devout Pharisee
4. faithful to the Old Testament law

His Jewish heritage and practices had been extremely important to him prior to his conversion (Acts 9:1–16), but Jesus showed him that just being Jewish did not make him righteous before God. Good works were not the means to salvation. True righteousness comes from personal faith in Christ, so Paul no longer placed his faith of winning God's merit through heritage or good works. Knowing Christ changed everything in his life.

3:7. While these credentials and accomplishments are impressive, Paul placed no "stock" or confidence in them. Jewish observers would place him at the top of the religious elite. He placed it all in the debit or loss column. Why? Nothing belonged in the profit column except Christ. His relationship with Christ is far superior to his Jewish background.

3:8. Paul emphasizes his point by restating it. The things of the world—all human accomplishments—are viewed as **rubbish** or garbage in comparison to gaining Christ. Paul's focus changed completely. No longer did personal religious ritual and obedient religious acts occupy center stage. All eyes were on Christ and on him alone. Paul wanted to know Christ.

3:9. Why such single-minded devotion to Christ? Because he is the only source of righteousness—that is, of right relationship with God. Righteousness comes as a gift from God and is by faith in Christ, the true way to God in contrast to human merit or works. Here is Paul's doctrine of salvation and philosophy of life. In regards to eternal salvation, humans deserve nothing, can achieve nothing, and have no reason for pride or self-assurance. God has done everything: created, disciplined, had grace, given his Son Jesus on the cross for our sin, raised Jesus, declared us righteous and justified, adopted us as his children, and promised us resurrection and eternal life. The only human part in all this, in faith, is to accept what God has done.

3:10–11. Demonstrating the lack of importance of earthly things, Paul expressed what life truly meant to him. He desired resurrection from the dead, so he sought the way that promised resurrection. The Damascus road experience transformed him. He discovered that Judaism with its traditions, regulations, and rituals could not guarantee resurrection. Only the resurrected One could. This changed Paul's aim in life. He wanted to **know Christ and the power of his resurrection**. To know Christ meant much more than knowing about him in his mind.

Knowledge is a relationship term of intimacy. Paul wanted the closest possible personal relationship with Christ, a relationship pictured in baptism as buried to the old life of sin and raised to a new life of righteousness. To know Christ in this way meant he was ready to share in Christ's sufferings, even if that meant sharing his death. Paul's longing to share with Christ comes through strongly in Galatians 2:20: "I have been crucified with Christ and I no longer live, but Christ lives in me. The life I live in the body, I live by faith in the Son of God, who loved me and gave himself for me." In everyday living, Paul maintained that his life and the lives of his readers should reflect the difference that Christ makes.

Knowing Christ Expresses Godly Motivation (vv. 12–16)

> **SUPPORTING IDEA:** *We have not attained completion as a Christian but press on toward maturity in Christ.*

3:12. Paul's description of his desires pointed forward to a goal. He had not "arrived." Not yet mature, he was still very much in the race of the Christian life. The perfection he would have at the future resurrection was not yet attained. He still had to deal with what in Romans 7 he calls "the flesh," an innate pull to sin. He had to deal with his sinful body and was only too aware of the need for further spiritual growth. He purposes to **press on** as he had not attained the intense personal knowledge of Christ that he desired and had not become all that Christ wanted him to be. He did not press on out of personal power or will. He did so because Jesus had chosen him and on the Damascus road grabbed hold of his life. Paul always held God up as the source of every part of the salvation experience. A fact of the Christian life is that the more you mature the more you realize how much further you have to go to become like Christ.

3:13. Paul, in this verse, underlines his denial of personal power or attainment and his single-minded focus. To describe that focus, he employs the image of a runner in a race who hopes to win the prize. He cannot look back. He cannot cloud his mind with past memories. He strains every muscle in his body to achieve forward motion. Eyes focus on the finish line. Paul forgets the guilt of persecuting the church. He forgets the pain of prison and physical punishment. He forgets the frustration of disobedient church members and false teachers. He looks ahead to see the resurrection, where he will meet Jesus face-to-face.

3:14. With this focus he pursues his goal intently. His goal is **to win the prize for which God** had called him in Christ Jesus. He wants to hear God call his name and summon him to the victory stand, where he will meet Jesus face-to-face and know him in perfect intimacy. Earthly prizes do not last. Eternal prizes do. The goal can never be realized on earth. It is a goal that pulls us heavenward. Note 1 Corinthians 9:25: "Everyone who competes in the games goes into strict training. They do it to get a crown that will not last, but we do it to get a crown that will last forever." In the late 1950s, Jim Elliot, former husband of author Elisabeth Elliot, gave up his life to reach a hostile tribe in the jungles of Ecuador. His words have been immortalized: "He is not a fool who gives up what he cannot keep to gain what he cannot lose." While Paul was not spiritually where he thought he would ultimately be, he intended not to be distracted by anything as he pursued his goal (Heb. 12:1–2). Both discipline and determination are required to accomplish this objective.

3:15. Paul believed that all spiritually **mature** Christians would agree with or would share his philosophy toward life. **Mature** translates the same Greek term as did *perfect* in verse 12. Paul pointed to a difference of opinion as to the meaning of perfection. His opponents thought they had obeyed the law and achieved perfection in this life. Paul knew he would never obtain perfection. The only persons who could claim to be part of the "perfect ones" were those who knew that running the race and seeking the goal was the only mark of perfection possible on earth. If they thought **differently**, Paul was confident God could cause them to change their minds, since Paul's human arguments could not. Paul was content to shed some light on the subject.

3:16. As followers of Christ, we are responsible to live out or put into practice what we have learned. We are not perfect, but that is no excuse not to run the race and seek the prize. God is calling us to the victory stand. We must run as hard as we can to cross the finish line.

Ⓓ Knowing Christ Exposes Reckless Living (vv. 17–21)

SUPPORTING IDEA: *Follow my example of living, not the example of those who walk after the world.*

3:17. Paul's example was Christ. He then lived out the Christ model as he ran the race. He appealed to his readers to follow his example. Some already followed that example, so they, too, serve as models for the Philippians. They had a choice. They could model their lives after those advocating falsehood and fail to win the prize or they could model their lives after Christ.

3:18. The apostle with great emotional anguish described the reality of life. Many did not follow the example of Christ or Paul. He labels such people **enemies of the cross of Christ**. The Christ way is a cross way, a suffering way. The enemies' way is a pride way, a self-achievement way, a way of present perfection. It never leads to suffering.

3:19. The enemies' way or philosophy of life has a different focus, a different goal, a different source of pride, and a different result. Paul describes these somewhat ironically, giving double meaning to his words. At the same time, he wrote against Jews who emphasized achieving perfection by obeying the laws, he also had in mind Greeks and Romans who threw off all restraints and lived very sensual lives. Their emphasis was on the physical and the material. These people were called "antinomians" (against the law) as they were against any rules or laws. They wanted to live in complete freedom of any restraints on their physical desires.

Contrary to the gospel of Christ Paul preached, the enemies focus on **their stomach** or their own physical desires rather than on God. From a Greek perspective such a focus is purely physical. Thus, in practice, their physical desires have become their god. From a Jewish perspective, the stomach represents food allowed or not allowed by Jewish food laws. Their god has become self-protection from ritual pollution, thus the preservation of their self-perceived perfection.

Their goal is earthly things. For the Greeks these are things that give prominence and pleasure in this life. For the Jew, these are rules, regulations, and rituals humans have devised on earth trying to please God in heaven.

They **glory** or take pride in **shame**. For the Greek such shame would be meaningless rituals for all their gods, rituals often involving sexual practices and prostitution. For the Jew such shame would be in their attention to the "shameful" body parts, namely their preoccupation with circumcision as a requirement for perfection with God. All such pride is misplaced, for it centers on human achievement. For Paul all glory is in Christ and what he has done (3:3). Thus Jew and Greek faced a **destiny** of **destruction**. Instead of winning the prize and participating in resurrection, they would face eternal hell.

If you have become a Christian, Satan, the evil one, has lost the battle for your soul. He seeks to distort your Christian walk with false doctrine opposed to the teachings of the Bible. In many cases, Satan uses unsaved people to tempt and lead Christians astray. They will show you a different way to the salvation Paul preached, a way that avoids the cross and satisfies the human appetite. Such a way leads to the destruction of hell. So every person faces the decision: Paul's way and resurrection or the human way and hell.

3:20. While on earth, believers in Christ are foreigners or aliens away from their true home. In stark contrast to the enemies of the cross, the Christian's **citizenship is in heaven**. Earthly goals and self-centered desires fade in importance. Mature, godly believers live in anticipation not in participation. Believers know the Lord Jesus Christ is coming back from heaven. He will fully establish the kingdom of heaven, where we have citizenship. While we wait, we participate in kingdom activities, not worldly activities.

3:21. Why look to the future rather than the present for satisfaction and joy? Because in the resurrection, Jesus has shown that he is sovereign. Everything is **under his control**. We have no reason to pamper and value the earthly body. It passes away. Jesus has another body for us, one like his resurrected body. It can take up citizenship in heaven with the resurrected Christ. The joy there is so great, we can forsake any pleasures earth might give. The apostle gives more details of this event in 1 Corinthians 15:51–54.

Our bodies get sick, hurt, desire sinful pleasures, grow old, and eventually die. Followers of Christ have the hope that life in this world is not the end. Someday, we will have a perfect body that will never die, a body like the one the Savior now has (1 John 3:2). Chapter 3 communicates the joy that Paul had in knowing Christ. Through his growing experience with the Son of God, he shared how this relationship is superior to false teaching, the pride of life and reckless living. Instead, he anticipated the day when he would be like his Savior and live forever in perfect joy with him.

MAIN IDEA REVIEW: *Righteousness cannot be gained by our works; it is found only by faith in Christ. Therefore, forsake all things, just to know him; and press toward the goal of spiritual maturity, keeping in view the goal of your eternal home in heaven.*

III. CONCLUSION

Two Mistakes about God

People make two big mistakes about God. First, they think they can go to heaven by good works. Like the woman crawling across the rough, rocky, Mexican square, they think they can earn the right to go to heaven. Most people think that they can get to heaven by believing in God and doing good things, but listen to what the Scriptures have to say about our good works:

"All of our righteous acts are like filthy rags" (Isa. 64:6).

"For it is by grace you have been saved, through faith—and this not from yourselves, it is the gift of God—not by works, so that no one can boast" (Eph. 2:8–9).

Good people do not go to heaven, because goodness is not the requirement to get into heaven. Perfection is. Like Paul in this passage, we can be a very good, religious person; but without Christ, we can never be good enough to go to heaven.

People make a second mistake about God. They think they have forever to put their faith in Christ. Mistakenly, they think they can indefinitely put off this decision. Yet for many the sands of time run out.

I read recently of a man who, while walking on the beach, found a used magic lamp washed up on the shore. When the genie answered his rub, he told him that the lamp contained but one remaining wish. The man pondered for a moment and then requested a copy of the stock page of a local newspaper, dated one year in the future. In a puff of smoke, the genie was gone, and in his place was the financial page. Excited, the man sat down to peruse the stock prices, one year in the future. As the paper fell to his lap, it turned over to the obituary column found on the back side of the stock quotes. The name on the top of the list caught his attention. It was his.

The Bible tells us that "now is the time of God's favor, now is the day of salvation" (2 Cor. 6:2). Like the man in this story, we never know when we will be listed in the obituary column. Now is the time to believe in Jesus Christ and receive him as your Savior.

PRINCIPLES

- God will never love you more, or love you less, than he does right now.
- Perfection, not goodness, is the entrance requirement to heaven.
- Being a member of a church does not make you a Christian anymore than being a Pharisee made Paul a child of God, or anymore than walking into a garage will make you a car.

- Jesus paid a debt he didn't owe because we owed a debt we couldn't pay.
- Believing in Christ cancels the debt we owe God for our sins and gives us a right relationship with him and eternal life in heaven.
- When we lean on his power (v. 10), learn from his pain (v. 10), and rest in his plan (vv. 12–14), we grow closer to Christ.
- "This life in light of eternity will be nothing more than a bad night in a cheap hotel" (Mother Teresa).

APPLICATION

- Quit trying to earn God's favor by good works.
- Thank Christ that he loved you enough to die for you.
- Put your faith in him now.
- View suffering as the opportunity to know Christ better.
- Loosen your grip on this world by giving away something to meet a need that you see.
- Close your eyes and visualize heaven. See Jesus, your loved ones, heaven's peace and beauty. Now ask God to change your priorities by this vision of your future.

IV. LIFE APPLICATION

Do I Know You?

Paul begins chapter 3 with knowing Christ as one's Savior (3:1–11). Then he talks about knowing Christ in a deep, personal, intimate way (3:12–21). Paul wanted more than just fire insurance. He wanted more than a passport to heaven. He wanted to have a satisfying, intimate relationship with Christ.

Some time back, a fellow whom I knew only by acquaintance, listed my name as a reference on his resume. I was happy to help him; but when the future employer called me and began asking me questions, all I could say was, "I don't really know." You see, I knew him, but I didn't know him personally and intimately. Paul says in verses 8–9 that he knows Christ by acquaintance. In verses 10–11, he says, "But I am not content to leave it at that. I want to know him personally and intimately."

After stating that he wants to know Christ personally and intimately, Paul mentions three things about Christ he wants to pursue, three ways to know Christ better—to lean on his power (v. 10), to learn from his pain (v. 10), and to rest in his plan (vv. 12–14). First, to lean on his power is God working in us and through us, rather than relying on our own ability. Second, to learn from his pain is to accept the comradeship we have when we suffer for him. Such suffering allows us to appreciate the pain he suffered for us on the cross.

In addition, suffering weans us from affections to this world and bonds us with the priorities and values of eternity. Finally, to rest in his plan is to pursue his will for our lives rather than our selfish ways. When we do these three things, we get to know Christ better.

Augustine once wrote of God, "Thou hast made us for thyself, and our hearts are restless until they rest in thee." A deep relationship with God, through Christ is the deepest desire locked up in the heart of every person. Focus entirely on knowing him and fulfilling his will for your life, and you will know the greatest joy in all the world.

V. PRAYER

God in heaven, I have tried to win your love for so long. I now understand that, like Paul, all my good works are just rubbish. They cannot make me right with you. I now believe in you, Jesus, and open my life to you as my Savior and Lord. I now realize that my restlessness is merely an invitation to find deep joy and satisfaction in an intimate relationship with you. Like Paul, it is my chief desire to know you and to fulfill your plan for my life. In your name, I pray. Amen.

VI. DEEPER DISCOVERIES

A. Dogs (v. 2)

Dogs (*kyon*) is employed here in a nonliteral, figurative sense. It is most often a designation for scavenger dogs. Before addressing the figurative sense, we must understand the literal role of dogs in Bible times. Dogs served as watchdogs for herds (Isa 56:10; Job 30:1) and the home (Exod. 11:7). Some were trained for hunting (Ps. 22:16–17,21). Yet, instead of companions or household pets, most dogs in the ancient world were scavengers, feeding on garbage and filth, fighting among themselves, and menacing people. To the Jew these canines were despised and unclean.

Just like stray dogs, Paul's false-teaching opponents snapped at his heels and followed him from place to place, "barking" their false doctrines. They were dangerous troublemakers. These false teachers were adding a type of legalism to the Christian gospel. They thought it was absolutely necessary for Gentile converts to Christianity to become circumcised and observe the Jewish Old Testament law. In effect, they were teaching that one must become a Jew before one could become a Christian! By calling them dogs, Paul used a term of reproach and contempt that Jews commonly used in referring to non-Jews (Gentiles). In Revelation 22:15, the apostle John uses *dogs* to refer to those excluded from the New Jerusalem who will spend a Christless eternity.

B. Mutilators of the flesh (v. 2)

Paul described his enemies as **mutilators of the flesh**. The Greek term *katatome* means "mutilation, cutting in pieces." The apostle asserts this as a play on words to denote those whose circumcision results in destruction or a false gospel.

These Jews had lost the true meaning of God's covenant with Abraham (Gen. 17:10). They made the Christian life a set of rules while neglecting the true gospel. They had so distorted the meaning of circumcision (v. 3) that it had become nothing but a useless surgery (mutilation).

Anyone who adds anything to the gospel as a requirement for salvation is a false teacher. Neither circumcision nor any other religious practice can save a person from his sins. Only faith in Jesus Christ can do that.

C. Circumcision (v. 3)

Circumcision (*peritome*) means "a cutting around." In ancient Israel, circumcision was a religious rite performed on the eighth day after a male's birth. The father or another designated person would remove the foreskin of the penis with a sharpened stone or knife.

Circumcision was commanded of Jews in the Old Testament in covenant with God as a sign of being a member of the chosen nation. M. H. Woudstra in *The Evangelical Dictionary of Biblical Theology* writes:

> The special meaning of circumcision for the people of Israel is found in Genesis 17 and occurs within the context of God's renewed covenant promise to Abraham, following the initial contractual relationship (Gen. 15). On the second occasion, God again promised lands and offspring to the still childless patriarch and gave him the sign of circumcision, which was to be imposed upon Abraham and his descendants as a token of covenant membership (Gen. 17:10). For the Israelites, circumcision was a religious rite and was intended to mark the beginning of covenant solidarity for Abraham's descendants rather than describing the historical origins of the procedure (ed. Walter A. Elwell, Grand Rapids: Baker Book House, 1984, 98).

Merrill F. Unger adds:

> Circumcision was formally enacted as a legal institute by Moses (Lev. 12:3; John 7:22–23) and was made to apply not only to one's own children but also to slaves, home-born or purchased and to foreigners before they could partake of the passover or become Jewish citizens (Exod. 12:48). As spiritual purity was demanded of the chosen people of God, circumcision became the external token of the covenant between God and his people. It secured to the one subjected to it all the rights of the covenant, participation in all its mate-

rial and spiritual benefits while, on the other hand, he was bound to fulfill all the covenant obligations (*Unger's Bible Dictionary*, Chicago: Moody Press, 1966, 206).

In the church age, physical circumcision is not a requirement for entrance into a relationship with God (1 Cor. 7:17–19). Faith, not circumcision, was the basis of God's covenant with Abraham (Rom. 9:9–12). Circumcision of the heart, that is a spirit of trust and obedience, is what God desires (Rom. 2:29).

In Philippians 3:3, Paul is emphasizing that the true circumcision is a changed heart, not a changed body (Deut. 10:16; Jer. 4:4). Believers in Christ are said to be circumcised in him (Col. 2:11).

D. Pharisee (v. 5)

Judaism in New Testament times was diverse, including Pharisees, Sadducees, Herodians, Zealots, and Essenes. Pharisee comes from the Semitic word *pharisaioi* meaning "the separated ones, separatists." These laymen— not priests—came from the middle class and were primarily businessmen, merchants, and tradesmen. They were exacting interpreters of Old Testament law and strongly committed to strict adherence to it. They controlled the synagogues and exercised great control over the general population. They built up a body of oral tradition designed to adapt the ancient precepts of the written law to the changing situations of later days and thus safeguard their principles against being dismissed as obsolete or impracticable. In this way they were distinguished from their chief rivals, the Sadducees, who maintained the authority of the written law alone, rejected the Pharisees' belief in the resurrection of the dead, and in the existence of orders of angels and demons (see Acts 23:8). They banded together in local fellowships.

Josephus, who claims to have regulated his own life by Pharisaic rule from the age of nineteen, reckons that there were some six thousand Pharisees in his day (*Ant.* 17.42). The Pharisees were particularly scrupulous in observing the Jewish food laws and the rules about tithing. They tithed garden herbs as well as grain, wine, and olives (Matt. 23:23; Luke 11:42) and avoided eating food that was subject to tithing unless they were sure that the tithe had been paid on it.

D. A. Hagner explains:

> Even more pernicious than the teaching of the Pharisees, however, was the gap between their profession and their practice. Their over-concern with externals led almost naturally to a neglect not only of the weightier parts of the law, but also of the inner man and matters of the heart. The resultant hypocrisy Jesus described in the words of Isaiah (29:13 in Mark 7:6f.), about a people who honor the Lord with their lips while their hearts are far from him. In fact, the Pharisees were intent upon cleansing the outside of the cup and plate whereas the

inside remained dirty (Matt. 23:25–26); they were like whitewashed tombs, disguising an inner corruption (23:27–28). Some of this may well have been the inevitable product of the Pharisaic legalism. What was not inevitable, however, was the pride of which the Pharisees were simultaneously guilty. Their motive in holding to their observances was a wrong one. 'They do all their deeds to be seen by men,' said Jesus (23:5). They loved the special honor that was paid to them as men who were reputedly serious about their godliness (23:6–36), but their pride was totally without foundation. The truth was, as Jesus summarized it, "they preach, but do not practice" (23:3).

Pharisaic opposition to Jesus is a persistent theme in the Gospels. They opposed Jesus because he refused to accept the teaching of the oral traditions. Not only were they ardent opponents of Jesus, but of the early Jewish Christians. Yet, all Pharisees are not condemned in the Scriptures. Nicodemus was genuinely a seeker of truth (John 3:1–21), spoke out for justice on behalf of Jesus (7:50), and remained a follower of Jesus even after the disciples had fallen away (19:39). Joseph of Arimathea (Mark 15:43) was probably a Pharisee who did not agree with the decision to crucify Jesus (Luke 23:51). Fearing the Jews, he became a secret disciple of Jesus (John 19:38) and took care of Jesus' body after the crucifixion. Many other Pharisees may well have believed in Jesus secretly (*The Zondervan Pictorial Encyclopedia of the Bible*, ed. Merrill Tenny, Grand Rapids: Zondervan, 1975, 4:750–1).

E. Resurrection from the dead (v. 11)

Not only did the Lord Jesus Christ rise from the dead, but someday all men will be resurrected (see 1 Cor. 15). All humanity has a corporate destiny before God (Acts 24:15). The Bible clearly promises resurrection of the believer. Isaiah 26:19 and Daniel 12:2 give the clearest Old Testament statements about resurrection (compare Pss. 17:15; 49:15; 73:24–25).

Paul's teaching on resurrection stood over against the Sadducees, who, holding only the books of Moses as authoritative, refused to believe in resurrection. It also opposed the Greek idea of immortality that thought a part of every human would never die. Paul, using Jesus' resurrection as his model (Rom. 8:11; 1 Cor. 15:12–14; Col. 1:18), saw resurrection as a transformation of the present body, a body that in its entirety faced death and decay (Rom. 8:22–23; 1 Cor. 15:44; Phil. 3:20–21). Resurrection is a miraculous victory over death, not a natural escape of the soul from death. It changes a physical body that dies into a spiritual one that lives forever.

Both believers and unbelievers will experience resurrection (Acts 24:14–15; compare Matt. 16:27; 25:1–46; Mark 13; Acts 17:31; Rom. 2:5; 2 Cor. 5:10; Heb. 9:27), one group finding eternal blessed life with God in heaven, the other eternal separation from God in hell. Scholars debate whether both groups will appear at one judgment or whether the wicked will be judged at a later time than the righteous (see Rev. 20:4–6,11–15).

In Philippians 3:11, Paul is looking for the imminent return of Christ. He wants to be sure that he joins the righteous in the resurrection that brings the Christian hope to reality. He knows this will be the case only as he exercises faith in Christ and rejects faith in any human accomplishments. Thus Paul keeps the goal in focus. He is not expressing doubt about his salvation but giving testimony to his own determination to stay with Christ despite his opponent's fervent demands to add rituals and rules to faith. Assurance of the resurrection gave perfect reason to reject the opponents and adhere to faith in Christ alone.

F. Made perfect (v. 12)

Teleioo, **made perfect,** conveys the idea of "bring to an end, bring to its goal or to accomplish." It can imply, "becoming mature or having reached its end." It does not refer to sinless perfection; rather it connotes completeness, like the maturity of an adult compared with that of a child.

Our English word *perfect* has the idea of flawless or sinless. Absolute perfection or sinlessness, a reality in heaven, is never achieved in this life on earth. In the lives of obedient Christians, the Holy Spirit conforms them more and more into the image of Christ. One day God will bring believers into absolute spiritual maturity. Until that wonderful day occurs, life in this world will be a challenge.

G. Prize (v. 14)

Without doubt, Paul had in mind the prize or trophy that one wins in an athletic contest. Yet, instead of an earthly prize, he was eyeing a heavenly one. Paul is mentally projecting himself forward to the time when both living and dead will meet the Lord in the air and triumphantly proceed to heaven (1 Thess. 4:13–18). Until that day he will not have fully attained his goals, being still confined to a body which he describes as "this body of death" (Rom. 7:24)—still plagued with physical suffering and the advancing limitations of age. These are all part of the race as far as Paul is concerned, but like a runner his prime interest is in attaining the prize and finishing the race.

VII. TEACHING OUTLINE

A. INTRODUCTION

1. Lead story: Trying to Earn Salvation
2. Context: In the third chapter of Philippians we learn that joy (v. 1) is found in knowing Christ. After exposing the false teachers (vv. 1–3) and

the human pride that keeps people from a personal relationship with Christ (vv. 4–11), we are challenged to have as our number one motivation, the desire to know Christ, personally and deeply. Finally, Paul cautions us to avoid reckless living that can sabotage this godly pursuit.

3. Transition: From this chapter, we learn that knowing Christ and pursuing his plan for our lives is the source of all joy, happiness, and peace. You will learn to avoid the distractions of religiosity and carnality in this vital pursuit. So experience joy as you pursue Christ and his plan for your life!

B. COMMENTARY
1. Knowing Christ Exposes False Teachers (vv. 1–3)
2. Knowing Christ Exposes Human Pride (vv. 4–11)
3. Knowing Christ Expresses Godly Motivation (vv. 12–16).
4. Knowing Christ Exposes Reckless Living (vv. 17–21)

C. CONCLUSION: DO I KNOW YOU?

VIII. ISSUES FOR DISCUSSION

1. What false teachings tempt members of your church? Why? How does your church deal with false teachings? With false teachers?
2. What fleshly qualifications do you have that tempt you to put confidence in them? Have you considered them "a loss" for Christ? What changes has this brought into your life?
3. What is righteousness? How do you become righteous before God? Does God consider you righteous right now?
4. What goal are you absolutely determined to accomplish in life? How does this compare to the goal towards which Paul pressed forward?
5. Who is following your example as a Christian? Where is that example leading them? Can you recommend that someone follow your example? Why or why not?

Philippians 4

Peace in the Midst of Trouble

Quote

"Most Christians are being crucified on a cross between two thieves: yesterday's regret and tomorrow's worries."

Warren Wiersbe

Philippians

IN A NUTSHELL

In chapter 4, Paul charges the Philippian Christians: Do not worry about the future, but pray about your concerns. Only think about good things, and God will give you peace. Even though I have learned to be content with little, I am grateful for your gift to me, and I am happy that God will bless you for it. God will take care of you.

Peace in the Midst of Trouble

I. INTRODUCTION

The Parable of Death

Death was walking toward a man who stopped him and asked, "What are you going to do?" Death said, "I'm going to kill ten thousand people." The man said, "That's horrible!" Death said, "That's the way it is; that is what I do."

As the day passed, the man warned everyone he could of Death's plan. At the end of the day, he met Death again. He said, "You said you were going to kill ten thousand people, and yet one hundred thousand people died." Death explained, "I only killed ten thousand. Worry and fear killed the others."

Worry is one of the biggest problems we face in life, and it tends to get worse as we get older. Its destruction is sure. Charles Mayo of the Mayo Clinic in Rochester, Minnesota, said, "Worry affects the circulation, the heart, the glands, the whole nervous system, and profoundly affects the health." Corrie Ten Boom knew the destructive force of worry when she said, "Worry does not empty tomorrow of its sorrow; it empties today of its strength." Its destruction starts like a little trickle through the mind and cuts out a furrow until it becomes a Grand Canyon and all other thoughts drain into it.

Do you ever engage in imaginary, "what if" thinking? Do you ever blow things up in your mind by jumping to a conclusion or making a mountain out of a molehill? Have you ever looked at a dilemma and imagined the worse-case scenario? If you engage in any of these draining, negative mind games, then you need to know that God's plan for you is peace and joy not worry. His plan for you is rest not stress, peace not turmoil.

In this final lesson from Philippians, you will learn how to keep worry from robbing you of your joy. You will discover how to have peace and joy in your relationships with God and others.

II. COMMENTARY

Peace in the Midst of Trouble

MAIN IDEA: *Believers are to rejoice always, not to worry but to pray, and to keep our minds fixed on good thoughts. As you do, you will experience God's peace, knowing that God will bless your generosity.*

Ⓐ Joy in Friendship (v. 1)

> **SUPPORTING IDEA:** *Friends standing fast in the Lord bring joy to other Christians.*

4:1. Again Paul demonstrates his love and friendship for the church at Philippi. He addresses them as **my brothers** and **dear friends,** that is, as equals under God not as a superior church authority to subordinate members. In this most personal of his writings, Paul expressed his fond affection and the pain of separation by telling them that he both loves and longs for them. They are his **joy and crown** because their growth in the Christian life makes him proud. He points back to everything he has written in the previous three chapters as the reason to maintain a firm foundation in the Lord. He points forward to the following verses to show how to **stand firm.** He remains ever concerned with believers' spiritual lives. Deeper spirituality can come but only by heeding the rapid-fire list of imperatives Paul is about to throw at us.

Ⓑ Joy in Unity (vv. 2–3)

> **SUPPORTING IDEA:** *Be at peace, and help one another.*

4:2. Paul addressed a specific situation in the Philippian church, a quarrel between two Christian sisters—**Euodia** and **Syntyche.** This discord may be why he wrote what he did in Philippians 2:1–4. Although he believed their conflict would negatively affect the entire church, Paul did not reveal the nature of their problem or take sides. He did appeal tactfully for unity by asking them **to agree with each other in the Lord. To agree** is a strong Pauline word which NIV translates with several different English equivalents (*phronein,* 1:7; 2:2,5; 3:15,[16 KJV],19; 4:2,10; compare Rom. 8:5; 11:20; 12:3,16; 14:6; 15:5; 1 Cor. 13:11; 2 Cor. 13:11; Gal. 5:10; Col. 3:2; 1 Tim. 6:17). The word basically means "to think, form an opinion," or "to set one's mind on something." It came to mean to be in agreement, to live in harmony. This is the picture of the Christian church standing firm in Christ.

4:3. Paul asked a specific member of the congregation to **help these women.** Despite numerous guesses, no one knows who the **loyal yokefellow** was. Some even think Paul referred to the entire church. At least he set a precedent for church disputes to be settled by mediation within the church. Paul uses strong, urgent language to insist that the church get the problem solved and get back to the Christian position of standing firm "in one spirit, contending as one man for the faith of the gospel" (1:27; compare 2:2–4). Disagreements even among mature Christians are not new. Mature Christians do not allow these disagreements to interfere with love and unity in the body of Christ.

Quarreling is not the nature of the church nor was it of the women involved. They had fought alongside Paul like gladiators in the arena to spread the gospel message. God had written their names in heaven's registry of citizens alongside all the others to whom he promised eternal life. Paul sets the women on an equal level with others whom the Philippian church knew as faithful soldiers of the cross. Paul names one specifically—Clement. We know nothing else about him. The third bishop of Rome was named Clement, but we have no evidence to connect the two persons.

Ⓒ Joy in God's Peace (vv. 4–9)

SUPPORTING IDEA: *Rejoice in the Lord, pray in all things, and keep your mind on positive thoughts, and as you do, God's peace will be yours.*

4:4. Again Paul returns to the key theme of this letter: joy. He calls believers to **rejoice** at all times and repeats the call for emphasis. This includes the bad times as well as the good (compare Jas. 1:2–5). Christians should be known as joyful people. Such joy resides not in circumstances or positive attitudes toward life. Joy reigns in the heart only when Christ is Lord of life. Joy is always **in the Lord.**

4:5. A practical way to have joy is by exhibiting **gentleness** to all. This lets the church and world see that you belong to the Lord. The Greek word *epieikeus* means "yielding, gentle, kind." It includes the ability to go beyond the letter of the law in treating others, to provide something beside strict justice. It does not insist on personal rights or privileges. Christ embodied such gentleness in his dealing with all people (2 Cor. 10:1; compare 1 Tim. 3:3; Titus 3:2; Jas. 3:17; 1 Pet. 2:18). Why should we surrender personal rights for others? **The Lord is near.** In both time and space, God is available to us. He is not far removed in heaven but present in our hearts to hear and relate to us. His nearness also means he knows us and what we are. In time, God is near, for he is coming again. Then we will receive our rewards for living like Christ rather than like the world.

4:6. Joy replaces anxiety in life, so Paul advises the Philippians not to be **anxious about anything.** The cure for anxiety? Prayer! Worry and anxiety come from focusing on your circumstances such as imprisonment or persecution which Paul and the Philippians faced. Anxiety or worry doesn't accomplish anything, but prayer does (Jas. 5:16). Jesus warned against worry which demonstrates a lack of trust in God (Matt. 6:25–34).

4:7. **The peace of God** comes from prayer involving both asking God for earthly needs and thanking God for his presence and provision. The expression appears only here in the New Testament. God's peace reflects the divine character, which lives in serenity, totally separate from all anxiety and worry. Such peace is like a squad of Roman soldiers standing guard and protecting you from worry and fret. Such peace is not a dream of the human mind. The human mind cannot even comprehend this kind of peace, wholeness, and quiet confidence. Such peace protects the two organs of worry—**heart** and **mind that** produce feelings and thoughts. Such protection is real, available in Christ Jesus. Those who do not trust and commit their life to Christ have no hope for peace.

4:8. Continuing his strong imperative style, Paul suggested what should occupy our minds rather than anxiety and worry. Paul understood the influence of one's thoughts on one's life. Right thinking is the first step toward righteous living. What is right thinking? It is thinking devoted to life's higher goods and virtues. Thus Paul picked up a practice from secular writers of his day and listed a catalog of virtues that should occupy the mind. Such virtues are not limited to the Christian community but are recognized even by pagan cultures.

True is that which corresponds to reality. Anxiety comes when false ideas and unreal circumstances occupy the mind instead of truth. Ultimately, thinking on the truth is thinking on Jesus, who is the truth (John 14:6; Eph. 4:21). **Noble** refers to lofty, majestic, awesome things, things that lift the mind above the world's dirt and scandal. **Right** refers to that which is fair to all parties involved, that which fulfills all obligations and debts. Thinking right thoughts steers one away from quarrels and dissensions to think of the needs and rights of the other party. **Pure** casts its net of meaning over all of life from sexual acts to noble thoughts to moral and ritual readiness for worship. Thinking on the pure leads one away from sin and shame and toward God and worship. **Lovely** is a rare word referring to things that attract, please, and win other people's admiration and affection. Such thoughts bring people together in peace rather than separating them in fighting and feuding. **Admirable** is something worthy of praise or approval, that which deserves a good reputation. Pondering ways to protect one's moral and spiritual image in the community leads away from worries about circumstances and possessions that project a different image to the community and which thinking cannot change.

The catalog of virtues Paul sums up in two words: **excellent** and **praiseworthy.** The first encompasses what is best in every area of life, the philosophical good for which every person should strive. Here it is especially the ethical best a person can achieve. The second term refers to that which deserves human praise. The catalog of virtues thus reflects the best life a person can live and the best reputation a person can thereby achieve in the community.

Finally, in this verse, Paul gets to his point: think on these things. That, joined with prayer will relieve all anxieties and lead one to praise God and live life the way he desires.

4:9. Is such noble thinking possible. Paul says, "Yes, it is. Look at my example." This is not braggadocio or pride. It is the state every Christian should live in, a state of being an example for all who observe you. The example includes Paul's teaching, the tradition he received from the apostles and passed on, his reputation for Christian living, and the Christian lifestyle they saw him practice. If they obey Paul, God will bless them with his peace (see v. 7; John 14:27; 16:33).

Joy in Contentment (vv. 10–13)

SUPPORTING IDEA: *Expressions of love from fellow believers enrourage us, but contentment comes not from physical circumstances but from relying on divine strength.*

4:10. Paul shows his attitude of gratitude by expressing joy over their gifts which Epaphroditus had delivered to him (Phil. 2:25), gifts which continued a long history of the Philippian church's supporting Paul (see 4:16; 2 Cor. 11:8–9). The gifts provided a problem for Paul. He consistently refused to accept payment for his ministerial work, not wanting to burden the churches (1 Cor. 4:8–13; 9:1–18; 2 Cor. 11:7–10; 1 Thess. 2:5–12; 2 Thess. 3:7–12). Thus he never used the term *thank you* as he wrote the Philippians, and he delayed using the term *gift* until verses 17–18. He concentrated instead on the attitude of the Philippians and the relationship the gift represented. He used a unique verb to express the freshness of their **concern** for him, saying it had blossomed afresh like a flower in springtime.

Why the Philippians had a time when they could not show concern for Paul we do not know. Perhaps it had to do with the distance to his Roman imprisonment, the lack of opportunity to send messengers that far, or some problems in the Philippian church. Paul cast all that away as past history. The emotion of the moment was joy at renewed relationship and renewed expression of care for one in trouble (see v. 14).

4:11. Paul makes clear that he was not hinting for another gift. He has solved his economic problems. How? Not with new resources but with a new attitude. He is **content** no matter what his circumstances. What is such contentment? It is a term apparently taken over from Stoic philosophers describing an inner spirit of freedom and discipline, the ability to conquer circumstances and situations rather than be conquered by them. Such an attitude is the exact opposite of worry and anxiety.

4:12–13. Paul spoke from experience. He had been through the extremes: surplus and poverty. He knew how to weather the dangers of both. This was his secret. Greek and Roman religions had secret initiation rites. Some religions and philosophies prided themselves on secret knowledge. Paul had a different kind of secret. His secret was his reliance on Christ, a reliance gained through his Christian experience. Stoics relied on personal will to gain contentment. Paul did not claim such personal inner strength. His strength came from Jesus living in him. Paul was in Christ and thus content no matter what his circumstances.

J. Vernon McGee writes:

> Whatever Christ has for you to do, He will supply the power. Whatever gift He gives you, He will give the power to exercise that gift. A gift is a manifestation of the Spirit of God in the life of the believer. As long as you function in Christ, you will have power. He certainly does not mean that he is putting into your hand unlimited power to do anything you want to do. Rather, He will give you the enablement to do all things in the context of His will for you (McGee, *Thru the Bible*, V:327–8).

The Christian life is not only difficult; it is also impossible unless we acquire the power to live it through Christ. To be sure, this truth does not come naturally to us but must be learned.

E Joy in Christ's Provision (vv. 14–20)

SUPPORTING IDEA: *Give what others need, and you will find that God will supply all your needs.*

4:14. Sometimes the Lord works through his redeemed people to meet human needs. Contentment did not do away with troubled circumstances. Paul knew operating from a Roman jail cell, chained to a Roman soldier, was not operating from a position of power. He was in trouble. The present Epaphroditus brought from Philippi helped. Paul wants the Philippians to know this and to know how commendable he considered their loving action to be.

4:15. The Philippians' gift was not unexpected. They had treated Paul this way before in the early days of his ministry in Europe (Acts 16:12–40). Paul described their relationship with him at that time in technical accounting terms. No other church entered into a financial partnership with him. In a sense, the Philippian letter is Paul's official receipt, acknowledging and giving credit for the church's gift to him.

4:16. Paul went directly from Philippi to Thessalonica (Acts 16:12–17:1). Though we have no record of them, there the Philippians began sending him gifts (compare 2 Cor. 8:1–9). Thus Paul acknowledges the depth and length of his relationship with the Philippian church. He also acknowledged that he had need even when he learned to be content.

4:17. Again the apostle reveals that the motive for his thankfulness of their partnership in his ministry was not to secure another gift. His letter was not a fund-raising attempt. He wanted them to realize that their deeds would not go unnoticed. God is marking them down in the credit column of the heavenly ledger. They have a deposit in heaven that will yield rich dividends. (See Jesus' words in Matt. 6:19–21.)

4:18. Paul finds another way to show he is not writing to ask for another gift. He retains his accounting vocabulary. The letter he sends with Epaphroditus is his receipt marked "paid in full" and more. His storehouse is full. His needs were met through the Philippians' gifts. These good deeds not only satisfied Paul but were **a fragrant offering, an acceptable sacrifice, pleasing to God.** Giving to God's servant for God's work is a gift to God, a first-class offering (compare Rom. 12:1; Heb. 13:16).

4:19. Their obedience and generosity will bring God's reward. This is Paul's promise to the Philippians, according to the NIV. However, other translators follow different manuscript evidence or interpret the Greek tense differently and read this as Paul's prayer that God may fulfill all their needs. Either reading gives encouragement and expectation to the readers. As they met all of Paul's needs (v. 16), so God will meet all their needs. God does this out of the abundance of his treasury, a glorious resource without limits. How does one draw from these unlimited resources? Through Christ Jesus. Only those in him have access to God's account and can ask him to meet their needs.

4:20. Paul concluded the body of the letter with a doxology praising God. The thought of God's providing our needs in Christ naturally led to praise and thanksgiving. The God of glory and honor is not far removed from us, however. He remains **our . . . Father** ready to bring love and resources to meet our needs. Thus, glory belongs to him forever—into the unseen ages.

▉ Conclusion (vv. 21–23)

> **SUPPORTING IDEA:** *Believers seek fellowship with one another and wish the best for one another in Christ Jesus.*

4:21. Final greetings with a benediction of grace are a regular feature of Paul's letters. He concludes this letter by sending his greetings and the greetings of the Christians with him in Rome. **The saints** are all the members of the Philippian church set aside to serve God. They are saints not because of holy lives they live but because they are in Christ Jesus, the source of holiness and thus of sainthood.

4:22. Caesar's household does not necessarily mean the blood relatives of the Roman emperor. Probably, Paul was referring to those employed by the emperor, perhaps including the Roman guards that had become believers, possibly as a result of Paul's confinement.

4:23. The realization of this benediction would hopefully increase the harmony of the church by causing each believer to cherish **the grace of the**

Lord Jesus Christ and bring a joyous peace among them. This fulfilled Paul's opening statement in Philippians 1:2.

> **MAIN IDEA REVIEW:** *Believers are to rejoice always, not to worry but to pray, and to keep our minds fixed on good thoughts. As you do, you will experience God's peace, knowing that God will bless your generosity.*

III. CONCLUSION

Painting Peace

A number of years ago a very rich man wanted a painting that would portray peace. He commissioned three artists to paint peaceful scenarios. After a month the artists returned with their paintings completed. Each painting was placed in the foyer, covered by a veil, waiting the moment of revelation.

The first artist unveiled his painting of a beautiful mountain scene. The mountains were covered with green aspens and spring flowers. The snow-capped, majestic peaks rose up to meet a blue, cloudless sky. The rich man said, "I like it. This mountain scene is indeed peaceful."

Then the second artist removed the cloth veil draped over his masterpiece. His painting was of a beautiful ocean view. The sand was crystal white. The sea was blue and tranquil. The sun was slowly setting in the sky as its reflection danced across the placid sea. In the center of the picture were two people relaxing in lawn chairs at sea's edge, their feet dangling in the water. The rich man was delighted. He said, "I love the beach. I love this. What a splendid portrayal of peace."

The third artist reluctantly pulled the veil from his painting, and the rich man looked with puzzlement. This artist had painted a waterfall scene. In this scene a raging river is falling hundreds of feet, crashing on the rocks below. The rich man said, "How is this peaceful? I've stood beside a waterfall, and it's anything but peaceful. The sound of the water is deafening. All I see is turbulence. Where is the peace?"

Then, the third artist said, "Look closer, sir. Notice I painted the waterfall from the side. Look closely under the fall, behind the water, and you'll see a cleft in the rock. Do you see it?"

Leaning forward, the rich man replied, "Yes, I see it, and I also see a bird perched in that cleft. The artist responded, "That's it, sir! That's the peace! In the midst of the noisy turbulence, the bird has found a peaceful place. That, my friend is real peace; the ability to find peace in the midst of troubled chaos."

The point of this powerful story is the point of Philippians. Very seldom do we in the midst of stressful relationships and undaunting demands get to escape to the peaceful mountains or tranquil sea. Like the waterfall scene, most of life is lived in the middle of noise, rushing activity, turbulence, chaos, with things crashing down all around us. This realistic painting of peace brings good news. In the midst of the trouble, Jesus is the cleft in the rock. We can find peace in him. He is the shelter in the midst of the storm.

Peace is not the absence of trouble. It is not circumstantial bliss or "life without a hitch." Rather, peace is the presence of Christ in our lives. When we come to Christ in the midst of troubling relationships and dilemmas, we find both the "peace of God" (v. 7) as well as "the God of peace (v. 9).

Jesus said, "Come to me, all you who are weary and burdened, and I will give you rest" (Matt. 11:28). Peter comparably said, "Cast all your anxiety on him because he cares for you" (1 Pet. 5:7). As you perch in the cleft of the rock, as you abide in Christ, may you, in the midst of chaos and worry, enjoy "the peace of God, which transcends all understanding " (Phil. 4:7). Always remember, joy comes in the midst of worry and stress through the person and peace of Christ!

PRINCIPLES

- Worry is the toxic waste of unbelief.
- All worry is atheism, because it is a want of trust in God (Bishop Fulton Sheen).
- Tomorrow is the result of today's thoughts.
- Happiness is the by-product of bringing happiness to others.
- Happiness is not something you go out and get; it's something you go out and give.
- Your attitude toward money is an EKG revealing the spiritual condition of your heart.
- God will meet your needs (4:19), if you will meet the needs of others (4:14–18).

APPLICATION

- Reconcile your strained or broken relationships.
- Trust God with your greatest worry.
- Limit sensual stimulation by controlling the TV habit.
- Pull up any weeds that you have let grow in the garden of your mind.
- Begin to lay up treasure in heaven by giving freely to build God's kingdom.
- Start finding your contentment, not in material things, but in Christ.
- Share with a friend what God has taught you from this chapter concerning joy.

IV. LIFE APPLICATION

Pete Maravich and Spiritual EKG

Since the giving of money is a great source of joy and happiness, it comes as no surprise that Paul ends his letter (4:10–23) talking about money. While many people in America would be willing to sacrifice the misery of others to gain their own happiness, the Bible teaches a different definition of happiness. Paul contends that joy and happiness are the by-products of what Christians give, not what they receive. Joy and happiness are not something you receive when you go out and get. Rather, they are what you get when you go out and give. Zealously, he argues that joy and happiness are not something you get through financial acquisition. To the contrary, you can only gain joy and happiness through financial contribution. Hoarders worry about their money, while givers experience great peace and contentment in Christ (v. 13).

Some years ago, unexpectedly, Pete Maravich, one of the greatest college basketball players ever to play the game, dropped dead from a heart attack. He still holds the record for the most points scored by a college player. He had a marvelous ten-year professional career in the National Basketball Association. The sad thing about his death was that a simple EKG could have revealed his congenital heart problem and saved his life.

Paul teaches in this chapter that your attitude toward money is an EKG. It will give you an accurate readout of the state of your spiritual heart. Your attitude toward money, Paul teaches, will tell you more about your spiritual life than any other factor in your life. Your attitude toward money is an EKG that will tell you:

1. the depth of your concern for the cause of Christ (v. 10)
2. the source of your contentment (vv. 11–13)
3. the wisdom of your investments (vv. 14–17)
4. the sincerity of your worship (v. 18)
5. the quality of your faith (v. 19)

With each financial contribution we make toward God's kingdom and the cause of Christ, we credit our account in heaven (v. 17). In a sense, all I really have is what I give away. A rich tycoon died and went to heaven. Saint Peter led him on a tour. As they passed a beautiful mansion, he asked Peter, "Is this my place?"

Peter said, "No, that is your maid's place."

The rich man exclaimed, "My maid's place! Wow, I can't wait to see what I get." Walking on, they came upon a really huge mansion, bigger than the White House. The tycoon said, "Then, is that my place?"

"No, that's for your gardener," Peter said.

"My gardener lives here!" the man shouted. "Then my place has got to be incredible."

As they went down another street, they came upon a little shanty. Peter said, "Welcome home. This is your place." Alarmed, the tycoon snorted, "My place? What are you talking about? I was worth five hundred times what the maid and gardener were worth.

Peter replied, "I'm sorry, but we did the best we could with what you sent us."

V. PRAYER

Dear God, the struggles of life constantly rob me of peace. Too often, I fret and worry. Too often, I feel the stress and strain of anxiety. You are the God of peace, so I ask for grace to live peacefully with others. Remind me to pray in faith and not to worry in unbelief. Empower me to think pure and holy thoughts. Teach me the peace of generosity. For it's in the name of the Prince of peace that I pray. Amen.

VI. DEEPER DISCOVERIES

A. Stand firm (v. 1)

The key phrase in 4:1 is that a Christian—to win the battle against Satan and the world—must **stand firm** *in the Lord.* Again, this thrust reminds us of Paul's final words to the Ephesian Christians. He wrote, "Finally, be strong *in the Lord* and in *his* mighty power" (Eph. 6:10). No Christian will ever win the race purely in his own strength and through human effort. Philippians 4:1, then, is a summary statement—a concise reminder of the strategy Paul had already clearly presented and illustrated. This verse is also introductory—a transitional statement to prepare the Philippians for some final thoughts and exhortations.

B. Yokefellow (v. 3)

This word (*syzugos*), meaning "true comrade or companion," is found in the New Testament only here. It is made up of a word referring to an ox yoke and a preposition meaning "with." Some consider the word to be a proper name, while others believe it was a reference to a particularly well-trusted associate of Paul. Opinion varies as to whom Paul referred. Possibilities include Epaphroditus, Lydia, Timothy, Luke, Barnabas, or Silas. Some have speculated that Paul had a wife who was his "yokefellow." Apparently the Philippians knew whom he meant, but we are left to guess.

C. Peace of God (v. 7)

In the world of turmoil in which we live, the peace of God is an attractive concept. Yet it is not always understood. We sometimes fight images in our mind of angels slouching on couches, listlessly picking at a harp, trying, after a million years, to think of a new tune. To English-speakers, peace generates images of war being finished. For us, peace is an absence of conflict either internal or external. The biblical idea of peace is much broader, however.

Old Testament Hebrew speaks of *shalom*, completeness, wholeness, living well. It may refer to wellness of body (health) or a right relationship between two people or parties. The New Testament parallel term is *eirene*, a term not so broad in meaning as *shalom* but often carrying Hebrew overtones in the New Testament contexts.

The peace of God means we are no longer enemies with God. Through the blood of Christ on the cross, God removed the enmity our sin caused with him. He did even more. He provided inner peace and personal fullness. Such peace with God allows us to know that present circumstances may be troublesome, but God will bring all things to his perfect completion in the end. That gives us a hope that produces calmness and stability, qualities only God can give. Peace with God is thus an inner calm derived from knowing God will cause everything to work together for good in our lives. This gift of peace follows our faith and settles over our lives. It gives us a satisfaction and richness we could know in no other way. Peace with God can be ours if and only if we believe and depend on the promises of God.

D. Macedonia (v. 15)

Macedonia includes the northern-most part of modern Greece and southern sections of present-day Bulgaria and the former Yugoslavia. It became a Roman province in 146 B.C. In Paul's day it was a senatorial province with Thessalonica as its capital. Other major cities included Amphipolis, Apollonia, Berea, Neapolis, and Philippi. Its geography consisted of high mountains, broad rivers, and fertile valleys. The region contained rich farmland, timber, deposits of gold and silver, and good harbors. The general language of Macedonia was Greek, while the official language of the Roman colony was Latin. The gospel came to Macedonia through Paul (Acts 16:9–12).

E. Thessalonica (v. 16)

Thessalonica was the capital city of the province of Macedonia. It was situated on the great road, Via Egnatia, whose five hundred miles of pavement connected Rome with the entire region north of the Aegean Sea. It was an important city for the spread of the gospel. Paul first visited and founded a church there on his second missionary journey after his ministry in Philippi (Acts 17:1–4). His initial letter to this church, First Thessalonians, believed to have been written around A.D. 51, is considered among the earliest New Testament books.

F. Riches in Christ (v. 19)

The Bible consistently and repeatedly portrays God and God alone as the Creator of all that exists. It insists that he creates and distributes all wealth. Several verses from Psalms draw the consequences of God's wealth: "I have no need of a bull from your stall or of goats from your pens, for every animal of the forest is mine, and the cattle on a thousand hills" (Ps. 50:9–10). Today, we would say that he needs no American Express card from us as he owns it all.

J. Dwight Pentecost pens:

> God can meet the multitude of needs of an infinite number of His children because He is infinite in the riches of His glory. A man who has limited funds will find those funds depleted as he gives to different causes; but if a man has unlimited funds, he can give without limit, and there will be no depletion of his supply. Since God is infinite in glory, God can give to an unlimited number of needs and still have an infinite supply left. When God gives to His obedient children, He gives according to His infinite riches in glory (*The Joy of Living,* Grand Rapids: Zondervan, 1973, 244).

VII. TEACHING OUTLINE

A. INTRODUCTION

1. Lead story: The Parable of Death
2. Context: Having told us how to have joy in adversity (chap. 1), joy in relationships (chap. 2), and joy in knowing Christ (chap. 3), Paul now tells us how to have joy in God's peace (chap. 4). We desperately need peace because worry constantly threatens to rob us of both peace and joy. Warren Wiersbe has said: "Most Christians are being crucified on a cross between two thieves: yesterday's regrets and tomorrow's worries."
3. Transition: While worry is one of the biggest problems we face, peace and joy are to be the lot of the Christian. Thus in chapter 4, Paul will tell us how to have peace in the midst of troubling relationships (4:1–5), troubling thoughts (4:6–9), and troubling finances (4:10–23). Listen while Paul teaches you to have peace in a troubling world. Apply what you are about to learn, and you will experience a "transfusion" of joy. For joy comes in the midst of worry and strife through the person and peace of Christ.

B. COMMENTARY
1. Joy in Friendship (v. 1)
2. Joy in Unity (vv. 2–3)
3. Joy in God's peace (vv. 4–9)
4. Joy in Financial Contentment (vv. 10–13)
5. Joy in Christ's Provision (vv. 14–20)
6. Conclusion (vv. 21–23)

C. CONCLUSION: PETE MARAVICH AND SPIRITUAL EKG

VIII. ISSUES FOR DISCUSSION

1. How do you think Paul would define *Christian joy?* How do you know that you are experiencing such joy in your life? Can you do anything to gain such joy? If so, what?
2. What would Paul tell you to do to be sure you are standing firm in the Lord?
3. What would you do if two faithful workers in your church suddenly began quarreling with one another?
4. What thoughts occupy your mind most of the time? How do these compare with the type of thoughts Paul recommended?
5. Are the ministers in your church facing any kind of financial difficulty? How can the church help them?

Colossians 1

The Truth about the Gospel and Christ

"It is not until a man finds his faith opposed and attacked that he really begins to think out the implications of that faith. It is not until the Church is confronted with some dangerous heresy that she begins to realize the riches and the wonder of orthodoxy."

William Barclay

LETTER PROFILE

- Possibly the first of Paul's prison epistles.
- The church at Colosse was not founded or visited by Paul but probably founded by Epaphras.
- Philemon and Onesimus were from Colosse.
- The letter was written to encourage a group of believers who were growing spiritually.
- The letter was written to warn a group of believers who were being confronted with false teaching which undermined the supremacy and sufficiency of Jesus.
- Very similar in style and vocabulary to Ephesians.

CITY PROFILE—COLOSSE

- Located one hundred miles east of Ephesus.
- Together with Hierapolis and Laodicea, Colosse was part of a tri-city area in the Lychus valley in what is now south central Turkey.
- Once an important city, by the time of Paul, Colosse had become a small market town.
- The population was a mixture of Jews and Gentiles (11,000 Jews by A.D. 62).
- The cities of the Lychus valley were prosperous despite frequent earthquakes.
- Manufacturing and exporting wool products were the principal industries.

AUTHOR PROFILE—PAUL

- Jewish-born in Tarsus, near the Lebanese border in modern Turkey.
- Roman citizen.
- Prominent, highly educated Jewish religious leader (Pharisee).
- Dramatically converted to Christianity, A.D. 35.
- Primary apostle to the Gentiles, tireless missionary.
- Imprisoned in Rome, A.D. 67, during Nero's reign.
- Died in prison, A.D. 68.

Colossians

I N   A   N U T S H E L L

In chapter 1, Paul tells the Colossian believers: Hello, Colossians. Timothy and I are pleased to hear from Epaphras that the gospel which is growing all over the world is bearing fruit in your lives as well. Because of this, we constantly pray that you stay focused on God's will so that your lives will be pleasing to him. Remember that Jesus, our Creator and Reconciler, deserves absolute supremacy in absolutely everything. I endure suffering and hard work on behalf of Jesus and his church to bring believers to maturity.

The Truth about the Gospel and Christ

I. INTRODUCTION

The Siren Song of Heresy

*T*he seductive allure of the counterfeit has confounded men throughout the ages. Homer, in his mythological tale *The Odyssey* personified the perils of deception in the story of the Sirens—mythological half-woman, half-bird creatures who lived on an island in the Mediterranean Sea. Their beautiful, melodious songs were so enchanting that passing sailors strayed from their charted course and crashed their ships on the rocky shoreline. The short-lived appeal of the Sirens' song quickly gave way to the horrible reality of a painful death as the creatures came down from the rocks and devoured the flesh of the shipwrecked sailors.

Two men overcame the powerful enticement of the Sirens but in very different ways.

Ulysses, warned of the fatal effect of the Sirens' song, remained fascinated with the prospect of hearing the beautiful sounds with his own ears. Understanding the human frailties of his crew and himself, Ulysses plugged the sailors' ears with beeswax and then had himself lashed to the ship's mast. As the ship sailed past the Sirens' rocky home, the sailors were unaffected by the sweet-sounding songs while Ulysses was physically restrained from acting on the desires that stirred within him.

Orpheus, a musician of legendary renown, took a different approach to escape the Sirens' snare. When the Argonauts sailed into the treacherous waters surrounding the deadly isle, Orpheus began to play and sing. The exquisite beauty of Orpheus's music was so genuine and compelling that the Sirens no longer held any appeal for the crew.

False teaching is much like the Sirens. It is purposely made to sound sweet. It's enticing. It's alluring. It's deceptive. And it's terribly dangerous. Whose lead should we follow as we navigate our way through the straights of deception—Ulysses or Orpheus?

From a prison cell in the year A.D. 60, a man who wore both the mantle of an apostle and the shackles of a prisoner wrote a letter to a group of believers he had never met. Paul wrote the Colossians the truth so they would not be the victims of false teaching.

While Paul was in prison, Epaphras, one of his most faithful coworkers, visited him and brought him a report on the congregation at Colosse. In many ways the report was good, and for this Paul was thankful (1:3–8). As we read the letter carefully, we detect a sharp note of alarm and concern as well. This letter is written as a piercing rebuttal to the alluring enticements of theological and practical heresy. The heresy running rampant in Colosse attacked and undermined the identity and sufficiency of Jesus the Christ. Paul set the record straight.

How do we overcome the siren song of heresy? Do we plug our ears like the crew of Ulysses? Orpheus shows us a better way. We should be so captivated by the sweet sounds of the truth that the siren song of heresy is easily ignored. That's what Paul does in Colossians 1.

II. COMMENTARY

The Truth about the Gospel and Christ

MAIN IDEA: *Knowing the truth about the power of the gospel and the person of Christ is the believer's best protection against deception.*

A Greeting (vv. 1–2)

SUPPORTING IDEA: *God's grace and peace in a person's life come from knowing the power of the gospel.*

1:1. Paul, the author of the letter to the Colossians, identifies himself as an apostle, one who is sent as a commissioned and empowered representative. Paul is not an apostle because of personal ambition: his title came to him by the will of God. Paul mentions Timothy, his loyal companion.

1:2. Paul's letter is written to a group of believers in Colosse. Paul gives them a threefold identification. First, he calls them holy. This means the Colossian believers, in fact all believers, are "set apart" by and for God. Next, Paul refers to the Colossian believers as faithful. As he does later in the letter, Paul commends the Colossians for their steadfast commitment to the gospel. Finally, Paul says the Colossians are brothers. They are one spiritual family despite differences in background, race, or any other purely human considerations.

Paul's greeting of grace and peace was the standard way of saying "hello" to other believers in the first century. Paul's desire is that the Colossians come to appreciate and appropriate these two blessings which are good gifts from God.

🅱 The Truth about the Gospel (vv. 3–8)

SUPPORTING IDEA: *The gospel message bears fruit in believers and grows all over the world.*

1:3. As Paul begins his letter to the believers at Colosse, he does not immediately take on the false teachers and their teachings. First, he tells the truth about the gospel and its positive effects in the lives of the Colossians.

The gospel should do for us what it did for the Colossians. The gospel of Jesus Christ, like a seed, is a dynamic force that shatters the hard, stony soil of sin and takes root as new life. By complimenting the Colossians on how the gospel had taken root and grown in them, as it has in all the world (v. 6), Paul encouraged them to remain faithful to the message of truth they heard and not be seduced into error by the alluring lies of the false teachers (see "Deeper Discoveries").

Paul assured the Colossians that when he prayed for them his prayers took the form of thanksgiving. Paul will tell them why in verses 4–8.

1:4. Just like a harvest of ripe apples or a rich cluster of grapes is evidence of life in the seeds from which they sprang, so the seed of the gospel bears fruit—a cluster of virtues—that proves there is spiritual life.

Paul lists these virtues in verses 4–5. He points out three fundamental traits of Christian character that ought to be evident in the life of those in whom the gospel seed has taken root: **faith**, **love**, and **hope**. These virtues should be increasingly evident in our lives if the seed is doing what it is designed to do. Faith begins the process.

Paul is initially thankful for the saving **faith** of the Colossian believers. Contrary to the belief of some, faith is not "believing what you know ain't so." Faith is not a blind jump into the dark. In biblical vocabulary, *to believe*, is a strong word. Faith is being persuaded or convinced that something is true and trusting it with your life. This faith is **in Jesus Christ.**

Faith is only the beginning. Faith in Jesus Christ should produce inclusive **love** for others in the faith. The false teachers at Colosse were telling the Colossians that the fruit or evidence of spirituality was keeping rules, being initiated into secret knowledge, or having ecstatic experiences. Paul counters this by saying that the real fruit of faith is love.

Paul tells us in Galatians 5:6, "For in Christ Jesus neither circumcision nor uncircumcision has any value. The only thing that counts is faith expressing itself through love." The love that faith in Christ produces possesses a unique quality. It's inclusive, and it's nonselective. We don't pick and choose whom we love: Paul specifically says that it is love **for all the saints.** It's easy to love the lovely or those who love you. Genuine Christianity is evident when we love the undeserving the same way God has loved us. Love is not a feeling; it is an attitude and an action. Love is sincerely wishing for another person's best interest and taking whatever action is necessary to see that it is accomplished.

1:5. The next fruit Paul mentions is **hope**. What is hope? Again, contrary to the belief of some, hope is not "wishing for something you know won't happen." Biblical *hope*, like biblical faith, is a strong word. Hope is looking forward with eager anticipation and strong confidence to the sure promises of God. Paul also says that our hope is secure because it is **stored up for [us] in heaven**. Our hope is safe and secure, locked away in heaven far above anything that may threaten its integrity. This confident expectation is what motivates us to be able to love inclusively and nonselectively. Paul tells us that faith and love **spring from the hope**.

Paul then reminds us of the source of this rich bounty of fruit in the lives of believers. The source is **the word of truth, the gospel**. The message of the gospel is **truth**. Paul emphasizes the truth aspect of the gospel by mentioning it twice in this passage (vv. 5–6).

This truth is good news. The term **gospel** means "good news" or "good message." The good news is that Jesus Christ has solved the problem of sin through his death, burial, and resurrection (1 Cor. 15:3–4). This message of truth and good news bears fruit in the lives of believers and should not be abandoned for the alluring lies of false teaching.

1:6. The gospel bears fruit not only in the lives of individual believers but **all over the world**. Paul wanted the Colossians to understand that the gospel is not just another mystery religion isolated in the Lychus Valley and Asia Minor. These Colossians were part of a grand movement of God because the message they had believed and embraced was the seed of truth that was springing up with rich fruit all over the world. It's just as true today as it was in A.D. 60. As Eugene Peterson translates this verse, "[The message] doesn't diminish or weaken over time. It's the same all over the world" (*The Message*, Colorado Springs: NavPress, 1993).

The gospel message is not just true and good; it's also a message of **grace**. *Grace* means "unmerited favor or undeserved kindness." Mercy is when God doesn't give us what we do deserve. Grace is God giving us what we don't deserve. He gives us heaven when we deserve hell; he grants us forgiveness when we deserve to be forgotten; he offers us life when we deserve death. It's all grace. None of the good things we receive from God are earned. Salvation didn't come to the Colossians because of their attachment to a complicated series of intermediate spirit emanations, or their adherence to a set of demanding rituals, or their adventures into the realm of ascetic experience. Those were the experiences the false teachers said were necessary to be truly saved and spiritual. Paul says, "No, it's just grace." Jesus died for us, and he offers us life. That truth, when adequately understood, takes root in our heart and bears fruit.

1:7–8. The gospel seed, which bears fruit in individual believers and grows all over the world, must be planted. God's plan is that those who have received the seed are to plant the seed. That was the case for the Colossians. The gospel came to them when they **learned it from Epaphras.** The most significant day in the history of Colosse was not the day Xerxes rested in the city on his march against Greece, nor was it the day Cyrus marched his Greek army through the city. No, the most significant day in the history of Colosse was the day Epaphras came to town and planted the seed of the gospel. No banners unfurled in the wind, nor did trumpets blare in the breeze; but lives were changed and destinies were eternally altered when the gospel was planted.

Epaphras came to Paul in prison with a good report on the spiritual progress of the Colossian believers. Part of that report was their **love in the Spirit,** which refers to the love that is produced by the enabling of the Holy Spirit (Gal. 5:22).

The Truth about Pleasing God (vv. 9–14)

> **SUPPORTING IDEA:** *God is pleased when believers grow in knowledge and character and when they express gratitude for their salvation.*

1:9. Paul's letter to the Colossians began with a prayer of thanksgiving. That prayer, based on the good report of Epaphras, reminded the Colossian believers of the power of the gospel so they would not be seduced by the siren song of heresy. The theme of prayer continues in verses 9–14, but the focus shifts from thanksgiving to intercession. Paul prays that the believers will live lives that are pleasing to God. Does it take deep knowledge, strict living, or a rapturous experience to please God? That's what the false teachers were telling the Colossians. We, like the Colossians, need to know the truth about what pleases God so we won't be enchanted by error.

Paul tells us why he prays and what he prays for. When Paul says **for this reason,** he is looking back to the good report he received from Epaphras. Paul prays for believers who are doing well. He asks that they continue in the process of growth. The focus of much prayer is on those who are struggling and not doing well. While those are good prayers, Paul reminds us of the need to pray for those who are doing well since they are prime targets for enemy attacks. Many of our prayers ask for immediate relief from circumstantial or personal difficulties. While some of these prayers are good, Paul wants us to include prayers for spiritual growth and long-term development.

Paul's prayer is that God fill believers **with the knowledge of his will.** Paul wants the Colossians to know God's will and then let that knowledge control them. God's will is not a spiritual Easter egg he hides from us. No, God wants us to know **his will** and so clearly reveals that will in his Word. A mere knowledge of God's Word is not what will please him. We need to be controlled by that knowledge. The word **fill** means to control. To be filled with something (an emotion like fear or jealousy) means to be under its controlling influence that causes us to do things we might not do otherwise. Being controlled by God's will should cause us to do things we might not otherwise do—things like enduring rather than giving up, like being patient with others rather than getting angry with them.

The knowledge and control of God's will comes **through all spiritual wisdom and understanding**. This is more than simple intelligence. **Wisdom** refers to the comprehension of truth, while **understanding** refers to the application of truth. Being controlled by God's will means believers comprehend the principles of Scripture and then put them into practice.

1:10. Being controlled by God's will is not an end in itself; it is only a means to an end. The goal is to **live a life worthy of the Lord and . . . please him in every way.** The request of verse 9 was made so that the Colossians would live lives which please God. The word **worthy** refers to conduct that is expected and appropriate for God's children.

If pleasing God is the goal, how do we achieve it? Paul spells that out very clearly in verses 10–12. By bearing fruit, growing in knowledge, being strengthened for adversity, and giving thanks for salvation, we please God.

First, believers please God when they are **bearing fruit in every good work.** Good works are not a means to achieve salvation, but a natural result of it. Good works in the life of the believer please God because good works are God's plan for the believer (Eph. 2:8–10).

Second, God is pleased when believers are **growing in the knowledge of God.** The more we know of God's character, his ways, and his expectations, the more we are able to bring our lives into conformity with what pleases him.

1:11. Third, our lives please God when they are characterized by **endurance and patience.** Life is often difficult and challenging. At times, circumstances are less than friendly. At those times we need **endurance**—the ability to pass through any experience and trust God to see us through. At times, people are less than friendly. At those times we need **patience**—the capacity to be long-suffering with people and not retaliate when we are wronged or irritated.

We all know from experience, however, that staying steadfast through the circumstances and being patient with people is tough stuff. It's often beyond our ability. Right! The good news is that we aren't left alone with only our own resources to meet the challenge. Paul reminds us that God's power is available. Believers can please God with endurance and patience as they are **strengthened with all power according to his glorious might.** It is proper for a Christian to ask God to strengthen him to do God's will. God will do this. Sometimes it is immediate, and other times it is gradual, similar to the way a person is strengthened over time physically. As we yield ourselves to God in trust and obedience, we will be strengthened to do his will.

1:12. Finally, believers please God when they are **joyfully giving thanks to the Father** for the blessings of salvation. Just as Paul was clear to spell out specific means to please God, he is equally clear about the blessings of salvation for which we are to give thanks. This time we are given a list of three: God qualified us, rescued us (v. 13), and brought us into a new kingdom (v. 13).

God, the Father, has **qualified** believers for sharing in the blessings of salvation. We don't qualify ourselves by our moral achievements or personal worthiness. In grace, God qualifies us when we trust Christ as the atoning sacrifice for our sin. That this salvation is ours by grace is seen in our participation in the **inheritance**. We don't earn an inheritance. We receive it.

1:13. Being qualified is only one reason to be thankful. He has **rescued us from the dominion of darkness.** God delivered us from the ruling power of darkness, and the good news doesn't end there. God has also taken a positive step: he has **brought us into the kingdom of the Son he loves.** God has transferred us; he has moved us from one place to another. He has taken us from Satan's dark realm and placed us into the bright light of Jesus' kingdom.

1:14. God's work of salvation, for which believers are joyfully to give thanks, is pictured further with **redemption** and **forgiveness.** To redeem someone means "to buy them back and set them free." Jesus' death was the price paid to buy us back and set us free from sin. Because of Christ's death on our behalf, we are set free from both the penalty and the power of sin.

Forgiveness parallels redemption. *Forgive* literally means "to send away, to cancel." Through the death of Jesus, God has canceled the debt of our sin. It was a debt we could never repay; but since Jesus paid the debt for us, God has forgiven the debt.

Paul wants us to know the truth about pleasing God so that we won't be victims of the well-disguised lies of those who might lead us astray.

𝔻 The Truth about Jesus (vv. 15–23)

SUPPORTING IDEA: *Jesus is the visible manifestation of God and our eternal Creator and Reconciler, who has supremacy in the universe and the church.*

1:15. When Paul wrote to the Colossians, he was countering a clever company of false teachers who sought to replace the Colossians' enthusiastic devotion to Christ with only a mild approval of him. They didn't encourage anyone to forget Jesus altogether; they just said he wasn't the only show in town. According to these false teachers, Jesus got equal billing with a vast number of emanating spirits flowing out of God. They said Jesus could be prominent, but he certainly wasn't preeminent. In contrast, Paul—along with telling believers the truth about the gospel and pleasing God—tells us the truth about Jesus.

Jesus is the **image** of God. The word for *image* was used in Paul's time for likenesses placed on coins, portraits, and for statues. It carries the idea of correspondence to the original. It is the nearest equivalent in ancient Greek to our modern photograph. Jesus is the perfect representation of God. This verse and others (John 1:18; 1 Tim. 1:17) tell us that God is **invisible.** J. B. Phillips translates verse 15, "Christ is the visible expression of the invisible God." Hebrews 1:3 tells us that the Son is the radiance of God's glory and the exact representation of his being.

Not only is Jesus the perfect picture of God, but he also holds the highest rank in the universe. Jesus is **the firstborn over all creation. Firstborn** is a term of rank more than it is a word of time (see Ps. 89:27). The right of the firstborn was the right of privilege and priority. It was the honored position in the family. In the case of the patriarchs, we know that the honored position didn't always go to the first son born in time. Jesus is the firstborn—the highest rank—in all of creation.

1:16. Jesus holds the highest rank in creation because he is the Creator of **all** things. There is nothing in the created order that Jesus did not create (see also John 1:3). Because he is the Creator, Jesus has absolute supremacy over all creation, including any spirit beings who were being worshiped by the local heretics. Since only God can be the Creator, this means that Jesus, the perfect image of God, is even more than an image. He is divine. He is God.

1:17. Jesus is eternally existent (an attribute that can only be true of God) because he is **before all things.** Jesus is also the powerful sustainer of the universe. Because of him all things **hold together.** His power guarantees that the universe is under control and not chaotic.

1:18. Jesus is sovereign over creation. He is also sovereign over the **church,** the new creation. Jesus is sovereign over the church because he is the **head.** While scholars debate whether **head** should be understood as "origin" or "authority," both are certainly true of Jesus in relationship to the church. Jesus began his church, and HE is its source of life and vitality. Jesus is also sovereign over his church. The church takes its direction from Jesus and is under his authority. While both concepts are true, the context of supremacy certainly lends itself to the idea of authority.

The church is the **body** of believers who owe their allegiance to Jesus. The position of supremacy in everything (and particularly the church) belongs to Jesus because of his resurrection and work of reconciliation. He is the **firstborn from among the dead.** Again, **firstborn** here has nothing to do with time. Others preceded Jesus in rising from the dead. Lazarus is one example (John 11:38–44). Jesus is first in rank. Others were raised only to die again. Jesus was the first person to rise, never to die again. He is the first person to conquer death, and all other resurrections are based on his.

The glorious truth for us is this: because of his resurrection, we are assured of our own resurrection (1 Cor. 15:20–23).

1:19–20. Jesus has supremacy over all things because all of God's **fullness** resides in Jesus: He is the full embodiment of God's attributes and saving grace. Through Jesus, God is able to **reconcile to himself all things.** Reconciliation is the removal of hostility and the restoring of friendly relations to parties who have been at war. Paul also calls reconciliation **making peace through his blood, shed on the cross.** What God has done is to move toward us to restore harmony, patch things up, cease hostilities, bury the hatchet, smoke the peace pipe, and heal the breach.

1:21–22. This concept of reconciliation is not just a universal theory; it is a personal truth. Jesus' death allows God's enemy to become God's friend. Before the miracle of reconciliation, the Colossians, and all unbelievers, were at odds with God. We were **alienated,** that is we were separated, estranged. We were alone, an outsider, exiled, shut out, cut off, locked out. Ephesians 2:11–12 gives us another sad perspective on our estranged position before reconciliation.

Paul then tells us we were once God's **enemies** in two ways. First, we were **enemies in [our] minds.** Our thoughts and our attitudes were hostile to God. Before we trusted Christ, our entire way of thinking was contrary to God's. For us, and for those who have yet to be reconciled, the problem was and is simple. We refused to accept God's evaluation of us as being sinners. We would also not accept God's remedy for the situation—dependance on Christ.

Second, we were enemies in [our deeds], **because of [our] evil behavior.** It's not just that we thought wrong; we also acted wrong. Despite our active opposition to God, he **reconciled** us through the **death** of Jesus. Jesus died for a race of rebels to offer them a chance to become his allies.

The outcome of this reconciliation is present peace and a future presentation of ourselves before God. The slate of sin has been wiped clean, and we look forward to the day we will stand before God **holy in his sight, without blemish and free from accusation.**

1:23. The if of verse 23 should not be misunderstood. This verse is not saying that we will be presented holy and blameless if we remain faithful, as if our eternal salvation depends on our performance. The Greek construction of the **if** is not an expression of doubt but an expression of confidence and is better translated as since. Paul is not in doubt about whether the Colossians will remain faithful (see Col. 2:5). He is confident that because they have understood what it means to be reconciled they will remain faithful to the gospel that reconciled them. He writes this as an expression of confidence and as a warning to avoid the religious fads of the false teachers of Colosse.

⟦E⟧ The Truth about Ministry (vv. 24–29)

SUPPORTING IDEA: *Ministry is the hard work of bringing all believers to maturity in Christ.*

1:24–25. In his effort to keep believers from falling prey to the seductive sounds of false teaching, Paul tells us the truth about authentic ministry. It involves suffering. It's aim is maturity. It's hard work.

It is not surprising to find Paul talking about suffering for the sake of the gospel since he knew suffering "up close and personal." He wrote the letter to the Colossians from prison. He wasn't there because prison was a great place for Paul to work through writer's block. He wasn't there because he found it such a pleasant place. Paul had encountered suffering. Yet Paul was able to **rejoice** in what he suffered. Why? Because he suffered on behalf of others and because his suffering allowed him to identify with Jesus Christ. When Paul says he is filling up **what is still lacking in regard to Christ's afflictions,** he isn't saying that Jesus' suffering on the cross was insufficient. Paul was enduring suffering on behalf of Christ. The world hated Jesus Christ; and now that he is not around to persecute, they persecute his followers (see John 15:18–21). Paul's attitude is Jesus took the blows meant for me; I'll take the blows meant for him. Suffering brings about an identification with the Savior that nothing else can (see Phil. 3:10).

Paul endured his sufferings **for the sake of the body.** Paul was willing to suffer on behalf of the church because he saw himself as the church's **servant.** God gave him a **commission** to proclaim the gospel, and suffering was included with the commission.

1:26–27. Paul calls the message he was responsible to announce a **mystery.** The word **mystery** should not evoke images of Agatha Christie or Sherlock Holmes. The term really means secret. It is something that was **kept hidden for ages and generations** but is **now disclosed to the saints.** What's the secret? That God has chosen to include the **Gentiles** in the blessings of salvation (see Eph. 3:1–6). What's the secret? Jesus Christ is the secret. He opens the door to everyone. The unprecedented secret is that all are included. The unprecedented truth is that Jesus Christ lives in all who trust him. Not only does he live in us; he is our **hope of glory.**

1:28–29. Authentic ministry isn't just about suffering. It's also hard work. Paul makes this clear by calling his work **labor** (to work to the point of exhaustion) and **struggling** (literally, agonizing). The good news is that this hard work is motivated and enabled by God's **energy, which so powerfully works in [us].**

Paul tells us his objective or aim in enduring the suffering and hard work—to **present everyone perfect [mature] in Christ.** The goal of spiritual experience is not to chase the fads or jump on every new religious band-wagon. The goal is spiritual maturity. By reminding believers of this simple truth, Paul hopes to help us avoid the enticing sounds that might lead us away from maturity and into deception.

MAIN IDEA REVIEW: *Knowing the truth about the power of the gospel and the person of Christ is the believer's best protection against deception.*

III. CONCLUSION

Countering the Counterfeit with Truth

Counterfeits are dangerous because they can look so much like the genu-ine article. The casual observer sees no obvious difference between real and imitation. For example, a counterfeiter prints bills that look enough like real money that the victim accepts them at face value when, in fact, they are worthless. False teaching is pretty much the same way.

How can we learn to recognize deception when it is intentionally cloaked in the appearance of truth? Here is how that problem is handled in the bank-ing industry. Bank tellers attend a training class to learn how to identify coun-terfeit money. During the entire course of training they never study a counterfeit bill. Instead, they spend all their time studying the genuine arti-cle. They learn to recognize the texture of the paper, the colors of the ink, the clarity of the images, and the design of the bill. When they finish their train-ing, the tellers have such an intimate knowledge of authentic currency that counterfeits are obvious by comparison.

We can learn to recognize false teaching in much the same way. If we devote ourselves to studying the genuine article, the truth of Scripture, then we don't need to know the particulars of every heresy we encounter. An inti-mate knowledge of the Word of God is the only defense we need against all the different deceptions in our world.

The truth about the gospel and Christ is that the gospel changes lives all over the world and Christ has supremacy over all of creation.

PRINCIPLES

- The gospel is a dynamic force which grows in individuals all over the world.
- Believers who are doing well need our prayers.
- Pleasing God is possible only when his will is the controlling influence in our lives.

- Jesus has the right of absolute supremacy since he created us and reconciled us.
- Believers should expect suffering.
- Increasing spiritual maturity ought to be the aim of every believer.

APPLICATIONS

Thank God for the blessings of his salvation:
- Sunday—Grace
- Monday—Rescue
- Tuesday—Inheritance
- Wednesday—Redemption
- Thursday—Forgiveness
- Friday—Reconciliation
- Saturday—Hope

Honestly ask yourself, "Does Jesus have absolute supremacy in my life?"

Determine to be so saturated with God's truth that you won't be tantalized by religious error.

IV. LIFE APPLICATION

Mild Approval of Jesus?

In *The Joyful Christian*, C. S. Lewis writes, "We may note in passing that [Jesus] was never regarded as a mere moral teacher. He did not produce that effect on any of the people who actually met Him. He produced mainly three effects: Hatred - Terror - Adoration. There was no trace of people expressing mild approval" (New York: Macmillan Publishing Co., 1977, 72, 74).

Mild approval. Mild approval is what you give to a book you just read, a film you just watched, or a restaurant you visited recently. Mild approval is good, to be sure, but mild approval is not a "rave review." It's nothing to get really excited about. It's casual. It's restrained.

It's impossible to give Jesus Christ mild approval when you understand him. Jesus Christ can be ignored or adored, but you can't give him mild approval. Jesus is our Creator, our Redeemer, and our Judge. You can't be casual about that.

Paul tells us in Colossians 1 that Jesus has the right of absolute supremacy because of who he is and what he has done. Absolute supremacy. That means first place in everything. That means Jesus deserves preeminence and not mere prominence in our lives. As believers we must always be on guard against allowing anything to occupy the place in our lives which only Jesus deserves.

We must also be on guard against the more subtle danger of allowing Jesus a place of equal standing along with the other things that clutter our lives.

Often it's the good things that nudge Jesus aside. Ministry and religious activity can take the place of utmost importance. Our children can occupy the top spot. Our dates or our mates can be idolized. Acquisition of stuff or achievement and status can become the things for which we live. None of these are bad in themselves, but if Jesus stands in line behind or beside them, we're just giving Jesus mild approval.

Jesus is the image of the invisible God, the eternal Creator and powerful Sustainer of the universe. Jesus is our Redeemer whose death rescued us from the domain of darkness and transferred us into the kingdom of light. We may ignore him. We should adore him. But mild approval? Never!

V. PRAYER

Gracious Father, we are grateful for the continuing work of the gospel in our lives. May the truth of that good news provoke in us faith, hope, and love, protect us from deception, and provide for us a focus on Christ as supreme and sufficient for all our needs. Amen.

VI. DEEPER DISCOVERIES

A. The Colossian Heresy

The letter to the Colossians was written to warn believers against the seductive and dangerous presence of doctrinal heresy. On that scholars agree. However, they do not agree on the precise nature of the heresy. Some argue for a teaching of a specific, identifiable group. (J. B. Lightfoot suggests it is a radical form of Essene thought; F. F. Bruce implies it was possibly Merkabah Mysticism; while many believe it to be an early form of Gnosticism.) Others argue that the Colossian heresy is religious syncretism, a kind of blending together of several elements, a sort of hodgepodge of heresy. Still others understand the heresy to be the reflection of the cultural milieu of the area without any specific focus. In this view the general culture would have threatened to distract the Colossian believers from the centrality of Christ in their faith (see P. T. O'Brien, Word Biblical Commentary).

Whether the error Paul warned believers against was a specific system, a hodgepodge, or simply the reflection of a non-Christian culture, we can look at the letter and ascertain the elements of error. In some of his other books like Galatians and 1 Corinthians, Paul sets forth the teachings of the heresy. In Colossians, however, he simply offers a rebuttal to the heresy. In so doing he provides enough information for us to deduce the basic teachings of the heresy. At its core the heresy undermined the supremacy and sufficiency of

Jesus Christ. Heretics told believers they needed something more than their relationship with Jesus to bring them to genuine spiritual experience. What were the elements of the error?

1. Background: Philosophical Dualism. One of the central notions of Gnosticism was that all of reality could be divided into the categories of spirit and matter. Spirit was good, and matter was evil. This notion led to the belief that God could not have created the world since it was matter and matter was evil. Therefore, a series of intermediary spirit beings emanating out of God was postulated, each one being less God than the one preceding. This notion of dualism also spawned the idea of rigid self-denial. If matter was evil, then matter was to be avoided. Heretical teachers forbid people to marry and ordered them to abstain from certain foods (see 1 Tim. 4:3a).

The first flaw with this idea is that matter is not evil. God created all food to be received with thanksgiving by those who believe and who know the truth. Everything God created is good; nothing is to be rejected if it is received with thanksgiving (1 Tim. 4:3b–4). Jesus created everything, including spirit beings: **For by him all things were created: things in heaven and on earth, visible and invisible, whether thrones or powers or rulers or authorities; all things were created by him and for him** (Col. 1:16). The error of denying the full deity of Jesus is confronted in Colossians 1:15: **He is the image of the invisible God.** And in Colossians 2:9: **For in Christ all the fullness of the Deity lives in bodily form.**

In addition to this philosophical basis for the heresy, the heresy asserted that Christ was not sufficient for salvation; to be complete, a person needed more rules, more knowledge, and more experience.

2. More rules: Legalistic ritualism. Paul claims rigid self-denial looks good but has no true spiritual power: **Since you died with Christ to the basic principles of this world, why, as though you still belonged to it, do you submit to its rules: "Do not handle! Do not taste! Do not touch!"? These are all destined to perish with use, because they are based on human commands and teachings. Such regulations indeed have an appearance of wisdom, with their self-imposed worship, their false humility and their harsh treatment of the body, but they lack any value in restraining sensual indulgence** (Col. 2:20–23). A second ritualistic element of the heresy probably had Jewish origins, similar to the problem Paul faced with Judaizers in Galatians. Judaizers taught that salvation or spirituality were the result of strict adherence to a code of rituals or rules. Paul replied: **Therefore do not let anyone judge you by what you eat or drink, or with regard to a religious festival, a New Moon celebration or a Sabbath day. These are a shadow of the things that were to come; the reality, however, is found in Christ** (Col. 2:16–17).

3. More knowledge: Secret hierarchicalism. Gnosticism also thought true spiritual experience was obtained by a "higher" or "secret" knowledge. Not

everyone had this special knowledge. Only the initiated—those who had acquired this knowledge by legalism or experiences (see below)—were complete. This teaching established a hierarchy of those who were "in" and those who were "out." Paul met this error head on: **in [Christ] are hidden all the treasures of wisdom and knowledge. I tell you this so that no one may deceive you by fine-sounding arguments** (Col. 2:3–4); **see to it that no one takes you captive through hollow and deceptive philosophy, which depends on human tradition and the basic principles of this world rather than on Christ** (Col. 2:8).

In Christ (the full manifestation of God) we find all the wisdom and knowledge we ever need. We possess such knowledge as we get to know him and allow his Word to take up comfortable residence in our lives. We don't need more knowledge. We just need to know Christ more. We don't need knowledge of more. We need more knowledge of Christ. The path of growth, centered on knowing Christ, is available to all believers (2:19).

4. More experiences: Ascetic mysticism. The teachings Paul attacked included a focus on experience that led them to **false humility and the worship of angels** (2:18). These experiences were based in visions of **what he has seen** as well as **idle notions**(2:18). Such visions took the focus off of Christ and led to a focus on experiences. This threatened to move the Colossian believers to a place where they would lose **connection with the head** (2:19) who is Christ. The false teaching claimed that fullness could not be found in Christ alone. Paul is quite clear in stating that Jesus is the fullness of God and we have fullness in him (2:9). Jesus is God and nothing less, so cancel the quest for something more.

B. Apostle (v. 1)

Paul begins this correspondence, as he does many of his letters, by describing himself as **an apostle of Christ Jesus.** Paul had no personal contact with this particular church (2:1). Except for here and Rome, he wrote as founder of the other churches. One of his associates, Epaphras, was the church planter sent to Colosse (1:7). Paul's connection to and authority over the church was based solely on his role as an apostle.

What does it mean to be an apostle? A popular explanation appeals to the root of the word and claims that an apostle is a "sent forth" one. An apostle is much more involved than one simply sent forth. The word carries the idea of one sent forth with a message and with the authority of the sender. Richards summarizes the meaning of apostle: "An apostle is an envoy, sent on a mission to speak for the one sending him and having the sender's authority" (Lawrence O. Richards, *Expository Dictionary of Bible Words,* Grand Rapids: Zondervan, 1985, 60). These two ideas of the apostle's having authority and being the one who carries a message are foundational for Paul's role in the church at Colosse where he had never been.

When a replacement was selected for Judas Iscariot, some general guidelines were set down for those who qualified as an apostle (Acts 1). The eleven remaining apostles determined that Judas's replacement must have been with them from the time of Jesus' baptism by John until the ascension. The reason for that requirement was that the apostle must be a witness of the resurrection (Acts 1:22). When Paul was defending his apostleship in the book of 1 Corinthians, he focused on the requirement of being a witness to the resurrection (1 Cor. 9:1) as well as his ministry among them (1 Cor. 9:2) as the evidence that he was indeed an apostle.

In Colossians, Paul begins from the position of the authority of an apostle but also from the heart of a pastor. He is thankful for them (1:3), he prays for them (1:9), he is concerned for them (2:1), and finally he writes the letter out of intense concern for their spiritual health and growth (especially 2:19). Paul, the authoritative apostle and compassionate pastor, wrote to a church he had not started but nevertheless one in which he played an important role.

C. Faith, hope, love (vv. 4–5)

The triad of faith, hope, and love are foundational in Pauline theology: "And now these three remain, faith, hope, and love. But the greatest of these is love" (1 Cor. 13:13). The three appear together throughout Paul's letters (Rom. 5:2–5; 1 Thess. 1:3; 5:8; Gal. 5:5–6) as well as in Hebrews and 1 Peter (Heb. 6:10–12; 10:22–24; 1 Pet. 1:3–8,21–22).

In Paul's thanksgiving for the Thessalonians, we see that faith leads to work or action. Love produces labor or toil in the life of the believer. Finally, hope produces endurance (1 Thess. 1:3). These three work together to make us active, hard-working believers able to endure the struggles of living in a fallen world because the higher agenda of God and his kingdom are central.

Faith has to do with the memory of the past. Faith involves God's redemptive acts both in our own lives and in the lives of his people throughout history. Gabriel Marcel defined *hope* as the "memory of the future."

In that sense, hope is that vision of the future that sees the hand of God in continued guidance and protection. Only when the memory of God in the past and the memory of God in the future are operative in the life of the believer can love be an active reality in the present.

Dan Allender provides a look at the other side of faith, hope, and love (Allender, *The Wounded Heart*, Colorado Springs: NavPress, 1990). He shows that far too often the believer is not controlled by a memory of God's redemptive acts in the past but by memories of betrayal and abandonment. Rather than a location of hope and expectation, the future can be a place where we experience the greatest feelings of ambivalence. When betrayal colors our past and ambivalence is the lens through which we see the future, the present is experienced as a place of powerlessness in which we feel unable to love. Without the memory of God in the past, it would be foolish to have faith. Without the memory of God in the future, hope is impossible. Without faith and hope, love will never be a reality.

While the actual events of our past cannot be changed, the way in which we frame those events can be shaped to lead us to faith. This faith, and love, which is the crowning jewel of this triad, have their genesis in hope (Col. 1:5). The Colossians were models of this great triad of Christian virtue and examples for us to follow.

D. Gospel (v. 6)

What is the gospel? *Gospel* (*euangelion*) means "good news." We encounter many kinds of good news. Occasionally, we read a story in a newspaper or view a report on television that truly is good news. As positive as these might be, they fade in comparison to the good news of the gospel found in the pages of the Bible. The gospel is the good news that Jesus Christ has solved the problem of sin through his death, burial, and resurrection. Paul tells us exactly what the gospel is:

> Now, brothers, I want to remind you of the gospel I preached to you, which you received and on which you have taken your stand. By this gospel you are saved, if you hold firmly to the word I preached to you. Otherwise, you have believed in vain. For what I received I passed on to you as of first importance: that Christ died for our sins according to the Scriptures, that he was buried, that he was raised on the third day according to the Scriptures, and that he appeared to Peter, and then to the Twelve. After that, he appeared to more than five hundred of the brothers at the same time, most of whom are still living, though some have fallen asleep. Then he appeared to James, then to all the apostles, and last of all he appeared to me also, as to one abnormally born (1 Cor. 15:1–8).

That is good news. Christ died for our sins. The gospel isn't the bad news of condemnation; it's the good news of salvation.

E. Spiritual wisdom and understanding (v. 9)

The knowledge of the will of God comes through spiritual wisdom and understanding. Wisdom that comes from the world cannot apprehend the nature of God's design for us. Human intellect does not grasp the outworking of that design. Only spiritual wisdom and understanding can understand and grasp God's work. Wisdom (*sophia*) involves knowing the true nature of reality and knowing how truth can be applied to life. Such wisdom must be combined with understanding (*suneisis*), the ability to see relationships between truths and come to correct conclusions about life. Paul's wording here flies in the face of the false teaching at Colosse. The heretics looked for a secret knowledge available to only a few initiated members (see above "the Colossian heresy") who had knowledge (*gnosis*). Paul showed that believers do not need a special knowledge; believers need a full knowledge (*epignosis*) of God's will. God makes this full knowledge available to them. The spiritual nature of the wisdom indicates that it is an inward ministry of the Holy Spirit to the believer's spirit.

F. Strengthened, power, might (v. 11)

In verse 11, Paul brings together a number of words for power and strength to show that growth must come from a powerful source outside the believer. Only God's power and glorious might provide such a source.

Paul prayed that we will be **strengthened with all power,** using two forms of the word *power* (*dunamis*): literally, "powered by power." The connotation of the Greek word *dunamis* is "transforming power." The nature of this power is not explosive, as some would indicate by showing that our word *dynamite* developed from the Greek word. Reading a later development of a word into the New Testament is often misleading. The focus of this word in the New Testament is on the transformation that comes when this power is present. This power is often associated with the Holy Spirit (see Acts 1:8).

Paul relates this power to the standard (*kata*) of God's glorious might. The might (*kratos*) required for growth is power able to overcome resistance (see Heb. 2:14 where the power of death is overcome). In the New Testament this word indicates that God's glorious might is needed for growth in light of the many factors opposing it. The power available to believers is transformative and mighty, able to overcome anything that would stand in its way. Only as a result of that kind of power can endurance, patience, and joy be an integral part of the believer's life.

G. Inheritance (v. 12)

See Ephesians 1:14, "Deeper Discoveries."

H. Rescued (v. 13)

Paul uses a stark word (*ruomai*) to describe God's deliverance of the believer from darkness. The force of this word indicates that the believer was in acute danger and has been delivered from an alien power in a highly dangerous situation. Paul uses the word three times in 2 Corinthians 1:10 to catch the drama of the deliverance: "He has delivered us from such a deadly peril, and he will deliver us. On him we have set our hope that he will continue to deliver us."

I. Domain of darkness, kingdom of the Son he loves (v. 13)

Believers were under the authority (*exousia*) of darkness before their conversion. The non-Christian lives life under the authority of darkness in contrast to the light available to believers (1:12). Darkness is the realm of opposition toward God (John 3:19, especially Eph. 6:11–12) and the place of sin (1 John 1:6; 2:11), the realm where Satan enforces his authority. The realm of darkness is a place of authority and rule without true relationship, while the realm of light is a community of relationship headed by the Son of God. The kingdom is Christ's kingdom, of which believers are citizens (Eph. 2:19; Phil. 3:20). The Christian has been rescued from the dangerous rule of darkness and transferred into a community which is indeed a kingdom of light, headed by Christ.

Peter O'Brien summarizes the thought well:

> Like a mighty king who was able to remove people from their ancestral homes and to transplant them (metesthsen; the same verb is used in Josephus [Ant. 9:235] of Tiglath-pileser's removal of the Transjordanian tribes to his own kingdom: . . .) into another realm, God has taken the Colossians from the tyranny of darkness (Chrysostom aptly noted that "power" equals "tyranny" here) where evil powers rule (Luke 22:53) and where Satan's authority is exercised (Acts 26:18), transferring them to the kingdom in which his beloved Son held sway (WBC, 27–28).

J. Images of salvation (v. 14)

Throughout his letters, Paul uses a number of images related to salvation. Here he speaks of redemption. Each of these metaphors, like the many sides of a radiant diamond, add to the beauty and glory of the believer's salvation.

1. From the court room (justification) Romans 3:21–31
   The sinner stands before God accused and guilty. God declares the sinner righteous.
2. From the marketplace (redemption) 1 Corinthians 6:20 (see "Deeper Discoveries" on Eph. 1:7)
   The sinner stands before God as a slave. God grants freedom by payment of a ransom.
3. From the bank (forgiveness) Ephesians 1:7
   The sinner stands before God in debt, and the debt, having been paid by another, is canceled.
4. From the home (adoption) Ephesians 1:5 (see "Deeper Discoveries" on Eph. 1:5)
   The sinner stands before God as a stranger; God makes the sinner a member of his family.

5. From the battlefield (reconciliation) 2 Corinthians 5:18
The sinner stands before God as an enemy and becomes a friend when God makes peace.

K. Image (v. 15)

Christ does not bear the image in the same way that man bears the image of God. Man is made in the image of God, and in that he is similar to God. Christ is not made in the image, but he actually is the image of God. The word for *image* (*eikon*) contains the idea of representation and manifestation. Christ represents God in the same way a portrait represents a person. The portrait is not intended to be seen as an inferior copy but an actual representation of the real person. The image is also a manifestation of the real person as well. While God is invisible, he is manifested in the incarnation of Christ.

For every one who is alive today, Abraham Lincoln is an invisible figure in one sense. Our eyes have never seen him. We have never met him. However, we all know what he looks like because we have seen images of him on portraits; a quick look in most pockets will reveal his image on a penny. His image on the penny is his representation and manifestation. It is actually Abraham Lincoln we see there. In the same way, God, who is invisible, is represented and manifested in Christ. It is actually God we see. Christ being the image of God does not mean he is like God but that he is God.

This concept reminds us of a story of a little boy who looked up in the sky and asked his mother if God was up there. When she assured her inquisitive son that he was, he replied, "Wouldn't it be nice if he would put his head out and let us see him?" God has put his head out; we have seen him. He has done more than that. He stepped out of heaven, became a man, and lived among us. He could not only be seen, but he could also be touched. Jesus is God in a body. He is the perfect picture of God.

L. Firstborn (v. 15)

Over the years the term "firstborn over all creation" has been misunderstood, creating doctrinal heresies. In the first century, Arius, and in modern times, the Jehovah's Witnesses, understood the phrase to mean that Jesus was the first created being. They concluded that Jesus is not eternal and, therefore, he is not God. The context will not support this understanding. Verse 17 clearly states that he was before all things, and verse 16 tells us that he created all things. If he was before all things and created all things, then he cannot be part of that creation; thus, he is not a created being at all. He is eternal.

When Paul states that Christ is the firstborn over all creation, he is not making the assertion that Christ is a created being. Rather, *firstborn* (*prototokos*), in this context, indicates supremacy and priority in rank as it does in numerous other verses (Acts 26:23; Rom. 8:29; 1 Cor. 15:20; Rev. 1:5). Wilhelm Michaelis

(*Theological Dictionary of the New Testament*, ed. by Gerhard Kittel, Grand Rapids: Eerdmans, 1968, VI, 879) states that this word indicates Christ's unique supremance over all creatures as the Mediator of their creation. The clear thrust of Paul's argument is that Christ should have supremacy (1:18), and this designation of Christ being the firstborn supports that argument.

M. Thrones, powers, rulers, authorities (v. 16)

Part of the Colossian heresy included the worship of angels (2:18). The hierarchical list of thrones, powers, rulers, and authorities is likely a listing of the rankings within the angelic host (compare Eph. 1:21; 3:10; 6:12; 1 Cor. 15:24). The differences among the lists indicates that Paul was not necessarily trying to be exhaustive in his list or even setting forth a rigid order within the angelic host. The other references to these angelic forces present them as hostile toward God. In making the assertion that Christ is the Creator of the angelic host, the point is clearly made that the angels are not to have a place of priority or even equality with Christ. Only Christ can have the place of supremacy.

N. Supremacy—preeminence (v. 18)

The theological goal in this entire section is to demonstrate that Christ is to have supremacy (*proteuon*) in all things. He is to take first place in all realms. This was precisely the problem at Colosse. Christ was in danger of taking an equal or even subservient place. No! Paul cries. He must be first. The great third-century preacher Chrysostom writes, "For everywhere he is first; above first; in the church first; for he is the head; in the resurrection first."

O. Peace (v. 20)

In the New Testament, peace is not merely the absence of hostility, but it also includes the presence of a relationship. Over the years the United States has been at war with various countries. Clearly, when war is present there is no peace. The United States, however, has had various relationships with other countries that, although far short of war, cannot be described as peaceful. During the early 1990s, the president of the United States withdrew "most favored nation" status from the People's Republic of China because of human rights violations. Making application of the biblical idea of peace, we can say that the United States would not have been at peace with China during that period of time. While there was no war per se, there was still no peace because the relationship was being withheld.

Christ has made peace with us. This not only means he is no longer at war with us and we are not at war with him, but it also means we have relationship with him. We have "most favored people" status as a result of the peace which his blood purchased.

P. Reconciliation (v. 22)

The reconciliation Christ brought about is more than a theological term. Such an active term should have an impact on how we live. The Scripture makes three things clear about reconciliation:

1. Reconciliation is a reason to rejoice.

   "Since we have now been justified by his blood, how much more shall we be saved from God's wrath through him! For if, when we were God's enemies, we were reconciled to him through the death of his Son, how much more, having been reconciled, shall we be saved through his life! Not only is this so, but we also rejoice in God through our Lord Jesus Christ, through whom we have now received reconciliation" (Rom. 5:9–11).

2. Reconciliation is a blessing to be practiced.

   "For he himself is our peace, who has made the two one and has destroyed the barrier, the dividing wall of hostility, by abolishing in his flesh the law with its commandments and regulations. His purpose was to create in himself one new man out of the two, thus making peace, and in this one body to reconcile both of them to God through the cross, by which he put to death their hostility" (Eph. 2:14–16).

3. Reconciliation is a message to share.

   "Therefore, if anyone is in Christ, he is a new creation; the old has gone, the new has come! All this is from God, who reconciled us to himself through Christ and gave us the ministry of reconciliation: that God was reconciling the world to himself in Christ, not counting men's sins against them. And he has committed to us the message of reconciliation. We are therefore Christ's ambassadors, as though God were making his appeal through us. We implore you on Christ's behalf: Be reconciled to God. God made him who had no sin to be sin for us, so that in him we might become the righteousness of God" (2 Cor. 5:17–21).

VII. TEACHING OUTLINE

A. INTRODUCTION

1. Lead story: The Siren Song of Heresy
2. Context: In the first chapter of Colossians, Paul reminds believers of two positive truths to stabilize them as they face false teaching. Paul tells the believers at Colosse that the gospel of Christ was a powerful force which was bearing fruit in their individual lives as well as all over the world. This gospel was not to be abandoned. Paul also tells believers that Jesus Christ has absolute supremacy over all of creation since he is the Creator and Redeemer. When believers understand these truths, they will not be caught in the tantalizing traps of false teaching.

3. Transition: As we look at this chapter, we see the need to maintain a steadfast commitment to knowing the truth in order to be able to detect and resist error. The gospel is the truth. The truth about Jesus is that because of who he is, and what he has done, he deserves first place everywhere and in everything.

B. COMMENTARY

1. Greeting (vv. 1–2)
    a. Author—Paul (v. 1)
    b. Recipients—believers in Colosse (v. 2)
    c. Greeting—grace and peace (v. 2)
2. The Truth about the Gospel (vv. 3–8)
    a. The gospel is the truth (vv. 3–5)
    b. The gospel bears fruit in believers (vv. 4–6)
    c. The gospel grows all over the world (vv. 7–8)
3. The Truth about Pleasing God (vv. 9–14)
    a. Pleasing God is being controlled by his will (v. 9)
    b. Pleasing God is growing in character (vv. 10–11)
    c. Pleasing God is being grateful for salvation (vv. 12–14)
4. The Truth about Jesus (vv. 15–23)
    a. Jesus is the perfect picture of God (v. 15)
    b. Jesus is the eternal Creator (vv. 16–17)
    c. Jesus is the universal Reconciler (vv. 18–23)
5. The Truth about Ministry (vv. 24–29)
    a. Ministry involves suffering (vv. 24–27)
    b. Ministry aims at maturity (v. 28)
    c. Ministry is hard work (v. 29)

C. CONCLUSION: COUNTERING THE COUNTERFEIT WITH TRUTH

VIII. ISSUES FOR DISCUSSION

1. What is the relationship between faith in Christ and love for the saints?
2. What kinds of prayers do you make for your church?
3. What have you learned about Jesus from Colossians 1? How would you teach this to a new Christian?
4. What does reconciliation mean? How are you reconciled to God?
5. What is lacking in Christ's affliction? How can you fill it up?
6. What mystery was kept hidden for ages? How was it disclosed?

Colossians 2

The Truth about Christ and Christians

I. INTRODUCTION
Don't Look for Treasure You Already Have

II. COMMENTARY
A verse-by-verse explanation of the chapter.

III. CONCLUSION
Fullness at the Table

IV. PRAYER
Tying the chapter to life with God.

V. LIFE APPLICATION
Keep Your Eye on the Ball

An overview of the principles and applications from the chapter.

VI. DEEPER DISCOVERIES
Historical, geographical, and grammatical enrichment of the commentary.

VII. TEACHING OUTLINE
Suggested step-by-step group study of the chapter.

VIII. ISSUES FOR DISCUSSION
Zeroing the chapter in on daily life.

Quote

"The greatest danger regarding cults . . . is complacency—considering ourselves and our children to be immune from their attraction. If Christ is not the center of a Christian's life, that Christian is ripe for another spirit...."

Paul Fox

 **IN A NUTSHELL**

In chapter 2, Paul tells the Colossian believers: Faithful friends in Colosse, I want you to know that even though I am concerned about you I am delighted to know that you are still standing firm in your faith in Jesus. You received Christ as Lord, now continue the process of growing up in him. Don't allow anyone to deceive you with fancy talk that promises much and delivers nothing.

Remember that fullness is found only in Christ, and you participate in that fullness. You have complete salvation and complete freedom in him, so don't allow yourselves to be intimidated into thinking that genuine spirituality is found in keeping rules, having experiences, or denying yourselves. All those things foster pride and have no value in keeping the flesh in check.

The Truth about Christ
and Christians

I. INTRODUCTION

Don't Look for Treasure You Already Have

In his book *Souls on Fire*, Elie Weissel tells a remarkable tale. In far away Krakau, in days when sleep was often disturbed by dreams, there lived one Isaac, son of Yechel. Isaac was a poor man whose family seldom ate their fill. One night in a vivid dream, he saw the distant city of Prague. He saw a river flowing through the city, and under a particular bridge he saw a buried treasure. When he woke the next morning, the dream had not faded. Its clear and vivid images remained etched on his mind. That night the dream returned. And the next night. Every night for two weeks, Isaac had the same dream in which he saw the city of Prague, the river, the bridge, and the buried treasure hidden beneath the bridge.

Finally, he decided to walk all the way to Prague to see for himself if the dream might be real. After several days he arrived in the city. Even though he had never been there, he recognized it and knew it well from his dreams. He found the bridge, went under it to search for the treasure, and then suddenly was grabbed firmly at the back of his neck by a soldier who dragged him away to prison for interrogation.

The soldier sat him in a chair and said, "All right, Jew, what were you doing prowling around under that bridge?" Not knowing what else to say, Isaac decided to tell the truth, "I had a dream that there was buried treasure under that bridge, and I was looking for it."

Immediately, the soldier burst into mocking laughter, "You stupid Jew, don't you know that you can't believe what you see in your dreams? Why, for the last two weeks I myself have had a dream every night that far away in the city of Krakau, in the house of some Jew by the name of Isaac, son of Yechel, there is a treasure buried beneath the sink in his house. Wouldn't it be the most idiotic of actions if I were to go all the way to Krakau to look for some Jew that doesn't exist. Or there may be a thousand Isaacs, son of Yechel. I could waste a lifetime looking for a treasure that isn't there." With uproarious laughter, the soldier stood him up, opened the door, gave him a good kick, and let him go.

Naturally, Isaac, son of Yechel, walked back to Krakau, back to his own house, where he looked beneath the sink in his own kitchen, found the treasure buried there, and lived to a ripe old age as a rich man. The treasure was at home all along.

This truth applies to Christians as well: our treasure is in Jesus Christ, who resides in us. We don't have to look anywhere else. Paul wrote to the Colossians because false teachers were telling them that Jesus Christ was not sufficient; they needed some additional spiritual experiences. They taught that Jesus himself was inadequate and this inadequate Jesus couldn't provide all they needed for a full spiritual experience.

Paul countered this claim by telling the Colossian believers, as well as their modern counterparts, that Jesus is the fullness of God and that because of their relationship with him, they have been given fullness. The treasure is Christ, who is in them. Paul tells them in this chapter not to look for other treasure when the true treasure is already theirs.

II. COMMENTARY

The Truth about Christ and Christians

MAIN IDEA: *Knowing the truth that fullness, forgiveness, and freedom are found in Jesus strengthens believers against attractive but empty deception.*

A Our Absolute Fullness in Christ (vv. 1–10)

SUPPORTING IDEA: *Jesus is fully God, and we are given fullness in him.*

2:1. Paul feared the Colossian believers would allow themselves to be caught in a web of deception cleverly spun by people promoting false doctrine. **Struggling** reveals the nature of Paul's concern. The Greek word means "anxiety or concern." Paul is not struggling because he is in prison. His struggle is not external; his is an intense inner struggle on behalf of believers in Colosse, **Laodicea, and for all who have not met [him] personally** (possibly a reference to believers in Hierapolis, or Colosse).

Paul had his eyes open to the presence and the appeal of false teaching. He was concerned that the Colossians not have theirs closed. Like Paul we need to have a wide-eyed awareness of the appeal of error. We have no excuse for having our eyes closed to the existence of error, because the Bible is full of warnings (Rom. 16:17–18; Gal. 1:6–9; Acts 20:28–31; 1 Tim. 1:3–7; 6:3–5; 2 Tim. 4:3–4; 1 John 4:1).

2:2–4. Paul tells how to avoid being deceived. These verses contain three elements which add up to a loving, learning community. Paul's goal is that believers be (1) **encouraged in heart** which happens as they are (2) **united in love**, (3) and as they are settled in their **understanding** of the truth.

Encouraged can either mean "comfort, cheer up" or "encourage, strengthen." Within the context of this letter, the idea of strengthen fits best, since there is no hint of sadness or distress for which the Colossians need comfort. They need strength to equip them to stand strong against the error they face.

Strengthening takes place as believers are **united in love**. United in love translates a Greek participle and could be rendered "by being united in love" (NASB) rather than "and united in love" (NIV). The imagery of **united** is that of a body being held together by ligaments to make a strong unit. Unity and solidarity create strength. False teaching is naturally divisive. A person left alone, with no support, is much more vulnerable than a cohesive unit.

What creates unity? **Love**! Concern for one another. Relating to one another as brothers and sisters, with loyalty and support. When we are united in love, .we will be strengthened in heart. Then we will have assurance in understanding.

A loving, learning community will produce believers who are settled in their **understanding** of the truth. Believers who link themselves with fellow believers, who care for one another, and who grow in their understanding of Jesus Christ will stand a good chance of remaining stable and confident.

Understanding has a very definite object: Jesus **Christ, in whom are hidden all the treasures of wisdom and knowledge**. In contrast to the false teachers at Colosse, who said that wisdom and knowledge were hidden away in mystical experience and higher knowledge, Paul says that **all** wisdom and knowledge are **hidden**, or deposited, in Christ. He is all we need. We will never mine all the treasure found in a full knowledge of Jesus Christ:

- In Colossians 1, we see that Jesus is the Lord of creation and reconciliation.
- In Colossians 2, Jesus is the fullness of deity, the forgiver of sins, and the conqueror of satanic forces.
- In Colossians 3, Jesus is the resurrected Lord, and our life.
- In Colossians 4, Jesus is the one worthy of devoted service. The false teachers claimed that spiritual experience was found in "secret" knowledge, available only to the initiated elite. Paul says that the only **mystery** (literally "secret") we need to know is Christ.

If believers come to a settled understanding that true treasure is found only in Christ, they won't be deceived by **fine-sounding arguments**. This term literally means "pithy words." False teaching promotes itself through "smooth talk," but it's still just "high sounding nonsense." We need to be careful of lies that come all dressed up in persuasive speech when all they do is hide naked error.

2:5. The bad news in the Book of Colossians is that believers were under attack. The good news is that they were standing strong. Paul, **though . . . absent . . . in body,** is **delight[ed]** to see how **orderly . . . and . . . firm [their] faith in Christ is. Orderly** and **firm** are military metaphors which paint the picture of the Colossians not breaking rank or defecting. When the enemy attacked, the Colossians maintained a solid front.

2:6–7. Believers can avoid the deception of verse 8 not by just maintaining a solid front but by moving forward with steady progress. When we stop going forward, we stall; when we stall, we can fall. **We received Christ Jesus as Lord.** Now we are to **continue to live** with him as our Lord. **Live** literally means walk. Step by step, day by day, we are to conduct our affairs in conscious submission to the lordship of Jesus Christ. Life is a journey, and we are not expected to sprint through it. We are just to make steady progress.

Steady progress is possible when we are grounded or **rooted.** Christians are not to be tumbleweeds with no roots, blown about by every wind of doctrine. We avoid this when we are firmly rooted in Jesus Christ. Roots don't exist for themselves: they exist to give the plant strength and help the plant grow. We are to be **rooted** and then **built up** and **strengthened.** We are to grow. How are we to grow? We are to grow **in the faith [we] were taught.** We have no need to seek secret or "higher" knowledge. We are to grow in knowledge of the truth already revealed in Christ. Finally, Paul wants us **overflowing with thankfulness.** This comes when we recognize that we are complete in Christ, that we have every opportunity to grow spiritually in him. A thankful believer is not easily led away from Christ. A discontented, grumbling, whiny believer, however, will be easy prey for false teachers who are more than willing to offer "just what you've been missing."

2:8. Believers face the very real threat of being captivated by false teaching and lured away from an unswerving devotion to the absolute supremacy of Christ. Paul's warning now becomes direct: **See to it that no one takes you captive. Captive** means "to carry away" or "kidnap." Here it refers to someone being carried away from the truth into the slavery of error.

Philosophy threatened to carry the Colossians away from the truth. This is not a blanket indictment against all philosophy. The reference here is to the particular philosophy, as seen in Paul's description that follows, being promoted by the false teachers. This **philosophy** is **hollow and deceptive,** literally, an empty deception which stands in stark contrast to the **fullness** in Christ (1:19; 2:9). The **hollow and deceptive philosophy** of the false teachers promises much but delivers nothing.

Paul provided the Colossians with the two origins of this **philosophy,** neither of which is **Christ.** First, Paul says this empty deception is based on **human tradition.** William Barclay says, "It was a product of the human mind; and not a message of the Word of God" (Barclay, 164).

The second source of this empty deception was **the basic principles of this world.** The Greek phrase (*stoicheia tou kosmou*) means "component parts of a series." It sometimes refers to elementary teaching like the ABCs. Sometimes, and most likely here, it refers to elemental powers or cosmic spirits. Paul mentioned spirit beings previously (1:16), telling us that Christ created the spirits which the false teachers venerated. Paul will mention them again (2:10,15), telling us that Christ defeated the spirit beings. Paul's warning is clear. Don't allow yourselves to be kidnapped by an empty deception based on human ideas and defeated spirit beings. Referring to the false teachers and their philosophy, Eugene Peterson translates this phrase, "They spread their lies through the empty traditions of human beings and the empty superstitions of spirit beings" (Peterson, 501).

2:9–10. When false teaching attacks, it usually attacks on two fronts: (1) the person of Jesus Christ and (2) the believer's identity in him. False teachers fail to acknowledge that Jesus Christ is God and undermine his uniqueness as the God-Man. False teachers propose that "something more" is needed to make the earnest disciple complete. It may be new knowledge, freshly revealed to the cult leader; it may be ecstatic experiences which are supposed to usher the individual into new vistas of insight; it may be legalistic activity which demonstrates sincerity.

Paul addresses both lies in verses 9–10 where he tells us that we are full in the full one. Jesus Christ is completely God, and we are complete in him. We just need to grow. The Christian always grows by nutrition (feeding on his Word) and not by addition.

Paul tells the Colossians that because **in Christ all the fullness of the Deity lives in bodily form,** they have no excuse for being deceived. The sum total of deity resides in Jesus, the incarnate Word of God (John 1:1,14). **All the fullness** is actually a tautology (saying the same thing twice in different words) and serves to underscore that the "fullness" is found exclusively in Christ. Fullness is not found in the host of spirit beings supposedly emanating from God. They are not the fullness of God; Christ is. The fullness living in Christ **in bodily form** points not only to Jesus' **Deity** but also to his humanity. This is a direct argument against the idea that matter is evil and that the fullness of God could not be found in Jesus, who assumed human flesh.

False teachers seek to kidnap believers by empty deception. Because of their vital union with Jesus, the full one, believers have **been given fullness** (John 1:16; Eph. 3:19; 4:13). This spiritual fullness is found **in Christ, who is the head [authority] over every power and authority.** It is futile to look for spiritual fulfillment or maturity in any other place than Jesus Christ, who is the treasure house of all wisdom and knowledge and the fullness of deity.

B ▪ Our Total Forgiveness in Christ (vv. 11–15)

SUPPORTING IDEA: *Jesus is our crucified conqueror, and we are forgiven by him.*

2:11–13a. Jesus Christ is fully God, and we are full in him. But what does spiritual fullness mean? How is it ours? In verses 11–15, Paul completes the argument of verses 9–10. Paul begins his explanation of fullness with complete salvation. The metaphors Paul chooses to explain our full salvation are **circumcision** and **baptism**. The point of these metaphors is that we are saved totally and exclusively through the work of God, not through any human activity.

No religious ritual can make us **alive with Christ**. Paul picks two familiar rituals in these verses, but he clearly is not talking about the physical acts of **circumcision** and **baptism**. Instead, he is talking about the spiritual reality behind the physical rite. The Jews were masters at physical rites. In Genesis 17, God instituted circumcision as a physical sign of the Abrahamic covenant. Every male was to be circumcised as tangible testimony that he was in a covenant relationship with Yahweh. The Jews began mistakenly to think that the physical ritual was sufficient all by itself.

The Bible is clear even in the Old Testament (Deut. 10:16; 30:6) that physical circumcision saves no one. This becomes even more unmistakable in the New Testament (Rom. 2:28–29). The circumcision Paul is talking about in Colossians 2:11 is the spiritual operation of putting away or cutting away—not of a piece of flesh—but the **putting off of the "sinful nature"** (NIV) or the "old man" as it is referred to in Romans 6. What we were in Adam—sinful, fallen, corrupt—Christ destroyed. This happened at the moment of salvation when we were spiritually baptized into Jesus Christ. The **baptism** Paul is talking about (v. 12) is the spiritual baptism where we are united and identified with Christ in his death, burial, and resurrection (Rom. 6:1–7).

How does **the putting off of the sinful nature** take place? Is it a simple outpatient procedure that can be done in virtually any medical clinic? No. For all our modern medical sophistication, no surgery can cut out our **sinful nature** and give us new life. This is an operation only God can perform. Paul tells us it is not **done by the hands of men** (v. 11).

2:13b–14. The second reality of spiritual fullness is total forgiveness—the cancellation of a debt we could never pay. [God] **forgave us all our sins.** Paul gives us a detailed description of what forgiveness involves.

In verse 14, Paul speaks of a **written code** with **regulations**, which stands **against us** and is **opposed to us**. The word Paul used here refers to a certificate of indebtedness or a signed confession of guilt which stood as a perpetual witness against the debtor. It was an ancient IOU.

Two things comprise this certificate of indebtedness: the **regulations** of the law and our offenses. Both of these stand against us and highlight our debt. What does God do with this signed confession of guilt? He cancels the debt. The word **canceled** also means "to wipe out, wash over, or erase." God erases the document and cancels the debt.

How can he do that? Doesn't that make the law cheap when guilty people are set free without having to pay for their crimes? Absolutely not. God himself paid the debt when his Son died on the cross. God upheld the holiness of his own law when Jesus died to pay the penalty for our sin. God not only erased the document, but he also **took it away**, by **nailing it to the cross**. When Jesus died, the condemning document was destroyed. We are fully forgiven.

2:15. Spiritual fullness means complete salvation, full forgiveness, and absolute victory. We have spiritual fullness because of our participation in the conquest of the cross.

On the cross a cosmic drama was played out as God, in Christ, battled and gained victory over the powers of evil. Jesus Christ not only paid the penalty to atone for sin, but he also won a decisive victory over Satan and all the host of supernatural beings who were in league with him. Verse 15 tells us that Jesus Christ **triumphed** over the **powers and authorities by the cross**. The cross was the consummation of a life of conquest of Christ over Satan. As early as Genesis 3:15, God promised that a conqueror would come to crush the head of the serpent. Satan attempted to destroy Jesus through the efforts of Herod, but he was unsuccessful. Satan attempted to destroy Jesus with his own temptation in the wilderness. Again, unsuccessful. On the cross Jesus consummated his victory. As he died, he defeated Satan because he died to forgive sin. Sin was Satan's trump card. Jesus defeated Satan and his evil league on the cross—first by being there and then by abolishing sin's condemning power.

We have a tendency to think of the death of Christ as his defeat and the resurrection as his victory. No. Christ won a victory over sin and Satan on the cross. The resurrection was God's vindication of the victory already won. The resurrection was a declaration of power that Jesus is the Son of God; it is public demonstration that confirms that his death had been effective for the forgiveness of sin.

Jesus also **disarmed** the **powers and authorities**. He broke their power and stripped them of their controlling influence over humans. Jesus celebrated his victory by making a **public spectacle** of the conquered powers. The picture comes from a common Roman military practice. When a general won a victory, a triumphal procession made its way through the streets, with the successful general leading the way. His army followed, singing songs of conquest and reveling in their victory. Bringing up the rear would be the defeated king and his warriors, subjected to public ridicule and paraded for all to see.

On the cross, Jesus won a decisive victory, making clear to the universe that Satan is a vanquished foe. This does not mean that we will not have conflict. The devil has been defeated, but he has not yet conceded defeat. He has been overthrown, but he has not yet been fully eliminated. Satan continues to harass us. When we understand our identity in Christ, we can live above Satan's control.

C Our Complete Freedom in Christ (vv. 16–23)

SUPPORTING IDEA: *Jesus is our life source, and we are free through him.*

2:16–17. The fullness and freedom that are ours in Christ ought to motivate us to maintain our devotion to the one who gave us that fullness and set us free. We have no reason to become enslaved by legalistic living, mystical experience, or rigid self-denial. Because of our fullness in Christ (declared in 2:10 and described in 2:11–15), Paul tells us that we should not allow others to **judge** us. The term **judge** means "pass unfavorable judgment on, criticize, or find fault with." We are not to allow others to intimidate us or question our spirituality.

How might others attempt to convince us that our spirituality is suspect? Apparently some in Colosse tried to convince the believers that spirituality was based on how well they observed certain codes of behavior. Paul mentions diets (**what you eat or drink**) and days (**religious festival, New Moon celebration, Sabbath day**). The false teachers said that the truly spiritual maintained a particular diet and properly observed all the right holy days.

What about this? Is the Christian bound to strict observance of diets and days? No. Two passages of Scripture make this clear (Heb. 9:10; Gal. 4:8–11). Here in Colossians 2:17, Paul informs us that rule keeping is just a **shadow**: there is no real spiritual substance. The **reality** (literally the "body" which casts the shadow) is **found in Christ**. Again and again, whatever the topic, Paul brings believers back to Christ.

Legalism—measuring your own or someone else's spirituality by the ability to keep man-made rules—is a rigid, confining, and lifeless way to live. It is easy because all it requires is a list of rules coupled with dutiful compliance. Wisdom or the skillful application of biblical principles to life's situations is unnecessary. Just comply. Legalism is not only rigid and lifeless, but it also fosters hypocritical pride. The Pharisees (ancient and modern) prove that. A focus on conformity to a code can cause one to forget things like arrogant pride, smug judgmentalism, anger, and a host of other dark sins that never seem to make the list.

2:18–19. Fullness and freedom mean that believers need not be drawn into the quest for exciting experiences. Apparently, the false teachers were telling the believers at Colosse that mystical visions and deeper experiences were necessary to make them truly spiritual. Once again, Paul brings the issue back to Christ.

Scholars debate whether the **worship of angels** referred to the angels being the objects of worship (the worship given to angels) or to the worship that the angels perform. Either are possible, but the former seems most likely. The mystical experience began with initiation into ascetic rituals (possibly referred to in Col. 2:21) which led to supernatural visions in which the individual was ushered into the heavenly realms to worship the angels who emanated from God or to join with the angels in the worship of God. The worshiper would then return with all kinds of stories about **what he [had] seen** in his vision. The Colossians were being told that if they really wanted to reach new levels of spirituality they needed to engage in these kinds of experiences. The mystical journey was intended to restore a lost dimension to spiritual experience.

Paul says this kind of spiritual quest is in fact a dangerous distraction. The person loses **connection with the Head, from whom the whole body** grows. The vision becomes the focus; Jesus becomes secondary. As a result growth is stunted, and believers are **disqualif[ied] . . . for the prize.** This phrase is actually one Greek term meaning "act as umpire against you." It could mean "let no one pass critical judgment against you," or it could mean "let no one deprive you of spiritual reward" because you have become distracted by a quest for experiences. Paul does not want Christians to be robbed of assurance and made to feel unspiritual, unfaithful, and in need of something extra—something more and higher than the cross.

This quest for superspiritual experience, like the legalism of the previous verses, fosters pride. The experience seeker **delights in false humility,** but **his unspiritual mind puffs him up with idle notions.** Believers may have spiritual experiences of varying kinds. Experiences themselves are not evil. When we try to make our experience the standard for all believers or when we measure our own or someone else's spirituality on the basis of that experience, we're being arrogant and unspiritual.

Christ is central. Not rules. Not experiences. Christ.

2:20–23. Paul's final warning is against asceticism—a religious philosophy which teaches that depriving the body of its normal desires is a means of achieving greater holiness and approval from God. Paul nullifies this notion as well. Again, Paul mentions the **basic principles of the world** and **human commands and teachings** (Col. 2:8). He is telling the Colossian believers to move on to maturity and to get past the elementary stages of spiritual life. He has told them that they are free, so why would they **submit to rules**?

Self-denial as a self-imposed form of spirituality is all appearance. Paul says it has **an appearance of wisdom**. It certainly looks spiritual when someone goes through all sorts of sacrifices supposedly to bring them closer to God. Asceticism has taken different shapes over time: wearing thick hair shirts close to the skin (as if itching is spiritual); sleeping on hard beds; whipping oneself; or prolonged fasting.

Paul tells us that asceticism is all appearance and no value. Paul says this kind of behavior has no **value in restraining sensual indulgence**. In other words, all this external performance has no effect on internal urges. Alexander Maclaren said, "There is only one thing that will put the collar on the neck of the animal within us, and that is the power of the indwelling Christ." When Jesus is given control, he not only gives us the Holy Spirit to fight against the flesh, but he also gives us new desires as well. We don't need rules for the outside because we have the Spirit on the inside. We simply need to yield to him.

MAIN IDEA REVIEW: *Knowing the truth that fullness, forgiveness, and freedom are found in Jesus strengthens believers against attractive but empty deception.*

III. CONCLUSION

Fullness at the Table

Imagine for a moment that you are poor and needy. You are desperate. Ragged, shabby clothes. You haven't eaten in several days. You are cold, and you are tired because you have been walking all day. Darkness advances swiftly. You notice some lights in the distance through the trees. Your aching stomach urges your throbbing feet to keep going just a little farther. As you draw closer, you see the lights are a blaze of white against the night. It's a huge house. Curtains are drawn back to reveal activity inside. You inch closer for a better look, until your face presses against the window. You stand there for a few moments without being noticed—shocked at what you see. It's a feast. A huge table is covered from end to end with more food than you've seen in months—green vegetables, steaming meat, cold drinks, warm bread. Your stomach rumbles; your mouth waters. You feel faint from hunger. As a butler is serving the guests, the master of the house glances over and notices your face pressed against the window. He thinks to himself, *Here is a needy person.* He motions for the butler to go out and speak to you. Your first instinct is to try to get away fast, because you think they want to punish you for trespassing. The butler calls out to you, "Please, the master would like you to come in and dine at the table." So you go in—and eat. Your great need has been met by the fullness of the table.

In a similar way, our great spiritual need has been met by the fullness of the table of blessings in Christ. Jesus Christ is the fullness of deity, and from his fullness he has given us spiritual fullness. Why look elsewhere? Why look for treasure we already have? As believers we have the awesome opportunity to feed at the table of spiritual blessing in Christ.

The truth about Christ and Christians is that Christ is the fullness of God, and Christians have been given fullness in him.

PRINCIPLES

- The threat of false teaching is cause for serious concern.
- Vital involvement in a loving, learning community is a defense against deception.
- Ongoing growth in the believer's life is a defense against deception.
- Jesus Christ is fully God.
- Every believer has spiritual fullness because of vital union with Christ.
- Every believer has experienced full forgiveness.
- Jesus defeated Satan on the cross and stripped him, and all his demons, of their power over mankind.
- Spirituality is not a matter of rules or experiences, but a relationship with and obedience to Jesus Christ.

APPLICATIONS

- Involve yourself in a local assembly where you can learn and grow in Christ with fellow believers.
- Reflect on a regular basis the essential truths that will keep Jesus central:
    1. Jesus is fully God. Nothing needs to be added to him.
    2. You have fullness in him. Nothing needs to be added to you.
- Be on the alert for false teaching. Don't be naive and think it was just a first-century problem.
- Don't allow yourself to be intimidated by those who tell you that you need something more. Just keep growing in your walk with Christ.

IV. LIFE APPLICATION

Keep Your Eye on the Ball

In his book *Keep in Step with the Spirit*, J. I. Packer reminds us of the need to keep Jesus Christ central. He warns of the danger of becoming preoccupied with the Spirit rather than the Savior to whom the Spirit points. Such warning applies to anything which might distract us from Jesus Christ.

> Should our interest shift from knowing the Son to knowing the Spirit, two evils would at once result. On the one hand, like the Colossian angel worshippers, we should impoverish ourselves by ". . . not holding fast to the Head, from whom the whole body, nourished and knit together through its joints and ligaments, grows with a growth that is from God" (Colossians 2:19). On the other hand, we should enmesh ourselves in a world of spurious "spiritual" feelings and fancies that are not Christ related and do not correspond to anything that actually exists except Satan's web of deceptions and his endless perversions of truth and goodness. We should not take one step down this road. Questions about the Holy Spirit that are not forms and facets of the basic question, How may I and all Christians—and indeed all the world—come to know Jesus Christ and know him better? ought not to be asked. This is a basic mental discipline that the Bible imposes on us. In golf it would be described as keeping your eye on the ball (Old Tappan, NJ: Fleming H. Revell Co., 1984, 92).

Spirituality is not a matter of knowing more Bible facts or having all the doctrinal wrinkles ironed out. Spirituality is not a matter of conformity to a code of rules. Spirituality is not a matter of exciting experiences. Knowledge, rules, and experiences all foster pride. Finally, spirituality is not a matter of recipes: "Do these three things two times a day and you'll be spiritual." Spirituality is not mechanical. These things seem so spiritual but are nothing more than distractions.

What then is genuine spirituality?

An Attitude: Trust

An attitude of trust means that I confidently rely on, put my weight on, Jesus Christ. Whatever life throws at me, I trust him. In my business practices, do I trust God rather than manipulate? Can I trust that he will provide and reward me even if I do what others think foolish? Can I trust him when things don't go my way?

A Behavior: Obedience

"If you love me, keep my commandments," Jesus said. Spirituality is loving obedience to Jesus Christ, not legalistic conformity to a man-made code. It's loving obedience to the Word of God, not chasing the flash and pizzazz of experiences. Simple, loving obedience.

Spirituality is an attitude of trust and a behavior of obedience. Life is challenging; and as we face it, God simply wants us to trust and obey. Spirituality is not a matter of rules or experiences but a relationship with, and obedience to, Jesus Christ. Let's keep our eye on the ball.

V. PRAYER

Sovereign Lord, as we look to Christ in whom all the fullness of deity dwells, may we live lives worthy of him and consistent with his fullness which has been given to us. Keep us satisfied with Christ when all the world around us is clamoring for more. Amen

VI. DEEPER DISCOVERIES

A. Struggle (v. 1)

Louw and Nida define the Greek word for *struggle* (*agon*) as, "to engage in intense struggle, involving physical or nonphysical force against strong opposition" (*Greek English Lexicon*, New York: United Bible Societies, 1988, II:496). The same word can describe an actual race (compare Heb. 12:1). The Word pictures an athlete agonizing during training to be victorious in competition. The strenuous demands of the contest would exact a physical and emotional toll on the participants. Paul used strong words to describe the intensity of his concern and his labor for the growth of the Colossians (1:28–29). Paul's struggle was on behalf of the believers at Colosse and Laodicea; the finish line would be reached when the believers were encouraged in heart, united in love, and assured in understanding the mystery.

B. Laodicea (v. 1)

Laodicea, a small town about eleven miles west of Colosse, was one of three principle cities in the Lychus River Valley. (Hierapolis, mentioned in 4:13, was the third). Known for its production of black wool, Laodicea was situated at an important crossroads of two trade routes. One route went from the western port cities of Ephesus and Miletus, through Laodicea, and on eastward to Syria. The North-South route traveled from Pergamum in the north to Attalia in the south. Its location on these two prominent trade routes made Laodicea a thriving commercial center in Southwest Asia. By the time

Paul wrote this epistle, Laodicea had eclipsed Colosse as the dominant city in the region.

The city is most well-known in the Bible as the city of the "lukewarm church" in Revelation 3:15–16. The city was quite familiar with lukewarm water because its water supply came from a hot spring, was piped into the town, and arrived lukewarm. An earthquake destroyed the city in A.D. 60, but it recovered without any aid from the Roman Emperor Nero. Eventually, the site of the city was abandoned, and another town was built closer to the springs. Paul refers to Epaphras throughout the book and demonstrates his concern for the people of Colosse, Laodicea, and Hierapolis. It would seem that Epaphras had started churches in all three cities.

C. Fine-sounding arguments (v. 4)

Literally "pithy words," the phrase translated as **fine-sounding arguments** is loaded. The term is used rhetorically to refer to speeches based on logical reasoning rather than demonstration. In one court case, the word is used to describe a criminal's attempt to persuade the court to let him keep stolen goods (see Lohse, 83). The indication is that those who use these fine-sounding words are constructing plausible, but false, arguments to manipulate others. As Paul states in verse 8, for such people the truth is not a concern. Their philosophy is hollow and deceptive. Clearly, this is persuasive speaking in the worst sense. Given the context in which Paul uses the word, images of the stereotypical used car salesman come to mind.

D. Metaphors of growth (v. 7)

Paul uses four participles to describe the manner in which believers should live and grow. The first three participles are passive indicating that divine activity is predominant. Dan Wallace writes that with the passive voice, "no volition—nor even necessarily awareness of the action—is implied on the part of the subject. That is, the subject may or may not be aware, its volition may or may not be involved. But these things are not stressed when the passive is used" (*Greek Grammar beyond the Basics*, Grand Rapids: Zondervan, 1996, 431). Believers are being rooted, being built up, and being strengthened. Clearly God is the one rooting, building, and strengthening. The last participle changes to active voice, indicating the response of the believer to God's work in his life. "In general it can be said that in the active voice the subject performs, produces, or experiences the action or exists in the state expressed by the verb" (Wallace, 410).

Of particular interest is the fact that the first participle ("being rooted") is a perfect participle. The other participles are present. The perfect is used when the author is describing an event which has been completed in the past and has continuing results in the present.

In summary, God has rooted the believer in Christ at the time of conversion in a completed sense, but that rooting is having continuing results in the present. At the same time God, in an ongoing process, builds up and strengthens the faith of the believer, which results in the believer's active response in thankfulness.

1. Rooted: This perfect passive participle indicates a condition that results from some past action. The past action is their conversion when they received Christ (2:6). As a result of their conversion, they are firmly rooted like the foundation of a building. The word (*rizao*) can also be used in a horticultural context: the roots of a plant are set, providing a firm foundation for the growth of the plant itself. However, in this context as well as in Ephesians 3:17, an architectural metaphor applies. This suggests that the term might best be understood as part of an extended metaphor of building that develops with the three participles. The term is often used this way. Believers are first foundationally rooted as a result of their conversion. Then a spiritual structure is built on the foundation.

2. Build up: This present passive participle indicates God's continual activity needed for growth. The believers are continually being more and more built up. After laying the foundation, God erects the structure. This is a process which takes time, but believers are encouraged not to grow weary along the way. God is in the process of making us into a museum of divine artwork.

3. Strengthened: This present passive participle again focuses on the continual and progressive nature of God's activity. The believers are being more and more strengthened. Once the foundation has been laid and the building has been erected, the building itself settles in and is made increasingly stronger. Again, the activity of God is primary, and yet the results are ours to enjoy. That is why we are finally overflowing with thankfulness.

4. Overflowing: This present active participle gives the natural response of the believer to the work of God in his life described in the three previous participles. As God does his work of laying the foundation, building the structure, and strengthening the entire building, the believer will—like a geyser—overflow with thanksgiving for all God has done for him.

If these metaphors are all joined together, the image is of a beautiful building, designed by a master architect, constructed by the world's best builder, approved as worthy by the most stringent code inspector, and enhanced by a lovely fountain in front—placed there in honor of the architect, builder, and inspector who are all the same person.

E. In Christ all the fullness of deity lives in bodily form (v. 9)

Jesus Christ was God in a body. This passage describes both Christ's deity and his humanity. The God-Man was both fully divine and fully human. *Deity* (*theotes*) is used to refer to the essence of God as opposed to the attributes (*theiotes* as in Rom. 1:20) of God. Christ possesses the fullness of the essence of God.

The evidence for the deity of Christ has been affirmed throughout the history of Christianity. Christ has the attributes of deity, performs the actions of deity, is given the titles of deity, and claims deity of himself. In addition the apostles also claim deity for Jesus as well.

Christ Possesses the Attributes of Deity
1. Eternity (John 8:58; 17:5; Isa. 9:6; Mic. 5:2)
2. Omnipresence (Matt. 18:20; 28:20; John 3:13; 1:50)
3. Omniscience (Matt. 16:21; Luke 6:8; John 2:24,25; 6:64; 21:17)
4. Omnipotence (Matt. 28:18; Mark 5:11–15; Phil. 3:21)
5. Immutability (Heb. 1:10–12; 13:8)
6. All attributes of deity belong to Christ (Col. 2:9)

Christ Performs the Work of Deity
1. Creation (John 1:3,10; Col. 1:16; Heb. 1:2)
2. Preservation (Col. 1:17; Heb. 1:3)
3. Forgiveness of sins (Mark 2:1–12; Luke 5:24; Col. 3:13)
4. Power to raise the dead (John 5:21; 11:43)
5. Judgment of the world (John 5:22,27; 2 Cor. 5:10)

Christ Accepted the Worship Due Deity
1. John 5:23
2. Luke 24:52

Christ is Given the Titles of Deity
1. Son of God (Matt. 26:63–64; Mark 1:1; John 10:36)
2. Son of man (Dan. 7:13; Mark 2:10)
3. YHWH (Luke 1:76 [compare Mal. 3:1]; Rom. 10:13 [compare Joel 2:32])
4. God (John 1:1,18; 20:28; Heb. 1:8)

Jesus Claimed to Be God
1. By claiming to be YHWH (Luke 1:76)
2. By accepting worship (Matt. 28; John 9)
3. By identifying himself with God in context of monotheism (John 10:30; 17:5).
4. By explicit claims (John 8:58)
5. By claiming to do what only God can do (John 5:19–27; Matt. 12:5–8)
6. By accepting the titles of deity (John 20:28; Matt. 16:16)

The Apostles Claim that Jesus Is God
Apostolic assertions for Christ's deity can be found in John 1:1; Colossians 1:19; 2:9; Hebrews 1:8, and Titus 2:13. (The grammar of this verse demands an interpretation which combines God and Savior as a reference to

Christ by virtue of Granville Sharp's Rule. The rule states that in an article, "noun, *kai*, noun construction" the two nouns have the same referent.)

Messianic Proof of Christ's Deity

1. The Old Testament says "Messiah is God."
      Isaiah 7:14: Immanuel
      Isaiah 9:6: Mighty God
      Isaiah 40:10: LORD God
      Daniel 7:13–28: Ancient of Days
      Micah 5:2: From Everlasting
      Zechariah 12:10: YHWH
      Zechariah 14:16: Lord of Hosts (or LORD Almighty)
      Psalm 45:6: God (Heb. 1:8)
      Psalm 110:1: LORD—(Matt. 22)
      Psalm 118:22: Stone (used 4 times in New Testament)
2. Jesus is Messiah (Hebrew basis for Greek christos or Christ)
      Matthew 16:16–17,20
      Mark 8:29
      Luke 9:20
   Jesus alone fulfills all the prophecies.
3. Therefore Jesus is God.

Having set forth the biblical teaching that Christ is both human and deity, the next theological task is to set forth the relationship between these two natures in Christ. This is commonly referred to as the Hypostatic Union. In discussing this topic, the student of Scripture may describe the union but have limited understanding of the details of that union.

The orthodox statement of the Hypostatic Union, first set forth by the Council of Chalcedon in A.D. 451 (a meeting of early Christian leaders to clarify scriptural truth), says:

> In agreement, therefore, with the holy fathers, we all unanimously teach harmoniously that we should confess that our Lord Jesus Christ is one and the same Son, the same perfect in Godhead and the same perfect in manhood, truly God and truly man, the same of a rational soul and body, consubstantial with the Father in Godhead, and the same consubstantial with us in manhood, like us in all things except sin; begotten from the Father before the ages as regards His Godhead, in the last days, the same, because of us and because of our salvation begotten from the Virgin Mary, the Theotokos, as regards his manhood; one and the same Christ, Son, Lord, only-begotten, made known in two natures without confusion, without change, without division, without separation, the difference of the natures being by no means removed because of the union, but the property of each nature being

preserved, and coalescing in one person (prosopon) and one hypostasis (hupostasis)—not parted or divided into two persons (prosopa), but one and the same Son, only begotten, divine Word, the Lord Jesus Christ, as the prophets of old and Jesus Christ himself have taught us about him, and the creed of our Fathers has handed down (J. N. D. Kelly, *Early Christian Doctrines*, rev. ed. San Francisco: Harper & Row, Publishers, 1978, 339–40).

This excellent treatment is true to Scripture in affirming, without minimizing, the deity and humanity of Christ. This statement grew out of a debate in response to a number of various approaches to the two natures. During the debate, the church seemed to be much more suited to identifying the wrong teaching without making a positive statement of the right teaching. Chalcedon is the final positive statement of the orthodox position, although it is somewhat negative in tone telling us more about what the union is not, than what it is.

In keeping with the practice of the church throughout history, the following discussion will identify the unorthodox views of the Hypostatic Union in order to focus more properly on the orthodox view.

Only six variations of the unorthodox position have been conceived; other offerings are merely variations of those six, which appeared in the first five centuries. The errors fall into three groups of two each:

Errors Concerning the Deity of Christ

1. *Ebionitism*: Jesus was a normal man possessing unusual but not superhuman or supernatural gifts of righteousness and wisdom. The literal son of Joseph and Mary, he was the predestined Messiah but only in a natural sense. Ebionitism denies the deity of Christ.

2. *Arianism*: Jesus is the absolute uniqueness of God, but he is a created being, made by God. Christ is similar to God, but he is not God. Arianism diminishes the deity of Christ.

Errors Concerning the Humanity of Christ

1. *Docetism*: Christ only appeared to be a man. Jesus was not actually born to Mary; he merely passed through her. Docetism denies the humanity of Christ.

2. *Apollinarianism*: Christ had a human body and a human soul, but the divine logos replaced a human spirit. Thus, Jesus was nearly human but not totally so. Whereas Docetism denied the humanity of Christ, Apollinarianism diminishes the humanity of Christ.

Errors Concerning the Two Natures of Christ

1. *Nestorianism*: Jesus actually has two separate and distinct natures: the human Jesus, and the divine Christ, who appeared in the form of

Jesus of Nazareth. This is a separation of the two natures of Christ into two persons.

2. Monophysitism: The divine nature of Christ is not fully divine, and the human nature is not fully human. The union of the two natures resulted in a new mixed nature that is Christ. Thus, Monophysitism, also known as Eutychianism, is a mixture of the two natures.

Orthodoxy

The orthodox position was carved out of the reaction to the unorthodox positions. Charles Ryrie's summary of the nature of the union is helpful. "There is no mixture of the divine and human attributes (as Eutychians taught), no change in either complex (as Apollinarians taught), no dividing of them and no separating them so as to have two persons (as Nestorians taught). Orthodoxy says two natures comprising one person or hypostasis forever" (*Basic Theology,* Chicago: Moody Press, 1986, 250).

Millard Erickson has set forth five principles, which he labels, "Basic Tenets of the Doctrine of Two Natures in One Person." These are helpful in formulating an exposition of the orthodox statement of Chalcedon.

1. The incarnation was more a gaining of human attributes than a giving up of divine attributes. This is directly related to the issue of the *kenosis.*

2. The union of the two natures means that they do not function independently. The divine nature of Christ was in some way limited by the circumstance of being in union with the human nature, but this is not a full limitation of his divine ability. Erickson provides an excellent illustration to make the point clear: if the world's fastest sprinter were running in a three-legged race, his union with another runner would limit his ability to run in that circumstance, but it would not limit his ability in himself to be the fastest sprinter in the world. In the same way Christ was limited by the circumstance of being in a human body, but this is not a real limitation of his deity.

3. Christ is fully God and fully human. This must be understood from the point of view that Christ reveals to us what *fully God* and *fully human* actually mean. Christ was not fully like us. We are fallen humanity, and he is full humanity. Christ has the same nature as Adam before the fall, which is not like our nature.

4. The incarnation is God becoming man, not man becoming God.

5. It is helpful to think of Jesus as a very complex person.

F. Power and authority (vv. 10,15)

(See "Deeper Discoveries" on 1:16.)

G. Sinful nature (vv. 11,13)

The NIV translates the Greek word *flesh* (*sarkos*) as sinful nature. The usage of the word *flesh* in the writings of Paul indicate that it is the locus of the sinful desires of man (see especially Gal. 5:19–21). It is not a physical element of man; rather it is a part of his nature, or better, it is his nature. The flesh is acting out what comes naturally as opposed to acting out what comes spiritually or by the Spirit. Louw and Nida provide an excellent summary when they write that the sinful nature is,

> . . . the psychological aspect of human nature which contrasts with the spiritual nature; in other words, [it is] that aspect of human nature which is characterized by or reflects typical human reasoning and desires in contrast to those aspects of human thought and behavior which relate to God and spiritual life. . . . Some scholars understand the meaning of *sarx* as being a person's "lower nature" rather than simply "human nature," but the distinction between lower nature and higher nature seems to be primarily arising out of typical Greek thought rather than out of the Semitic background which seems to be so pervasive in the use of the term sarx in such contexts in the NT. There are, of course, contexts in which sarx does refer to that psychological factor in man which serves as a willing instrument of sin and is subject to sin (Louw and Nida, 322–3).

H. The written code (v. 14)

The NIV's translation of **written code** (*cheirograpon*) does not capture the financial nature of the term well. The NASB's "certificate of debt" is closer to the meaning. The Greek language uses several terms for *debt*. This particular term combines the two words *hand* and *writing*, giving rise to the KJV translation of "handwriting." The emphasis of this term seems to be that the record of the debt owed would be signed by the debtor. Fragments from New Testament times have been recovered which have handwritten signatures on such records of debt (Deissmann, *Light from the Ancient East*, London: Hodder and Stoughton, 1910, 331). This term shows that we have signed an IOU which is evidence of the enormous debt we owe to God.

I. What you eat or drink, religious festival, new moon celebration, sabbath day (v. 16)

Regulations against eating certain types of food are found in Leviticus 11 and Deuteronomy 14:1–21. Clean and unclean animals are sorted out, and unclean animals are forbidden. Laws regulating drink are less common but some may include Leviticus 10:9 which regulates the priest's consumption of wine; Leviticus 11:34 which prohibits drinking from an unclean vessel; and

Numbers 6:3 which requires the man under a Nazarite vow to abstain from wine, strong drink, and even grape juice. While these regulations were not universally applicable to all Jews, the fact that they were applied to the elite (priests and Nazirites) may have appealed to the notion of the heresy at Colosse that created a class of those who were initiated and above the others.

The three terms **religious festival, New Moon celebration,** and **Sabbath** are often linked in the Old Testament as days set aside and dedicated to God (Hos. 2:13; Ezek. 45:17; 1 Chr. 23:31; 2 Chr. 2:4; 31:3). Regulations about religious festivals in general are found in Leviticus 23 and include Passover (vv. 4–8); Firstfruits (vv. 9–14); Feast of Weeks or Pentecost (vv. 15–22); Trumpets (vv. 23–25); Day of Atonement (vv. 26–32); and Tabernacles (vv. 33–44). The New Moon celebration is frequently spoken of in the Old Testament (Num. 10:10; 28:11; 1 Sam. 20:5,18; Ps. 81:3; Hos. 2:11; Amos 8:5). This was a monthly celebration. The final word "sabbath" is in the plural, which may indicate both the celebration of the weekly sabbath (Lev. 23:1–3) and the Sabbath Year (25:1–7). None of these rituals qualify believers for membership in a higher class of spiritual worshipers. They belong to the old order of relationship to God before Christ. Christ has shown us the way of the cross, the way of God's costly grace.

J. A shadow of things that were to come, the reality, however, is found in Christ (v. 17)

Only Christ is reality. The Old Testament and all of its regulations were simply a shadow cast backward from Christ. Christ is also casting a shadow forward over our lives now. Only he is real. We live in what C. S. Lewis called the "Shadowlands." In this life of shadows faith calls us to believe that "Real life hasn't begun yet. This is only shadows." We eagerly await real life when we will see reality, when we will see Christ. At that time we will be like him, for we will see him as he is (1 John 3:2.) At that time, we will be real; we'll no longer live in the shadows, but in the radiance of his reality.

VII. TEACHING OUTLINE

A. INTRODUCTION

1. Lead story: Don't Look for Treasure You Already Have
2. Context: In the second chapter of Colossians, Paul continues to counter the error of the false teachers, who were attempting to capture the Colossian believers with clever deception. Paul was concerned but encouraged that the believers were still maintaining a firm commitment to Christ. To ensure that they not be enticed by error, Paul made two simple but profound truth statements: Jesus is the

fullness of deity, and believers are given fullness in him. Since both these things are true, believers should not be intimidated into thinking they need to add anything to their spiritual experience.

3. Transition: As we look at this chapter, we see the truth about our Savior and ourselves. Jesus is fully God (and fully man), and we are complete because of our association with him. It is ridiculous to attempt to add anything to something (or someone) that is full. It is unfortunate (and unnecessary) that many believers fail to understand the facts and advantages of fullness. Colossians 2 makes the truth unmistakably clear.

B. COMMENTARY

1. Our Absolute Fullness in Christ (vv. 1–10)
2. Our Total Forgiveness in Christ (vv. 11–15)
3. Our Complete Freedom in Christ (vv. 16–23)

C. CONCLUSION: KEEP YOUR EYE ON THE BALL

VIII. ISSUES FOR DISCUSSION

1. What philosophies and human traditions would Paul warn you about if he were writing today? How do you present the Christian truth over against these?
2. What does Paul regard as true circumcision?
3. What did God do in the cross of Jesus?
4. What rituals and legalisms threaten to replace the gospel today as the means to salvation?
5. How does the church grow? What threatens its growth?

Colossians 3

❦

The Truth about Christians and Spirituality

❦

"*S*pirituality involves the whole of human life; nothing is nonspiritual. . . . In fact, spirituality is to be expressed primarily in the ordinary everyday affairs and relationships of our lives."

Ranald Macaulay and Jerram Barrs

Colossians

IN A NUTSHELL

*I*n chapter 3, Paul tells the Colossian believers: Fellow believers in Colosse, since you have been given new life by Christ, who is now exalted in heaven, it is only right that you focus your aspirations on heavenly things.

The new life you have because of your identification with Christ should cause you to discard the ugly remnants of your former lifestyle and display the Christlike character appropriate to your new life. The Word of Christ should take up comfortable residence in your hearts, and all your activities and relationships should be viewed with spiritual significance.

The Truth about Christians and Spirituality

I. INTRODUCTION

Skating in Circles

*D*an Jansen is an Olympic Gold Medal speed skater. You may remember him as the man whose sister, Jane, died of leukemia just before the 1988 Winter Games in Calgary. He desperately wanted to win the gold medal in honor of his sister. He failed in Calgary. In the 1992 games in Albertville, France, he again came away empty. Four years later, in Lillihammer, Norway, he won the gold in the one thousand meters and set a world record. It was an emotional moment when he skated his victory lap holding his nine-month-old daughter in his arms. Her name was Jane.

After the Olympics, Jansen was asked how he had overcome so much adversity and kept going. He reflected back to a time when he was twelve years old and had lost a meet. His father drove him home, and Dan pouted all the way. His father was silent until they arrived home. Then, as Dan was going to bed, his dad came into his room and said, "Son, life is more than skating in circles," and walked out. Jansen said that one comment changed his whole perspective on life.

Dan Jansen didn't quit skating in circles. He just had a bigger picture. His father's words gave him a higher perspective on life, and his skating took on new significance. Dan Jansen will be remembered for doing something ordinary in an extraordinary way.

Ever feel like your life is just skating in circles? The drudgery of the same old routines can make life seem like that. With an earthbound perspective, life really is little more than skating in circles. The repetitive cycles of infancy, adolescence, and old age; work, rest, and more work; marriage, children, and grandchildren; diapers and dishes; progress and regress can seem awfully ordinary and terribly tedious.

God, however, does not want us simply to endure the tedium. Our ordinary activities can be infused with spiritual significance. Paul calls us to a bigger picture, a higher perspective in Colossians 3. He calls us to look as high as the heavens to gain perspective for our earthly endeavors.

II. COMMENTARY

The Truth about Christians and Spirituality

MAIN IDEA: *Knowing the truth about Christian living invites us to live an ordinary life in an extraordinary way.*

Ⓐ The Foundation of Christian Living (vv. 1–4)

SUPPORTING IDEA: *Genuine spiritual living is built on the believer's association with the risen Christ.*

3:1. Colossians 3:1–4 is a hinge between the primarily doctrinal section of chapters 1–2 and the primarily practical section of chapters 3–4. These verses conclude the polemic against the false teachers with further exaltation of the supremacy of Jesus, and they provide the starting point for the alternative to the false teaching with exhortation to make Christ central in all areas of life.

The false teachers at Colosse have attacked the supremacy and sufficiency of Jesus Christ. They have made him less than fully God and have attempted to seduce believers into thinking that genuine spirituality is to be found in obtaining more knowledge, keeping more rules, or having more experiences. In chapter 2, Paul told us the truth about Christ (he is fully God) and Christians (we are given fullness in him). Now we learn the truth about Christians and spirituality.

Genuine spiritual experience begins with understanding our identification with Christ. Paul tells believers that they **have been raised with Christ.** The believer eagerly anticipates the future bodily resurrection mentioned in Romans 8:11 and 1 Corinthians 15:22–23,50–55. This is not, however, what Paul has in mind here. This reference to resurrection refers to a past event: we **have been** raised. The reference is to our identification with Jesus in his death, burial, and resurrection. Paul referred to this earlier in 2:12–13 and in Romans 6:1–10. He means that because of our identification with Jesus we have been granted new life which gives us the capacity to live a new kind of life. That new kind of life will be described in detail in the following verses.

The reality of our resurrection with Jesus should produce in us new motivations and new minds. Paul tells us that **since we have been raised** we are to **set [our] hearts on things above.** Believers are being urged literally to seek, pursue with diligence **things above.**

Paul continues his Christ-centered focus by assuring us that Christ is **above, seated at the right hand of God.** In contrast to the false teachers who demoted Jesus, Paul reminds us that Jesus is seated in the position of honor, majesty, and authority.

3:2. Coupled with our new motivation is a new mind. Believers are exhorted to **set [their] minds** on the same things their hearts were set on—**things above.** Paul expands his thought here by including the negative contrast—**not on earthly things.** This does not mean that believers are to live in a kind of mystical fog or neglect the affairs of earth with endless contemplation of eternity. This means that believers are not to be concerned only with the trivialities of the temporal. We are to be preoccupied with the things that get top billing in heaven. Heavenly values are to capture our imaginations, emotions, thoughts, feelings, ideas, and actions. The believer is to see everything, including **earthly things,** against the backdrop of eternity. With a new (resurrection) perspective on life, the eternal is to impact the temporal.

3:3. Paul now provides the basis for his preceding exhortations. The exhortations are based in a past reality, a present truth, and a future expectation. Paul begins with a glance back. He tells believers, **you died.** Believers have "died to sin" (Rom. 6:2), which means that the believer is no longer under the influence of sin's dominating power. Paul told the Colossians one chapter earlier that they had **died with Christ to the basic principles of this world** (Col. 2:20), which means that the believer is not subject to the cosmic powers of darkness. The old order of things (slavery to sin and evil forces) is gone.

The glance back gives rise to the glimpse **now.** In the present our **life is hidden with Christ in God.** The reference to **hidden** can refer to "safety or secrecy." In fact, both are probably in view. Our life is doubly secure since it is **with Christ in God.** This is a comforting reminder of the truth found in John 10:28–29: no one can snatch the believer out of Jesus' hand or the Father's hand. The believer is secure. The term **hidden** (*kekruptai*) can also mean "concealed, unseen." This means that the believer's life is unknown or not understood by the watching world (compare 1 John 3:1–2). The unseen realities will be revealed. Paul now turns his attention to that glorious truth.

3:4. Paul has taken a glance back and a glimpse at the present; his focus now shifts to a gaze ahead. The believer's identification with Christ brings not only a past break with sin and a present security, it also means a glorious future. The believer awaits the time **when Christ . . . appears. Appears** refers to an open display. **When Christ appears [we will] also appear with him in glory.** What has been **hidden** will be revealed. The secret will be out. As Barclay says, "Some day the verdicts of eternity will reverse the verdicts of time" (Barclay, 178).

Paul takes the idea of identification a step further. Not only is life shared by identification with Christ; Christ is life itself (Phil. 1:21; Gal. 2:20). For the believer, life isn't merely activity, details; life isn't acquisition or accomplishment. Life is Christ. He is the focus of our aspirations, the reason for our existence.

Four times in four verses, Paul mentioned Christ. Jesus is central and supreme. Paul doesn't want believers to forget that. Jesus is seated above in the position of honor. Believers are identified with him. With this solid foundation, the lives of believers can be transformed.

B The Transformation of Christian Living (vv. 5–17)

SUPPORTING IDEA: *Genuine spiritual living is behaving in accordance with the character of Christ.*

3:5–7. Paul's exhortation to **set** our **hearts** and **minds on things above** (v. 2) finds concrete expression in the verses which follow. With the old life gone and the new life a present and future reality, believers are to discard behaviors typical of the old life and display behaviors characteristic of new life. Paul is concerned that believers keep Christ (not angelic mediaries, not mystical experience, not legalistic ritual, not secret knowledge) at the center of their spiritual experience. Christ has given us new life, and the believer's objective is to conform his life to the image of Christ. The transformation of our lives is the genuine expression of spirituality.

Christ changed our life (3:1–4); **therefore**, it is up to us to change our lifestyle. Change starts with discarding the old. Paul employs two graphic metaphors to convey his ideas: (1) putting to death, and (2) putting off old clothes and putting on new clothes.

We are to **put to death** the practices of the past. Several images are used in the New Testament to portray Christian living. The believer is a disciplined "athlete" who strives to win the prize (1 Cor. 9:24–27; 1 Tim. 4:7–9; 2 Tim. 2:5). The believer is a faithful "soldier" who endures hardship to please his commanding officer (2 Tim. 2:3–4). The believer is a tenacious "wrestler" engaged in a fierce struggle with a crafty foe (Eph. 6:12). Here Paul tells us that the believer is to be a ruthless "executioner" who eliminates the behaviors of the past.

In verses 5–7, Paul tells us what things are to be eliminated and gives us two reasons for their elimination. In telling believers to **put to death** certain behaviors, Paul is calling for complete extermination, not careful regulation. What must go? Paul gives us an "outside in" perspective. He starts with external actions and then moves to the internal drives which cause the conduct. In his "vice lists" Paul mentions three categories of behavior: (1) perverted passions, (2) hot tempers, (3) sharp tongues.

First on the list is **sexual immorality** (*porneia*), a broad, general term for all kinds of illicit sexual behavior. God created sex to be enjoyed by one woman and one man in the confines of marriage. Any sexual activity that does not fit that definition is not to be part of a believer's life. The perverted passion list continues with mention of **impurity**. This reminds us that immorality is "unclean" or dirty and incompatible with the purity of our Savior. Believers are not to be slaves of their **lust** or **evil desires**.

With his mention of **greed** (KJV "covetousness"), Paul moves outside the sexual arena and into broader, internal areas. The Greek *pleonexia* means "a desire to have (*echein*) more (*pleon*). "Greed is the assumption that all things and passions exist for our own benefit. John Chrysostom called it a "silly weakness about silver." Greed is the internal, sinful desire to satiate ourselves with more, more, more. Paul equates **greed** with **idolatry**. To act as if everything exists for us is to place ourselves in the place of God himself. All things were created **by him and for him** (Col. 1:16), not for any of us. To make the acquisition of things or the satiation of desires our ambition is to demonstrate that our aim is too low—**earthly things** rather than **things above**.

Paul wants believers to view these vices from a **things above** or divine perspective. Why are these behaviors and attitudes to be **put to death**? First, because they are the very things which will bring **the wrath of God**, which is his future judgment. Secondly, these behaviors and attitudes are to be eliminated because they reflect the way we **once lived**. A transformed lifestyle should be the trademark of our new life.

3:8. In verse 8, Paul switches metaphors. The exhortation remains the same, but the picture changes. The imagery behind the call to **rid yourselves**, in verse 8, and **take off** and **put on**, in verses 9 and 10, is that of taking off clothes. Believers are to discard their old, repulsive habits like a set of worn-out clothes. They are then to adorn themselves with the kind of behaviors that will make them well dressed and appropriately fashionable.

Not only are perverted passions to be eliminated (vv. 5–7), believers must also **rid [themselves]** of a hot temper. **Anger** (*orge*) is a settled feeling, the slow, seething, smoldering emotion that boils below the surface. **Rage** (*thumos*) is a quick, sudden outburst, the blaze of emotion which flares up and burns with intensity.

Between the sins of the hot temper (anger, rage) and the sins of the sharp tongue (slander, filthy language), Paul mentions **malice**. The Greek term (*kakian*) refers to "ill will, the vicious, deliberate intention of doing harm to others." This ill will may work itself out through angry outbursts or sinful speech.

Slander (*blaspemian*) is basically defamation of character. To slander someone is to injure their reputation. This term is sometimes used in reference to God; but in this context, it probably refers to slanderous speech against another person. **Filthy language** refers to "obscene or abusive speech."

3:9–11. Perverted passions, hot tempers, and sharp tongues are to be removed as part of the life-transformation process. These things, along with **[lying] to each other**, are not appropriate behavior for our new life in Christ.

The remnants of the former lifestyle are to be discarded **since [we] have taken off [our] old self with its practices.** What is the **old self** (literally "old man") and the **new self** (literally "the new")? The "old man" refers to more than an individual condition ("sinful nature") and also has a corporate aspect. The corporate aspect of "the new" (man) is unmistakably seen in verse 11. What has been **put off** and what has been **put on?** Our former associations, the old humanity has been **put off,** and we now have a new association, the new community. As members of the new community, we are to conduct ourselves in ways which will enhance harmony in the community. Notice how the sins mentioned in the previous verses disrupt community and damage human relationships.

As individuals, and as believing communities, our objective is to be a part of the transformation process of **being renewed in knowledge in the image of its Creator** (Christ). Within the new community all barriers are abolished. Distinctions which normally divide people—racial (**Greek or Jew**); religious (**circumcised or uncircumcised**); cultural (**barbarian** or **Scythian**); social (**slave or free**)—no longer have significance. The reason human categories no longer matter is that **Christ is all,** which means Christ is central and supreme. Our relationship with him is really all that matters. Unity within the community is based on the fact that Christ **is in all.** He indwells **all** believers and permeates all our relationships. This does not mean that people cease to be Jew or Greek, slave or free, etc. It does mean that within the new community those distinctions don't matter. The false teachers at Colosse were fond of dividing people into categories—elite versus ordinary, spiritual versus not so spiritual. The truth is, all believers are equal; all believers are to discard any and all behaviors and attitudes which are inappropriate for our new life.

3:12–14. Verses 12–17 contain the virtues that stand in contrast to the vices mentioned in the preceding verses. With the old discarded, the character of Christ is to be displayed in its place. The transformation process includes more than don'ts. There are some dos as well.

Since the old humanity has been **put off** and the new community has been **put on,** believers are **therefore** to **clothe** themselves with the kind of behavioral apparel that fits their new life. The famous story "The Emperor's New Clothes" by Hans Christian Andersen has many possible applications for believers. One of them would be the simple lesson that we are not to be foolish like the emperor and take off our old clothes and put nothing back on. Before listing the appropriate attire, Paul reminds believers that they are **God's chosen people, holy and dearly loved.** These are exalted titles formerly used as designations for the nation of Israel (Deut. 4:37; 7:7–8) but now applied to the new community in Christ (1 Pet. 2:9–10).

William Barclay has an insightful comment on the nature of the virtues listed now:

"It is most significant to note that every one of the virtues and graces listed has to do with personal relationships between man and man. There is no mention of virtues like efficiency, cleverness, even diligence and industry—not that these things are not important. But the great basic Christian virtues are the virtues which govern and set the tone of human relationships. Christianity is community" (Barclay, 188).

The first piece in the believer's fashionable wardrobe is **compassion**, which refers to "heartfelt sympathy for those suffering or in need." The next item in the believer's wardrobe is **kindness**, the friendly and helpful spirit which meets needs through good deeds. This is the concrete action of compassion. If the believer is to be fully dressed, other Christlike characteristics are to be worn as well. The believer is to be clothed with **humility**, which is a proper estimation of oneself (Rom. 12:3). **Humility** is not a self-debasing attitude (like the "false humility" of 2:18 and 2:23) but an attitude that is free from pride and self assertion. The believer is to be clothed with **gentleness**, sometimes translated "meekness." **Gentleness** has been described as "power under control"; the picture of a powerful horse under the control of its master is a helpful image. The attitude behind **gentleness** is an attitude of refusing to demand one's rights. The believer is to be clothed with **patience** which is the capacity to bear injustice or injury without revenge or retaliation.

The idea of putting up with the abuses and offenses of others continues with Paul's call to **bear with each other**. Believers are to go beyond quiet resignation positively to **forgive whatever grievances [they] may have against one another**. Believers have been fully forgiven by Christ (2:13–14), and the forgiven are obligated to become forgivers. The standard for this forgiveness is Christ himself.

Paul saves the most important item of clothing for last. Without love, all the other virtues may amount to mere moralism and little else (a thought found also in 1 Cor. 13:1–3). When love is present, there is harmony and unity in the community. It is not clear whether **love** binds the virtues together, completing a lovely garment of Christlike character, or whether **love** binds the members of the community together in mature oneness. Perhaps the ambiguity is intentional. Both ideas make good sense.

3:15. To maintain **perfect unity** (v. 14) believers are to **let the peace of Christ rule in [their] hearts**. **Rule** literally means "to act as umpire." The Colossians were told earlier not to allow false teachers to "act as umpire against" them (2:18). However, when disputes arise, the believer is to let the **peace of Christ** make the call. Whatever will lead to peace must be the deciding factor so that peace will be preserved.

3:16. If believers are to be transformed into the character of Christ, the **word of Christ** should find a home in our hearts. It should not come and go, show up occasionally, or be something we visit like a vacation spot. As Eugene Peterson translates this phrase, "Let the Word of Christ—the Message—have the run of the house. Give it plenty of room in your lives" (Peterson, 504).

The parallel between Colossians 3:16–4:1 and Ephesians 5:18–6:9 must not be missed. The structure and terminology are almost identical. The Ephesians passage exhorts believers to be filled with the Spirit, whereas the Colossians passage exhorts believers to let the Word of Christ dwell in them. The two concepts must be synonymous. The external results are the same. The internal effect is the same. The believer is to be "under the influence" of the **word of Christ** and the indwelling Holy Spirit. The reason for the Colossians' emphasis on Christ is expected in a book so devoted to his centrality and supremacy. **Let the Word of Christ dwell in you richly as you teach and admonish one another with all wisdom, and as you sing psalms, hymns and spiritual songs with gratitude in hearts to God** (v. 16). When the **word of Christ** finds a comfortable home in individual believers and in the new community, there will be teaching (positive instruction), admonishing **one another** (negative correction), and thankful worship, evidenced by singing and **gratitude**.

3:17. The life transformation process is to include any and all areas and activities of life. In all places, in all ways, the believer is to honor the **name of the Lord Jesus**. Genuine spirituality is not found by following false teaching which leads away from Christ. Genuine spirituality is found in having our lives transformed into the character of Christ.

C The Relationships of Christian Living (vv. 18–4:1)

SUPPORTING IDEA: *Genuine spiritual living is bringing relationships into compliance with the example of Christ.*

3:18. The arena of relationships is our best testing ground for spiritual authenticity. Thinking above has practical results here below. True spirituality deals with "real life." The false teachers promoted ideas which made spirituality the possession of the special few who tapped into "higher" knowledge, engaged in mystical experiences, or conformed to a code of rules. Paul points believers in another direction. Spirituality is nothing grand, romantic, or impossible. It is submitting to the supremacy of Christ which will transform our character and revolutionize our relationships.

When Paul penned Colossians, the "household" consisted of three sets of relationships: (1) husband and wife, (2) parent and child, (3) master and slave. Paul addresses each relationship and gives instructions for each party. **Wives** are to **submit to [their] husbands. Submit** is a call to recognize and respond to the God-ordained authority of the husband. Submission does not diminish the equality or destroy the dignity of the wife. Christ himself is the model for equality with God and submission to the one with whom he is equal (1 Cor. 11:3; 15:28; Phil. 2). To function properly, any institution must have clear lines of authority and submission. The family is no different. The wife's submission is **fitting in the Lord. Fitting** means "proper or appropriate." Submission is God's desire and design for Christian wives, so it is to be obeyed by those who belong to the Lord.

3:19. The husband, though given a role of authority, is not to treat his wife as a "subject." The husband's call is to sacrificial **love.** Love is meeting the needs of others regardless of the cost to self. Again, the model for this is Christ himself. The parallel passage in Ephesians 5:22–33 makes this clear. The husband is to love his wife "just as Christ loved the Church and gave himself up for her" (Eph. 5:25). When husbands lead with love, the submission of the wife will more naturally follow. In contrast to the **love** to which he calls husbands, Paul commands that the Christian husband **not be harsh** with his wife. He is not to use his authority to be overbearing, critical, or bitter.

3:20. Children are charged to **obey [their] parents.** Obedience is the simple process of hearing, understanding, and responding. Once more, Christ provides the example (see John 6:38; 15:10). God is the one who commanded obedience to parents (Exod. 20:12), so naturally obedience **pleases the Lord.**

3:21. Just as the authority of the husband is not to lead to harshness with the wife, the authority of **fathers** is not to lead to the kind of behavior that will **embitter [their] children. Embitter** means "to provoke or irritate." The Christian father is not to overcorrect or harass his children, **or they will become discouraged,** which refers to "a listless, sullen resignation—a broken spirit." To be discouraged as a child means to think things like, *I'll never get it right,* or, *All he does is criticize,* or, *He'll never love me.* John Newton is reported to have said, "I know that my father loved me—but he did not seem to wish me to see it." Christian fathers should be sure their children are as sure of their love as they are of their authority.

3:22–25. The section on servants and masters is somewhat expanded in comparison to the "family" section. This may be due to the unique situation in the church at Colosse, where the runaway slave, Onesimus, was returning to his master, Philemon (Col. 4:9; Phlm.). The category of slave-master would be equivalent to our modern employee-employers. The arena is the workplace.

Slaves are to **obey** their **earthly masters.** Paul reminds those under authority that they have a master in heaven who observes their internal attitude and external performance (vv. 24–25). Christian employees are to render sincere service. The employee is not to work only when the boss is looking. The employee is to recognize that in the final analysis he is **working for the Lord, not for men** and so do his best. Such work will be rewarded. Remember, God does not play favorites. He "rewards" wrong motives and work as well as good.

4:1. All Scripture is God breathed (2 Tim. 3:16). Chapter divisions are another story. The separation of Colossians 4:1 from the preceding context is obviously one case where the line was drawn too early. The admonition to **masters** clearly belongs with the section dealing with relationships. **Masters** (those in authority), like husbands and fathers, are not to abuse their authority. They are to treat their workers fairly with justice. Why? They, too, **have a Master in heaven.**

Paul began chapter 3 by urging believers to "look above." He has closed the chapter in the same way. Wives are to "look above" to Christ as their example of submission; husbands are to "look above" to Christ as their example of love; children are to "look above" to Christ as their example of obedience; slaves are to "look above" to Christ as their impartial rewarder; masters are to "look above" to Christ as their heavenly judge.

Spirituality is a matter of understanding our identification with Christ, having our lifestyle transformed, and honoring Christ in our relationships. Ordinary sounding stuff, but with Christ at the center, it becomes extraordinary indeed.

MAIN IDEA REVIEW: *Knowing the truth about Christian living invites us to live an ordinary life in an extraordinary way.*

III. CONCLUSION

Image Quest

Sir Robert Ballard had a quest. His quest was the *Titanic.* He wrote, "My lifelong dream was to find this great ship, and during the past thirteen years the quest for her had dominated my life." The false teachers were on a quest. Their quest was for "something more." For them, Jesus was not supreme and hardly sufficient to provide the full experience of spirituality. So they set off on a quest for something more.

What is a "quest"? It's a pursuit, a search, an adventurous journey. Robert Ballard would understand that and so would the false teachers at Colosse. What about you? What's your quest? Or better yet, what is God's quest? God does have a quest. His is an "image quest"—the adventurous journey of seeing us conformed to his Son's image. We read about that in Romans 8:29: "For those God foreknew he also predestined to be conformed to the likeness of his Son." And see it in Colossians 3:10 where we are **being renewed in knowledge in the**

image of [our] Creator [Christ]. Character qualities in his children—that is God's quest (Adapted from Charles R. Swindoll, *The Finishing Touch: Becoming God's Masterpiece*, Dallas: Word Publishing, 1994, 464–6).

God's quest is to see the character of his Son in his children. Our quest should be the same.

The truth about Christians and spirituality is that Christians have been given new life, and spirituality is living that new life in everyday activities.

PRINCIPLES

- Jesus Christ has the position of highest honor and authority.
- All believers are identified with Christ and given new life.
- A heavenly perspective impacts our earthly activities.
- Jesus Christ indwells all believers.
- Christ is our model of love and obedience in our relationships with others.
- The categories of "spiritual" and "nonspiritual" are false. All of life is spiritual.
- Spirituality is obedience in the ordinary.

APPLICATIONS

- Do some personal inventory. Based on what you think about most and how you spend your money and time, honestly evaluate whether you have set your heart and mind on things above.
- Which area needs your immediate attention: perverted passion, hot temper, sharp tongue? Begin working on it today. Don't make excuses. Ask for assistance from a trusted friend.
- We all live in a web of relationships. Give regular time each week to pray for each of your relationships.

    Monday—with your spouse
    Tuesday—with your children
    Wednesday—with your parents
    Thursday— with your boss
    Friday—with your workers or coworkers

IV. LIFE APPLICATION

No Categories Please

In her devotional book *Diamonds in the Dust*, Joni Eareckson Tada clarifies the nature of spirituality:

Have you noticed how some activities seem more spiritual, more sacred than others? Singing hymns, teaching church school, or preparing a care basket for a sick friend—all of these seem exalted. But what about when you drive to the gas station for a fill-up? Or when you count up coupons for the clerk at the supermarket? Or while you're waiting for the salesperson to wrap what you've bought?

We do it all the time—separate "religious" activities into one group and "regular" into another. But Leviticus 19 addresses that problem. In one verse Moses says, "Do not steal," yet the verse next to it states, "Do not go over your vineyard a second time or pick up the grapes that have fallen" (Leviticus 19:10). Again he says in one verse, "Love your neighbor as yourself" and the verse following, "Do not mate different kinds of animals" (Leviticus 19:18–19).

Why didn't Moses group together all the spiritual activities and leave those nonessential things for another chapter? It's no mistake that God spoke these commands in one breath, mingling "spiritual" and "nonspiritual." In God's eyes, all of life's activities are sacred. (*Diamonds in the Dust*, Grand Rapids: Zondervan, 1993).

Everyday affairs are the arena of spirituality. Spirituality is not esoteric knowledge, nor exciting experience, nor extreme legalism. Spirituality is the development of character. Spirituality is integrity in relationships. Spirituality is obedience in the ordinary. It's wives respecting their husbands, husbands loving their wives; kids honoring their parents, parents loving their kids; workers doing good work, bosses being fair. All of life is spiritual with no categories. As Joni says, "Remember that, the next time you wash dishes."

Without a heavenly perspective ordinary activities can seem an awful lot like skating in circles. By looking above and obeying below, ordinary activities take on grand significance. Who knows? We may even win the gold. After all, God promised to reward us in "whatever we do."

V. PRAYER

Reigning Christ, renew us daily so that our relationship with you will have an impact on every relationship we have. Amen.

VI. DEEPER DISCOVERIES

A. Since, then, you have been raised with Christ (v. 1)

The Greek language provides a number of options for framing an "if . . . then" sentence. The manner in which a sentence is framed makes it either a first-class condition, a second-class condition, or a third-class condition. This Greek sentence is a first-class condition. The first-class condition is a sentence in which the first part of the sentence—the condition—is assumed to be true for the sake of argument. (See Dan Wallace, *Greek Grammar Beyond the Basics*, Grand Rapids: Zondervan, 1996, 679–712 for an excellent discussion of conditional sentences.) The context of the sentence determines whether the statement is actually true. Clearly, in this context the condition is actually true. Paul makes that point clear (v. 3) by stating the fact: they died with Christ. The Colossian believers have been raised with Christ; therefore, it is natural to assume that they will be setting their hearts on things above.

B. Set your hearts (v. 1)

Set your hearts (*zeteite*) literally means "seek" and has a broad range of meanings: trying to find the location of something or someone (Mark 1:37), trying to find information by careful investigation (John 7:52), desiring something (Rom. 9:6), or attempting to obtain something (Mark 8:11). This context certainly points to an attempt to obtain the virtues which Paul will set forth as belonging to the things above. The emphasis of this entire chapter is on the changed lifestyle that should grow out of identification with Christ.

The way we live is the ultimate test of maturity. This is not a once-for-all effort that transforms a believer into a saint in a day. The present imperative used here emphasizes the continual nature of the activity. Constant attention must be paid to focus on the changed life which Paul sets forth.

C. Things above, earthly things (vv. 1–2)

"Things above" (*ano*) as opposed to "earthly things" (*ges*) are not spatial references asking us to focus on the events in heaven rather than events on earth. Rather, "things above" are to be seen as ethical qualities set forth in the following lists. **The things above** are the virtues which the believer is to put on (3:12–4:1) The things of earth have an ethical character as well; the earth is presented as the theater of sin where the vices of life are played out.

D. Christ is seated at the right hand of God (v. 1)

To be seated at a person's right hand was to occupy a place of special honor. This is likely a quote of Psalm 110:1 and shows again the supremacy of Christ, the only one qualified to sit beside the divine throne in heaven (compare Eph. 1:20).

E. Put to death (v. 5)

Paul changes from present to aorist imperatives at this point. Earlier the believer is encouraged with present imperatives continually to keep seeking and thinking about a heavenly perspective. The aorist imperative here emphasizes the "action as a whole, without focusing on duration, repetition, etc." (Wallace, 485). The force of this word is strong. Louw and Nida indicate that when the word is used figuratively it means: "to cease completely from activity, with the implication of extreme measures taken to guarantee cessation—'to stop completely, to cease completely'" (Louw and Nida, New York: United Bible Societies, 1988, I, 661). The NIV's **put to death** captures the strength of Paul's expression more clearly than the NASB's "consider."

F. Whatever belongs to your earthly nature (v. 5)

This very unusual phrase can be translated literally: "the members which are upon the earth." Bodily members can be presented to sin as instruments of wickedness, or they can be presented to God as instruments of righteousness (Rom. 6:13,19). The members themselves are not the problem. The problem lies in the use of the members. To complicate matters, the members have a bent toward sin; they are oriented toward the earth, rather than toward things above (vv. 1–2). The "law of sin" is in the "members of my body" (Rom. 7:23). This earthly orientation must be put to death.

G. Vice lists (v. 5)

Vice lists and virtue lists are common in Pauline literature (Rom. 1:29–32; 1 Cor. 5:9–11; 6:9–10; Gal. 5:19–23; Phil. 4:8; 1 Tim. 3:1–13; Titus 1:5–9). These lists were common in nonbiblical literature as well. Paul's lists seem to have been adapted for each individual situation.

H. Image (v. 10)

By repeating a word he used earlier, Paul ties his argument together in an interesting fashion: While Christ is the image (*eikon*) of God (1:15), the believer is being renewed to the image (*eikon*) of God. Man was created in the image of God and thus bears certain similarities to God (Gen. 1:27): man is rational, moral, volitional, emotional, and relational, just as God is. In the fall the image of God was marred but not lost (Gen. 3:1–24). In identification with Christ, the believer is in the process of becoming more and more like Christ and thus is having the image renewed (compare Rom. 8:29; 1 Cor. 15:49; 2 Cor. 3:18; Phil. 3:21).

Here Paul is setting forth the logical extension of 2:9. Christ is the image of God in all its fullness. We have been given fullness in Christ. Therefore, we are being renewed into the image of God. That should impact the way we live.

I. Chosen people (v. 12)

(See "Deeper Discoveries" on Ephesians 1:4.)

J. Let the Word of Christ dwell in you richly (vv. 16–17)

Scripture closely connects the ministry of the Holy Spirit, the function of the Word of God, and the goal of becoming like Christ as can be seen in a comparison of four passages:

1. "Let the word of Christ dwell in you richly as you teach and admonish one another with all wisdom, and as you sing psalms, hymns and spiritual songs with gratitude in your hearts to God. And whatever you do, whether in word or deed, do it all in the name of the Lord Jesus, giving thanks to God the Father through him" (vv. 6–17).

2. "Do not get drunk on wine, which leads to debauchery. Instead, be filled with the Spirit. Speak to one another with psalms, hymns and spiritual songs. Sing and make music in your heart to the Lord, always giving thanks to God the Father for everything, in the name of our Lord Jesus Christ" (Eph. 5:18–20).

These two passages show that being "filled with the Spirit" and letting "the word of Christ dwell in you richly" result in the same lifestyle change. The person will be teaching others, singing praise to God, and offering thanks. The verses following both of these passages show that an impact will be seen in all the believer's relationships. What then is the connection between being filled with the Spirit and letting the word of Christ dwell richly within us?

3. "So I say, live by the Spirit, and you will not gratify the desires of the sinful nature" (Gal. 5:16).

4. "Rather, clothe yourselves with the Lord Jesus Christ, and do not think about how to gratify the desires of the sinful nature" (Rom. 13:14).

Galatians shows us the key to controlling the sinful nature is living by the Spirit. Romans makes the key clothing yourself with the Lord Jesus Christ. What is the connection between the ministry of the Spirit and Christlikeness in the life of a believer? The answer seems to come in understanding the ministry of the Spirit.

In *Keep in Step with the Spirit*, J. I. Packer describes the ministry of the Holy Spirit as a "Floodlight for Fools." The Spirit is always pointing us toward Christ and showing us what he is like (John 15:26). In similar fashion Scripture contains the record of what Christ was like here on earth. When Scripture and Spirit come together, the picture becomes clear. The Holy Spirit is always pointing us to Christ. Therefore, if we are filled with the Spirit, we will be conformed to the image of Christ (Old Tappan, N. J.: Fleming H. Revell Company, 1984, 65–6).

VII. TEACHING OUTLINE

A. INTRODUCTION

1. Lead story: Skating in Circles

2. Context: In the third chapter of Colossians, Paul makes the nature of true spiritual experience very clear. Having warned the Colossian believers against enticing, but empty, portrayals of spirituality—secret knowledge, hard-line legalism, exciting experiences, rigid self-denial—Paul gives a straightforward description of true spirituality. True spirituality is a changed life and Christlike relationships in every arena of life.

C. Transition: As we look at this chapter, we see the need to allow the Word of Christ to take up comfortable residence in our lives, so that we may develop in Christlike character and so our relationships with others please God. Spirituality is living an ordinary life in an extraordinary way. That is only possible through the power of the new life we have in Christ.

B. COMMENTARY

1. The Foundation of Christian Living (vv. 1–4)
2. The Transformation of Christian Living (vv. 5–17)
   a. Discard the remnants of your former life (vv. 5–11)
   b. Display the character of your new life (vv. 12–17)
3. The Relationships of Christian Living (vv. 18–4:1)
   a. Christian living at home (vv. 18–21)
   b. Christian living at work (vv. 22–4:1)

C. CONCLUSION: NO CATEGORIES PLEASE

VIII. ISSUES FOR DISCUSSION

1. Where is your mind set? Why?
2. What is the greatest hope you have in life?
3. What habits and practices do you need to put to death?
4. What characteristics do you need to clothe yourself with? What Christian clothing are you already wearing?
5. Describe the relationships within a Christian household? Why are these superior to the relationships the world advocates?

Colossians 4

The Truth about Spirituality and Service

"*The* most important question is not how much work is being done but how much Jesus is doing through you. Look up; God's ceiling is unlimited. Learn to look on Jesus, and more and more you will find that Jesus is directing your wandering look toward the Holy Spirit."

Corrie Ten Boom

Colossians

IN A NUTSHELL

In chapter 4, Paul tells the Colossian believers: Fellow believers in Colosse, be diligent and alert in your prayers. Please pray that God will give me opportunities to share clearly the message of Christ even while I'm in this prison. In your own dealings with unbelievers, may you be wise with your lives and winsome with your words.

All of the men who assist me and who are such a comfort to me send you their greetings. I am sending a letter to the Laodicean believers, and I want the two churches to exchange and read one another's letter. May God's grace sustain you all.

The Truth about
Spirituality and Service

I. INTRODUCTION

My Heroes Have Always Been Normal

*J*anice Munson, 39, and her husband, Dan, were on a shopping trip in Littleton, Colorado, when they came up behind a silver minivan moving along at a very slow pace. The minivan swerved first onto the shoulder, and then into oncoming traffic. Janice glanced into the minivan and was startled to see that the driver appeared to be asleep.

Dan engaged his flashers and began waving his arm and blinking his headlights to warn approaching traffic. Janice knew she had to act. Without a word to her husband, she jumped from the car. Within seconds, she was running alongside the van. She grabbed the door handle, banged on the window and yelled, "You're going the wrong way!" The woman only stared back vacantly.

Janice swung the door open and vaulted inside the moving vehicle. She slammed the gearshift into park, bringing the van to an abrupt stop. Seconds later, a stream of cars coming from the opposite direction whizzed safely past the van and its occupants. Afterwards, police told Janice that the van driver was a diabetic suffering from insulin shock. She was taken to a nearby hospital, treated, and released ("Heroes for Today," *Readers Digest,* October 1994, 23–24).

In *A World without Heroes,* George Roche defines *heroism* as "an extraordinary act of goodness, performed by 'ordinary' persons from whom we do not expect it" (Hillsdale, Michigan: Hillsdale College Press, 1987, 23). True of Janice Munson, just a thirty-nine-year-old wife and mom who risked her life to save lives. Extraordinary action. Ordinary people.

That's true of biblical heroes as well. We tend to make biblical characters into super saints. A careful look reminds us that they were just normal. Sure, some of them accomplished great things: we read of their accomplishments in the biblical record. Their records also include some embarrassing flaws. Remember Abraham's deception, Sarah's doubt, David's adultery, Peter's denials, Mark's desertion? They were just normal folks God used to accomplish his purposes. My heroes have always been normal.

In Colossians 4, we meet some normal people. As the letter closes, Paul introduces us to his partners in ministry. Through these normal heroes God accomplished his work.

The truth about spirituality is that it's obedience in the ordinary, by the ordinary. Genuine spiritual living is not for the favored few, as the false teachers would have us believe. What about service for the Christ who has supremacy? Does such a supreme Savior use only "special" people? Of course not. The truth about spirituality and service is that they're both open to ordinary people like you and me.

II. COMMENTARY

The Truth about Spirituality and Service

MAIN IDEA: *Knowing the truth about spirituality and service calls us to live lives of prayer, wisdom, and faithfulness.*

A Communication: Sharing Our Most with God (v. 2)

SUPPORTING IDEA: *Believers should pray with diligence, awareness, and thanks.*

4:2. Paul has reminded believers that they are identified with an extraordinary Christ who has absolute supremacy. He has called believers (ordinary people) to live their ordinary lives in an extraordinary way. How is the believer to accomplish such a challenging assignment? Is assistance available? Yes. The believer is not alone in a world of temptation and deception. Strength and perspective are always available by looking above in prayer. Paul exhorts believers to pray with (1) diligence, (2) awareness, (3) gratitude.

Prayer should be done with diligence. **Devote** means "be busily engaged in," persist in, or give constant attention." Prayer in the believer's life is not just an option for occasional emergencies. If believers are to withstand the constant pressures of a fallen and unfriendly world, an attitude of persistence and perseverance in prayer is needed.

Watchful literally means "stay awake" and refers to an attitude of being spiritually alert. Using the same term, Peter encouraged his readers to "be self-controlled and *alert.* Your enemy the devil prowls around like a roaring lion looking for someone to devour" (1 Pet. 5:8, emphasis added). Believers need to be alert because Satan wants to devour them. Colossians tells believers to be alert because false teachers want to deceive them. Believers need to be aware of the evil forces which seek to tantalize and capture them. If believers wish to be wide awake in their prayer life, the insight of C. S. Lewis can be helpful:

> No one in his senses, if he has any power of ordering his own day, would reserve his chief prayers for bedtime—obviously the worst

possible hour for any action which needs concentration. . . . My own plan, when hard pressed, is to seize any time, and place, however unsuitable, in preference to the last waking moment. . . . The body ought to pray as well as the head" (*The Joyful Christian,* New York: Macmillan Publishing Co., 1977, 88-89).

Finally, Paul calls believers to **thankful** prayer. Believers who pray with gratitude for God's blessing will be less likely to be led astray by the lures and lies of the enemy.

🅑 Conversation: Sharing Our Message with Unbelievers (vv. 3–6)

SUPPORTING IDEA: *Believers should share the gospel with clarity, wisdom, and grace.*

4:3–4. The believer is to share his most with God through diligent, watchful, grateful prayer, but the believer's prayers are not to be centered only on self. Paul asked the Colossian believers to **pray for us** (his partners in ministry), **too**. This request, however, is broader than Paul and his associates. Paul's request is that the Colossians pray for him so he can share the message of **the mystery of Christ** with those who have not yet joined the family of faith. Paul could have prayed for many things. He reminds us that he is **in chains**, a clear reference to his imprisonment. He could have prayed for release or relief. He didn't though. He prayed that God would **open a door [of opportunity] for [his] message.** Paul knew God can open doors of opportunity even for those behind prison doors.

Proclaim means "to make clear and plain." Paul desired not only opportunity; he also requested clarity. Paul's desire was that even in his less than ideal circumstances he might bring others to faith in Christ. Paul's prayers were answered. Philippians, like Colossians, was written while Paul was imprisoned. In that letter Paul writes, "Now I want you to know, brothers, that what has happened to me has really served to advance the gospel. As a result, it has become clear throughout the whole palace guard and to everyone else that I am in chains for Christ" (Phil. 1:12–13). As Paul closed Philippians (4:22), he sent a special greeting: "All the saints send you greetings, especially those who belong to Caesar's household," no doubt a reference to the palace guards and others with whom Paul had contact during his imprisonment. The answer to his request in Colossians continued later in his life as well. Acts 28:30–31 tells us, "For two whole years Paul stayed there in his own rented house and welcomed all who came to see him. Boldly and without hindrance he preached the kingdom of God and taught about the Lord Jesus Christ."

Even as Paul brings his letter to a close and as he prays for opportunities to evangelize, **Christ** remains central. He is the exalted Creator and Redeemer in chapter 1. He is the fullness of deity, and he conquers by his cross in chapter 2. He is seated in majesty and authority in chapter 3. In chapter 4, it is Christ who is proclaimed.

4:5. Paul shifts his evangelistic interest from himself to the believers at Colosse. If believers are to be effective in sharing the message, they must **be wise in the way [they] act toward outsiders.** Wisdom enables us to combine boldness with tact. Wisdom enables us to employ the proper approach in specific situations and with particular individuals. If believers are to be effective in sharing the message, they must also **make the most of every opportunity.** The literal translation of this phrase is redeem [buy back] the time. It refers to "snapping up every opportunity that comes." Believers can look to the example of the man who penned the words for encouragement. Paul, the prisoner, exploited every opportunity to share the message.

4:6. For the sharing of the message of Christ to be effective, the wise walk must be accompanied with flavorful talk. The believer's talk is to be gracious, rather than gruff, and charming, rather than coarse. The believer's talk is to be **seasoned with salt.** Salt was used for two purposes in Paul's time. It was used as a preservative to keep food from spoiling. This would mean the believer's speech is to be free from corruption, wholesome. Salt was also used as an additive to give flavor to food. If this meaning lies behind the figure, then the believer's speech is to be interesting, witty, tactful, and appealing. Perhaps the best understanding of the reference to **salt** is that the believer's speech is to be both wholesome and appealing. Paul wants believers to **know how to answer everyone.** He tells them to answer with speech which is gracious, wholesome, and appealing.

C Community: Sharing Our Ministry with Believers (vv. 7–18)

SUPPORTING IDEA: *Believers find comfort, help, and brotherhood with other believers.*

4:7–9. How was Paul able to maintain his perspective while in prison? With so many churches so close to his heart, how was he able to keep up with helping each one face their own unique challenge? Was he a superman? No. He had help.

In the concluding verses of the letter to the Colossians, Paul does more than send along personal greetings. He gives us a glimpse into his fellowship of encouragement. Verses 7–18 are more than a mere list of names. They are real, ordinary people, who helped Paul carry out an extraordinary ministry for the sake of an extraordinary Savior. We, too, will need others if we are to maintain the vitality in ministry which Paul exemplifies.

We might call **Tychicus** the trusted assistant. He is an example of faithfulness in little things which led to greater things. He was sent to inform the Colossians of Paul's **circumstances and encourage [their] hearts.** He was probably the carrier of the letter to the Colossians as well as the letter to the Ephesians (Eph. 6:21). In later years **Tychicus** was a relief minister for Titus (Titus 3:12). As Paul approached death, he sent **Tychicus** to care for the church at Ephesus (2 Tim. 4:12).

Accompanying the trusted assistant is Onesimus, the runaway slave from Colosse. We read his story in the Book of Philemon, a companion volume to Colossians. Everyone knew what the local boy had done. The story of Onesimus is a story of grace and hope. The slave becomes a **dear brother.** Only the gospel (1:3–8) can cause such a radical and absolute change.

4:10–11. Aristarchus, the devoted companion, was always there when Paul needed him. He was with Paul in prison. In Acts 19:29, **Aristarchus** was with Paul during the Ephesian riot; in Acts 27:2, he was with Paul in shipwreck. Adversity did not lessen his affection.

Mark, the recovered friend, made a mistake and a recovery. Mark abandoned Paul on his first missionary journey; as a result, Paul refused to take him along on the next trip (Acts 15:37–39). The career of John **Mark** appeared to be over, but Barnabas, his cousin, nurtured and encouraged him and salvaged him. He was with Paul as Colossians was written. At the end of Paul's life, he said Mark was useful to him (2 Tim. 4:11). Mark had been recovered, and Paul wanted the Colossians to **welcome him.**

Jesus Justus, the unsung hero, also brought **comfort** to Paul. Little else is known about Jesus (Jewish name) Justus (Roman name) except that he was a source of consolation to Paul.

4:12–13. Every church and ministry needs an Epaphras, the prayer warrior, also from Colosse. He was mentioned earlier (1:7) as the man responsible for bringing the gospel to the Colossians. For Epaphras prayer was not a game, it was a battle. He prayed continually, fervently, and with purpose. Aware of what the Colossians were facing, he knew their need was to grow to maturity in Christ in order to continue to resist the alluring lies of the false teachers.

4:14. One of Paul's most enduring companions was his **dear friend Luke,** the talented specialist. A man who gave his many considerable gifts to God, Luke was a doctor, historian, author, and friend. When Paul wrote Colossians, **Demas** was still at Paul's side. Unfortunately, Demas became a worldly defector. At the end of Paul's life, Demas fell in love with the world and forsook Paul (2 Tim. 4:10).

4:15–16. Paul sends a **letter** and **greetings** not only to Colosse, but also to **Laodicea.** The church in each city was to read its letter and then share it with the church in its sister city. Just what the letter to the Laodiceans was remains a mystery, but we know it must have had some significance for all believers in the Lychus valley. Later, a Latin letter to the Laodiceans circulated in some churches and is included in publications of the New Testament Apocrypha, but it was certainly not written by Paul.

4:17. Archippus may have been the son of Philemon and Apphia and the pastor of the church that met in their home (Phlm. 2). He is challenged to **complete the work [he] received in the Lord.** Perhaps he needed this word of encouragement so as not to give up in the face of the fierce battle with the false teachers.

4:18. Paul closed his epistle with an assurance of his personal interest in the Colossians and a request that they **remember** him and his circumstance of being in **chains.**

MAIN IDEA REVIEW: *Knowing the truth about spirituality and service calls us to live lives of prayer, wisdom, and faithfulness.*

III. CONCLUSION

Putting Things in Their Proper Place

Dr. A. C. Dixon once wrote, "When we rely on organization, we get what organization can do; when we rely on education, we get what education can do; when we rely on eloquence, we get what eloquence can do; and so on. I am not disposed to undervalue any of these things in their proper place— BUT when we rely on prayer, we get what God can do."

Colossians is all about proper place. False teachers were attempting to remove Jesus Christ from his proper place of absolute supremacy. Paul tells believers that the proper place for their ambitions is heaven above and not earth below. Prayer certainly has a prominent place in Colossians. The letter begins with two prayers (1:3–8 and 1:9–14) and closes with two references to prayer (4:2 and 4:12). Sandwiched in between are our responsibilities: know the truth and avoid error; live out our new life by developing character and deepening relationships. If ordinary people, like you and me, are to have any hope of fulfilling those compelling responsibilities, then prayer must have its proper place in our lives.

The truth about spirituality and service is that spirituality is keeping Christ central, and service is for ordinary people who love their Savior.

PRINCIPLES

- Prayer should be more than an occasional emergency; it deserves our constant attention.

- Believer's prayers should be conducted with a keen sense of spiritual alertness.
- Evangelism begins with praying for opportunities.
- Opportunities for evangelism are everywhere.
- Opportunities for evangelism must be seized.
- Faithful evangelism is a matter of combining a wise walk with flavorful talk.
- God uses ordinary people to accomplish his work.
- Vital ministry is accomplished through a team of people.

APPLICATIONS

- Evaluate the effectiveness of your prayer life. Are you diligent or haphazard? Do you give God the best moments of your day or the moments that fade into sleep? Determine to be a prayer warrior like Epaphras.
- Pray that God will give you opportunities to share your faith.
- Seize the opportunities God gives you to share your faith.
- Learn a gospel presentation so that you share with clarity.
- Make yourself and your gifts available to the Savior. God is in the business of doing extraordinary things with ordinary people who faithfully serve his extraordinary Son.

IV. LIFE APPLICATION

Celebrating Faithfulness

We live in a celebrity crazed society. *Time* film critic Richard Schickel says celebrities have become "the chief agents of moral change in America." Why? Because they're so moral? No. Simply because they're celebrities, and we listen to celebrities.

Scripture tells us that God has chosen to use the foolish things of the world to confound the wise, the weak to shame the strong—yet we fall into the celebrity trap, too. We have a tendency to make super saints of biblical characters and believe that God's work is accomplished only through "big names" with highly visible gifts. God's work is accomplished through "no names" as well as "big names."

Chuck Colson reminds us of that encouraging truth. He tells of a Prison Fellowship visit to Washington, D.C., saturated with media coverage. The governor of Maryland was present along with camera crews and reporters. The program included an internationally known gospel singer and Colson as the featured speaker. At the closing exercises, several inmates gave their testimonies. One man said, "I really appreciated Chuck Colson's message, and I was stirred by Wintley Phipp's singing. Herman's testimony reached me right where I was at. But frankly, those things really didn't impress me so much as did the ladies among the volunteers who, after the crowd and TV cameras left, went into the dining hall, with all the noise and confusion, and sat at the table to have a meal with us. That's what really got to me" (Charles Colson, "Ordinary People," *Moody Monthly*, May 1987, 12).

Our world may be obsessed with celebrities, but God most often builds his kingdom through the faithful obedience of ordinary people. Have you fallen into the celebrity trap? Convinced God can't use you? The truth is, he can. All it takes is availability, reliance on his enabling power, and faithfulness in the ordinary grind of life. So get involved. Dig in. Get your hands dirty. Keep it up. Most of us will never be "big names," but the only "big name" that really matters is Jesus.

V. PRAYER

God, may we enter your presence often, thanking you for your work in our lives, asking for opportunities to share your grace, and joyful as we find the fellowship and encouragement that comes from Christian community.

VI. DEEPER DISCOVERIES

A. Salt (v. 6)

Salt was plentiful in Palestine, both from the Mediterranean and the Dead Sea. Salt was both a preservative and a seasoning. The Old Testament emphasizes the preservative nature of salt. Salt is added to the meal offering to signify the lasting nature of the covenant (Lev. 2:13; Num. 18:19; 2 Chr. 13:5). New Testament passages seem to emphasize the seasoning function (Matt. 5:13; Mark 9:49–50; Luke 14:34; Col. 4:6). In each of these instances, salt is seen as a valuable commodity. Due to the addition of impurities and to chemical changes which took place during humid weather which causes the sodium chloride to leech out, the outer layer of salt could be lacking in flavor in many instances. It was then discarded as worthless (see Matt. 5:13). Here in Colossians 4:6, Paul speaks of salt as an additive to give flavor, that meaning being emphasized by the use of the word seasoned (*artuo*). This type of speech is engaging and clever but is not the **fine-sounding arguments** used by the false teachers in Colosse (2:4). The believer's speech is to be witty and compelling because it is connected to truth not because it lacks truth.

B. Hierapolis (v. 13)

Hierapolis was the third primary city in the Lychus River Valley, about six miles across the Valley from Laodicea and fourteen miles from Colosse. The city was famous for hot springs thought to have medicinal value. Many pagan cults grew up around the beautiful springs. Hierapolis had hot water; Colosse had cold water; and Laodicea had tepid water. Hierapolis is not mentioned anywhere else in the New Testament, but it seems to be a place where Epaphras had started a church alongside the churches in Colosse and Laodicea.

C. Nympha (v. 15)

Nympha is not mentioned elsewhere in the New Testament. A church met in the house of this friend of Paul. Beyond that we do not know much. Even the gender of Nympha is debated. The form of the name in the Greek, an unaccented accusative, allows for the reference to be to a man or a woman. This explains the textual variations in gender with reference to the church in either "her house" (NASB, NIV), "his house" (KJV), or even "their house" (RSV). The manuscript evidence can be used to argue for any of the options. In the end the identity of Nympha remains a mystery.

D. The church in her house (v. 15)

House churches were common in the New Testament. In addition to the church which met in Nympha's house, we know that a church also met in the house of Philemon (Phlm. 2). In Acts we find that believers met in the house of Lydia at Philippi for encouragement (Acts 16:15,40). Priscilla and Aquilla seem to have had a church meet in their house in the different cities in which they lived: Rome (Rom. 16:5) and Ephesus (1 Cor. 16:19). In Corinth, Paul used the house of the converted synagogue leader Titius Justus as a church for some period of time (Acts 18:7).

History tell us that churches did not own property for the purpose of meeting to worship until after A.D. 200. Before that time the church met outdoors (Acts 16:13) or in the synagogue for short periods of time (Acts 17:2,10).

E. In my own hand (v. 18)

This reference to Paul's writing in his own hand may mean he wrote the entire letter; more likely he used a secretary or amanuensis (scribe who listened to dictation and wrote the letter) who would have copied down Paul's words, and then Paul simply wrote the final greeting in his own handwriting to authenticate the letter. Paul mentions his own signature in a number of his letters (1 Cor. 16:21; 2 Cor. 10:1; Gal. 6:11; 2 Thess. 3:17; Phlm. 19). This personal signature guarded against forged letters which would claim to have come from Paul (2 Thess. 2:2) and gave emphasis to what Paul was saying (Gal. 6:11).

VII. TEACHING OUTLINE

A. INTRODUCTION

1. Lead story: My Heroes Have Always Been Normal
2. Context: In the fourth chapter of Colossians, Paul brings the letter to a close with an exhortation to be diligent in prayer and prudent in dealing with unbelievers. If believers are to be successful in the spiritual battle of avoiding error, they must rely on the power of prayer. Believers are not to forget that the gospel, which changed their lives, must be shared wisely, graciously, and clearly if it is to have impact on unbelievers. Paul concluded with greetings from the team of coworkers who faithfully helped him in ministry.
3. Transition: As we look at this chapter, we see that vitality in personal lives and public ministry is a matter of prayer and community. No one lives the Christian life alone. God is available through prayer. Other believers are available for encouragement. Prayer and community allows ordinary believers to serve their Savior, and their world with extraordinary results.

B. COMMENTARY

1. Communication: Sharing Our Most with God (v. 2)
   a. Praying with diligence.
   b. Praying with awareness.
   c. Praying with gratitude.
2. Conversation: Sharing Our Message with Unbelievers (vv. 3–6)
   a. Evangelism calls for perspective and clear proclamation (vv. 3–4)
   b. Evangelism calls for wisdom and an opportunistic walk (vv. 5)
   c. Evangelism calls for grace and flavorful talk (v. 6)
3. Community: Sharing Our Ministry with Believers (vv. 7–18)
   a. Faithful servants are a source of encouragement (vv. 7–11)
   b. Fervent servants are a source of support (vv. 12–13)
   c. Friendly servants are a source of community (vv. 14–18)

C. CONCLUSION: CELEBRATING FAITHFULNESS

VIII. ISSUES FOR DISCUSSION

1. For whom are you praying? What do you expect to happen as a result of your prayers of intercession for other people?

2. Do you have answers for the questions people raise about your faith? In what situations do you talk with unbelievers about your faith? How can you find more opportunities to do so?

3. What description would other members of your church use to characterize your Christian life?

4. Do you have incomplete work for God? What is your plan for completing it?

Glossary

abba—The Aramaic word for *father* used by Jesus to speak of his own intimate relationship with God.

Abraham—The first Hebrew patriarch.

allegory—A means of presenting or interpreting a story by focusing on hidden or symbolic meanings rather than the literal meaning.

antinominism—The false teaching that since faith alone is necessary for salvation, one is free from the moral obligations of the law.

apostles—Men chosen by Jesus as his official messengers.

ascension—Act of going to heaven in bodily form from earthly life.

atonement—Meaning reconciliation, was associated with sacrificial offerings to remove the effects of sin, and in the New Testament refers specifically to the reconciliation between God and humanity effected by the death, burial, and resurrection of Christ.

baptism—The immersion or dipping of a believer in water symbolizing the complete renewal and change in the believer's life and testifying to the death, burial, and resurrection of Jesus Christ as the way of salvation.

Berea—City in Macedonia to which Paul escaped after the Jews of Thessalonica rioted.

body of Christ—The church, the unity in Christ of diverse Christians.

covenant—God's agreement to complete the salvation of sinners based on Christ's saving work.

day of the Lord—God's time of decisive intervention in history.

Diana (Artemis)—Roman (Greek) goddess of the moon; daughter of Zeus; cared for nature; mother goddess; fertility goddess; identified with Ephesus (see Acts 19:28).

docetism—A heretical belief which taught that God did not take on human flesh in the form of Jesus and that Jesus only *seemed* to have a physical body.

elect—Those whom God has chosen to follow him and obey his commandments.

faith—A response which takes God at his word and acts upon it. Faith provides assurance of things we can only hope for and a certainty about things we cannot see.

Galatia—Geographical name derived from Gaul because its inhabitants were Celts or Galli.

Gentiles—People who are not part of God's chosen family at birth and thus can be considered "pagans."

gnosticism—A view fully developed after A.D. 100 that emphasized salvation through a secret knowledge and a dualistic worldview with equal powers of good and evil.

grace—Undeserved acceptance and love received from another, especially the characteristic attitude of God in providing salvation for sinners.

Herodians—An aristocratic Jewish group who favored the policies of Herod Antipas and thus supported the Roman government.

incarnation—God becoming human; the union of divinity and humanity in Jesus of Nazareth, qualifying him to be the agent of God's saving plan for humanity.

Jerusalem—Capital city of Israel in the Old Testament; religious center of Judaism in the New Testament; also name of the heavenly city John describes in Revelation (New Jerusalem)

Jerusalem Council—The meeting at which the apostles and elders of Jerusalem defended the right of Paul and Barnabas to preach the gospel to the Gentiles without forcing converts to obey the Jewish law.

justification—The act/event by which God credits a sinner who has faith as being right with him through the blood of Jesus (Rom. 3:21,26; 4:18,25; 5:10,21; 1 Pet. 3:18).

Law—The revelation of the will of God in the Old Testament and to the later elaboration of the law referred to as the "traditions of the elders" in the New Testament.

Mercy—A personal characteristic of care for the needs of others. The biblical concept of mercy always involves help to those who are in need or distress.

Moses—The leader that God used to bring the Israelites out of slavery in Egypt.

Essenes—Members of a Jewish sect that existed in Palestine during the time of Christ. Not mentioned in the New Testament, they were ascetics who practiced community of goods, generally shunned marriage, refrained from attending Temple worship, and attached great importance to the study of the Scriptures.

orthodoxy—Holding right beliefs as opposed to heretical beliefs.

pagans—Those who worship a god or gods other than the living God to whom the Bible witnesses.

paraclete—Greek word of Helper and Counselor as promised by Jesus; looking to the coming of the Holy Spirit.

Paul—An important apostle chosen by Jesus after his resurrection; wrote thirteen New Testament epistles (letters).

Pharisees—The largest and most influential religious political party during New Testament times.

redeem—To release something or someone by paying a price.

resurrection—The doctrine, event, and act of persons being brought from death to unending life at the close of the age.

righteousness—The actions and positive results of a sound relationship within a local community; the right relationship created by God between himself and a person of faith.

Sadducees—A religious group which formed during the period between the Testaments when the Maccabees ruled Judah.

salvation—The experience of life as a believer in Christ; being rescued from condemnation on the judgment day because of Christ's sacrifice and one's trust in him.

sin—Actions by which humans rebel against God, miss his purpose for their life, and surrender to the power of evil rather than to God.

zealots—Militant radicals who act with great zeal for a cause. The term came to designate a particular segment of the Jewish population who continually tried to overthrow foreign oppression, especially the Roman rule in Palestine.

Bibliography

General Reference:

Bauer, W. *A Greek-English Lexicon of the New Testament,* (BAGD) 2nd ed. Chicago: University of Chicago Press, 1979.

Butler, T. C., ed. *Holman Bible Dictionary,* (HBD). Nashville: Holman BiblePublishers, 1991.

Dockery, D. S., ed. *Holman Bible Handbook,* (HBH). Nashville: Holman BiblePublishers, 1992.

Elwell, W. A. *Evangelical Dictionary of Theology.* Grand Rapids: Baker Book House, 1984.

————. *Evangelical Commentary on the Bible.* Grand Rapids: Baker Book House, 1986.

————. *Evangelical Dictionary of Biblical Theology.* Grand Rapids: Baker Book House, 1996.

Galatians:

Barclay, W. *The Letters to the Galatians and Ephesians.* The Daily Study Bible, rev. ed. Edinburgh: St. Andrews, 1976.

Boice, J.M. *The Expositer's Bible Commentary,* vol. 10. Grand Rapids: Zondervan, 1976.

Bruce, F.F. *The Epistle to the Galatians.* NIGTC. Grand Rapids: Eerdmans, 1982.

Burton, E. D. *A Critical and Exegetical Commentary on the Epistle to the Galatians.* ICC. Edinburgh: T. & T. Clark, 1921.

Cole, R.A. *The Epistle of Paul to the Galatians.* TNTC, rev. ed. Grand Rapids:Eerdmans, 1989.

Fung, R.Y.K. *The Epistle to the Galatians.* NICNT. Grand Rapids: Eerdsmans, 1988.

George, T. *Galatians.* The New American Commentary. Nashville:Broadman & Holman Publishers, 1994.

Hansen, G.W. *Galatians.* IVPNTC. Downers Grove, IL: InterVarsity, 1994.

Lightfoot, J.B. *Saint Paul's Epistle to the Galatians.* 1st ed. 1865, repr. Grand Rapids: Zondervan, 1957.

Longenecker, R.N. *Galatians.* Word Biblical Commentary. Dallas: Word, 1990.

Luther, Martin. *A Commentary on St. Paul's Epistle to the Galatians,* repr. Grand Rapids: Baker, 1979.

Machen, J.G. *Machen's Notes on Galatians,* ed. J.H. Skilton. Nutley, NJ: Presbyterian & Reformed, 1977.

Ridderbos, H.N. *The Epistle of Paul to the Churches of Galatia.* NICNT. Grand Rapids: Eerdmans, 1953.

Stott, J.R.W. *The Message of Galatians.* Downers Grove, IL: InterVarsity, 1968.

Westerholm, S. *Israel's Law and the Church's Faith: Paul and His Recent Interpreters.* Grand Rapids: Eerdmans, 1988.

Ephesians:

Abbott, T.K. *A Critical and Exegetical Commentary on the Epistles to the Ephesians and to the Colossians.* ICC. Edinburgh: T. & T. Clark, 1897.

Arnold, C.E. *Ephesians: Power and Magic.* SNTSMS 63. Cambridge: UniversityPress, 1989.

Bruce, F.F. *The Epistles to the Colossians, to Philemon, and to the Ephesians.* NICNT:Grand Rapids: Eerdmans, 1984.

Carson, D.A., D. Moo and L. Morris. *An Introduction to the New Testament.* Grand Rapids: Zondervan, 1992.

Lincoln, A.T. *Ephesians.* Word Biblical Commentary. Dallas: Word, 1990.

MacArthur, J. F. *Ephesians.* Chicago: Moody Press, 1986.

Martin, R.P. *Ephesians, Colossians, and Philemon.* IntC. Louisville: John Knox, 1992.

Stott, J.R.W. *The Message of Ephesians: God's New Society.* Downers Grove, IL: InterVarsity, 1979.

Vaughn, C. *Ephesians: A Study Guide Commentary.* Grand Rapids: Zondervan,1977.

Philippians:

Barclay, W. *The Letters to the Philippians, Colossians, and Thessalonians.* The Daily Study Bible, rev. ed. Philadelphia: Westminster Press, 1975.

Bruce, F.F. *Philippians, A Good News Commentary.* San Francisco: Harper & Row, 1983.

Hawthorne, G.F. *Philippians.* Word Biblical Commentary. Waco: Word, 1983.

Martin, R. P. *The Epistle of Paul to the Philippians.* Tyndale New Testament Commentaries, rev. ed. Grand Rapids: Eerdmans, 1987.

Melick, R. R., Jr. *Philippians, Colossians, Philemon.* The New American Commentary. Nashville: Broadman, 1991.

Motyer, J.A. *The Message of Philippians.* Downers Grove, IL: InterVarsity, 1984.

O'Brien, P.T. *The Epistle to the Philippians.* NIGTC. Grand Rapids: Eerdmans,1991.

Scott, E.F., and R.R. Wicks. *The Epistle to the Philippians.* Nashville: Abingdon, 1955.

Silva, M. *Philippians.* WEC. Chicago: Moody Press, 1988.

Colossians:

Bruce, F.F. *The Epistles to the Colossians, to Philemon, and to the Ephesians.* The New International Commentary. Grand Rapids: Eerdmans, 1984.

Lincoln A.T. *Paradise Now and Not Yet.* SNTSMS 41. Cambridge: University Press,1981.

Martin, R.P. *Colossians and Philemon.* New Century Bible Commentary. Grand Rapids: Eerdmans, 1981.

Meyer, H.A.W. *Critical and Exegetical Handbook to the Epistles to the Philippians, Colossians and to Philemon.* Winona Lake, IN: Alpha, 1979.

Moule, C.F.D. *The Epistles of Paul the Apostle to the Colossians and Philemon.*Cambridge: University Press, 1977.

O'Brien, P. *Colossians, Philemon.* Word Biblical Commentary. Waco: Word, 1982.

Wright, N.T. *The Epistles of Paul to the Colossians and to Philemon.* TNTC. Grand Rapids: Eerdmans, 1986.